The State after Statism

The State after Statism

NEW STATE ACTIVITIES IN THE AGE OF LIBERALIZATION

Edited by
JONAH D. LEVY

HARVARD UNIVERSITY PRESS

Cambridge, Massachusetts
London, England   2006

Library of Congress Cataloging-in-Publication Data

The state after statism : new state activities in the age of liberalization /
   edited by Jonah D. Levy.
      p.   cm.
   Papers presented at three workshops held at the University of California,
Berkeley, in October 2002, May 2003, and November 2003.
   Includes bibliographical references and index.
   ISBN-13: 978–0–674–02276–8 (cloth : alk. paper)
   ISBN-10: 0–674–02276–9 (cloth : alk. paper)
   ISBN-13: 978–0–674–02277–5 (paper : alk. paper)
   ISBN-10: 0–674–02277–7 (paper : alk. paper)
   1. Industrial policy—Congresses.   2. Comparative economics—Con-
gresses.   3. Economics—Political aspects—Congresses.   4. State, The—
Congresses.   I. Levy, Jonah D.

HD3611.S755   2006
330.12'6—dc22   2006041101

To Julien, Elijah, and Charlotte
who have taught me the joys
of new missions and responsibilities

Contents

II THE STATE AND SOCIAL GROUPS

III THE MARKET-MAKING STATE

Tables and Figures

Preface

This book seeks to fill a gap in existing understandings of the transformation of the state among the affluent democracies. By and large, the debate in comparative politics, political economy, and international relations has focused on alleged threats to the state, on the forces supposedly narrowing existing state activities, without considering the possibilities for states to take on new missions. It has also tended to conceptualize change in terms of "more" or "less" state intervention, while neglecting shifts in the goals and instruments of that intervention.

I first became aware of the limits of the debate about the state in the context of my research on French economic and social policy. France has long stood as an archetype statist (or *dirigiste*) political economy, but in the early 1980s, for a combination of economic and political reasons, the statist economic model entered into crisis and was repudiated. Twenty years later, after a series of liberalizing reforms by governments of the Left and the Right alike, virtually nothing remains of *dirigiste* industrial policy. And yet, during this same period, state spending has continued to expand, both in absolute terms and measured as a share of gross domestic product (GDP). The reason is that while French authorities have wound down *dirigiste* industrial policy, they have initiated a variety of social and labor market programs that have taken public spending to new heights. State activism has shifted, rather than falling away.

Initially, I assumed that the developments I had detected were idiosyncrasies of French politics, of a lingering *Colbertiste* attachment to state activism. But then I began to notice that other scholars of the affluent democracies were making similar observations. Across a variety of arenas—from women's employment to new technologies, to corporate governance, to services, to trade—state authorities seemed to have adopted a market logic and become very busy and assertive in the process. State officials were changing their goals and instruments, but they were by no means curbing their ambitions.

To advance the discussion, I invited a number of leading scholars to think systematically about the new state activities among the affluent democracies. In particular, each contributor was asked to describe the new state missions in his or her area of research, to compare these missions to traditional state activities, and to consider the reasons for and implications of these shifts. Two main conclusions emerged from the empirical cases. The first is that contemporary developments in the economy, technology, society, and politics are not just challenging existing state activities but also creating demands and opportunities for new state intervention. The second is that the spread of a liberal, market logic has been an especially powerful prod to state activism. In short, the move to the market has been, at the same time, a move to and through the state. I hasten to add that although these claims are informed by both the cases and comments of my collaborators, I alone bear the responsibility for any errors or excesses in judgment.

This book is the product of a series of three workshops held at the University of California, Berkeley, in October 2002, May 2003, and November 2003. I wish to thank the University of California's Institute on Global Conflict and Cooperation (IGCC) and Institute of European Studies (IES) for funding the workshops. The Berkeley Roundtable on International Economy (BRIE), notably Genevieve Taylor and Whitney Whetstone, provided logistical support both for the workshops and for the project more generally. I am especially grateful to Mark I. Vail, who operated in a dual capacity. Vail not only coauthored a fine chapter in the volume, but he also served as a supremely able all-purpose assistant—summarizing conference presentations, organizing submissions by the contributors, formatting chapters, and helping shorten and edit the manuscript.

One of the great virtues of a collective volume is the opportunity to learn from the other contributors, and I have benefited enormously in this regard. My thinking about the state has been especially influenced by Chris Howell, who drew my attention to the role of economic change in driving new kinds of state intervention and to the limits of employer coordination, and by John Zysman, who expanded my understanding of the market-making state and new technologies. I further wish to thank Zysman for bringing me into the cozy confines of BRIE, recommending a number of the project participants, and helping shape the contours of the book, notably the focus on the affluent democracies.

A number of people have graciously offered comments and constructive criticisms at various phases of the project. Peter Gourevitch commented on several of the chapters at a meeting of the American Political Science Association in 2003, then later on the manuscript as a whole. Others who provided valuable feedback include Suzanne Berger, Stephen Cohen, Yong-Chool Ha, Peter Hall, Yohei Nakayama, T. J. Pempel, Richard Samuels, Steven Vogel, J. Nicholas Ziegler, and an anonymous reviewer for Harvard University Press. I also wish to acknowledge my editor, Michael Aronson, for both his substantive insights and his support in ushering the manuscript through the publication process. In addition, Barbara Goodhouse and Susan E. Badger copy-edited the manuscript, while John Grennan put together the index.

Finally, my greatest debt, as always, is to my wife, Helga Ying. Helga's capacities make those of any state, whether authoritative or infrastructural, look puny in comparison. I am supremely grateful that these capacities have been deployed on my behalf and that Helga remains my partner and bedrock, unendingly loyal and supportive, whatever state I may find myself in.

The State after Statism

The State Also Rises

The Roots of Contemporary State Activism

JONAH D. LEVY

THIS BOOK EXAMINES NEW STATE ACTIVITIES among the political economies of the affluent democracies.[1] In the past, such a subject would have been relatively uncontroversial. Andrew Shonfield's classic treatise (Shonfield 1965) portrayed the essence of "modern capitalism" as "the changing balance of public and private power" (the second part of the book's title). According to Shonfield, modern capitalism was characterized by the growth of public intervention in five areas: (1) the management of the economic system; (2) Keynesian demand stimulus, the welfare state, and expanded public expenditures; (3) the "taming" of "the violence of the market" in the private sector, thanks to government regulation, planning, and inter-firm cooperation; (4) policies to increase innovation and worker training; and (5) the pursuit of intellectual coherence through long-term planning. Taken together, these five sets of public initiatives had apparently ushered in a new age of capitalism. Enduring recessions were a thing of the past; fast, steady growth and full employment were now the order of the day.

Recent times have been less kind to the practices and institutions of "modern capitalism." Slow growth and mass unemployment have reappeared, confounding the efforts of state authorities to return to the postwar "golden age." Many of the characteristic policies described by Shonfield—Keynesian demand stimulus, nationalizations, strategic

industrial policy—have malfunctioned or been repudiated. Statist political economies, like France and Japan, have experienced profound
crisis. Meanwhile, the advanced economies most distant from Shonfield's ideal, the United States and Britain, have seemingly moved from
the back of the modern capitalist class to the front. Finally, even if
state economic activism is still deemed desirable by some, such activism is widely perceived to be less practicable in a world of globalization, triumphant neoliberalism, and US hegemony. Put simply, "the
changing balance of public and private power" described by Shonfield
seems to have shifted into reverse.

The contributors to this volume share the belief that many of the
characteristic policies described by Shonfield are no longer practicable.
The place of the state in the advanced economies is changing. But we
also believe that change should not be equated with eclipse. While old
forms of state intervention may be discredited and cleared away, new
interventions often emerge to take their place. *The state also rises*. For
this reason, the contributors to this book adopt a dynamic perspective
on state activism, examining what is new about the state, not just what
is old. All of the chapters analyze new state activities that we believe
are critical to the economic adjustment of the affluent democracies.

We choose to focus on the affluent democracies for three main
reasons. First, if we wish to understand the changing character of political economy in its most advanced form ("modern capitalism," to
use Shonfield's parlance), they are the obvious choice. Although
modern capitalist countries do not necessarily show the future to developing ones—indeed, the political dynamics may be quite different
across regions of the world—they tend to be at the forefront of
emerging changes and challenges in the global political economy.
Second, the affluent democracies are home to the overwhelming majority of the largest and most internationalized corporations. To the
extent that state intervention is a response to economic backwardness
and capital shortages (Gerschenkron 1962), then these countries have
presumably "outgrown" the need for such intervention. Third, the
affluent democracies possess the most expensive and far-reaching state
administrations in the world; hence these would appear to be most
susceptible to contemporary pressures for rollback. Indeed, the calls
for curtailing state spending and intervention among the affluent democracies often invoke the competitive pressures from less free-

spending and intrusive polities in the developing world. While focusing on the advanced economies, we believe that many of the analytical claims have implications for the state in developing and postcommunist countries as well (a theme to which I return in the concluding chapter to this volume).

The central contention of this book is that the contemporary context of globalization and liberalization has spelled not the erosion of state activism but rather the redeployment of state initiatives on behalf of new missions. State authorities have shifted from a market-steering orientation, which was the essence of modern capitalism in Shonfield's day, to a market-supporting orientation in the present period. Market support is not synonymous with state withdrawal, however. On the contrary, the move toward the market has generated a raft of new state missions. The new state activities described in this volume have emerged for the most part since the turn toward the market in the late 1970s and early 1980s. Chief among these new missions (which I describe at greater length in the book's conclusion) are (1) repairing the three main varieties of capitalism (liberal, corporatist, and statist); (2) making labor markets and systems of social protection more employment friendly; (3) recasting regulatory frameworks to permit countries to cross major economic and technological divides (from Fordism to post-Fordism, from the mechanical era to the digital era, from managerial capitalism to shareholder or finance capitalism); and (4) expanding market competition in industry and services, at home and abroad. The first two missions are of an essentially *corrective* nature, addressing dysfunctions that have emerged over the years, whereas the latter two are *constructive* in character, laying the foundations for future growth. All of these missions depend critically on the state's innovative capacity—on the forging of new state policies and regulations for a new competitive environment.

The market-supporting state after statism is not only very busy; in many cases, it is aggressive as well. Although it has become fashionable to argue that state authority is less central to economic adjustment than in the past, that states must negotiate rather than direct or that they are being eclipsed by more powerful actors and economic forces, the chapters in this volume paint a very different picture. Because the transformations associated with the move from market direction to market support are so controversial and so far-reaching, state officials often find themselves making choices that produce clear winners and losers. Such choices require a capacity to act unilaterally and decisively, even in the face of substantial societal opposition. In short, state activism, autonomy, and—in some instances—imposition remain central to the ability of the affluent democracies to meet the challenges of today's globalizing economy.

The dynamic and activist perspective on state intervention that animates this book contrasts with the dominant depictions of the changing place of the state in the advanced economies. In the next section, I review the contemporary debate about the changing place of the state, showing that this debate has focused on the alleged threats to traditional state activities while paying little or no attention to new state missions. Yet Section 2 demonstrates that these "threats" can have a Janus-faced quality with respect to state intervention. Many of the very changes portrayed in the conventional literature as challenging state intervention, most notably economic liberalization, are also creating opportunities for new kinds of state activism. Section 3 argues that the analytical approach of this book offers a more compelling understanding of contemporary economic and social adjustment than the employer-centered "varieties of capitalism" approach of Peter Hall and David Soskice (2001b). The fourth and final section outlines the central themes and organization of the book.

1. The Debate about the Changing Place of the State

The discussion of the changing place of the state has focused on the threats to established forms of state intervention. One camp asserts that new developments in the economy, technology, society, and ideology are posing significant challenges to traditional patterns of state intervention. Another camp counters that the pressures for change are weaker and the sources of inertia stronger than suggested by the first camp. Both literatures make important contributions to our understanding of the changed context for state intervention. That said, their common emphasis on threats to established state policies tends to neglect the possibilities for new forms of state intervention.

Threats to State Intervention

A large body of literature points to new developments that threaten state intervention in the economy. Although the effects of globalization have received the most attention, the list is considerably longer. Broadly speaking, developments in four areas are seen as constraining the possibilities for state activism: (1) the economy, (2) technology, (3) society, and (4) ideology.

Globalization is the most familiar of the arguments emphasizing economic change (Ohmae 1991, 1995; Horsman and Marshall 1994; Cable 1995; Strange 1995, 2000; Keohane and Milner 1996; Greider 1997; T. Friedman 1999). The growth of international trade, production, and financial flows places a number of constraints on state policy. Keynesian demand stimulus becomes impracticable, since much of this stimulus leaks, benefiting foreign rather than domestic producers. Keynesianism is further constrained by the threat of capital exit, that is, by the flight of mobile investors who disapprove of increased government spending and deficits.

Globalization also undermines industrial policy. Trade openness deprives governments of one of the key tools for nurturing infant industries, the possibility of insulating them from foreign competition. Most forms of subsidies are prohibited under the rules of the World Trade Organization (WTO) or European Union (EU) competition policy. Finally, given that companies are outsourcing production the world over, aid to industry, like Keynesian demand stimulus, may leak out of the domestic market, providing manufacturing jobs for workers in China or India rather than the United States or Germany.

On a more general level, globalization is said to raise the power of business relative to the state or organized labor, thereby forcing governments to accommodate business preferences for lower taxes, wage moderation, and regulatory relief. Capital is considerably more mobile than labor or the state, giving business a tremendous source of leverage. Companies can "regime shop," locating production and investment in the most tax-friendly, labor-friendly countries. In response, governments are forced to pare back spending and economic intervention, on pain of losing investment to more business-friendly locations. The result is a race to the bottom, not only in social protection and wages but also in state intrusiveness in the economy.

Globalization is not the only economic development that is said to threaten state activism. The problem of slow growth and mass unemployment has likewise strengthened the hand of business relative to other players. Governments, eager to revive the capitalist goose that lays golden employment eggs, are now paying special attention to the demands of employers, particularly when these demands are packaged as solutions to the problems of growth and unemployment. Finally, changes in the realm of production—the exhaustion of the so-called Fordist mass production model—have led to a crisis of the various institutional arrangements that accompanied that model (Piore and Sabel 1984). Several of the core economic vocations of the state in the Fordist era—matching demand to the rapid growth in productivity generated by mass production, stabilizing mass markets, channeling capital for large, up-front investments in expensive, dedicated equipment—have no place in today's more flexible, unstable, post-Fordist economy (Glyn et al. 1990).

Closely related to these economic arguments, many see new technologies as eroding the possibilities for state intervention. The information technology revolution has given global traders the capacity to send trillions of dollars around the world daily, far outstripping the currency reserves of individual nations (O'Brien 1992). This flood of footloose capitalism undermines the capacity of governments to sustain fixed exchange rates or to undertake policies at odds with financial orthodoxy. The ease with which money sloshes across borders also makes it difficult for governments to control tax evasion and money laundering. The Internet further weakens government controls, allowing all sorts of prohibited activities—such as pornography, gambling, and hate speech—to relocate offshore, beyond the reach of the regulators.

Changes in society are likewise portrayed as pressing in an antistatist direction. The spread of affluence and education has made citizens less deferential toward the state (Goldthorpe 1968; Rothstein 1998). They want to control their destinies, rather than being ordered around by an intrusive "nanny state." Citizens are also becoming more heterogeneous, hence less satisfied with the state's uniform, one-size-fits-all benefits. Finally, they are more autonomous and self-reliant, decreasing the demand for collective provision. In short, as "citizens" have become "consumers," the monopsonistic nanny state appears as antiquated as Ma Bell's rented rotary phones.

The final pressure on the state originates in the political and ideological realm. We live in an age of triumphant neoliberal ideology. Whether this triumph represents the superiority of the neoliberal model, the political pressures of the United States and associated in-

ternational organizations, or simply a policy fad, the inescapable conclusion is that markets are in and states are out (Evans 1997). Across
the affluent democracies (and beyond), state intervention is viewed
with tremendous suspicion, as prone to inefficiency, corruption, and
rent seeking. The dominant theme of would-be reformers is to roll
back dysfunctional state intervention, clearing the way for a market-
based allocation of economic resources. The reformist agenda has
moved from the left of the political spectrum to the right, from advocates of more state to advocates of more markets. Taken together,
then, changes in the economy, technology, society, and political ideology appear to be placing tremendous downward pressure on state
intervention.

Sources of State Resilience

The claim that the state's role in the economy is being significantly
eroded has not gone unchallenged, however. A second group of
scholars counters that the purported constraints on the state have been
greatly exaggerated. Collectively, they put forward four arguments for
the persistence of state intervention.

The first argument is that the world has not changed so much. In
the context of globalization, for example, it is noted that levels of trade
integration today scarcely exceed levels reached in the years prior to
World War I (Berger and Dore 1996; Hirst and Thompson 1996;
Garrett 1998b). Although capital flows have indeed grown exponentially, most of these flows are short-term portfolio moves, with little
impact on domestic loan rates. Thus, financial globalization has not
fundamentally altered the day-to-day operation of lending and borrowing.

Change is also limited in the political-ideological realm. Scholars
note that the alleged triumph of neoliberal values has not necessarily
made its way into the minds of the electorates of the affluent democracies, even on issues of taxing and spending (Steinmo and Swank
2002). In most cases, only a brief brush with neoliberal reform has
sufficed to turn public opinion in favor of stable or higher levels of
government expenditures, redistribution, and taxation. Relatedly, Paul
Pierson has demonstrated that popular support for the welfare state
held firm even at the epicenter of the neoliberal revolution—the

United States under Ronald Reagan and Britain under Margaret Thatcher (Pierson 1994). Enduring public support for social protection has made significant welfare retrenchment exceedingly difficult.

Another limit to change is that many of the constraints on state action that are attributed to recent developments actually existed in an earlier period. For example, although capital liberalization has enhanced business's exit option, it is not as if companies were powerless previously. Government actions have always been restrained by the need to assure business confidence, to create an environment in which privately held companies would be willing to invest (Lindblom 1977; Block 1982). In a similar vein, if globalization makes it difficult for a country to run sustained budget deficits, it is not as if big deficits were the macroeconomic strategy of choice in the 1960s, even for free-spending Scandinavian countries. On the contrary, needing to defend a fixed exchange rate and fearful of inflation, these countries tended to run budget surpluses (Stephens 1996; Huber and Stephens 2001).

The second argument for the persistence of state intervention is that the demand for state rollback is weaker than commonly portrayed. Much of this discussion has focused on the preferences of employers, who are assumed to be the driving force behind reforms in the current period (Hall and Soskice 2001a). Scholars of Germany note that employers derive many benefits from the country's highly structured industrial relations system and expansive welfare state, including a skilled labor force, labor management cooperation, and opportunities to pension off redundant workers at government expense (Thelen 1999). Despite the presence of a center-right government for much of the 1980s and 1990s, German employers did not push for Thatcher-style deregulation because the system worked well enough, especially for large companies. In the case of Japan, Steven Vogel shows that not only employers but also most citizens have opposed market-opening reforms that might bring lower prices (S. Vogel 1999). An important reason is that Japanese citizens have tended to see themselves as producers first, so that protecting jobs takes precedence over lowering grocery bills. Paul Pierson's analysis of support for the welfare state also operates in this spirit: the American and British publics were not nearly as enthusiastic about welfare retrenchment as the electoral successes of Reagan and Thatcher might have indicated (Pierson 1994). The broader analytical point is that key economic actors often do not hold the deregulatory preferences attributed to them by the literature on state decline.

The third argument against state decline acknowledges that the world may indeed have changed and that constraints on the state have grown, but counters that these constraints can be met with relatively small adjustments (Garrett 1998a; Mosley 2003). For example, international financial markets may not allow governments to run sustained budget deficits; Keynesian demand management is much less available as a policy option. But the prohibition on big budget deficits is not a prohibition on big government: budgets can be balanced at 30 percent of gross domestic product (GDP), as in the United States, or at 60 percent of GDP, as in Sweden. Relatedly, it is noted that while business has become harder to tax owing to international capital mobility, corporate taxation generally represents a small proportion of government revenues, in the neighborhood of 7 to 8 percent, making a fiscal crisis of the welfare state exceedingly unlikely (Ganghof 2000; Steinmo and Swank 2002; Steinmo 2003). What is more, most countries have been able to retain corporate tax revenues through a combination of simple antievasion measures and tax reforms that lowered rates, while eliminating exemptions and broadening the base.

The fourth argument for the persistence of state activism is one of path dependence. Institutions are sticky, and state policies, especially costly social policies, tend to rest on powerful political foundations. There is a reason why the US Social Security system is commonly referred to as the "third rail" of politics, and pension reform in Europe has proven even more politically parlous. Contemporary reformers do not make policy in a vacuum. They operate on a political terrain shaped by prior state policies—policies that have reinforced or even fostered powerful interests with an enormous stake in the perpetuation of existing programs (Weir, Orloff, and Skocpol 1988; Pierson 1994, 2000; Skocpol 1995). However persuasive the arguments of neoliberal economists and however significant the pressures of globalization, the capacity of state authorities to roll back existing commitments is highly constrained by the interests and public expectations that have grown up around these commitments. Globalization is countered by domestic politics.

The two rival camps examined in this section make essential contributions to our understanding of the changing place of the state.

The first camp identifies a number of pressures and constraints confronting state authorities. The world has changed since Shonfield. The title of this book is *The State after Statism*, a phrase that is meant to convey a more difficult and contested environment for state authorities. Gone is the heady optimism of Shonfield's opus, the belief that state policies to tame and steer the market are the hallmark of "modern capitalism." Gone, too, are many of the tools wielded by state planners in Shonfield's day. That said, the second camp offers a valuable corrective to overblown prophecies of state eclipse. There has been far less change in the world than meets the ear, and much of this change can be accommodated with relatively limited adjustments to existing arrangements.

Still, scholars in the second camp do not advance their criticism as far as they might. For the most part, they leave unchallenged the presumption that contemporary change pushes in a single direction, toward the reduction of state intervention. They differ mainly in their assessment of the strength of these pressures and of the capacity for political and institutional resistance, adopting a more sanguine position than the first camp on the possibilities for state persistence. They also tend to accept the first camp's metric of change as the decline of traditional forms of economic and social coordination, thereby confining politics and institutions to a kind of rearguard action. The logic of economic, technological, social, and ideological change is that state intervention should shrink, while national political and institutional forces resist this logic. Thus, politics is destined to defend an ever smaller, less relevant, and embattled sphere of state activity over time.

Because the existing scholarship focuses on the evolution of existing policies, it tends to slight new public initiatives. A clear example is the latest edition of *Political Science: The State of the Discipline*, sponsored by the American Political Science Association (Katznelson and Milner 2002). *The State of the Discipline* devotes seven chapters and over 200 pages of small text to a section titled "The State in an Era of Globalization." One of the chapters is even called "The State of the Study of the State." Yet nowhere in these 200 pages and seven chapters can one find analysis of new state missions and activities.

The contributors to *The State after Statism* see the changing place of the state in a more variegated light. Although economic, technological, social, and ideological changes may produce demands for reduced state intervention, such forces also create opportunities for new kinds of state intervention. There is a Janus-faced or dual-edged quality to these forces; they can push state intervention up as well as down. In other words, state activism can be renewed and replenished, rather than simply eroded. It can also develop in new directions, through new instruments, on behalf of new objectives. Indeed, framing the issue in terms of whether the state is growing or shrinking misses what is perhaps a more important set of changes—a shift in the purposes and modalities of contemporary state intervention.

Intellectual Antecedents

The dynamic and variegated perspective on state change of this book has three main intellectual antecedents. The first is a recent historical-institutionalist literature, perhaps best embodied by Wolfgang Streeck and Kathleen Thelen's *Beyond Continuity: Institutional Change in Advanced Political Economies*, which seeks to normalize and endogenize institutional change (Streeck and Thelen 2005). Streeck and Thelen argue that we need to think about institutional change as a continuing, everyday course of adjustment in comparative politics, not simply as an occasional response to deep crisis at so-called critical junctures. The authors map out five forms that institutional change can take (displacement, layering, drift, conversion, and exhaustion). Although such change tends to occur in an incremental, low-visibility manner, it can cumulate into significant institutional transformation. Streeck and Thelen also see economic liberalization as an important force behind recent institutional change, an understanding echoed by many of the contributors to this volume.

A second, related antecedent to this book is what might be termed the neo-Polanyian perspective on economic liberalization. This approach builds on Karl Polanyi's critical insight that market-making is itself a state activity, rather than simply the eclipse of the state, and that such activity tends to engender demands for state intervention to compensate and shelter those subjected to the market (Polanyi 1944). According to Polanyi, market-making entails a "double movement" of the state—first establishing the market, then embedding the market in social norms. Picking up on this second movement, the so-called domestic compensation literature (D. Cameron 1978; J. Ruggie 1983;

Katzenstein 1984, 1985; Rodrik 1997; Garrett 1998a, 1998b) has long noted that the countries most open to international trade tend to have the largest welfare states. In other words, the expansion of the state's social vocation has been essential to the expansion of international trade. In a contemporary vein, studies of neoliberal reformers, such as Margaret Thatcher of Britain, have likewise pointed to the increased role of the state in forging a more market-oriented political economy, whether by breaking the power of unions and other producer groups, imposing pro-competitive regulation on sheltered activities, reining in free-spending local government authorities, or bringing the public sector to heel (Gamble 1994; J. Richardson 1994; S. Vogel 1996). Finally, several scholars have suggested that the agenda of economic liberalization is shifting the state toward a new vocation: from the "welfare state" to the "competition state" (Cerny 1990, 1997); from the "positive state" to the "regulatory state" (Majone 1994, 1997); from the "Keynesian welfare state" to the "Schumpeterian workfare state" (Jessop 1993, 1994a, 1994b). Like Streeck and Thelen as well as the neo-Polanyian scholars, the contributors to this volume identify economic liberalization as an important driver of new state activities. That said, we see other drivers as well.

A third set of writings that has shaped the perspective in this book is an emerging, "enabling" perspective on globalization (Paul, Ikenberry, and Hall 2003; Weiss 2003c). This group of scholars argues that in response to globalization states may develop new capacities, rather than simply defending the old. In the apt phrase of Linda Weiss, globalization can be "enabling," rather than simply constraining. The chapters in this volume build on Weiss's insight that globalization can be enabling for state authorities, while extending it in two directions. First, we show that other social and economic changes besides globalization can open the door to new forms of state activism. Second, we offer a more complete empirical depiction of the state's new economic and social activities. While arguing that globalization can enable new state activities, Weiss's volume concentrates on fairly traditional state missions (social protection, public investment in infrastructure and human capital, and support for industrial upgrading), albeit often pursued in new ways. The chapters in this volume, by contrast, focus on activities that have not previously been core state vocations.

2.   Sources of Contemporary State Activism

The prevailing characterization of new developments in the economy, technology, society, and ideology as fundamentally challenging the place of the state is not only exaggerated but also misguided. The problem with this characterization is not just that new pressures on the state can be countered or resisted. It is that new developments can create opportunities for new state intervention, as opposed to simply constraining existing intervention. The chapters in this volume examine new forms of state intervention across the affluent democracies. A striking feature of these chapters is that the new intervention has often been spawned by the very forces identified in the previous discussion as potential constraints on state activism. This section focuses on the opportunities for state intervention created by economic, technological, social, and ideological developments. It illustrates these opportunities by drawing on the chapters in the volume.

Economic Change: Globalization and the Crisis of Mass Production

Economic change, notably globalization, has been widely portrayed as narrowing (or even eviscerating) state intervention in the economy. Scholars within this camp recognize that, historically, governments have expanded the welfare state to socialize some of the costs of economic adjustment prompted by trade openness. That said, they tend to quickly note that states may no longer be able to afford such compensation in the contemporary climate of fiscal competition (Keohane and Milner 1996; Rodrik 1997). Compensating displaced workers is by no means the sum total of state responses to globalization, however. Several of the chapters in this volume describe how globalization has expanded state goals and capacities.

Richard H. Steinberg's chapter looks at a relatively traditional form of globalization, the liberalization of international trade. For Steinberg, trade liberalization has always had an instrumental side, as the world's leading economic powers—first, the United States, then the United States and Western Europe together—have used the lure of market access to impose desired changes on developing countries. One example is the transformation of the General Agreement on Tariffs and Trade (GATT) into the WTO. This transformation occurred in 1994 when the United States and the EU formally withdrew from GATT, founded the WTO, and announced that in order to access American and European markets countries would need to join WTO, accepting a far more constraining set of rules than under the old GATT regime. Trade liberalization was thus an instrument of power politics.

Steinberg describes how the GATT/WTO regime is forcing countries to develop new kinds of state capacity in a range of areas. These new capacities include strategic trade institutions, antidumping procedures, technical standards, countervailing duty and safeguards law, intellectual property enforcement, and environmental protection. Trade liberalization also tends to shift authority within each country. Authority is shifting vertically, from the local to the national level. Authority is shifting laterally from the legislature to the executive, as illustrated by the use of fast track in the United States. The rationale is that governments need to be able to speak with one voice and to make binding agreements when engaging in international trade negotiations. Finally, authority is shifting within the national bureaucracy toward trade ministries and, within the trade ministries, toward external affairs departments.

John W. Cioffi's chapter deals with another dimension of globalization, the liberalization of financial markets. Cioffi observes that financial globalization is expanding the pool of international investors, most of whom possess limited local knowledge. It is also eroding the ties between banks and industry, even in Germany, the historic heartland of Gerschenkronian developmental banks. This growing relative importance of international investors, which Cioffi argues has ushered in a new age of "finance capitalism,"[2] has raised critical issues of corporate governance. Finance capitalism requires a corporate governance regime that allows international capital to invest with confidence. In both Germany and the United States, the two cases that Cioffi analyzes, state authorities have responded with new regulations and institutions to police markets, prevent insider trading, standardize accounting practices, and enhance transparency and disclosure. These reforms have extended the regulatory hand of the state into some of the most private, discrete, financial affairs of powerful multinationals. They have also imposed significant restrictions and costs on managers.

The development of finance capitalism has occurred, therefore, in tandem with the very controversial and contested development of new state capacities.

Globalization is not the only economic change fueling new state activities. Chris Howell describes how the breakdown of the Fordist model of mass production has led to extensive state intervention to recast industrial relations. Operating from a Regulation School perspective, Howell argues that broad shifts in the economy, such as the crisis of mass production or the emergence of the Internet, inevitably pose challenges to existing industrial relations systems. Typically, there is a surge in industrial relations conflicts during these shifts because the old institutions are maladapted to new economic conditions. While many scholars privilege the role of the social partners in adapting or recasting systems of industrial relations, Howell maintains that only the state can handle this task. The state possesses critical capacities that the social partners lack:

1. The state can narrate crisis. Failure becomes crisis discursively, and different interpretations of situations of crisis are always available. The state has a unique capacity in privileging one or another reading.
2. The state can solve collective action problems among employers and unions, who are often timid, divided, and concerned with short-term interests and have sunk costs in existing institutions. It can also anticipate and craft alliances among private industrial actors.
3. The state can extend laws and arrangements across the political economy, in effect, taking institutions "out of competition."
4. The state can use the public sector as a laboratory or demonstration effect for new industrial relations practices.
5. The state can reshape the organizational landscape, legitimizing and, in some cases, even creating new interest groups and class actors.

The state, for Howell, intervenes in industrial relations systems "because it cannot afford not to." State inaction risks the breakdown of industrial relations and the rise of strikes, inflation, unemployment, and generalized political crisis. In his discussion of industrial relations reform in Britain and France, Howell shows how state authorities played a central role in expanding labor market flexibility and decentralizing bargaining. State authorities, particularly under governments of the Left, have also enacted a number of reforms to take some of the harsh edges off the new industrial relations systems, expanding benefits and protections for vulnerable and low-wage workers.

Technological Change: The Digital Revolution and Telecommunications

The chapter by John Zysman and Abraham Newman shows that new technologies likewise present opportunities for state intervention. In a wide-ranging analysis of the "digital economy," Zysman and Newman compare the effort to commodify information today to the commodification of land, labor, and capital described in Polanyi's *Great Transformation* (1944). At a minimum, digital information is a new "lead sector," like textiles or automobiles in the past, that will introduce new products and drive economic growth. But the digital revolution has the potential to become a "great transformation" in the manner of the industrial revolution of the nineteenth century, transforming not just the economy but also society, governance, and community. For the digital revolution to become a "great transformation," however, Zysman and Newman suggest that state authorities will need to address an array of challenges: creating intellectual property rights in digital information; building or underwriting the networks that carry digital information; removing the barriers to the circulation of digital information; and insuring that digital information flows respect widely held social norms of privacy, free speech, access, and decency. Thus, tapping the full potential of powerful new digital technologies is an agenda for state activism, not state withdrawal.

The chapter by Peter Cowhey and John Richards, although focused on trade liberalization in global services, also draws attention to the essential role of the state in realizing the potential of technological change. Traditionally, telecommunications, one of the two sectors analyzed by Cowhey and Richards (along with airline traffic), has been regarded as a "natural monopoly." With economies of scale and scope limiting opportunities for effective market competition, telecom systems were either tightly regulated or directly owned and managed by the government. Gradually, however, a series of technological developments—the explosion of cheaper and higher-capacity, long-distance transmission technologies (satellites and undersea cables); the rise of the semiconductor, which revolutionized the economics of equipment; and the growth of networked computing (starting with large corporate networks) on a national and global scale—created possibilities for substantial gains from competition. Cowhey and Richards show that realizing these gains was not simply a matter of rolling back dysfunctional government regulations. Rather, telecommunications was first "deregulated" at the national level through a combination of privatization and intrusive pro-competitive reforms, a process reinforced by EU competition authorities. At the international level, establishing a global market in telecom services required that EU and US trade negotiators be able to guarantee foreign companies access to the national infrastructure and the right of foreign direct investment or ownership. Acquiring such authority was by no means given; indeed, regulators were unable to reach a similar deal in aviation. Ultimately, then, the movement from a monopolistic telecom industry to a competitive industry was the product not just of new technologies but also of new regulatory capacities at the US and EU levels that enabled authorities to recast market structures.

Societal Change: The Decline of Deference and the "Farewell to Maternalism"

Changes in society have likewise opened the door to new state intervention. The decline of deference and rising expectations of a more affluent society have challenged established patterns of policymaking. In the case of Britain, Michael Moran characterizes the traditional pattern as "club government," or self-regulation by amateurs drawn from the country's elites. Club government was rooted in a predemocratic and imperial ethos, in efforts by British elites to insulate governance from the effects of the ballot box as the masses gained the right to vote. Moran blames this pattern of self-regulation by amateurs, selected primarily on the basis of their social class, for dysfunctions in British policymaking and economic decline.

According to Moran, the election of Margaret Thatcher in 1979 touched off a period of "hyperinnovation" within the British state. Thatcher wielded the power of the state to break up club government, the self-regulation that characterized so many areas of policymaking, from industrial relations to education, to the financial sector, to the sporting establishment. More important, she and her successors constructed a new system of policymaking, designed to create a performance-oriented state, based on management by objectives. Under this system, self-regulation has been replaced by direct state regulation, with state agencies setting explicit, quantitative performance targets—from children's test scores to the number of medals won in the Olympics—and demanding results. Moran views this transformation as nothing short of revolutionary, borrowing James Scott's notion of "high modernism" to suggest that British reformers have been every bit as ambitious as Joseph Stalin or Mao Zedong (Scott 1998). Where Moran parts company with Scott is in his endorsement of the British high modernist project. The activist British state has replaced club government, a dysfunctional vestige of a premodern age, with a system of policymaking more open to contemporary values of democracy and accountability.

Another social change that has contributed to new state activities is the growth in female participation in the labor market described by Ann Shola Orloff. The affluent democracies have been moving from a "maternalist" model, under which mothers were expected to stay at home with their children, to a model of "employment for all," under which women are expected to enter the labor force. Orloff captures this shift nicely with the phrase "farewell to maternalism." It is not just changing social norms that are moving mothers into the workforce, however, but also deliberate social engineering. Orloff notes that state authorities are mobilizing an array of carrots and sticks to coerce or attract mothers into the labor force: welfare to work and labor market activation programs, tax reform, the expansion of child-care facilities, the development of part-time employment—the list goes on.

The mass entry of women into the labor market has triggered a fierce debate within feminist circles as to whether paid employment empowers women, giving them an independent source of earnings, or simply adds exploitation in the labor market to exploitation and inequality at home. Orloff argues that the answer depends critically on the character of state policies, particularly those affecting caregiving and women's employment. Underwriting mothers' participation in the labor market presents a challenge not only politically and culturally but also in terms of state capacities. Support for the breadwinner/ caregiver family was accomplished largely through "passive" means, such as cash allowances. In contrast, encouraging or mandating mothers' employment brings the state into more "active" modes. Employment initiatives demand more than a "check in the mail"— training, rehabilitation, job creation, and the like, are all critical. The package of resources and constraints offered by state authorities varies tremendously from one of Gøsta Esping-Andersen's (1990) "worlds of welfare capitalism" to the next, according to Orloff, with significant implications for the way in which women experience the "farewell to maternalism."

Politico-Ideological Change: Economic Liberalization

Ironically, one of the biggest sources of new state activities is the agenda of economic liberalization that is so often counterposed to state capacity. The chapter by Jonah D. Levy, Mari Miura, and Gene Park compares economic liberalization in the two archetype statist political economies, France and Japan. Traditionally, these two countries have been grouped together, but since the 1980s, France has largely dismantled its *dirigiste* or state-led economic development model, whereas Japanese authorities have introduced limited change, despite mounting evidence and criticism of the dysfunctions of Japanese industrial policy. Levy, Miura, and Park argue that this divergent trajectory stems primarily from divergent approaches to social policy.

The authors show that French authorities were able to roll back *dirigiste* policies because they put in place an elaborate system of social and labor market policies to cushion the blow to displaced workers. These "social anesthesia" measures did not come cheaply. The creation and expansion of early retirement programs, worker training opportunities, subsidies for low-income hires, public internships, and a guaranteed minimum income have pushed French state spending to historic heights, despite the winding down of expensive industrial policies. That said, France has clearly broken with the *dirigiste* industrial policy model.

Japanese authorities responded in a very different manner to the onset of slower economic growth, consciously deciding not to create a European-style welfare state, out of fear of runaway government spending and diminished work incentives. The problem, however, is that lacking a safety net to protect the losers of market-led adjustment, Japanese leadership has found it difficult to move strongly in a liberalizing direction. Moreover, many developmental policies have been diverted by considerations of job preservation. Japanese authorities are spending vast amounts propping up debt-laden banks, which are propping up, in turn, debt-laden companies because were those banks and their customers to shut down, millions of Japanese workers would lose their jobs, and Japan has no social safety net to take care of these people. The absence of a welfare state has meant that the ruling party has relied, for the most part, on costly measures to preserve employment that have actually slowed down the transition to a more market-driven political economy. The broader lesson told by Levy, Miura, and Park is that getting the *dirigiste* state out of industrial policy requires getting the state into social and labor market policy. De-*dirigisation* is an exercise in state redeployment, rather than simply rollback.

The chapter by Anton C. Hemerijck and Mark I. Vail offers another case of state activism to move political economies in a more market-rational direction. Hemerijck and Vail focus on two corporatist countries, Holland and Germany. Corporatist policymaking has been widely praised for providing social peace, wage restraint, cooperative industrial relations, and high-road production. But in the 1980s and 1990s in Germany and Holland, corporatism displayed a number of dysfunctions: it did not deliver wage restraint and job creation; it created severe insider-outsider cleavages; and it externalized the costs of economic adjustment to society. Hemerijck and Vail demonstrate that state authorities have responded to the crisis of corporatism by moving aggressively to make corporatist practices more market conforming or—failing that—to bypass or dismantle corporatist mechanisms altogether.

Hemerijck and Vail show that Dutch authorities induced the nation's social partners to restrain wages and expand part-time and temporary employment by threatening to enact legislation that would strip powers from both parties. This strategy, which the authors (borrowing from Fritz Scharpf 1997) describe as reform under the "shadow of hierarchy," was less effective in the area of social security. Consequently, state authorities essentially evicted the social partners from the management of these programs through either nationalization or privatization. The pattern of liberalizing reform in Germany has been more modest than the Dutch, according to the authors, because German authorities are constitutionally barred from intervening in wage bargaining and because governing coalitions have been constructed on a narrower base and have often lacked a majority in the second chamber of Parliament, the Bundesrat. Unable to wield state capacity to liberalize industrial relations, German authorities have tended to expand state policies to palliate for the failings of industrial relations, multiplying public internships, job subsidies, and labor market activation measures.

Moving from the domestic arena to the international arena, several of the chapters in this volume show how international market opening has often prompted new forms of state intervention. Richard Steinberg's account of trade liberalization, described above, relates how powerful countries have used the institutions of GATT and WTO, as well as the threat of market closure, to compel developing countries to open their markets and accept controversial rules on intellectual property. The chapter by Peter Cowhey and John Richards argues that the creation of global markets in network services, such as airline traffic and telecommunications, requires the existence or creation of certain kinds of state capacities. US and EU trade negotiators must be able to guarantee foreign companies access to essential facilities (landing strips in aviation, the "last mile network" between the main telecoms network and the individual in telecom) along with the right of foreign investment and ownership. Consequently, building a market for services has often entailed building state regulatory capacity. Finally, Zysman and Newman, while firmly rejecting notions that nation–states are being marginalized by the digital revolution, see a central place for international negotiations across a variety of forums (Internet Corporation for Assigned Names and Numbers [ICANN], World Intellectual Property Organization [WIPO], WTO, bilateral United States–EU) in forging the framework for the new technologies.

This section has shown that prevailing depictions of state activities as an established and shrinking stock are profoundly misleading. The state also rises. Rather than an eroding historical legacy, state intervention should be seen as a new response to some very contemporary economic, technological, social, and ideological developments. There is much more happening than state decline, on the one hand, or path-dependent inertia, on the other hand. The chapters in this book focus on the undertold story—on the initiation, adaptation, and transformation of state activities in the contemporary period.

3. State Coordination versus Employer Coordination

The emphasis of this volume on new state activities contrasts not only with the literature on growing constraints, much of it emanating from the international political economy subfield, but also with an increasingly influential perspective within the comparative politics subfield—the employer-centered "varieties of capitalism" approach advanced by Peter Hall and David Soskice (Hall and Soskice 2001a, 2001b). Hall and Soskice argue that there are two main forms of capitalism, a "liberal market economy" (LME), embodied by the United States and Britain, and a "coordinated market economy" (CME), associated with Germany. Both models are supported by clusters of complementary institutions that regulate relations among firms, labor, and finance. These clusters are a source of "comparative institutional advantage," providing vital resources to domestic businesses. As a result, both models are likely to prove enduring, notwithstanding the competitive pressures of globalization.

Hall and Soskice's *Varieties of Capitalism* makes a number of valuable contributions to the study of comparative political economy. First, it unpacks the somewhat counterintuitive logic of the Germanic coordinated market economy. Hall and Soskice show how a highly regulated and organized institutional environment may serve the interests of employers and business development. In so doing, they offer a powerful reply to the neoliberal contention that there is one best way to compete in the contemporary global economy, centering on deregulation, unconstrained markets, and significant increases in poverty and inequality.

Second, *Varieties of Capitalism* suggests that economic development derives from the resolution of coordination and collective action problems (organizing worker training in spite of the risk of poaching, encouraging interfirm cooperation in research and technology, forging agreement on common technical standards), not just the transfer of resources from one group to another. This perspective casts light on why a rich institutional ecosystem may be conducive to corporate profitability and investment. Because institutions help solve coordination and collective action problems, they support certain kinds of employer strategies, notably high-end manufacturing. In short, institutions generate economic resources as well as constraints.

Third, from a methodological standpoint, whereas much of the literature on capitalist diversity focuses on the macro- or mesolevels, Hall and Soskice provide a micro- or firm-level foundation for such diversity. Their borrowings from game theory and more formalistic approaches enable them to move beyond anecdotal, small-n comparisons, creating opportunities for quantitative testing.[3] This tack also broadens their audience. Hall and Soskice make their argument in a language that speaks not only to the choir of comparative political scientists, many of whom have long espoused such views, but also to those singing a different tune in the fields of business and economics.

While sharing many of the objectives and assumptions of *Varieties of Capitalism*, this volume advances a very different understanding of the role of the state. Hall and Soskice circumscribe the state in two fundamental respects. First, they all but eliminate the statist category from their typology, reducing the number of capitalisms from three to two (coordinated market economies and liberal market economies). Hall and Soskice evoke a possible (third) "Mediterranean" subtype, characterized by a large agrarian sector and a recent history of extensive state intervention, but this subtype is mentioned in only a single paragraph, and its features and logic are not elaborated systematically in the manner of the CME and LME ideal types. As for specific countries traditionally associated with the statist ideal type, Japan is attached to the Germanic CME model, its *keiretsu*, networks of business associations, and relational subcontracting highlighted, while the role of the Ministry of International Trade and Industry (MITI) and the planners is essentially ignored. Meanwhile, France finds itself in typological purgatory, neither CME fish nor LME fowl. Insofar as France is given a typological home, it is in the Mediterranean second division of European political economies, along with the likes of Portugal, Greece, and Turkey.

Hall and Soskice not only downplay statism as a variety of capitalism; they also marginalize the state and politics in discussions of how capitalist systems adjust to new challenges and changes in their environment. Hall and Soskice proclaim their approach to be a firm-

centered perspective, with employers the critical actor driving economic adjustment: "[T]his is a firm-centered political economy that
regards companies as the crucial actors in a capitalist economy" (Hall
and Soskice 2001a: 6). Political authorities are pushed to the sidelines,
playing at best a supporting role on behalf of the coordinating strategies of employers. To the extent that autonomous state initiatives
factor into Hall and Soskice's understanding, it is in a primarily negative capacity: the concentration of power in the executive branch may
enable leaders to unwind or damage the delicate institutional arrangements supporting CMEs. Some of the individual essays within *Varieties
of Capitalism* offer a more prominent place to the state (Thelen 2001;
S. Wood 2001), but these insights do not structure Hall and Soskice's
analytical framework, which makes employer coordination the central
determinant of economic development and adjustment.

Varieties of Capitalism is part of a growing literature that draws attention to the critical role of employers in driving economic and social
regulations among the affluent democracies (Samuels 1987; Swenson
1991, 2002; Evans 1994; Martin 2000; Mares 2003). This literature
offers a salutary corrective to traditional accounts that relegated employers to the role of passive policy-takers, dominated by an autonomous, "strong" state or a powerful labor movement. In a capitalist
economy, where profitability is essential to investment and employment, most reforms must meet with at least the acquiescence of employers in order to be sustainable and function effectively. Moreover,
scholars in this camp, after carefully combing historical archives, have
often been able to demonstrate that employers played a far more critical role than the traditional literature acknowledged in establishing
or orienting a range of public policies, from encompassing welfare
states to industrial policy, to centralized wage bargaining.

Hall and Soskice's *Varieties of Capitalism* takes this valuable corrective too far, however. Employers go from being nothing to being essentially everything. Yet several of the chapters in *The State after Statism* point to the limits of employer capacity to steer economic reform.
Employers often lack the resources or inclination to play the lead role
attributed to them by Hall and Soskice. This employer incapacity
stems from three main factors.

The first factor is that, in many cases, employers themselves are
part of the problem. Anton C. Hemerijck and Mark I. Vail describe

how in Germany and Holland the social partners privileged wages over employment, setting wages at levels too high to sustain adequate job creation. What is more, to limit the consequences for their members, the social partners abused the social security system, transforming disability and sickness programs into de facto early retirement programs. Michael Moran's analysis of British reform describes a failure of "club government" and "self-regulation" in critical sectors like industrial relations and the City of London. These failures accelerated British economic decline and set the stage for the "high modernist" project launched by Margaret Thatcher. In John Cioffi's analysis of corporate governance reform, US and German managers were the principal opponents of efforts to establish a system of "finance capitalism." Managers had no desire to be exposed to more intense scrutiny by international investors or to be deprived of instruments for masking disappointing financial results. Finally, in John Zysman and Abraham Newman's account of the digital revolution, the growing eagerness of companies to appropriate information that has long been in the common domain and to buy and sell sensitive personal data has raised widespread concerns that could potentially undermine the very basis of the emerging digital economy.

A second source of employer incapacity is internal divisions. The chapter by Peter Cowhey and John Richards shows that in many global services, such as telecommunications and aviation, there is no single, unified "business" position. Rather, users of services tend to favor liberalization (with varying degrees of intensity, depending on how critical these services are to operations), while providers and their suppliers tend to see competition as a threat. As John Cioffi relates, such divisions within the business community exist not only in liberal market economies, like that of the United States, but also in Germany, Hall and Soskice's archetype of employer coordination. Behind the relatively neutral language, "corporate governance reform" entails the strengthening of mobile, institutional investors at the expense of managers. Cioffi shows that managers have fought such reforms tooth and nail, whereas bankers and the financial community have been strong supporters. Moreover, the resistance and political battles have been every bit as bitter in Germany as in the United States.

A third limitation on employer coordination is that, as Chris Howell notes in his analysis of industrial relations reform, there are some things that only governments can do. Governments frame and narrate crises, change laws, experiment in the public sector, open spaces for negotiation among the social partners, extend agreements reached in one part of the economy to the rest, and provide side payments or compensation to the losers of new forms of economic adjustment. Although employers in France and Britain have spearheaded the introduction of labor market flexibility, they have done so at the invitation of the state, which has expanded the scope for decentralized firm-level or individual-level bargaining. Absent supportive state policies, Howell argues that the transformations of French and British industrial relations over the past twenty-five years would have been inconceivable.

The chapters in this volume paint a very different picture from Hall and Soskice of the state after statism. An essentially employer-coordinated political economy is a chimera because employers are internally divided, lacking in key regulatory capacities, and—in some cases—the source of economic difficulties in the first place. Conversely, the role of the state is both essential and evolving. As against the employer-centered approach of Hall and Soskice, the contributors to *The State after Statism* show that states are continuing to structure markets in important ways, that new state missions are emerging, that critical collective choices are being made, and that these choices are the product of power and politics, not just path dependence and employer "coordination."

4.   Contributions and Plan of the Book

The State after Statism makes four important contributions to the study of political economy among the affluent democracies. The first is to document and characterize the ways in which the state is changing (a theme to which I return in the concluding chapter). State intervention is a moving target. If we confine our investigation to existing forms of state intervention, to the question of whether these forms are surviving or being undermined, we miss much of what is happening. This approach to state intervention is the analytic equivalent of searching for the key under the lamppost. Instead, borrowing from Joseph Schumpeter (1950), we should think of state intervention as a process of "institutional creative destruction." Old forms of intervention may be discredited and cleared away, but new activities often emerge in their place. The issue is not so much whether the state is getting "bigger" or "smaller," on balance (however measured), but rather how the actions of the state are changing. Put another way, this book offers an alternative metric of state change: instead of just expanding or contracting, the state should be understood as evolving, as shifting in its purposes and modes of intervention. *The State after Statism* emphasizes four new state missions that have emerged on the basis of a fundamental reorientation from market direction to market support: (1) repairing the three main varieties of capitalism (liberalism, corporatism, and statism); (2) making labor markets and systems of social protection more employment friendly; (3) recasting regulatory frameworks to permit countries to cross major economic and technological divides; (4) expanding market competition.

The second contribution of *The State after Statism* is to identify the drivers of the new state intervention. As we have seen, the scholarly discussion of the relationship between economic, technological, social, and political change, on the one hand, and state intervention, on the other, has been singularly one-sided. With few exceptions, scholars have focused on the ways in which economic, technological, and social developments *constrain* state intervention, without considering the ways in which these developments might *drive* new forms of state intervention. *The State after Statism* provides a more balanced picture that—following and extending the lead of Weiss (2003c)—is sensitive to the Janus-faced character of social and economic change.

The third contribution of *The State after Statism* is to cast politics and the state in a more creative light. Politics is not just fighting a rearguard action, defending an ever-smaller and less relevant set of interventions, as posited by much of the international political economy literature. Nor is the state being displaced by employer coordination, as suggested by *Varieties of Capitalism*. Rather, political and institutional forces are crafting new policies to meet new needs. Globalization, technological breakthroughs, changing social norms, and the move to the market all create demands and opportunities for new forms of state intervention. Thus, state authorities are not simply defending existing policies; they are also forging new ones.

The fourth contribution of *The State after Statism* is to offer a more nuanced understanding of the politics of economic liberalization and market support. State and market are not locked in a zero-sum struggle, where the gains of the one come at the expense of the other. Rather, state activism is an essential component of the move to the market. Instead of an eclipse of the state, economic liberalization is perhaps best conceived of as a redeployment of state energies on behalf of new missions. It is an agenda for state activism, not withdrawal.

The State after Statism is organized into three parts. Each part is composed of three chapters and probes a different aspect of the new state intervention. Part I, "Varieties of State Intervention," examines the changing role of the state within the three principal models of political economy: liberalism (Moran), corporatism (Hemerijck and Vail), and statism (Levy, Miura, and Park). Part II, "The State and Social Groups," considers changes in the state's relationship to three key social groups: labor (Howell), business (Cioffi), and women (Orloff). Part III, "The Market-Making State," assesses the state's role in the development of markets in three areas: digital technologies (Zysman and Newman), global services (Cowhey and Richards), and international trade (Steinberg). In a concluding chapter, I characterize the new economic and social missions of the state and analyze the implications of these missions for our understanding of state capacity.

∼ I
Varieties of State Intervention

⁓ 1

The Transformation of the British State

From Club Government to State-Administered High Modernism

MICHAEL MORAN

FOR ABOUT THE FIRST TWO-THIRDS of the twentieth century, the British state was among the most stable and least innovative in the advanced industrial world. Since then, British institutions have been in turmoil, and the United Kingdom has been a pioneer of policy and institutional innovation.

Consider first the epoch of stability (or as I prefer, stagnation), especially notable in the half century or so after the end of World War I. The extensions of the franchise in 1918 finally established something close to formal democracy. Labour emerged as the Conservatives' main rival, ushering in a half century when partisan argument was organized around two class blocs. With the creation of the Irish Free State four years later, the single most contentious issue in British politics—the character of the United Kingdom itself—went underground for half a century. The consolidation of a unified civil service after Warren Fisher's appointment as Head of the Service in 1919 fulfilled the final conditions for the creation of a culturally homogenous metropolitan mandarin class. The biggest domestic change over the next half century was, simply, continuing, miserable economic decline.[1]

Now contrast the experience of the last thirty years. It has been an age of hyperinnovation in which Britain emerged as a pioneer of institutional and policy change. Consider just four examples:

1. *Privatization*. Harvey Feigenbaum and colleagues show that the scale of privatization in Britain, measured by standard indicators, was the greatest of any major industrial nation. Indeed, among the democracies, only New Zealand outstripped Britain (Feigenbaum, Henig, and Hamnett 1999: 1, 62).
2. *Public sector reform*. Christopher Pollitt and coworkers, in their comparative study of reform, measure reform along six dimensions, for instance, marketization and intensity of implementation. Britain is in the top rank of all (Pollitt, Lonsdale, and Ginne 1999: 42).
3. *Financial liberalization*. Throughout the 1980s and 1990s, a wave of liberalization swept over world financial centers. Britain was in the first wave again, notably through the Big Bang of 1986. The result was to consolidate London's place as a world financial capital and as Europe's leading financial center.
4. *Self-regulation*. This takes us to the heart of the illustrative case

Table 1.1. The transformation of firm regulation in Britain: regulation of the City

	Traditional regulation	Modern regulatory state
Role of the law	Law marginal	Law (Financial Services and Markets Act 2000) governs regulatory system
Mechanisms of public accountability	Public accountability rare	Public accountability via reporting to core executive and Parliament
Regulatory institutions	Regulatory institutions controlled by markets	Single regulatory peak institution, Financial Services Authority
Standard setting	Standards controlled by markets	Standards the result of public argument, debate, and regulatory prescription
Institutional stability	Institutions and practices stable, 1918–1980s	Institutions and practices in turmoil, 1980s–

used in this chapter. When David Vogel (1986) "set" British business regulation into comparative perspective two decades ago, he stressed the peculiarities of the British: the dominance of self-regulatory bodies; the extent to which self-regulatory institutions were private associations; in the unusual cases where the law was historically entrenched—like regulation of health and safety at work—the extent to which regulation was light touch and consensual; and the degree to which institutional structures bore a heavy imprint of their nineteenth-century origins.

Every one of these generalizations about British regulation now has to be radically revised. I illustrate the scale of the revision with the three simple accompanying tables. They focus on a single domain—broadly, corporate governance—and they show persistent features. I choose the City as my first illustration (Table 1.1), both because of its importance in the British economy and because it provided an institutional and ideological template for traditional British business regulation; I select accounting and auditing standards (Table 1.2) because these have emerged as key processes in the government of the firm; and I finally highlight the broader framework of corporate governance in Britain (Table 1.3).

Table 1.2. The transformation of firm regulation: accounting and auditing

	Traditional regulation	Modern regulatory state
Standard setting	Accounting and auditing standards fixed by professional convention	Accounting and auditing standards fixed by statute
Enforcement of standards	Accounting and auditing standards bodies controlled by profession	Accounting and auditing standards bodies, though nominally self-regulatory, increasingly have organization and membership prescribed by government
Institutional stability	Institutions and practices stable, 1918–1990	Institutions, standards, and powers in turmoil, 1990–

Table 1.3. The transformation of firm regulation: corporate governance

	Traditional regulation	Modern regulatory state
Status of the firm	The firm is a private association, not a state creation	Privatization revives a "concessions" model of the firm, where privileges of corporate status viewed as concessions by the state in return for acknowledging public obligations
Locus of corporate governance struggles	Key corporate governance relations are among shareholders	Internal issues of corporate governance like corporate reward are politicized throughout the 1990s
Organization of competition policy	Competition policy is controlled by business interests	Monopolies and Mergers Commission restructured as Competition Commission; Office of Fair Trading acquires new mandates and powers
Legal regulation	Legal regulation of firm activities—safety, pollution—is light touch and business friendly	Signs of incremental legalization of regulation of firm activities
Organization of public inspectorates	Public inspectorates are fragmented creation of historical evolution	Public inspectorates reorganized into central, comprehensive regulatory bodies
Institutional stability	1918–1980: corporate governance stable and "depoliticized"	2002–2005: White Paper and proposed legislation—latest in a decade of constant reform

The sketches in these tables are very "broad brush," but they show two striking features:

• A long-term shift from stability to almost perpetual policy innovation.

• A long-term rise in the importance of the state as an organizer and controller of systems of regulation.

I have focused on corporate governance in this example because space demands selectivity. But my contention is that a similar picture—of hyperinnovation and rising state surveillance—emerges when we look at other regulatory domains: of professions; of all levels of education; of industrial relations; of the internal operation of the state machine; of sport and the arts. I return to some of these illustrative cases later in the chapter.

This picture of growing state surveillance presents serious problems of interpretation and explanation, because the prevailing account of the British revolution of the last generation suggests a very different pattern of state withdrawal, collapsing hierarchies, and the spread of self-governing networks. I call this prevailing view a theory of the postmodern state. It comes from many quarters. Students of the European Union (EU) into which the British state is being integrated picture it precisely as postmodern—in James Caporaso's phrase: "abstracted, disjointed, increasingly fragmented, not based on stable or coherent coalitions" (Caporaso 1996: 45). It is, in Giandomenico Majone's (1996) formulation, a "regulatory state" where, following the collapse of Keynesianism, the state has withdrawn to the role of regulator—a balancer rather than a driver of social forces. In public management practice the image is of a state that has shifted from rowing to steering, to use David Osborne and Ted Gaebler's dazzling image (1992: 25–48). In the new literature on the sociology of organizations, there is claimed to be a shift to "soft bureaucracy" as an alternative to Weberian hierarchies (Courpasson 2000). R. A. W. Rhodes summarizes the paradigm in a characteristically pungent way:

> The shift from government to governance in the differentiated polity is my preferred narrative. . . . It focuses on interdependence, disaggregation, a segmented executive, policy networks, governance and hollowing out. Interdependence in intergovernmental relations and policy networks contradict the authority of parliamentary sovereignty and a strong executive. Institutional differentiation and disaggregation contradict command and control by bureaucracy. (R. Rhodes 1997: 199)

To maintain this paradigm in the face of the evidence of the state's transformed role—notably its invasion precisely of those self-governing networks that were once central to British regulation—involves serious intellectual contortion. I propose something simpler: that we view the state now developing in Britain as an exercise in high modernism, not postmodernism. I take the notion of high modernism from James Scott (1998).[2] Its characteristic marks are:

- The growth of central control to impose ambitious projects of social transformation—whether these are waging war, collectivizing agriculture, or reshaping a failing market economy.

- A drive for synoptic legibility to the center as a precondition of control—a drive that in Britain manifests itself in a boom in auditing and the development of Michael Power's (1997) "audit society."

- A consequent emphasis on the importance of measurement, part of an attempt to convert the tacit knowledge of insiders into explicit knowledge more widely available. The process is thus bound up with the notions of modernization and democratization that are examined in Theodore Porter's (1995) history of the growth of quantification in social life.

Where has the British version of high modernism come from? To understand, unsurprisingly, we have to go back to origins.

1. Club Government, Incompetence, and Stagnation

The best single characterization of the British system of government in the age of stagnation has been offered by David Marquand. The state became a large-scale interventionist state over the course of the twentieth century, but this interventionist state was run by an oligarchic system of club rule. In Marquand's words: "The atmosphere of British government was that of a club, whose members trusted each other to observe the spirit of the club rules; the notion that the principles underlying the rules should be clearly defined and publicly proclaimed was profoundly alien" (1988: 178). The club system was not confined to the heartlands of the British executive, though it was peculiarly at home in the metropolitan ruling elite, for instance, at the top of the civil service; it also provided the defining features of British business regulatory ideology.

This club system originated in something familiar: the special timing of British economic development. Britain not only pioneered industrialism; it also pioneered the institutional forms—such as company law, the invention of agencies to regulate the firm, the conception of the firm as an economic actor—that accompanied the transition to industrialism. Britain invented these forms, notably in the middle decades of the nineteenth century, when the state had some particularly premodern features: the bureaucratic and fiscal resources available to government were by modern standards tiny; notions of state intervention, especially to control business, were in their infancy; political life was dominated by bourgeois and aristocratic oligarchies; and democratic, accountable government was viewed mostly as a threat—notably a threat to property and order from the working class that was being created by industrialism.

These were the conditions under which the wider ideology of club rule was formulated, and the particular ideology of business regulation crystallized. Where the state did equip itself with law and regulatory institutions—such as in factory inspection and in air pollution regulation—it fashioned the laws and regulatory practice to accommodate business preferences (Carson 1970, 1974, 1979). Where it created the legal framework for corporate governance, as in the critical company law acts passed between the 1840s and the 1860s, it defined the company as a legal creature that was the product of a private contract among its owners, the shareholders. (This is a major theme of John Parkinson [1993].) In the critical domain of financial markets, it invented a system of regulation centered on a privately owned, and privately controlled, central bank and an ideology of "self-regulation" that was the very crystallization of the notion of club rule. "Clubs" such as the Stock Exchange and banking cartels ruled the markets; "practical" knowledge—which meant the tacit knowledge of club insiders—was elevated over the formal knowledge of experts or the formal rules that might have been contained in laws passed by Parliament.

Club rule was invented before the rise of the formally democratic, interventionist state, but it was adapted as a defensive mechanism by governing elites against the threat of that new state. The first two decades of the twentieth century were critical. The working class emerged as a distinctive, independently organized political interest; something close to formal democracy was established in the franchise reform of 1918; and, briefly, there appeared the frightening specter of revolutionary socialism from Eastern Europe, coupled with the equally brief employment of revolutionary language by the political instrument of the newly enfranchised working class, the Labour Party. Yet the outcome of all this turmoil resembled Edmund Burke's verdict on

1689: not a revolution consummated but a revolution averted. These decades saw the institutionalization of the club system: the final consolidation of the metropolitan civil service elite into a single unity under Warren Fisher's headship; the transformation of the Bank of England, under Montague Norman, its first permanent governor, into a professionally organized manager of the financial markets; a burst of quango creation—for instance, in the spheres of research and university funding—establishing institutions that allowed interests to run their own affairs unencumbered by public accountability. (Quango, literally, but not very revealingly, stands for Quasi-Autonomous Non-Government Organization; in practice, quangos are constitutional hybrids of public and private agencies which allow the extension of public control over hitherto autonomous domains of civil society.)

The club system could absorb an extraordinary amount of institutional change. In the 1920s, for example, public ownership of the new technologies of broadcasting was established; the new corporation, the British Broadcasting Corporation (BBC), soon became almost paradigmatic of club rule. The wider system of nationalized corporations likewise was absorbed into a culture of informal understandings, backstairs manipulation, and evasion of public accountability—with disastrous consequences for economic performance and responsiveness to consumers. Even in those few cases where the state equipped itself with a modern-looking regulatory institution, the club culture prevailed. Here is Stephen Wilks on the early decades of the Monopolies and Mergers Commission, established in 1948 to regulate monopolies and cartels in the domestic economy. The commission's practice was to emphasize

> [t]he avoidance of legal process and the determined retention of room for bargaining implied in ministerial discretion. They emphasize the accommodating approach taken towards industry and the respect for reasonable business behavior and voluntary compliance with inquiries and recommendations. Additionally, they stress the tendency to "negotiated legislation" in which the views of business were given considerable weight. (Wilks 1999: 10)

The age of club rule was also necessarily an age of amateurism, incompetence, and stagnation. It had to be an age of amateurism because to insist on professional competence was to threaten the tacit knowledge controlled by club insiders. And it had to be an age of stagnation because to open the system to institutional reform was to raise awkward questions about transparency and accountability—to expose, in other words, the anachronism of an oligarchic system of rule, originally created in predemocratic circumstances, persisting into an age of formal democracy. The transformation to an age of hyperinnovation and high modernism therefore required something deepseated: a mixture of secular cultural change and deep systemic crisis. How this happened and with what consequences for the state I examine next.

2. The Crisis of Club Rule

Crisis and policy failure were inscribed in the nature of the club system. The lack of transparency in the policy process meant that a high level of fiasco could be accommodated. Expectations about the standards of performance required of public institutions could be depressed; failures could be minimized, forgotten, or explained away as the inevitable product of complex social affairs. Some striking examples, from different dates, include the following. (For an anthology of incompetence, see Patrick Dunleavy [1995].)

- The catastrophic mismanagement of currency policy in the 1920s, culminating in the return to the gold standard.

- The equally catastrophic postwar mismanagement of British policy on European unification, in part the product of fatuous advice from an incompetent civil service elite.

- The Suez fiasco.

- The inability to master complex project management when characteristic modernist projects were occasionally attempted, as in the fiascos of the high-rise housing projects of the 1950s and the 1960s and the Concorde supersonic aircraft, a project embarked on with an amateurism that would have been comic, had not the costs been so great.

- Low expectations of performance from professional groups inside the club system: a seriously underperforming state school system

that damaged the interests of the poorest children; an autocratic
health-care system that was run for the convenience of the medical elite, not the wishes of patients; and a complacent university
sector that ostentatiously cultivated a delusionary and self-
regarding amateurism.

• A consensual and business-friendly system of business regulation
that turned a blind eye to abuses as various as the endangering
of workers' lives (examples stretch from North Sea oil explora-
tion to the control of asbestos), large-scale financial fraud (the
Lloyds Insurance market), and crooked business practices (the
ubiquity of insider trading in the City of London until the
1990s).

Simple fiasco and policy failure were therefore never going to be
enough to undermine club government; it had learned to live with
them. Club government was almost swept away by two forces, however: the grand systemic crisis of the 1970s and the slower ebbing away
of the wider culture on which club rule rested.

The story of this grand systemic crisis is well known and need only
be summarized briefly here. The crisis came to a head in the early
and mid-1970s. At its root lay the end of the great thirty-year period
of global economic expansion—the end of the "thirty glorious years."
That buoyant epoch had concealed the weaknesses of the British
economy, masking relative economic decline and widespread institutional incompetence behind full employment and rising real prosperity.

The last couple of years of life of the Heath government destroyed
many illusions. The latter half of 1972 saw the abandonment of that
government's brief experiment with economic liberalism and deregulation and the introduction of a disastrous attempt to run a prices and
incomes policy on command lines. The consequences of that latter
catastrophe continue to shape our politics more than thirty years on.

The destruction of the Heath experiment in command economics,
mostly at the hands of the miners in 1973–1974, caused the greatest
constitutional crisis since the General Strike. It destroyed Edward
Heath's premiership and leadership of the Conservative Party and in
the longer run destroyed the kind of conservatism that he stood for.
It led directly to the accession of Margaret Thatcher to the party

leadership and then the premiership, to the rise of Thatcherism, and thus to the great economic reforms of the 1980s. But as the connection with wider problems of the international order showed, this was much more than a crisis of Heathite conservatism.

Economic catastrophe pursued Heath's immediate successors, leading to the *annus terribilis* of 1976, when a runaway crisis of the currency forced the British government into the humiliating acceptance of policies dictated by the International Monetary Fund (IMF). That episode provoked a wider crisis in the British governing elite, comparable in magnitude to the Great War crisis of 1940. That sense of crisis intensified in the "Winter of Discontent" of 1978–1979. A typical "club"-type bargain between the Labour government and the trade union movement broke down, leading to widespread industrial unrest and highly public disruption to fundamental public services, like garbage collection. The agonies of the 1970s produced revolutionary change. That revolution, still by no means finished, wrought profound institutional and policy transformation in the 1980s and 1990s.

The circumstances of the 1970s opened the door to a modernist response. In other words, crises encouraged elites, as a condition of survival, to embark on a large-scale transformation both of the institutions of the state and of civil society in order to accomplish aims of almost utopian scale: to refit British government and society so as to compete successfully in global markets. Why this response occurred, and occurred so dramatically, remains a considerable historical puzzle. Plainly, the sheer intensity of the British crisis had something to do with its radical character. A case can also be made for the influence of agency, in particular, for the impact of a particularly powerful, determined, and able prime minister. And a case can also be made in more impersonal, structural language: notably, much that happened involved the transmission of the imperatives of global competition to an economy uniquely sensitive to global economic forces. In this last connection, the reshaping of regulation and market practices in the City of London during the 1980s seems best understood as an attempt to come to terms with the global financial services revolution.

This is the substantive sense in which the last quarter century has been an age of high modernism in Britain: it has been dominated by a project that matches anything documented in Scott's wider account of high modernism. Although attempted in a liberal society with democratic political institutions—albeit institutions that for much of the twentieth century operated imperfectly by democratic criteria—it is as ambitious in its own way as the collectivization of Soviet agriculture, Mao Zedong's Great Leap Forward, or Tanzanian villagization. The language of economic liberalism and of state withdrawal that accompanied this project was not simply rhetoric. It showed itself in real policy changes involving deregulation of a wide range of markets. But, in a manner Karl Polanyi would have appreciated, the road to a more market liberal society was cleared and sustained by massive state intervention and a sharp rise in state control of regulatory systems.

The turn to a highly interventionist reshaping of civil society is therefore traceable in part to the sheer intensity of the crisis that was experienced in Britain in the mid- and late 1970s. But there is another face to the British revolution. It has not been a stable project of high modernism. Britain turned into a laboratory of hyperinnovation, where revolutionary change spread with great speed across virtually the full range of the domains of British society: the system of business regulation, as sketched above; the core institutions of the welfare state, like the National Health Service; all levels of the education system; the regulation of hitherto autonomous domains of civil society, like sport; even the regulation of the institutional life of political and administrative elites themselves, changes that in the case of the public service can be documented in the work of Christopher Hood and his colleagues and in the wider public sphere can be traced in the efforts of the Committee on Standards in Public Life to codify norms of behavior for public servants (Hood et al. 1999; Committee on Standards in Public Life 1995, 1996, 1997a, 1997b, 1998, 2000a, 2000b).

To understand why this has happened, we must recall one of the key functions of club government: to protect elites in a range of policy domains from the agents of formal democracy, like elected politicians. A key reason for the institutional turmoil of recent decades has been the collapse of the defenses of the club system and the invasion of hitherto enclosed policy communities by a wide range of new actors, notably elected politicians. The connection between this growing overt politicization and hyperinnovation can be seen with remarkable clarity in the fields of schools and health policy, where there has been a torrent of innovation, as politicians intervene to seek to steer social subsystems hitherto dominated by relatively autonomous professional elites. (For a closer examination of school inspection, see below.)

The collapse of these defenses of the club system is due not only to the intensity of the systemic crisis of the 1970s but also to wider social change that undermined, long term, the cultural conditions for club government. Since the club system was an exercise in constraining the institutions of formal democracy, its effectiveness depended heavily on the existence of a wider culture of subjection—on deference, to resort to a once-fashionable language. This was the culture that ensured that the once threatening Labour Party was, even by the middle of the 1920s, drawn into accepting traditional constitutional understandings; that the values disseminated by key institutions such as the BBC reflected the values—and even the accents—of a metropolitan elite; and, at the other end of the social scale, that citizens accepted without undue questioning the decisions of professionals like teachers and doctors.

The collapse of deference—of the culture of subjection—in the 1960s and 1970s has been thoroughly documented (Goldthorpe 1978: 194–212; Kavanagh 1980; Beer 1982: 107 ff.). Its long-term decay was inevitable since at heart it was an anachronism: an attempt to secure the foundations of oligarchy in conditions of formal democracy. But the proximate sources of collapse in an astonishingly short time span are less certain. For Samuel Beer, it reflected a kind of change in Zeitgeist: the rise of a new romanticism across British society, which resulted in a wide-ranging questioning of authority (Beer 1982: 119). Plainly, the growing accumulation of policy failure even before the systemic crisis of the mid-1970s must also have been a contributory factor, even though the club could live with a huge amount of incompetence.

There was also one ticking time bomb whose final detonation in the 1960s helped destroy the deferential cultural foundations of club rule: the dissolution of empire, which, beginning with the loss of India in 1947, accelerated in the later 1950s and early 1960s. The club system was irrevocably bound in with the social hierarchies of imperial Britain—and with the collapse of empire between the 1940s and the 1960s, there collapsed also the social and cultural foundations for hierarchy provided by the imperial system. Some of the key themes emerge in David Cannadine's (2002) study of the hierarchies of empire. Cannadine's work examines how the empire was represented, both visually and linguistically, and how these representations were connected to understandings of the hierarchies that supported empire.

But these hierarchies were not confined to the imperial possessions: as Cannadine himself stresses, they also helped define hierarchies at the metropolitan center and were thus part of the key to domestic patterns of deference (121–135). Critical moments of consolidation and dissolution of the club system coincide with critical moments in the history of imperial cultural creations.

Perhaps the single most important few years in the consolidation of the club system were those around the end of World War I, when there was a need to domesticate formal democracy and the even more frightening specter of a wave of revolutionary socialism emanating from the European mainland (Cowling 1971). As we saw earlier, these were also years when key institutional innovations were made at both the center of the machine and in quasi-government. Virtually the same moment (1917) also saw an important cultural innovation, the creation of the Most Excellent Order of the British Empire, spanning Knight or Dame Grand Cross (GBE) to humble Member of the British Empire (MBE). This order was designed to unify the hierarchical cultures of domestic society and its imperial domains. It rapidly emerged as the centerpiece of the domestic honors system, "the order of Britain's democracy" (Cannadine 2002: 181). The external imperial collapse could not but affect the domestic system. The history is full of striking coincidences, both large and small: the grand coincidences of the end of empire in the two decades after the close of World War II, followed in the 1960s by the collapse of deference and then the wider collapse of club hierarchies across British government and society; the smaller coincidence of the liquidation at the end of the 1990s of the last significant relic of empire—Hong Kong—and the virtually simultaneous near liquidation of a domestic institutional relic of the predemocratic system, the hereditary House of Lords.

It is also full of ironies. The single movement that did most to destroy club government and create the new state animated by the spirit of high modernism—Thatcherism—also fought in the Falklands a war over a relic of empire; and the stunning electoral victory of 1983, which did so much to empower Thatcherism's most radical instincts, may also have been due in part to that military victory. That connects to perhaps the greatest of all ironies: the high-modernist project that so fiercely assaulted club government was launched by a Conservative Party government—by a party that had in the recent past been itself a byword for club rule. Understanding why the Conservatives were instrumental in this way is part of solving the wider historical conundrum posed by the radical character of the British response to crisis. As we gain a perspective on the key events of the closing decades of the twentieth century, it emerges as one of the great issues in the historiography of the period. Simplifying somewhat, future historians can probably choose between two contrasting accounts—or, if they are ingenious, can try to combine them in some way. One obvious possibility is that the changes were driven by larger forces than party—by the depth of the British crisis, by the impact of global forces. On this account, they just happened to occur during the Conservative Party's watch on the bridge. A contrasting account could single out the intense traumas suffered by the Conservatives in the mid-1970s; the way these subjected traditional Conservative ideology to peculiarly intense scrutiny; and by the way this in turn helped the rise of a unique historical agent—a prime minister of outstanding determination and ability.

3. The Resolution of the Crisis as High Modernism

The core of my argument thus far is that for about the first two-thirds of the twentieth century Britain operated a system of club government. Inherited from a predemocratic era, club government insulated elites from the institutions of democratic politics and excused them from accounting for their incompetence. The price was the cultivation of an amateurish system of government by club insiders, which produced massive policy failure, human misery, and national decline. The great systemic crisis of the 1970s opened the door for the state to embark on a characteristically modernist project: reshaping civil society and its own institutions in the name of national efficiency and competitiveness. The collapse of the culture of deference that had underpinned club rule created the conditions in which this revolutionary project could be attempted. I here try to illustrate this process by sketches of three very different policy domains: the transformation of financial regulation; the transformation of sports regulation; and the transformation of the regulation of the school system. The importance of the first of these is virtually self-evident: the regulation of the City was the paradigmatic model for the club system. The case of sport is important for a variety of reasons. Before the changes summarized here, sport was an almost entirely autonomous domain of civil society and furthermore a domain that exemplified many of the institutional and ideological features of club "gentlemanly" rule. The transformation therefore dramatizes how far the state is now engaged in the reshaping of civil society. School inspection I choose because it shows an extraordinary surge in overt central control in an area of the welfare state that had for most of the twentieth century simply been handed over to the control of the teaching profession—and that as a result was marked by a culture of incompetent provision and low expectations, especially for the poorest children in Britain.

The Transformation of Financial Regulation

The transformation of financial regulation has taken place in two giant steps. The first occurred in the Financial Services Act of 1986, a law that was partly prompted by a series of frauds and collapses among financial investment firms and partly by pressures from modernizers in the state bureaucracy and the biggest firms, who wanted more effective controls to position the City as a key location in the global financial services industry (S. Vogel, 1996: 93–117). It accompanied, and was a corollary of, one of the most important state-directed episodes in economic modernization: the "Big Bang" that deregulated City markets with the aim of securing London's place as a leading world financial center.

The Big Bang is both analytically and substantively important: analytically, because it involved a drastic reshaping of a part of civil society that had been dominated by club rule; substantively, because it was stunningly successful, converting the economy of the southeast into one of the most successful in Europe. The 1986 legislation is ideologically significant because it saw a large step in the direction of a hierarchical system of state-backed controls, while nevertheless trying to retain the language, and some of the institutions, of club-based self-regulation. It systematically organized all the main markets into a hierarchy of self-regulatory organizations (SROs). These self-regulatory organizations gained monopoly control over the markets—that is, membership of, and obedience to their rules, was a condition of entry. In turn, their own rules and internal government were subjected to oversight by an overarching self-regulatory organization, the

Securities and Investments Board, which in effect licensed the individual SROs. All this greatly increased the degree to which the self-regulatory system was codified: the SROs of necessity acquired rule books, and these rule books over time became more detailed and more elaborate and of course acquired legal force. The Securities and Investments Board spoke the language of self-regulation and, as a gesture toward independence, was constituted as a corporate body financed by a levy on the industry. But the power it wielded over the SROs was based on statute, its own constitution was prescribed in law, its leading officers were publicly appointed, and it was required to report to Parliament and to the central state in Whitehall (Margaret Reid [1988] tells the whole story).

This remarkable advance in the direction of a corporatist hierarchy in financial self-regulation did not endure. The passage of the 1986 Financial Services Act was followed by more than a decade of instability in financial regulation: periodic regulatory crises and scandals as well as internal struggles within the financial services industry, as scandal and failure pushed the regulatory authorities toward more controls, while supporters of traditional light-touch self-regulation tried to preserve as much as possible of the old order. That struggle has culminated for the moment in the changes associated with the passage into law of the Financial Services and Markets Act of 2000 (Financial Services Authority 2001). The act completes in a radical way the transformation of self-regulation begun in 1986. Some vestiges of the old forms of self-regulation, admitted, do still remain. The new institution charged with implementing the act, the Financial Services Authority (FSA), is a company limited by a guarantee financed by a levy on the industry, thus conferring "ownership" on the regulated themselves. But this is a weak echo of the voice of the old world of self-regulation. The Authority (originally established in advance of the law in 1997 but deriving its powers from the statute of 2000) has some claim to be the most impressively empowered financial services regulator in any leading world financial center. If, for instance, we compare the system usually taken as the model of tight legal control, the United States, we find a striking contrast: all the powers over the full range of markets and institutions that are concentrated into the hands of the FSA in London are in the case of the United States dispersed among a wide range of regulatory bodies at the state and federal levels.

The FSA in effect licenses all institutions and products and does so by virtue of power conferred by statute. It has thus displaced the Bank of England from any significant role in prudential regulation of markets or institutions. Authorization, standard setting, supervision, and enforcement—all come within its powers (Financial Services Authority 2001: 9–19). The creation of the Authority amounts to the diffusion into the financial markets of a major recent institutional innovation in the British system, the specialized regulatory agency empowered by law. (Other important examples include the regulation of food safety and the regulation of human fertility.) As a regulatory agency, the Authority has a radically different relationship with the central state from that enjoyed by the old institutions of City regulation and by the Bank of England. The Treasury appoints its Board, it reports annually to the Treasury and the House of Commons, and it is required to give evidence to the Commons' Treasury Select Committee (Financial Services Authority 2002).

To summarize: In just about fifteen years since the middle of the 1980s, self-regulation of financial markets was transformed. There were radical changes along at least three dimensions: a sharp increase in state surveillance; a growth in the volume and complexity of rules, including legally prescribed rules; and the development of a comprehensive hierarchy of controls operated by a single, legally empowered regulator. That regulator—equipped with great legal powers, harboring an increasingly assertive sense of regulatory mission, and subject to powerful popular pressures to respond to cases of regulatory failure—is emerging as a major actor in both the regulatory politics of the markets and the bureaucratic politics of the central state.

The changes have a distinctly "modernist" cast in the sense identified in this chapter. That is, they take social domains that were largely independent of public control, that were the result of fragmented, gradual historical change, and that relied heavily on informal controls and tacit knowledge, then transform them into something recognizably modernist in workings and ambitions. There has been a radical shift to formality, including legally backed formality, in regulatory relationships; a shift from tacit to explicit knowledge, in the form of more elaborate codification of rules and more elaborate and onerous reporting requirements; and the reorganization of regulated domains into a reshaped set of hierarchically organized institutions subject to systems of close formal reporting and central surveillance.

It is true that the FSA's actual behavior has hardly yet been adversarial. It has certainly been nothing like as draconian as the new schools' inspection agencies described below. Nor is that surprising: the Authority is dealing with some of the most powerful interests in global markets, and they cannot be bullied in the manner experienced by teachers. The complacent and self-congratulatory tone in the reaction of the British financial regulatory elite to the recent US accounting scandals shows that much of the old culture remains embedded. But, nevertheless, the 2000 legislation and the creation of the FSA have brought an irreversible change in the institutional forms and working assumptions of City regulation in the United Kingdom.

The Transformation of Sporting Regulation

Sport is of growing substantive importance for some well-documented reasons. For long a major cultural domain of civil society, professional sport in particular has in recent decades assumed a growing economic significance, both in the resources that it directly commands and because of its impact on other domains—the shape of competition in the media being an obvious instance (Holt and Mason 2000: 92–120).

Until the 1960s, sport was paradigmatic of the British tradition of self-regulation: "Sport was almost the quintessential voluntary activity, part of that long tradition of British voluntarism in which people pursued a wide variety of cultural, intellectual and social activities not because the state wanted them to but because they freely chose to" (Holt and Mason 2000: 146). It is true that there was an earlier tradition that connected sport to ideologies of imperialism and to projects for channeling and controlling the energies of potentially disruptive parts of the working class (Holt 1989: 202–279; S. Jones 1988: 15–41). But the organization of the most important sports as it crystallized in the later decades of the nineteenth century was characteristically clublike in nature, in exactly the sense used in this chapter: it involved the domination of individual sports by metropolitan oligarchies often—as in the cases of cricket and horse racing—integrated informally with upper-class "gentlemanly" cultures (Birley 1995a, 1995b).

It is possible to track over the postwar period an incremental growth in both state support for sport and some institutional change. The first British minister of sport was appointed in 1964, and a Sports Council, chaired by the minister, was formed in the same year. The council, however, still enjoyed only an advisory status (Coghlan and Webb 1990: 21; Holt and Mason 2000: 150). Despite the institutional innovations of the 1960s, therefore, the traditional picture of autonomous self-regulation still survived at the end of the 1980s. The role of the state in sporting regulation had not changed greatly since the golden age of sporting codification in Britain in the closing decades of the nineteenth century.

That pattern of autonomy changed radically in the 1990s. On the institutional front, Sport England was established in 1997, replacing the Great Britain Sports Council. (Separate Sports Councils now exist for the different nations of the United Kingdom.) Sport England is a public institution charged with important executive functions in implementing a national strategy for sport. It is accountable to Parliament through the Department for Culture, Media, and Sport, and the secretary of state appoints its council. Its primary roles are to develop and maintain the nation's sporting infrastructure. In pursuit of this, it allocates substantial moneys, a mix of exchequer grant and lottery funding (Sport England 2002).

UK Sport also came into existence in 1997. It is primarily concerned with enhancing performance in elite sports and with managing sporting international relations, notably the diplomacy of bidding to host prestigious international events such as the Olympics and the soccer World Cup. In its own words, "[T]he work of UK Sport is targeted towards developing and supporting a system capable of producing a constant flow of world class performers" (UK Sport 2002). One of its most important instruments in achieving this is the distribution of a mix of exchequer funding and lottery grants to over forty sports in return for a commitment by individual sporting governing bodies to achieve agreed performance targets.

At the back of these changes lies a radical alteration in the way the British state has begun to view sport. One of the most important shaping motives has been the desire to raise British performance at the elite level, as an index of British national prestige. The first important public sign of this desire in the 1990s was the publication in 1995 of *Sport: Raising the Game* by the Department of National Heritage. This publication was a response to perceived poor British results in showcase events like the Olympics (Department of National Heritage 1995, 1996). *Raising the Game* was the immediate stimulus for the reorganization that created Sport England and UK Sport in 1997, and as the title suggests, it was mostly concerned with the problem of managing performance in elite sports. Elite sporting success thus achieved significance beyond either sport's internally generated standards of excellence or the life goals of autonomous individuals. It became an index of national and state achievement. The consequences of *Raising the Game* also anticipate a theme that will be important when we turn in a moment to the new world of schools inspection: the micromanagement of service delivery. As a result of *Raising the Game*, the physical education curriculum in schools was changed to place more emphasis on participation in competitive team sports (Department of National Heritage 1996: 2).

By the time Labour was elected to office in 1997, therefore, a powerful force—the desire to use elite sport as an instrument of state policy—was already reshaping this domain of civil society. There was colonization by a state intent on using sporting success in the pursuit of national prestige. The new government added a novel element: a desire to use mass sport as an instrument of social policy, notably as a way of combating social exclusion and promoting public health. These elements all come together in *A Sporting Future for All*, the national strategic plan published in 2000 (Department for Culture, Media and Sport 2000).

A Sporting Future joins together the two concerns of elite performance and mass participation. It lays down as fundamental principles of policy the objectives of achieving lifelong participation and reducing "unfairness in access to sport" (Department for Culture, Media and Sport 2000: 11). It announces that the governing bodies of sports must adopt inclusive policies to widen the range of participation and expects all major sporting bodies in receipt of significant television revenue to set aside a minimum of 5 percent of receipts for grassroots participation (19). But it is in the organization of elite sport that we see most clearly the shift to instrumentalization and integration into a wider national sporting strategy. The strategic plan notes the history of failures in elite sport (cricket, tennis, soccer World Cup.) It then uses the New Public Management language of target setting and performance achievement to announce a new relationship between sport and the state:

We will be asking the Sports Councils to move to a more open appraisal of the individual performance plans. All the various sports—and the athletes, coaches, and performance directors— must be fully aware of what is required of them. The focus will be much more closely on target setting by national governing bodies and on the achievement of targets by individual performers and teams. (44)

The way this works in detail is explained by the description of the World Class Performance Programme, a system of public subsidies for elite athletes:

Awards are made to the governing bodies of sport following their submission of performance plans setting out the future targets for their sports. . . . The level of support received by individual athletes is dependent on their individual performance. Competitors are graded according to their ranking or their results in world championships. (Department for Culture, Media and Sport 2002)

My argument in these passages is that we are seeing the working out of a characteristically high-modernist project. There is occurring the reshaping of hitherto autonomous domains of civil society in the light of objectives prescribed by institutions of the central state.

The Transformation of School Inspection

School inspection is both substantively and analytically an important case. It is substantively important because education provision was a major part, and a pioneering part, of the modern interventionist state. The state sector has long accounted for about 90 percent of the cost of primary and secondary education (Hood et al. 1999: 140). It is analytically important because it was a domain where several different parts of the state—a partially autonomous profession, layers of government below the level of the metropolitan, and the central state itself—inhabited a "secret garden" of regulation (139). This was a world where the "British" style of informal, cooperative regulation was deeply embedded and where the scrutinizing gaze of the state had all but disappeared. The secretary of state at the beginning of the present upheavals once estimated that under the old system it would take central inspectors 200 years to complete inspection of all schools (cited in Hood et al 1999: 147). It was also a domain where, despite the fact that the teachers were a client profession of the state, they had won an operational autonomy that compared well with the autonomy of traditionally "self-regulated" liberal professions.

Much of this was turned upside down in the 1990s, following the passage of the Education Reform Act (1988) and the Education (Schools) Act of 1992. The formation of the Office for Standards in Education (OFSTED) as the state body concerned with the regulation of standards in education in 1992 heralded a significantly different regulatory approach (Gray and Wilcox 1995: 133–148). Gone was the conception of the schools inspector as a kind of gentle encourager of the dissemination of high culture; in its place was a ferocious insistence on the inspector as the driver of standards in the name of national efficiency. In OFSTED was created an institution that in culture and working practices was far removed from the main interests that had supported the old cooperative system. At the same time, there was a marked increase in the formal organization and institutional density of the regulatory system. In place of the fairly simple, small regulatory community that had joined an educational elite and a mandarin elite, there now developed a large, overlapping, and often competing range of regulatory bodies.

By the late 1990s, in addition to OFSTED, there existed individual local authorities, the kingpins of the historically displaced system, who still nevertheless retained significant roles; a Funding Agency for Schools; a Schools Curriculum and Assessments Authority; and several others, including "all purpose" regulators such as the Audit Commission and the National Audit Office, who intervened unpredictably in the regulatory system (Hood et al. 1999: 143–144). At the same time, there developed a marked shift in regulatory style, especially after the appointment of a new chief inspector of schools in 1995, toward a more adversarial and judgmental system. This was in turn associated with a move to more explicit, quantitatively expressed regulatory standards, notably in the use of standardized attainment tests and targets and a policy of "naming and shaming" those who failed to meet targets. (I rely on Pring 2001 for this account of changes in regulatory standards in teaching.)

The return of a new administration in 1997, though it ultimately displaced some individuals, changed little. The Labour government was convinced both that educational standards were an electorally sensitive issue and that fostering human capital and the skill base were the keys to international competitiveness. Indeed, the pressure to achieve targets probably intensified over the early years of New Labour's period in power, as the publication of the second Blair Administration's skills strategy in 2002 showed (see Department for Education and Skills 2002).

In summary: In the space of less than a decade, a cooperative, enclosed, oligarchic world had been broken open. Micromanagement of the school system from the center was now so great that ministers were forming views even on such details as particular methods of teaching (Blunkett 2001). In the course of the 1990s, the country acquired one of the most ambitious schemes of school inspection in the world. Brian Wilcox and John Gray's summary catches the ambitions of all this:

> The system of inspection inaugurated by the 1992 Act represented an unprecedented attempt to apply a universal model of inspection of ambitious frequency and comprehensiveness, carried out by independent inspectors drawn from a wide range of backgrounds and operating on a competitive commercial basis. We doubt if any more ambitious programme of school-by-school evaluation and review has ever been mounted anywhere in the world. (Wilcox and Gray 1996: 2)

In its form and ambitions, this new inspection system looks anything but a turn to reflexive regulation, soft bureaucracy, and steering through dispersed networks. Far from being smart casual postmodernism, it looks to be one of the clearest cases of the new regulatory state in Britain, as the incarnation of buttoned-up high modernism. Its origins can be traced right back to one of the main sources of change in the modern British state—the great economic crisis of the 1970s and the consequent first appearance of a "great debate" on education, a debate that was stimulated by the belief that the malaise of the economy was in part traceable to a malfunctioning school system. (For the context, see Richard Laughlin and John Broadbent [1997:

278–280].) Thus, there is a direct connection between these institutional upheavals and the birth of the wider modernist project of reshaping British economy and society to compete more effectively.

4. The United Kingdom and High Modernism

In Scott's great study, high modernism is mostly a villain (Scott 1998). That is hardly surprising, for much of the work is about its totalitarian variants. Yet high modernism is, precisely, a characteristic feature of modernity, and it is therefore at home in democratic cultures. The great insight offered by Porter's study of quantification in social life is the connection he establishes between quantification and democratic accountability (Porter 1995). Measurement helps turn the tacit and occluded into the explicit and the transparent. It therefore turns knowledge—and thus control—once available only to insiders into something widely accessible. Hence, many of the characteristic features of high modernism—notably the drive for synoptic legibility— are democratizing features. That is partly why the new regulatory state built in Britain has met such furious opposition from traditional elites: in the most prestigious universities; in the civil service elite that Thatcher encountered in the early 1980s; in the old City; and, as I write, in the arguments surrounding the creation of a new regulatory system for broadcasting, in the BBC.

Because high modernism is an inscribed trait of contemporary states, it is not unique to Britain. Two things nevertheless make the British experience special. First, the trajectory of Britain's historical development meant that it "half modernized," entering the twentieth century with an economy and a government that were still shaped by the traditional traits summarized in this chapter as "club rule." Second, the great crisis of the 1970s meant that the British were challenged—and offered the opportunity through the agency of Thatcherism—to make a particularly brutal break with that half-modernized past.

Other states had earlier broken more decisively with traditionalism, and that perhaps helps explain why they have often seemed more competent at high-modernist projects than have the British. The ambitious project—typically involving a mix of high-technology innovation and the reshaping of some part of civil society—is a characteristic mark of high modernism. A well-known contrast lies in the experiences of the French and the British. For over a century, the French state has had a history of some spectacular successes in precisely such projects, from clearing the marshes of Aquitaine to building the TGV (*train à grande vitesse*—high-speed train).[3] Recent British experience is littered with project disasters. Rail electrification, the Millennium Dome, the re-building of the national football stadium, the new buildings for the Scottish Parliament and the Welsh Assembly, countless information technology (IT) schemes: you name it, the British can make a fiasco out of it. To make a mess of one project may be deemed a misfortune; to make a mess of so many shows incompetence in the face of high modernism.

There is nothing elusively cultural in these failures. They arise from incompetence in complex project management. At the root of this incompetence lies the social configuration of institutions in the public and private sector charged with project management and an education system that still cannot produce enough people with the appropriate skills—for instance, in numeracy—to fill the division of labor in complex projects. Thus, the great crisis of the 1970s and the Thatcher Revolution helped propel the British state in the direction of high modernism. But creating the conditions efficiently to realize high-modernist projects will be a much longer haul. And that haul will require anything but a retreatist, postmodern state: it will demand continuing control over, and reshaping of, civil society.

~ 2

The Forgotten Center

State Activism and Corporatist Adjustment
in Holland and Germany

ANTON C. HEMERIJCK AND MARK I. VAIL

Since the 1970s, a well-developed literature has explored the dynamics of policymaking in corporatist countries. This literature emphasizes a high degree of involvement of societal interests, particularly employers and trade unions, in public policy formation and implementation (Schmitter 1977; Streeck and Schmitter 1985; Lehmbruch and Schmitter 1982). A number of scholars have shown how regularized channels of deliberation, consultation, and negotiation between labor and capital have contributed to economic growth and social peace. Corporatist systems often perform better, politically and economically, than liberal political economies, where questions of economic distribution and the organization of production are addressed primarily through (or remain unaddressed by) markets. Although this rich body of work has provided an analytical framework for exploring policy and institutional regularities in nonliberal political economies, it has paid scant attention to the role of the state (except, perhaps, in the original establishment of corporatist bargaining). Yet the role of the state is crucial to understanding how corporatist polities respond to shifting social and economic challenges. This omission has resulted in a misleading image of corporatist systems as requiring little regulation once established, with the interests of social groups almost seamlessly producing policies concomitant with the public good.

The theoretical underdevelopment of the state in traditional accounts of corporatist governance, we suggest, renders them poorly equipped to account for recent political developments in many advanced industrial countries. Like much of the literature on corporatism, recent work on "varieties of capitalism" undertheorizes the role of the state in corporatist or "coordinated market economies" (Hall and Soskice 2001a). As a result, such work has difficulty accounting for the significant variation in performance and employment across corporatist political economies. It also offers limited analytical purchase on the political sources of this variation, including the nature of the party system, the ideological postures of unions and employers' associations, and the partisan character and strategic predilections of particular governments. Moreover, these kinds of political factors are critical for understanding variation, not just *across* corporatist polities but also *within* corporatist systems over time. In all corporatist systems, adjustment invariably entails significant and continued involvement by the state, whose purview for autonomous action is critical to promoting needed reforms and institutional change.

This chapter examines the role of the state in promoting adjustment in two prototypical corporatist political economies, Germany and Holland. Both have experienced economic difficulties, which have led state authorities to attempt to remedy perceived corporatist dysfunctions. In fact, we contend that it is in hard economic times, when the relative scarcity of resources engenders competition among social groups and increases discrepancies between private interests and public weal, that the state's coordinating functions are *particularly* important. This is true both when the state delegates authority to the social partners, as during the 1970s, and when it attempts to repair or compensate for the shortcomings of existing corporatist frameworks, as during the past two decades. Such adverse economic contexts tend to intensify pressures on policymakers, not only to formulate just and viable policies that reduce economic uncertainty but also to promote negotiation among social partners, who are more likely to dig in their heels in tough times.

Germany and the Netherlands represent excellent prima facie cases for a comparative study of the role of the state in corporatist systems. The state in both countries has a tradition of sharing political space with the social partners. Employers are well organized, especially among large- and medium-sized firms, and collective bargaining occurs predominantly at the sectoral level (Streeck 1995; Thelen 1991). Furthermore, the Netherlands and Germany both possess "Bismarckian" welfare states, characterized by occupationally distinct, employment-related social insurance programs, comanaged by worker and employer representatives, and financed by earmarked payroll contributions from employers and workers (van Kersbergen 1995; Esping-Andersen 1990; Scharpf and Schmidt 2000a; Ferrera, Hemerijck, and Rhodes 2000).

At the same time, the two countries are distinct in terms of the institutional frameworks within which their welfare states and industrial relations systems are embedded. State intervention has traditionally been very strong in Dutch industrial relations (Windmuller 1969), whereas in Germany, the constitutionally enshrined principle of *Tarifautonomie*, or "wage independence," has limited intervention in this area. Likewise, in the Netherlands, a decentralized but unitary state retains final authority across a wide range of policy domains, whereas in Germany, jurisdictional limits on state authority impose significant constraints on policymakers, not only in wage bargaining but also in a number of other policy areas (Katzenstein 1987). As a result, the mechanisms through which the German state has facilitated adjustment have tended to be more informal and subtle than those in the Netherlands, although, as we shall see, recent German governments have been anything but passive observers of social and economic change.

During the past twenty years, the Dutch and German states have been instrumental in promoting reform and compensating for the policy failures of corporatist institutions. Previously, corporatist policymaking, in Germany and the Netherlands as elsewhere, was widely celebrated for promoting social peace, wage restraint, and vibrant economic growth, and both countries served as standard-bearers for the possibilities of adjustment through organized political and social bargaining. Indeed, it was the souring economic climate and stagflation of the 1970s, and states' evident inability to cope with it singlehandedly, that led policymakers in many countries to delegate greater authority to the social partners. Stories of corporatist success yielded to narratives of failure, however, as new economic problems emerged, including sluggish or even stagnant growth, high levels of structural unemployment, apparently unbridgeable insider-outsider cleavages, and increasingly severe pressures on wage-based social policy financing. These experiences clearly demonstrated that although hard economic times may lead to a shift toward more corporatist-style bargaining structures, such structures are not self-sustaining. Rather, they require continual state intervention in order to function appropriately.

As the Dutch and German economic pictures darkened, the same corporatist institutions that had once been credited with underpinning national prosperity came to be seen as the sources of sclerosis and failed adjustment. In response, the state in both countries (beginning in the 1980s in the Netherlands and somewhat later in Germany) has employed a variety of forms of intervention in an effort to fix dysfunctional corporatist policymaking structures. At times, state authorities have used administrative and financial pressure to coerce the social partners into undertaking desired policy changes. In some extreme cases, they have bypassed corporatism and imposed policies of their own devising, while in a few instances they have suspended corporatist bargaining or even dismantled it altogether.

Germany and the Netherlands represent two salient examples of corporatist political economies in which state authorities have sought to correct institutional and policy dysfunctions. By and large, Dutch authorities have possessed greater capacity to modify corporatist behavior than their German counterparts. That said, state authorities in both countries have become increasingly active and assertive in recent years.

In the 1980s, the Netherlands witnessed a resurgence of corporatist bargaining in the wake of a severe recession, spiraling unemployment, and significant inflation. Under the threat of government-imposed austerity and mandated liberalization, the social partners chose to negotiate, with unions wishing to limit the pain resulting from reform and employers hoping to forestall a government takeover of the policymaking process. The resulting "Wassenaar accord," concluded in late 1982, provided for the de-indexation of wages, negotiations over work-time reduction and job creation, and the partial decentralization of wage bargaining. This agreement ushered in a period of vibrant, negotiated reform in the 1980s and early 1990s that underpinned the celebrated "Dutch miracle" of rapid job growth (Visser and Hemerijck 1997). In the areas of social security and labor market reform, however, the Dutch picture has been more mixed. The dysfunctions of corporatist policymaking have led to alternating patterns of state intervention, suspensions of corporatism in social insurance, and much to the chagrin of the social partners, independent state efforts to shape active labor market policy after the failure of a tripartite experiment in the early 1990s.

In Germany, the 1980s witnessed a series of relatively timid reforms in social and labor market policy, followed by a period of increasing state intervention in response to the seismic social and economic shocks of reunification in 1990. Thereafter, German governments of both the Left and Right worked to promote corporatist negotiation, most notably in the case of the tripartite Bündnis für Arbeit, or "Alliance for Jobs." The failure of attempts to reinvigorate corporatist wage bargaining and social protection reform in turn led German governments to adopt a series of second-best strategies for promoting adjustment, characterized by a more aggressive, interventionist state posture and waning receptiveness to the concerns of the social partners and political opposition. In labor market policy, for example, they have introduced a wide variety of training and placement programs, boosted subsidies to employers to create jobs, and stepped up pressure on the unemployed to search for work. In social policy, where there are fewer constitutional limits on their authority, governments have been even more successful in securing reforms, as in the case of the recent restructuring of the pension system. Although federalism and the frequent control of the Bundesrat, or upper house of Parliament, by the political opposition, place significant limitations on state capacity even in the realm of social security, governments have often been able to enact reforms in this area by buying off or otherwise undermining the opposition politically.

These nationally distinct patterns of state intervention provide clear support for the two central arguments of this chapter. First, they demonstrate that state capacity and strategy are crucial to understanding the dynamics of corporatist politics, particularly in periods of reform, fiscal austerity, and slow economic growth. Second, they illustrate that corporatism is a dynamic and evolving process of dialogue and political exchange between the state and social partners, rather than a fixed institutional structure producing stable and predictable political patterns and policy trajectories. In our contribution to this volume, we focus on wage policy, social policy, and labor market policy, domains that have moved to the center of recent reform debates. In each of these areas, the state has been instrumental in securing reforms, whether by promoting compromise among unions and employers, working indirectly to reshape the policy incentives faced by the social partners, or intervening directly to compensate for the failures of existing corporatist institutions. In exploring these policy areas, we show how national constitutional and institutional particularities shape both the options available to state authorities and the resulting character of their efforts to repair broken corporatist arrangements.

The remainder of this chapter provides a comparative analysis of state efforts to address growing problems in social security and labor market policy in the Netherlands and Germany. In the following section, we undertake a brief review of the literature on corporatism, emphasizing the extent to which leading scholars have addressed, or failed to speak to, the critical role of the state in corporatist governance. We then proceed with a detailed discussion of state initiatives and the politics of reform in the Netherlands, followed by a similar analysis of developments in Germany. We end with a brief conclusion, where we provide an overview of recent Dutch and German experiences and explore their import for scholarly studies of reform in corporatist political economies and the role of the state in corporatist adjustment.

1.   The State and Corporatist Policymaking

The corporatist literature of the 1970s and 1980s made important contributions to the revival of the study of institutions mediating between state and market in advanced capitalist democracies. In the midst of the allegedly "ungovernable" 1970s, there was significant empirical support for the hypothesis that the capacity of advanced industrial societies to cope with social conflict and improve economic performance is increased by an institutional infrastructure that incorporates the societal interests of organized capital and labor into national economic policy formation and implementation (Lehmbruch and Schmitter 1982; Berger 1981b; Goldthorpe 1984). Corporatist research during this period focused primarily on the organizational attributes of interest groups, arguing that tripartite incomes policies were almost indispensable tools of crisis management. In particular, so-called encompassing organizations, or highly centralized and concentrated functional interests, were believed likely to pursue responsible strategies of collective action supportive of the public goals of full employment and price stability (Olson 1982; Bruno and Sachs 1985; Lange and Garrett 1985; Goldthorpe 1984). To a considerable extent, corporatist success in achieving economic and social stability was seen as largely self-reinforcing, due to positive demonstration effects that promote trust among the social partners and between them and the state.

In the 1980s, however, many corporatist political economies ran into serious employment, fiscal, and monetary difficulties. The advent of such problems provided ammunition for neoliberal and other critics of political "interference" with market mechanisms. As the recovery of Western economies seemed increasingly elusive, a number of arguments were advanced for the putative demise of corporatism. One influential perspective took shape around the "Eurosclerosis" diagnosis, which suggested that the corporatist political economies of continental Europe were fraught with entrenched "insider-outsider" cleavages that impeded growth and reform (Olson 1982; Lindbeck and Snower 1988). Other authors were ready to predict "the end of organized capitalism" (Lash and Urry 1987), while still others discovered the "challenge of flexibility" (Baglioni and Crouch 1990), arguing that pressures to decentralize collective bargaining and the shift from Fordist, standardized mass production toward craft-based, diversified models were difficult to reconcile with corporatist interest intermediation (Piore and Sabel 1984; Locke, Kochan, and Piore 1995). Highlighting the historical correlation of corporatist success with Keynesian macroeconomic intervention, other observers suggested that the liberalization of international capital markets in the 1980s had sharply curtailed the political capacities of national governments to offer full employment in exchange for wage restraint through the use of fiscal and monetary policy (Scharpf 1991). Finally, with the introduction of the Stability and Growth Pact in the lead-up to the Economic and Monetary Union (EMU) and the resulting shift toward hard currency policies across Europe, many scholars feared that intensified regime competition would further jeopardize corporatist bargaining frameworks.

Yet the fiscal and monetary pressures associated with qualifying for

EMU did not generally lead to bold strategies of liberalization and deregulation. On the contrary, EMU seemed to spur a resurgence of national social pacts aimed at ensuring welfare state sustainability, as the shift to a hard currency regime unexpectedly brought the social partners in many countries closer together (Fajertag and Pochet 2000). This trend began in the Netherlands with the 1982 "Wassenaar" accord, followed by Denmark and Ireland in 1987, and Finland, Italy, Spain, and Portugal in the early to mid-1990s (D. Cameron 2001; M. Rhodes 2001a, 2001b).

The role of the state in reviving corporatist concertation has been relatively neglected by scholars of corporatism. From their earliest incarnations, most treatments of corporatist governance employed a rather narrow, "society-centered" perspective, emphasizing the organizational attributes of interest groups and largely neglecting the role of the state in what purported to be more or less self-regulating political economies. To be sure, the state played a significant role in some of the earlier corporatist literature, particularly with respect to the establishment of corporatist bargaining frameworks. According to Philippe Schmitter's famous definition, for example, "societal corporatism" is characterized by a "limited number of singular, compulsory, non-competitive, hierarchically ordered and functionally differentiated categories, *recognized, or licenced (if not created) by the state, and granted a deliberate representational monopoly*" (Schmitter 1979: 13).[1] Although such scholars acknowledged the importance of the state, they tended to limit their analysis of its role to the *initial* construction of corporatist systems, which thereafter were supposed to be more or less self-regulating. In so doing, they failed to recognize that the state plays a critical role, not only in the initial delegation of authority to the social partners (as occurred during the 1970s in many advanced industrial countries) but also, and perhaps even more important, in sustaining the viability of corporatist bargaining in the face of significant fluctuations in economic performance and shifting political and policy contexts.

The absence of a dynamic conception of the state continues to characterize more recent work, notably the emerging literature on "Varieties of Capitalism," founded by Peter Hall and David Soskice (Hall and Soskice 2001a). Viewing the political-economic dynamics of both coordinated market economies (CMEs), such as Germany, and liberal market economies (LMEs), such as the United States and Britain, as self-reinforcing and highly path dependent, Hall and Soskice overlook the role of politics and the state's capacity to engineer novel adaptive strategies, except to argue that, over time, government policies reinforce the tendency of both CMEs and LMEs to revert to established practices (Hall and Soskice 2001a: 62–64, 66–67). Accordingly, while Soskice and Hall admit that governments are important, they see their role as limited to supporting existing patterns of coordination, particularly in CMEs, in response to pressure from economic shocks, both exogenous and endogenous (63). As a result, not only is the state's role reduced to reinforcing established economic structures, but other political factors, including party dynamics and electoral strategies, are largely ignored.

Recognizing the neglect of the state in such approaches, a separate strand of research has, since the mid-1980s, attempted to develop a more complex, "state-centered" perspective (see, e.g., Evans, Rueschemeyer, and Skocpol 1985). This body of work has emphasized the state as an autonomous actor that critically affects the ways in which corporatist political economies adjust to shifting economic, social, and political challenges (e.g., Poggi 1990). Colin Crouch, in particular, has shown how organized interests define their strategies of collective action within an institutional setting involving distinctive state traditions and complex linkages between state and society (Crouch 1993). Insights such as Crouch's point to the fact that nearly all aspects of corporatist governance are profoundly affected by the state. He shows that the state plays several key roles related to the construction of corporatist frameworks and the support of vibrant political exchange within them. First, the state is an institutional regulator providing *Ordnungspolitik*, the legal framework and ground rules that govern corporatist negotiation among the social partners. Second, the state's legislative capacity in economic, social, and labor market policy has a direct influence on relations among the government, trade unions, and employer organizations. Third, the state frames and facilitates corporatist exchange, whether through side payments or threats to bypass corporatist institutions. As new policy pressures and dysfunctions arise over time, state intervention in each of these areas is required to sustain a responsive system of meaningful political exchange.

The state's authority to approve and ratify also implies the power to nullify undesirable agreements, enabling it to ensure bona fide processes of negotiation. In this respect, the multifarious role of the state in corporatist governance corresponds to Fritz Scharpf's notion of the "shadow of hierarchy" in strategic games (Scharpf 1997). For Scharpf, the ultimate availability of hierarchical intervention and state ratification of agreements among private interests helps to curb distributive conflict and opportunistic rent-seeking among bargainers. Likewise, state intervention is critical for combating the social partners' potential "externalization strategies," which involve unions' and employers' mutual agreement to protect their narrow interests at the expense of the collectivity. This "relative autonomy of the state" does *not* mean that state actors can change the institutional environment as if they were operating a lever, however. Rather, state responses to corporatist policy exchanges shape and are shaped in turn by both the institutional framework within which they operate and the strategies of organized interests with which they are confronted.

Even in the presence of an active state role in guiding corporatist bargaining, conflicts or collusion among the multiple interests involved can result in failure, a situation that Scharpf aptly labels a "joint-decision trap" (Scharpf 1985). The state is inevitably confronted with conflicts between recognized social partners, whose needs to represent rank-and-file demands effectively and regulate these claims are in constant tension. When the strain between what Wolfgang Streeck and Philippe Schmitter have called the "logic of influence" and the "logic of membership" is not successfully managed by the social partners, a "representation crisis" can result, jeopardizing the entire edifice of corporatist exchange (Streeck and Schmitter 1985). In such a situation, capital and labor pursue their own versions of the national economic interest, and their respective strategies are influenced not only by divergent ideologies and economic doctrines but also by perceptions of their respective roles in the political economy and their self-regarding concerns with organizational growth and survival.

At other times, the social partners may collude to defend mutually beneficial arrangements, thereby creating significant impediments to reform. In both cases, the state faces the challenge of reshaping unions' and employers' preferences in ways that are supportive of desired policy or institutional changes. Much depends on the state's capacity for "consensus engineering" to generate, maintain, and adjust agreements in the face of changing political-economic circumstances and potential collusion or conflict among the social partners that can produce obstacles to reform. The social partners' requisite willingness to accept sacrifices, on the understanding that they will not be exploited, but rather reciprocated, when the occasion arises, presupposes a high degree of mutual trust, which must be nurtured over time by enlightened state intervention.

Without effective consensus engineering, which relies heavily on actual or potential state intervention, corporatist institutions can become barriers to effective policy coordination, economic performance, and social peace. Under such conditions of a "joint-decision trap," the state becomes imprisoned in an institutional setting that no longer functions as intended. Faced with such a situation, state authorities can choose one of two options. On the one hand, they can work actively to reinvigorate societal consensus in an attempt to relaunch more responsive corporatist bargaining processes. On the other, they can distance themselves from corporatist arrangements in an attempt to extricate the state from its dependence on the support of the social partners. Such a strategy of "corporatist disengagement" constitutes a reaction to prolonged corporatist immobility and is often accompanied by a state's move to devise reforms directly rather than negotiating with the social partners. In extreme circumstances, the state may even dismantle parts of the corporatist apparatus.

This possibility noted, the availability of state-led corporatist disengagement is limited by the path-dependent character of established corporatist institutions, as the state's ability to dismantle or bypass corporatism very much relies upon the institutional capacities at its disposal. While enjoying a certain autonomy to address problems in an authoritative fashion, state actors will generally believe themselves to be in need of societal consensus and are thus reluctant to break out of the stagnant corporatist policy framework or dismantle corporatist institutions in favor of untried alternatives. In the event of failed corporatist bargaining, state actors tend to try first to persuade organized interests by offering them side payments and other incentives or work to adjust and recalibrate the corporatist model in order to revitalize joint policy formation and implementation. While corporatism functions best when there is a credible commitment on the part of the state not to intervene, accumulated failures on the part of the social partners to perform delegated policy functions create both opportunity and political pressure for the state to do just that. In the sections that follow, we examine state efforts to repair dysfunctional corporatist arrangements in Holland and Germany. We begin with the Dutch case, where the revitalization of corporatist wage bargaining in the 1980s and 1990s was prompted by an effective "shadow of hierarchy" supported by a high degree of institutionalized state capacity.

2.   State Responses to the Contingencies of Dutch Corporatism

In this section, we focus on Dutch reforms of wage bargaining, social security, and labor market policy and regulation. As these components of the political economy are governed by different mixes of associational self-regulation and government intervention, state strategies have varied widely. State initiatives have ranged from attempts to reinvigorate Dutch corporatism in the area of wage bargaining to deliberate efforts to dismantle corporatism in social insurance.

The Dutch political economy is furnished with a firmly established apparatus of bi- and tripartite boards for nationwide social and economic policymaking. The Foundation of Labor (STAR, or Stichting van de Arbeid), controlled by the central union and employers' organizations, is a private foundation, established in 1945 as a forum for meetings between the social partners. These meetings, attended by a delegation from the cabinet, occur twice per year, once in the spring when the budget is prepared and again in the fall when a new round of wage negotiations is about to begin. The Social-Economic Council (SER, or Sociaal-Economische Raad), founded in 1950, is a tripartite advisory board. Since its reorganization in 1995, employers and unions each have eleven seats, while the other eleven are occupied by independent Crown members appointed by the government, usually professors of economics, the president of the Central Bank, and the director of the Central Planning Bureau. The foremost Dutch economic forecasting agency, the Central Planning Bureau (CPB, or Centraal Planbureau), enjoys a great deal of influence as the key supplier of economic projections, on the basis of which the social partners define their strategies of collective action.

A distinctive feature of Dutch postwar economic policy has long been its state-led wage policy (Windmuller 1969). In the 1960s and 1970s, responsibility for wage policy reverted to unions and employers. However, since they were often unable to agree among themselves, negotiations frequently ended with state intervention. Problems intensified with the first oil shock in 1973. The center-left Den Uyl government opted for a strategy of fiscal stimulus. This set the stage for a conventional Keynesian corporatist package of fiscal reflation in exchange for wage restraint. The strategy failed, however, due to the refusal by increasingly radical trade unions to support the government's loose budgetary policies with wage moderation. In response, in 1974 and 1976, the state imposed a wage freeze, but to no avail. A center-right government was also forced to resort to wage intervention in 1979, 1980, and 1981.

Having failed to adjust to the first oil shock, the Netherlands experienced a severe recession following the second oil crisis in 1979. With unemployment running at 8.5 percent in 1982 and 11.0 percent in 1983 (Scharpf and Schmidt 2000b: 341), the highest rates since the Great Depression, the public grew increasingly frustrated with divided governments and repeated corporatist failures. Dutch economic problems during this period were further exacerbated by the so-called Dutch Disease. This term referred to the fact that the rising price of natural gas, of which the Netherlands had large deposits, created a large current-account surplus and put upward pressure on the Dutch guilder, in turn weakening the competitiveness of Dutch exports and import-competing sectors (van Rijckeghem 1982).

Elections in 1982 brought to power an austerity coalition of the CDA (the Christen Democratisch Appel) and the liberal VVD (the Volkspartij voor Vrijheid en Democratie), led by Christian Democrat Ruud Lubbers. His government presented itself as a "no-nonsense" administration that was "there to govern." Ready to take on vested interests, the new government immediately suspended cost-of-living indexation in wage agreements and social benefits, while freezing minimum wages, social benefits, and public sector wages. The stage appeared to be set for confrontation between the state and the social partners, especially the unions.

Surprisingly, the inauguration of the new government was met instead with a social pact, the now-famous Wassenaar accord of November 24, 1982, named after the Dutch town where it was concluded

(Visser and Hemerijck 1997). After a decade of corporatist failure, the Dutch social partners had come to recognize that promoting invest-ment, essential for job creation and the struggle against unemploy-ment, required a higher level of profits, hence a lower wage share. Moreover, the unions, weakened by the severe recession, were hardly in a position to engage in industrial conflict, whereas the employers' organization feared political interference in the form of a statutory, uniform reduction of the working week. As a result, the trade unions accepted protracted real-wage restraint in exchange for a so-called cost-neutral reduction of working hours and job sharing.

The Wassenaar accord marked a shift from the failed tripartism in the 1970s to successful bipartism in the 1980s and 1990s. Despite the celebrated voluntary character of the bipartite agreement, it is crucial to emphasize that Wassenaar was prompted by an effective threat on the part of the Lubbers administration to intervene in wage setting. Compelled by this "shadow of hierarchy," the social partners negoti-ated a bipartite deal. Once the accord was signed, the government withdrew this sword of Damocles. Helped by an international eco-nomic upswing, rising levels of profits and investment, and significant job creation, Lubbers's austerity policy paid off politically. In 1986, the center-right coalition was reelected, with gains for his CDA party. Two successive center-right governments thus successfully engineered a clear break with corporatist immobility of the 1970s.

This resurgence of corporatism significantly altered the relation-ships among unions, employers, and the state. A new pattern emerged, characterized by centralized dialogue over legislative and substantive policy issues, combined with sectoral wage bargaining based on the primacy of industrial self-regulation (van Toren 1996). In the wake of the Wassenaar accord, the tripartite Social and Economic Council also gained a new lease on life and issued a range of unanimous policy recommendations regarding youth unemployment (1984 and 1986), training (1986 and 1987), long-term unemployment (1986 and 1987), the minimum wage (1988), and part-time work (1989).

This new corporatism proved fairly robust, although it was certainly not free of conflict. Conflict occurred within the government in 1989, when the Christian Democrats exchanged their Liberal coalition part-ners for the Social Democrats after the breakdown of the coalition over environmental policy. There were also conflicts over economic policy. At the turn of the 1990s, German reunification boosted Dutch growth, but high interest rates soon dampened economic activity, leading to a reversal of employment gains. In this troubled context, the credibility and legitimacy of Dutch social partnership came under attack from parliamentary leaders, who maintained that consensual, negotiated adjustment occurred at too slow a pace to respond to economic crises.

Alarmed by mounting political pressures, the central employers' and union organizations moved closer together in the early 1990s. In another attempt to stave off government intervention, the social partners signed a multiyear agreement, the so-called New Course accord, in December 1993 (Hemerijck, van de Meer, and Visser 2000). This accord was an heir to Wassenaar but went further down the path of organized decentralization and flexibility. Employers abandoned their categorical refusal of shorter working hours, and unions promised further wage restraint. This accord also embraced a new balance between flexibility and security by reducing levels of protection of existing ("core") workers, while enhancing employment opportunities and social security benefits for part-time and temporary workers (Visser 1999). The New Course helped relaunch strong growth and job creation that would last for nearly a decade.

Though the social partners repaired the wage-setting system and introduced flexibility into the labor market, they were also guilty of externalizing the costs of economic adjustment onto the social security system. Rather than firing workers outright, employers, with the support of the unions, moved surplus employees into generous disability, sickness, and early retirement programs. Displaced workers largely preserved their income, but the cost of these programs was borne by (or externalized to) the general public. Unsurprisingly, in the late 1980s, this cartellike arrangement, common to many continental European countries, resulted in uncontrollable growth in the volume of social security claimants. In response, the second Lubbers coalition of Christian Democrats and conservative Liberals, in office between 1986 and 1989, enacted a package of cost-containment measures, including a reduction of the replacement rate of social security benefits from 80 percent to 70 percent of previous wages. Despite these cuts, in the second half of the 1980s, the number of people receiving disability benefits continued to rise, leading to an explosion in costs. As the number of disability claimants neared the politically sensitive figure of 1 million in 1989, out of an adult population of 7 million, Prime Minister Lubbers publicly dramatized the issue by saying that the country was "sick" and required "tough medication."

Lubbers I and II had exhausted the "price" strategy of bringing social expenditures under control by freezing and lowering benefits, supported by consistent wage restraint. Lubbers recognized that he needed the Social Democrats (the Partij van de Arbeid [PvdA]), led by ex-union leader and Wassenaar negotiator Wim Kok, in the government to share responsibility for the unfinished business of welfare reform. The PvdA reentered the government in 1989 as a partner in Lubbers's third cabinet. The government's chief goal was to raise the level of labor force participation, as opposed to keeping formal employment low by shunting excess workers into welfare programs (Wetenschappelijke Raad voor het Regeringsbeleid 1990).

The new government shifted to a "volume" policy, which aimed to reduce the number of benefit recipients. The social partners were less than enthusiastic about this objective, however. The Social Economic Council proved unable to draft a unanimous recommendation on changes to the disability insurance scheme. As a result, the government opted to act unilaterally. In the summer of 1991, after a great deal of agonizing, the government decided to restrict disability programs (Occupational Disability Insurance Act—Wet op de Arbeidsongeschiktheidsverzekering [WAO]) and close off other routes to labor market exit. The legal requirement that partially disabled WAO benefit recipients accept alternative employment was strengthened, and eligibility criteria for the WAO scheme were tightened. The proposal also included a reduction of replacement rates for all workers under the age of fifty. Benefits would ultimately decrease to 70 percent of the statutory minimum wage, plus an additional age-related allowance. Furthermore, workers under age fifty who filed disability claims would be subjected to new, stricter medical examinations. This episode had far-reaching political consequences, leading the unions to organize their largest postwar protest, with nearly 1 million participants, in The Hague. This unrest generated a profound crisis within the PvdA, nearly leading to Kok's resignation as party leader.

In 1992, the Public Audit Office (Algemene Rekenkamer) published a report highlighting the ambiguous distribution of power and responsibilities within the Dutch welfare state. The report suggested that the sluggish pace of reform was due in no small part to the social partners' broad policymaking and administrative authority within the social security system. In response, Parliament decided to use its biggest weapon, an All-Party Parliamentary Inquiry, involving testimony gathered by numerous legal authorities. The commission's inquiry (often referred to as the Buurmeijer Commission after the name of its chairman) was crucial in triggering path-breaking institutional changes in the Dutch social security system. In September 1993, the Buurmeijer report revealed what everybody already knew, namely, that social security was being misused by the social partners for the purpose of industrial restructuring and advocated a fundamental recasting of bipartite governance in Dutch social security. Unsurprisingly, the social partners disputed this diagnosis, but, confronted with the commission's conclusions, they were in no position to defend the institutional status quo.

The 1994 elections took place in the shadow of popular discontent over welfare reform, and the Lubbers-Kok coalition lost its majority, yielding 32 of its 103 parliamentary seats. Despite being stripped of 12 of its 49 seats, the PvdA became the largest party. The progressive Liberals (the Democrats 66) persuaded the PvdA and the conservative-liberal VVD to form a coalition, resulting in the first government since 1917 without a confessional party (Koole 1997). This new, so-called purple coalition, a mixture of socialist red and liberal blue, placed "jobs, jobs, jobs" at the center of its social and economic policy agenda. Its primary objective was maximizing employment, rather than combatting unemployment through labor-supply reduction. The PvdA, however, stipulated as a nonnegotiable condition for its cooperation that the level and duration of social benefits remain untouched.

The restructuring of Dutch social security by two successive purple governments under Wim Kok (1994–2002) is best characterized as a case of "managed liberalization" (van der Veen and Trommel 1999; OECD 2000a). This approach entailed two central components. In substantive terms, financial incentives were developed through a partial privatization of social risks. With respect to institutional design, a pathbreaking overhaul of the Dutch social security administration was enacted in several steps between 1995 and 2000 (Visser and Hemerijck 1997). The majority of programmatic changes placed a heavier financial burden for covering sickness and disability risks on employers, so as to create incentives for them to limit sickness- and disability-related absences, even as the state assumed a more active responsibility for the reintegration of sick-listed employees. Beginning with the privatization of the sickness scheme (through the Ziektewet [ZW], or Sickness Benefits Act) in 1994, the responsibility for the first few weeks of workers' sickness-related absence was transferred from the sectoral funds to individual employers. In 1996, all employers became responsible for coverage of benefits up to a maximum of twelve months, at a rate of 70 percent of the most recently earned wage (SZW 1998).

In May 1998, the Kok administration was reelected, rewarded by the voters for its excellent employment record and tough stance on social security reform. The blessings of the Dutch "Polder Model," something of an alternative to both neoliberal deregulation and traditional social democracy, were celebrated in the international media (Schmid 1996; Hemerijck and Visser 1999; Hartog 1999).[2] The economy grew by 2.9 percent per year in the 1990s, and the rate of unemployment fell to 3 percent, the lowest in the European Union (EU) after Luxembourg. With 1.4 million new jobs, labor force participation rose from 59 percent to 67 percent of the adult population. In 2000, a budget surplus of 0.3 percent of gross domestic product (GDP) was achieved, and the public debt was reduced from 80 percent of GDP in 1994 to 54 percent in 2001.

Before the second Kok administration took office in June 1998, the social partners reached an agreement in the SER on the privatization of certain aspects of the social security implementation system, in particular, sickness leave and job placement for the disabled. This privatization program pertained to the administration of social security provisions, but the newly formed "Purple II" Coalition argued that the intake of claimants in these areas, by contrast, could not be left to market forces. In late 1998, the basic outline for the newly integrated organizational structure was presented as part of the SWI process ("Cooperation, Work, and Income"). Subsequently, the SUWI report ("Structure of the Execution of Work and Income"), officially adopted in 1999, stated that social insurance organizations and employment boards should join forces in so-called Centers for Work and Income (CWIs). The new "Work and Income (Implementation Structure) Act," which radically altered the way in which a number of benefit schemes are implemented, came into force on January 1, 2002. The act reduced the role of the social partners in this area and granted more responsibility to the Ministry of Social Affairs and Employment. The Work and Income Board (Raad voor Werk en Inkomen [RWI]), with representatives from employers, employees, and local authorities, was set up to help formulate overall policy directions in the areas of work and income but lacked any real executive authority (SZW 2001).

Like most of its continental counterparts, the Dutch welfare state did not deploy active labor market policies until the early 1990s. The Dutch Public Employment Service (PES) had been a state monopoly since 1930. Since the mid-1970s, a dormant state monopoly ran job-placement offices, shunned by employers and skilled workers and over-run by the unemployed, for whom little could be done. Then, after long preparation, in 1991, a new tripartite employment service was created.

While the demonopolization of placement services and the tenuous combination of functional and regional decentralization represented a major break in Dutch labor market policy, corporatist innovation in this area failed to meet expectations. A 1995 official review of the new tripartite structure, written by a commission chaired by former Minister of the Interior Van Dijk (CDA), was overwhelmingly negative. The commission argued that the new PES had failed to take charge, decentralization had gone too far, finances were poorly managed, and decision-making procedures were cumbersome and unclear.

The social partners were furious about the Van Dijk commission's critique, which led ambitious Social Democratic Minister of Social Affairs and Employment Ad Melkert to seek alternative solutions rather than patching up incipient corporatist arrangements. From the advent of the period of purple coalition governments, Melkert launched a number of labor market policy instruments that were to remain independent of the tripartite PES (Visser and Hemerijck 1997). Special "activation" programs, or so-called Melkert jobs, were designed to promote participation among low-skilled workers, women, younger workers, foreign nationals, the long-term unemployed, and others who stood poor chances of labor market success. On the de-mand side, the "jobs, jobs, and more jobs" slogan was embodied in increased support for wage moderation through reductions in em-ployers' social contributions and greater tax incentives for workers to accept jobs, particularly at or near the minimum wage.

The introduction of the Jobseekers Employment Act (Wet Inschakeling Werkzoekenden [WIW]) in 1998 marked a critical step in the shift in the focus of state policy from seeking to expand the number of jobs to encouraging the unemployed and nonemployed to take those jobs that were readily available. Each new WIW entrant (or unemployment claimant) was required to undergo an assessment interview, which is officially the responsibility of the municipalities but in practice is often delegated to social service and employment organizations. In this interview, a person's chances for employment or further education are assessed, after which an individual route to either work or social activation is sought. Participation in this scheme is obligatory for the unemployed, and a refusal can result in the withdrawal of benefits (SZW 2001).

Since the mid-1990s, labor market flexibility has become an integral part of the new policy mix of labor market regulation and has enjoyed significant support from the social partners. Lower taxes and social contributions, made possible by improved public finances and a broader tax base, have been deployed to induce unions to accept both wage moderation and labor market flexibility. By "greasing the wheels" of corporatist concertation in this way, the government has been able to secure collective bargaining accords that encompassed the "flexicurity" approach that formed the core of its strategy for creating jobs. In 1995, unions and employers signed the first collective agreement for temporary workers, which introduced a right of continued employment and pension insurance after four consecutive contracts or twenty-four months of service for all workers, union members and nonmembers alike. The collective agreement for temporary work prepared the ground for the 1996 agreement on "Flexibility and Security," which in turn paved the way for a new Working Hours (Adjustment) Act in 2000. This measure gave all part-time workers an explicit right to equal treatment in all areas negotiated by the social partners, including wages, basic social security, training and education, subsidized care provision, holiday pay, and second-tier pension rights. In exchange for these added protections, unions accepted the liberalization of firms' right to hire and fire workers in core industries, where unionization rates were relatively high. It is important to emphasize that the initiative for flexicurity came from the social partners on the basis of an innovative collective agreement, which then gained the status of law through state legislation. Together with the incremental individualization of the tax system since 1984, flexicurity legislation has contributed to the "normalization" of part-time employment, which now encompasses nearly one-third of the workforce.

During the past twenty years, the story of Dutch social security and labor market reform has been marked by significant successes, which have nonetheless reflected some of the limitations of Dutch corporatism. In the area of labor market reform, recent administrations have been able to secure moderate wage agreements and increased labor market flexibility, both of which have contributed to major reductions in employment. Although the deals that have underpinned these happy outcomes have primarily been the work of the social partners, they have been concluded under a "shadow of hierarchy," involving the state's implicit or explicit threats to intervene in the event of the social partners' failure to act. In the domain of social security reform, the Dutch state has adopted a more aggressive posture, effectively nationalizing portions of the welfare state, in particular, the regulation of the intake of new claimants, in order to secure reforms that limit expenditures and the number of beneficiaries. If labor market outcomes have been governed by a "shadow of hierarchy," in other words, welfare policy outcomes have been shaped by hierarchy *tout court*, as the relatively capacious Dutch state has exerted increasing control over the policymaking process and eroded the long-standing prerogatives of the social partners. While the Dutch story reflects possibilities for corporatist renewal, then, it also demonstrates that such an outcome can depend on—and often is dependent on—a significant degree of state intervention within the policymaking process.[3]

3. The German State and the Dilemmas of Corporatist Social Protection Reform

Germany's path of adjustment has diverged from that of the Netherlands due primarily to institutional and political differences between the two countries. First, in contrast to the Dutch unitary, decentralized state, the prerogatives of German state authorities are limited by a federal distribution of political authority. An important institutional expression of German federalism is a bicameral Parliament, in which the *Länder*, or federal states, are represented in the upper house, the Bundesrat, which enjoys authority over a good deal of German legislation and is often controlled by opposition parties. Other limitations on the prerogatives of the German state can be found in particular policy areas, notably labor market policy, in which the constitutional principle of *Tarifautonomie*, unknown in the Netherlands, reserves authority over collective bargaining to unions and employers. Because of these constraints, German authorities have been unable to impose wage restraint in the Dutch fashion. That said, since the early 1990s, German governments have adopted an increasingly aggressive posture in the areas of labor market and social security reform, using what financial and institutional resources they do enjoy to promote significant policy change.

From its inception, the postwar German social market economy was designed to support a self-regulating, virtuous circle between vibrant job growth and generous social policies. The German approach was quite successful during the postwar boom and weathered the crises of the 1970s and 1980s relatively well (Scharpf 1984: 258). The chief policymaking goal before 1990 was to preserve the existing system and promote social peace by equitably dividing wealth between wages and profits and cushioning workers from the effects of (relatively rare) unemployment.[4] This strategy was ill-equipped to handle the strains resulting from German reunification in 1990, however, which forced the system into full-blown crisis. Millions of poorly adapted eastern workers entered the labor market, scores of uncompetitive eastern firms went bankrupt, the government's high-wage strategy for revitalizing the eastern economy accelerated job losses, and rising economic vulnerability put intense pressure on the welfare state. Over time, high rates of structural unemployment, increasing welfare expenditures, and repeated hikes in payroll taxes came to represent serious threats to the sustainability of the celebrated German model.

In response, successive administrations have undertaken initiatives designed to remedy the failures of corporatism and adjust the German political economy to new economic realities. The initial strategy of the center-right government of Chancellor Helmut Kohl—and, after 1998, the center-left administration of Gerhard Schröder—involved pursuing Dutch-style wage restraint through negotiations with the social partners. The government hoped that the social partners would strike bargains that would lead to significant employment creation.

In 1995, the Kohl government created the Bündnis für Arbeit, or

Alliance for Jobs, a standing forum for the government and social partners to develop social policy and labor market reforms jointly. Revived under Schröder in 1998, the Bündnis seemed to augur a period of reinvigorated corporatist bargaining. Despite much fanfare, however, the forum produced very little in terms of tangible policy results. Neither employers (who wished above all to increase labor flexibility and limit social contributions and tax burdens) nor unions (who were more concerned with protecting the wages of their older industrial membership than promoting jobs in emerging, largely non-unionized sectors) demonstrated much interest in making sacrifices for the noble but less proximate goals of reducing unemployment and ensuring the viability of social protection. As a result, the Bündnis degenerated into a talking-shop. In early 2003, the government finally allowed the organization to lapse, thereby recognizing a failure that been evident to many for some time.[5]

The failure of the Bündnis reflects the broader dilemmas faced by the German state in shaping labor market and social policies. Because the purview for state intervention in the labor market is limited by both the constitutional principle of *Tarifautonomie* and the prerogatives of the federal labor office, German governments have been unable to cast a "shadow of hierarchy" in the Dutch manner. As a result, wage restraint has remained elusive, despite high unemployment.

The collapse of the Bündnis led both Kohl and Schröder to adopt a second-best strategy for palliating the effects of the increasingly dysfunctional German wage-setting system, involving a series of federal labor market programs. If these initiatives reflected state authorities' recognition of their inability to repair the German collective-bargaining system, they also represented a significant departure from the traditional pattern of consensual, incremental economic adjustment and the relatively passive posture of the state with respect to social and labor market policy.

Initially, this second-best labor market strategy involved the creation of a number of federal job creation, placement, and retraining schemes in former East Germany (the DDR, or Deutsche Demokratische Republik). Spurred by the massive economic dislocation resulting from reunification, Kohl expanded labor market schemes designed to absorb large numbers of unemployed workers, preserve social stability, and begin the task of adapting the eastern workforce to a modern capitalist economy.[6] By the mid-1990s, around 450,000 easterners were participating in federal training programs, with another 400,000 employed in temporary job schemes. As a result, as early as 1991, spending by the Bundesanstalt für Arbeit, or Federal Labor Office (hereinafter BA) had become the largest single component of financial transfers from West to East. By the end of 1994, the number of people enrolling in labor market programs was actually above the level of registered unemployment (Knuth 1997).

As Germany's postunification slump deepened, state authorities moved aggressively on a host of other policies that affect employment, particularly under the Schröder government. A characteristic example involved reforms of the extensive network of early retirement schemes. Instituted in the 1980s, these programs exploded in the 1990s, with 809,000 people receiving benefits in 1999, not including disability pensions (OECD 2001: 37).[7] Around 20 percent of the population aged fifty-five to sixty-five in the West and 40 percent in the East were participating in related programs by 1996 (Manow and Seils 2000).[8] Although such policies have the politically desirable effect of reducing the formal unemployment *rate*, since retirees are not counted, they are extremely costly and have at best questionable effects on actual joblessness. In most cases, firms do not replace workers "retired" at the expense of the social security system (OECD 2001a: 31).

In the wake of the postreunification influx of unemployed eastern workers, the federal government attempted to limit recourse to early retirement schemes, in the process subtly assuming a degree of authority from the social partners. In particular, the government has worked within the BA to end some early retirement programs and boost subsidies for part-time jobs for older workers. It has done so in the hopes of increasing older workers' rate of exit from traditional employment, while providing them with an income in the labor market.[9] Although the dire state of the eastern economy has made curtailing these programs politically tricky (Ebbinghaus 2000: 534–535), state officials have continued to tighten eligibility restrictions (Trampusch 2002).

Recent governments have also worked to remedy sclerotic corporatist labor market arrangements, promoting low-wage jobs by reimbursing employers' social contributions and granting tax exemptions to low-wage workers. Although the Kohl government made tentative moves in this direction, such efforts gained momentum under the Schröder administration. For example, in April 1999, the government passed a law that provided for the reimbursement of taxes and contributions on all workers making slightly more than DM630 (about €320) per month (OECD 1999b: 85, 177). The goal of this measure was to encourage employers to create jobs by relieving them of the obligation to pay social contributions for low-wage positions, while encouraging workers to accept such employment by eliminating income taxes for those at the lowest end of the wage scale (Jacoby 2005; Streeck n.d.).

In other areas of labor market policy, the state has been able to adopt a more direct approach to creating jobs, working to compensate for the failures of corporatist wage bargaining by expanding policies of labor market activation (Vail 2003b). While the Kohl government focused its efforts largely in the East, the Schröder administration developed similar programs across the country. For example, the *Sofortprogramm zum Abbau der Jugendarbeitlosigkeit*, or Immediate Program for the Reduction of Youth Unemployment (suggestively referred to as "JUMP"),[10] created a wide range of training and apprenticeship measures, additional wage subsidies for firms that hire unemployed youth, and job-counseling services. The government devoted DM2 billion (€1.02 billion) annually (DM600 million of which came from the European Social Fund) to this policy, with the goal of creating 100,000 jobs for workers under age twenty-five.[11] Whereas the BA has traditionally administered such programs with almost total autonomy, JUMP was to be run jointly by BA and the Labor Ministry, reflecting the same gradual centralization of authority seen elsewhere in labor market policy. The BA claimed that 406,000 people benefited from the program between 1998 and 2002 (Bundesanstalt für Arbeit 2000a; Bundesministerium für Arbeit und Sozialordnung 2002).

Increased state intervention in the labor market can also be seen in the recent law for "Job-Activation, Qualification, Training, Investment, and Placement (*Vermitteln* in German), or *Job-AQTIV Gesetz*. This measure aims to reintegrate the long-term unemployed into the labor market, in the hopes of reducing long-term unemployment and cutting benefit expenditures. The law requires regional or local branches of the BA to create personalized profiles for each job seeker, offering "appropriate" job openings and providing tailored advice and counseling services. In return, the unemployed person is obligated to accept "reasonable" job offers and make a concerted effort to find work or else risk having his or her benefits suspended.[12] The long-term efficacy of this measure remains to be seen, but its contractual posture toward the unemployed—connecting the right to benefits to job seekers' obligations—reflects a major departure from the traditional view that unemployment (and other social) benefits are inalienable "rights" paid for by years of contributions.

Furthermore, while the BA still officially manages many such schemes, the federal government has assumed an increased degree of authority for their financing and administration, in order to increase the BA's responsiveness to worsening labor market conditions. In 1993, for example, the government passed a law providing that the Labor Ministry would directly set the BA's annual budget (Trampusch 2002: 28).[13] By 1999, federal authorities were financing nearly one-third of all employment programs, traditionally paid for by the BA through social contributions, and they have steadily increased the share of resources devoted to high-priority, active labor market policies (Blien, Walwei, and Werner 2002: 6). The government has also partially shifted welfare funding from social contributions to general taxation in an effort to reduce non–wage labor costs. In 1999, for example, a new tax (the controversial *Ökosteuer*) on environmentally "dangerous" activities and materials funded the replacement of 0.8 percent of annual pension contributions.

In 2002, state authorities began to assert greater control over the BA following the discovery that the agency had grossly inflated job placement statistics.[14] Since March of that year, the BA has been governed by a three-person executive board appointed directly by the federal government. The following summer, the Schröder government established the Hartz Commission, an independent panel of experts from government ministries, employers' associations, and unions, with a mandate to make recommendations for further labor market reforms. The commission called for reinforcing state influence over labor market policy, including increased federal funding for active labor market policies, the development of state-run temporary job agencies to promote flexible employment, and further reforms of the BA's administration and employment services (Hartz Commission 2002).[15] To be sure, such policies sought to contain damage from an embarrassing scandal, but they also attested to mounting concern about the apparent incapacity of Germany's tripartite labor market institutions to govern themselves effectively.

More recently, under the banner "Agenda 2010," the Schröder administration passed additional reforms that aimed to promote employment, reduce non–wage labor costs, and liberalize regulations on economically motivated layoffs and shop hours.[16] The most politically significant (and controversial) of these measures was the so-called Hartz IV reforms, which cut the length of eligibility for primary unemployment insurance (*Arbeitslosengeld*) from eighteen months to twelve months for all workers, with the exception of those older than fifty-five, who will continue to enjoy eighteen months of eligibility. Even more controversially, the measure reduced unemployment assistance benefits (*Arbeitslosenhilfe*), paid to workers at the end of their eligibility for the more generous unemployment insurance benefits, to the level of *Sozialhilfe*, the German basic income-support program.[17] The size of such a cut is quite significant, as it reduces unemployment benefits from 75 percent of previous wages to just a few hundred euros per month.

These reforms reflected the Schröder government's broader emphasis on pressuring the unemployed to find and accept work, even menial or low-paying jobs, such as the infamous "one-euro" jobs—so called because they pay only one euro per hour more than unemployment benefits—which an increasing number of jobless have been forced to accept. Such assaults on what have long since been seen as vested rights to social protection sparked a series of massive protests during 2004, with tens of thousands of Germans marching through the streets of several major cities for weeks to express their outrage at Schröder's perceived abrogation of the German social contract. As with its earlier measures, Schröder's government was willing to risk significant political capital in order to see through its labor market reforms. Indeed, the unpopularity of the reforms and their failure to produce immediate, tangible results contributed significantly to the SPD's (Sozialdemokratische Partei Deutschlands, or Social Democratic Party of Germany) setback in the 2005 elections. The measures prompted members of the left wing of the party to join the ex-Communist Partei des Demokratischen Sozialismus (PDS——Party of Democratic Socialism) in a new, far-Left party that drained away SPD voters, allowing the Christian Democratic Union (CDU—Christlich Demokratische Union) to become the largest party in Parliament. As a result, the Social Democrats were forced to cede the Chancellery to Angela Merkel and join the CDU as a junior partner in a "Grand Coalition." Ironically, if the SPD's defeat was prompted in no small part by dissatisfaction with Schröder's Agenda 2010, the likely effect of the election will be the continuation of cautious liberalizing reforms. Indeed, the grand coalition may prove able to move more aggressively than the Schröder government, given the absence of any significant parliamentary opposition.

Germany's corporatist labor market institutions have clearly failed to adapt to the darkened economic climate, leaving a policy vacuum that the state has begun to fill. Still, the state's capacity to fill this vacuum remains circumscribed. Although state-sponsored labor market reforms are credited with making the German economy more employment friendly (OECD 2001a; Bundesanstalt für Arbeit 2003), they have taken place against a backdrop of wage-setting arrangements that continue to price more than 10 percent of the workforce out of a job. The Kohl and Schröder governments gradually assumed a variety of responsibilities that formerly lay within the domain of the social partners. They increased public resources devoted to the labor market, introduced coercive (some would say punitive) policies vis-à-vis the unemployed, and developed a range of new policies that parallel existing programs managed by the BA. For all of their achievements, however, neither the Kohl government nor the Schröder administration was able to recast the wage-setting arrangements that lie at the heart of Germany's employment problem.

The recent increase in German state activism extends beyond the labor market, to areas such as tax cuts, corporate governance, and pension reform. In an effort to spur economic growth and job creation, German authorities have put forward a number of proposals, some of which have been passed into law, to cut taxes on businesses and wealthier citizens. Like the expansion of active labor market programs, tax cuts represent a kind of second-best strategy for creating jobs, given the difficulty of repairing the German wage-setting system. In a similar spirit, corporate governance reform, detailed in the contribution to this volume by John W. Cioffi, has focused in part on increasing the responsiveness of German firms to market conditions and allowing them more flexibility in responding to changing economic circumstances. As in the case of labor market reform, these tax and corporate governance measures have been very politically controversial and have antagonized major constituencies—labor, in the case of tax breaks for business, and managers, in the case of corporate governance.

In the area of pension policy, too, the German government has been surprisingly, and increasingly, interventionist and insular in its approach to reform. Such developments reflect an erosion of the traditionally consensual rapport between the major political parties in this area and increasing strains between the state and social partners. The differences between trajectories in labor market and pension policy result from the administrative structure of the pension system. Pension policy changes have long been administered by government experts—albeit in close consultation with the opposition, unions, and employers—in contrast to the tripartite administration of the labor market. Unimpeded by formal limitations such as *Tarifautonomie*, the German state has recently adopted a "go-it-alone" approach to pension reform, excluding unions and the opposition from the influence that they have traditionally enjoyed.

Created in 1957, the German pay-as-you-go pension system remained relatively untouched until 1989, when the Kohl administration raised the retirement age to sixty-five, established a 0.5 percent per year penalty for early retirement and an equivalent bonus for later retirement, and slightly modified the benefit-calculation system. Passed before reunification, this relatively modest measure, which preserved an average replacement rate of 70 percent and involved significant concessions to the opposition SPD and the trade unions, was unable to cope with the huge additional burden of eastern workers after 1990. Kohl introduced relatively limited austerity measures in 1997, but these were repealed by the new center-left government when it assumed power in 1998. Very quickly, however, the Schröder government realized that more fundamental changes would be required.

In 2000, Schröder's government released its own pension proposals, which went far beyond Kohl's 1989 measures and contravened the preferences of the SPD's union allies.[18] The initial draft envisioned a reduction in total average benefits from 70 percent to 64 percent[19] and, from this adjusted rate, an additional annual reduction of 0.3 percent for those retiring in or after 2011 (the disputed *Ausgleichsfaktor*, or "Equivalence Factor").[20] The measure also created a legal right to firm-level pensions and introduced caps on contribution rates and subsidies for low-wage workers' pensions. The reform's centerpiece and most controversial provision, however, was the unprecedented introduction of supplemental private accounts, into which each worker would deposit up to 4 percent of his or her annual income (beginning with 0.5 percent in 2001 and increasing by 0.5 percent annually until 2008), supplemented by generous government subsidies and tax exemptions (Bundesministerium für Arbeit und Sozialordnung 2000). In addition, the government committed to paying annual supplements to the system, increasing from DM8.1 billion (€4.1 billion) in 2001 to DM43.7 billion (€22.3 billion) by 2030 (SPD und Bündnis 90/Die Grünen Bundestagsfraktionen 2000: 4).

The proposals elicited sharp protests, as women's groups, the opposition Christian Democrats, pensioners' associations, and the left of Schröder's own party demanded major changes to the measures. Decrying a "privatization of social risk,"[21] unions demanded the preservation of total average benefits at 67 percent, the quashing of the *Ausgleichsfaktor* (said to disadvantage younger workers), increased state and employer support for firm-level pensions, and the abandonment of the proposal for private accounts. This last demand was the unions' highest priority, for they suspected that employers' exemption from contributing represented the beginning of the end for Germany's system of parity financing.[22]

Declaring itself willing to discuss "the details, but not the principle" of the reform, the government adopted a multipronged strategy to secure the reform's passage while making the fewest possible concessions.[23] The first move entailed separating the reform into two laws. The first law, involving changes in the basic pension regime, was opposed by the CDU/CSU and, to a lesser extent, by the unions. However, since the German Constitution makes the federal government responsible for guaranteeing social protection, and because the basic pension scheme does not affect the financial burdens of the *Länder*,[24] the law did not need the approval of the Bundesrat, where the CDU had the votes necessary to block it. As a result, the reform of the basic pension scheme, adopted by the Bundestag on January 26, 2001, and heralded by Walter Riester as "the greatest social reform of the post-war era,'" incorporated almost none of the CDU's priorities.

By contrast, the second law, which created the supplemental accounts, required a majority in both houses, and in particular the votes of Berlin and Brandenburg, both of which were governed by SPD-CDU "grand coalitions." As a result, the government could not ignore *Länder* concerns about the increased costs that the reform would entail. Nor could it disregard the CDU's opposition to both laws, centering on the *Ausgleichsfaktor*, said to deal a serious blow to "generational justice," the law's alleged lack of consideration for families with children, and the use of federal money to subsidize pensioners below the poverty level.[25] In navigating the law through the Bundesrat, however, the government employed a strategy that permitted it to preserve the law's core provisions. It agreed to delay the application of the law until 2002 in order to relieve some of the costs of implementation to the *Länder*, at an additional expense of DM1 billion (€511 million) to the federal government,[26] and offered DM21 billion (€10.7 billion) to cover administrative costs and subsidies to participating workers. This federal money and the lure of the administrative jobs that the law would create prompted Berlin and Brandenburg to support the reform.[27] Even in the face of CDU and public opposition, the clever navigation of the legislative process had allowed the first major structural reform since the pension system's inception in 1957.

In the case of pension reform, exclusion and control, rather than consensus and compromise, were thus the hallmarks of the government's approach. While the tripartite structure of German labor market policy and the principle of *Tarifautonomie* have called for a subtle and shifting combination of incentives and intervention, significant pension reform has rested on a more unalloyed interventionist strategy. These policy-specific dynamics noted, the German state has played a critical role in shaping reforms in both areas, even when it alone has not been able to dictate their character.[28] Although authorities have had to confront the constraints represented by inherited corporatist institutions, they have in many cases been able to exploit possibilities for more unilateral action.

4. Conclusion: The State and Future Prospects for Corporatist Governance

We have traced the experience of social protection and labor market reform in the corporatist political economies of Germany and the Netherlands since the 1980s, emphasizing the shifting and dynamic role of the state. As we have shown, *Staatsentlastung*, or relieving the state of a share of the burden of policymaking, cannot be taken for granted but rather requires skillful state action in order to encourage the social partners to adopt public-regarding strategies of collective action. This is particularly the case once preexisting corporatist institutions confront hostile economic conditions marked by fiscal austerity, slow or absent growth, structural unemployment, and intense pressures on welfare financing. When public-regarding behavior is in short supply, inherited corporatist arrangements can become significant barriers to effective reform, prompting the state to adopt riskier strategies of corporatist disengagement or legislative imposition. As a result, the state may regain a degree of autonomy vis-à-vis the social partners in important policy areas, but at the cost of increased policy and administrative burdens (or even confrontation).

As the cases of Germany and the Netherlands demonstrate, the particular character of state responses to corporatist failures varies significantly with both national institutional capacities and policy-specific legacies. Forms of intervention range from stimulating corporatist accords in wage bargaining and pensions to legislating corporatist agreements in labor market regulation, to bypassing corporatism in labor market policy, to dismantling corporatism in social security administration. In the Netherlands, where the state is unitary and decentralized rather than federal, authorities have often been able to intervene more directly than their German counterparts. That said, both Germany and the Netherlands have witnessed greater state assertiveness than in the past. At times, state authorities have been successful in rebalancing or relaunching corporatist policymaking, whereas at others they have "gone it alone" and suspended or even dismantled corporatist institutions that have failed to produce necessary reforms. Both German and Dutch policymaking have been vulnerable to national variants of Fritz Scharpf's "joint-decision trap," but they have also met with some success in overcoming this dilemma and lending renewed momentum to the reform process. These myriad forms of state intervention have begun to alter the character of politics and policymaking in two political economies that have long been celebrated as exemplars of gradual, consensually negotiated political-economic change.

The success of the Dutch, or "Polder Model," is often seen as the result of long-term compromise of the social partners over wage moderation during the 1980s and more flexible employment relations in the 1990s. In point of fact, the revitalization of corporatist wage bargaining in the 1980s and 1990s was prompted by a highly effective "shadow of hierarchy" that grew out of the 1970 Wage Law and was supported by a high degree of institutionalized capacity for autonomous state action. The state, for example, more or less forced the social partners into the pathbreaking Wassenaar and New Course accords of 1982 and 1993. It is important to note, however, that the institutional framework of the bi- and tripartite institutions of the Foundation of Labor and Social and Economic Council did not have to be invented but rather involved turning inherited corporatist structures to new purposes. The result was a synthesis of moderate wage increases with a high degree of flexibility at the microlevel, as well as rather smooth interplay among wage setting, monetary and fiscal policy, economic growth, and moderate inflation. Since Wassenaar, however, there has been limited political intervention in wage setting. Although the minister of social affairs and employment has the authority to declare (parts of) collective bargaining legally binding (or not) for all workers and employers in a certain branch of industry, in practice, extension is routinely applied. In other words, the Dutch state still has considerable power in industrial relations but has increasingly exercised this power indirectly.

In the realm of social security, governments in the 1990s had the courage to break with the joint control over the system exercised by the social partners. The field of social security has witnessed considerable institutional discontinuity and disagreement among unions, employers, and the government. Dutch welfare reform was an explicitly political attack on the privileged position of the social partners and their failure to adopt needed reforms. This "shadow of hierarchy" has provided the state with a considerable degree of authority over the course of welfare reform, even in situations in which intervention has been merely threatened, rather than used. It is not insignificant that in the past twenty years all of the major political parties, from left to right, in various grand coalitions, have undertaken welfare reform, often involving significant departures from established policymaking paradigms.

In the lengthy process of negotiated welfare and labor market reform in the Netherlands, the rules of Dutch corporatism have been rewritten, and the boundaries between the respective responsibilities of the state and social partners have been redrawn. In contrast to the bipartite "depoliticization" of collective bargaining since the early 1980s, characterized by a shift in the direction of de facto *Tarifauton-omie*, the last decade has witnessed a significant repoliticization of social security (Slomp 2002). This development has been accompanied by a shift in policy dynamics away from fighting unemployment through labor market exit, the continental welfare state's typical response to industrial restructuring. Instead, state authorities since the 1980s have sought to raise employment levels through organized wage restraint and, in the 1990s, through a social-liberal mixture of fiscal austerity, "flexicure" labor markets, and "activating" welfare policies. In each case, the policy agenda was set by the government, rather than the social partners. However, the respective cabinets of Ruud Lubbers and Wim Kok could never have been successful on a majority of social and economic policy issues without the support of the social partners. Furthermore, the second Kok administration's failure to achieve a structural reduction in inactivity rates, despite a fundamental overhaul of the Dutch social security system, demonstrates that suspending corporatism is no panacea.

In contrast to Dutch authorities, German policymakers have had to work within an institutional context marked by greater institutional, legal, and political impediments to unilateral state action. In the area of labor market policy, the German government continues to confront the legally enshrined principle of *Tarifautonomie*. At first, in the early to mid-1990s, German reform strategies tended to focus on efforts to revive moribund corporatist institutions and to reduce unemployment, in the Dutch manner, through the wage-bargaining process (except in the former DDR, where both active and passive labor market policies were instituted on a massive scale following reunification in 1990). With the failure of this strategy, the German government has turned to a series of second-best labor market policies. These have involved tax and corporate governance reforms, as well as policy initiatives to reduce unemployment, including job creation and training programs, increased pressure on the unemployed to accept available work, and curbs on traditional mechanisms of labor-supply reduction, such as early retirement schemes. While somewhat restricted in scope, all of these policies have been undertaken by state actors, largely independently of the social partners, who have seen their authority over German labor market policy shrink considerably.

In the domain of social policy, state intervention has likewise been critically important in shaping reform outcomes. Here the state is not constrained by the kinds of legal impediments that it faces in labor market policy. As a result, governments have been able to see through more ambitious reforms, again without significant input from either the social partners or political opposition. To be sure, German authorities have been in a somewhat weaker position than their Dutch counterparts, owing to the federal structure of the German political system and the frequent existence of blocking majorities in the Bundesrat. Such obstacles have not precluded significant social policy reform, however, as the 2000 pension reform demonstrates. Instead, German governments have had to seek other ways to secure reforms, such as making side payments to certain *Länder* represented in the Bundesrat and accepting some limited compromises over policy content. Although the existence of institutional constraints has resulted in more modest social policy reforms in Germany than in the Netherlands, these constraints have not prevented authorities from securing major changes in the German social protection system. If the political dynamics of the reform process have differed significantly by policy area, in both labor market and social policy, the German state has played a critical role in shaping both the character of the political agenda and policy outcomes.

The German and Dutch experiences offer several important lessons about the role of the state in corporatist political economies. First and foremost, corporatism is not self-regulating. The state is needed not just to establish the institutions of corporatist exchange but also to adapt the system to shifting economic challenges and social and political circumstances. Second, conventional notions of state capacity help explain differences in outcomes across the two countries. Because of greater state capacity (thanks primarily to unicameral government and the authority to intervene in wage setting), Dutch officials were able to introduce more far-ranging changes than their German counterparts. That said, different kinds of state capacity may be required for different tasks, reflecting the importance of flexibility on the part of policy makers in devising responses to varying political and economic circumstances. In contexts where the social partners carry the policy making burden, as in wage setting, the "shadow of hierarchy" and the availability of state intervention may be instrumental in persuading unions and employers to adopt needed reforms. In cases where losses must simply be imposed, by contrast, unilateral state action is often required. In all cases and across corporatist political economies, however, the state continues to play a vital role in promoting reform and economic adjustment.

~ 3

Exiting Etatisme?

New Directions in State Policy in France and Japan

JONAH D. LEVY, MARI MIURA,
AND GENE PARK

FRANCE AND JAPAN HAVE LONG BEEN SEEN as embodying the possibilities for state-led economic development (Shonfield 1965; S. Cohen 1977; Katzenstein 1978; C. Johnson 1982; Zysman 1983; Hall 1986; Tyson and Zysman 1989). In the postwar period, both countries experienced far-reaching economic and social transformation guided by state technocrats. Their apparent success was celebrated and, in some countries, notably Korea, emulated.

Over the past twenty years, however, all of the exemplars of state-led economic development have experienced profound crisis. In the early 1980s, France's vaunted *dirigiste* model was repudiated by a leftist government that had been elected on a pledge to take *dirigisme* to new heights (E. Cohen 1989; Hall 1990; Levy 1999, 2000). Japan's statist system, once the object of envy and fear among Japan's trading partners, is now blamed for the country's persistent economic stagnation since the early 1990s. And in the wake of the 1998 financial meltdown in East Asia, the Korean offshoot of the Japanese model has been relabeled as "crony capitalism."

The predominant interpretation of these crises portrays globalization (and, in the case of France, European integration) as having rendered state intervention obsolete. Whatever the merits of state activism in the past, today's internationalized environment leaves no place for free-spending, interventionist ways. In perhaps the most extreme version of this line of thinking, Peter Hall and David Soskice essentially reduce the "varieties of capitalism" from three to two by marginalizing the statist category, while appending Japan to the Germanic "coordinated" model and excluding France from the two main ideal types altogether (Hall and Soskice 2001b).[1] Even when politics and the state are acknowledged to matter, it tends to be in reactive and negative capacity. Scholars and pundits emphasize the reluctance of state authorities to cede power, particularly in Japan, which has prevented successful adjustment to a changing international economic environment.

At first glance, the comparison of France and Japan would seem to bolster this skepticism toward state intervention. If Japan is a case of halting and constrained adjustment, France is an example of statist rollback. Twenty years after the Socialists' break with *dirigisme*, virtually nothing remains of the institutions and practices associated with the *dirigiste* model. Planning, sectoral industrial policies, and ambitious *grands projets* have been abandoned; the vast majority of nationalized companies have been privatized; credit, price, and capital controls have been lifted; restrictions on layoffs and temporary and part-time employment have been eased; and a macroeconomic orientation emphasizing inflationary growth coupled with large devaluations has given way to one of the lowest inflation rates in Europe and a strong franc, culminating in European Monetary Union (EMU). By all accounts, France has become a much more market-oriented political economy, whose performance rests on the calculations of profit-seeking businesses, as opposed to state technocrats.

First impressions can be deceiving, however. Alongside the dismantling of the *dirigiste* model, French authorities have launched a number of expensive new programs, notably in labor markets and social protection. As Figure 3.1 reveals, state spending, which totaled 51.8 percent of gross domestic product (GDP) in 1983, at the height of Socialo-Communist voluntarism, has continued to rise in the post-*dirigiste* period, reaching 54.5 percent of GDP in 2003 (OECD 2004a). Thus, not only has the post-*dirigiste* French state failed to shrink; by some measures, it has become bigger than ever. In Japan as well, despite over a decade of ostensibly liberalizing reforms, public expenditures surged from 30.2 percent of GDP in 1989 to 37.7 percent in 2003 (OECD 2004a).

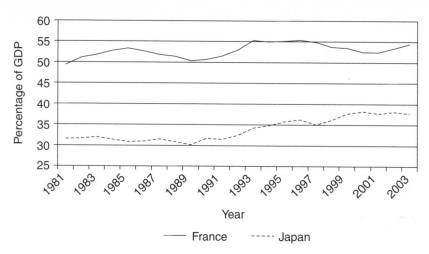

Figure 3.1. Public expenditures in France and Japan, 1981–2003. *Source:* OECD.

This chapter uses a comparison of France and Japan to cast light on the changing place of the state in today's global economy. We advance two main claims. The first is that the road to *dirigiste* rollback is paved with new state interventions. In France, de-*dirigisation* was purchased at the expense of expanded state activity in the social arena. Getting the state out of industrial policy required getting the state into social and labor market policy. The policy innovations of the past twenty years have been designed to pacify and demobilize potential opponents of market-led adjustment—what Jonah D. Levy has termed a "social anesthesia" strategy (Levy 2005a, 2005b). Once regarded as a "welfare laggard," France now has the biggest welfare state outside Scandinavia, and labor market spending also approaches Nordic levels.

Our second claim, inspired by the Japanese case, is that the failure or unwillingness to construct a European-style welfare state may limit the possibilities for economic liberalization. As Japan's economy began to slow in the 1970s, state authorities consciously decided to avoid creating a European-style welfare state. Officials, particularly within the Ministry of Finance, feared that generous social policies would lead to runaway government spending, and both bureaucrats and leaders within the conservative Liberal Democratic Party (LDP) believed that a welfare state would weaken work incentives and lead to social and economic degeneration. Instead, the LDP used state instruments to sustain employment by protecting declining and weaker sectors (Gao 2001). Thus, in Japan, employment itself, rather than a social safety net, has functioned as the main instrument of social protection. It has been more politically difficult for Japanese authorities to pursue liberalizing policies since, unlike in France, governments have not offered welfare policies as compensation to groups that would bear the costs of adjustment. Japanese officials have been loath to implement reforms that lead to large-scale job losses and have taken extensive measures, such as propping up debt-laden banks and quasi-bankrupt companies, to avoid them. What is more, many developmental policies have been diverted by considerations of job preservation.

Our chapter will show that France and Japan have taken very different paths over the past twenty years. We do not wish to suggest that one approach is intrinsically superior to the other. French authorities have been able to disengage from failing *dirigiste* industrial policies, but at the expense of job losses and high levels of public spending that have generated economic and social problems of their own. Japanese authorities have been able to preserve employment and key features of the postwar model—cooperative industrial relations, mutual support between finance and industry, close ties among suppliers and assemblers—but they have been less successful at unraveling costly assistance to uncompetitive businesses and banks. In short, France and Japan have made trade-offs. Interestingly, for all the differences between the French and Japanese adjustment paths, they share one point in common: neither has entailed the eclipse of the state. Indeed, notwithstanding the supposed imperatives of globalization, state spending as a share of gross national product (GNP) has increased in both countries.

Our chapter is divided into five sections. Section 1 examines the origins of the crisis of statism in the two countries. Section 2 explains why France and Japan responded to this crisis in different ways. Section 3 describes the French path of adjustment, which has combined the dismantling of *dirigiste* industrial policy with the expansion of state intervention in other areas, notably labor markets, social protection, and the promotion of small business. Section 4 analyzes the consequences of Japan's employment preservation strategy: halting liberalization and the growing use of state instruments for social purposes, especially job preservation. Section 5, the conclusion, explores the implications of the French and Japanese experience for understanding statist political economies and institutional change.

1.   The Crisis of the Statist Model

In the postwar period, France and Japan relied heavily on state guidance to rebuild and modernize their economies. Although each country pursued a distinct policy mix, the French and Japanese approaches shared a number of core features. These included (1) meritocratic elite schools that recruited and trained the nation's best and brightest youth for high-level positions in the state administration; (2) multiyear planning processes that established the priorities and parameters of the nation's economic development; (3) a variety of policy instruments that permitted state authorities to influence and channel resources to key sectors or even individual firms (strategic use of trade policy, subsidized credit, research aid, price rigging, etc.); (4) a political foundation of conservative hegemony that allowed planners to slight the needs of labor, favoring investment over consumption.

For some thirty years, statist arrangements served France and Japan well. Both countries modernized and prospered, becoming among the leading economies of the world. Beginning in the late 1960s in France and the 1970s in Japan, however, the statist model encountered a series of challenges and difficulties.

New Economic Challenges

The first challenge was economic. The statist approach was well adapted to efforts at industrial catch-up—to channeling resources to clearly identifiable strategic industries, copying and transferring existing technologies from the United States, and supporting domestic champions. As France and Japan approached US levels of development and technology, however, identifying "winners" became much more difficult. Moreover, technologies had to be developed, not simply copied and adapted. Finally, the champions of the next phase of industrialization were often renegades or start-ups largely unknown to the planners, rather than well-established multinationals (Piore and Sabel 1984; D. Friedman 1988).

In this less predictable environment, state planners were not always

able to replicate the successes of the early postwar period, and embarrassing failures multiplied, from the French Concorde to Japanese
fifth-generation computers (Zysman 1977; Padioleau 1981; Cohen and
Bauer 1985; Ziegler 1997) For reasons described below, such problems
afflicted the French variant of statism more than its Japanese counterpart, but neither country was immune.

A Less Hospitable International Environment

If the tasks confronting state authorities were more difficult, the international environment in which they operated was more constraining. The European Common Market, constructed in the 1960s,
greatly weakened the capacity of French planners to selectively protect
markets. For Japan, General Agreement on Tariffs and Trade (GATT)
rounds and pressure from the United States led to reduced tariffs and
measures to curtail its bilateral trade surplus. As early as the 1960s,
Japan began signing VERs (voluntary export restraints) and OMAs
(orderly marketing agreements) with the United States for industries
such as textiles, footwear, and steel. By the 1980s, the United States
began to limit Japanese access to key sectors, such as automobiles and
semiconductors. Attempts to ease the Japanese-US trade imbalance
led to the 1985 MOSS talks (market-oriented, sector specific), the
1989 Structural Impediments Initiative (SII), and the 1994 Framework
talks. US actions also undermined one of the key pillars of Japan's
developmental model—an undervalued yen. With the collapse of the
Bretton Woods system, the value of the yen spiked sharply. In the
wake of the 1985 Plaza Accord, the yen jumped again from about 260
yen to the dollar to close to 120 yen to the dollar by 1989.

In the case of France, the pressures of European integration undermined the *dirigiste* model in a second, more fundamental way (Hall
1990; Loriaux 1991). The 1983 U-turn and repudiation of *dirigisme*
were touched off by a currency crisis. The franc was overvalued because France's rate of inflation was much higher than that of its trading
partners, making it difficult for French businesses to compete. Traditionally, France had accommodated high rates of inflation through
periodic "aggressive devaluations" that not only neutralized price differentials but also conferred a temporary price advantage on French
companies (Hall 1986). Under the rules of the European Monetary

System (EMS), however, any devaluation required the consent of other EMS countries. Led by Germany, these countries resisted a large devaluation and demanded that France curb government spending, so as to reduce inflationary pressures. President François Mitterrand was forced to choose, therefore, between France's traditional statist growth strategy and European solidarity. His advisers were divided into two basic camps (Bauchard 1986; Hall 1986; D. Cameron 1996; Favier and Martin-Roland 1996). One side advocated a fortress France strategy, encompassing withdrawal from the EMS, a sharp devaluation of the franc, and tightened exchange and trade controls. The other side favored European solidarity, backed by a severe austerity program to eradicate inflation once and for all and stabilize the franc's position within the EMS. After much agonizing, Mitterrand opted for the latter option, and the process of *dirigiste* rollback began.

The Erosion of Conservative Hegemony

The third and perhaps most important challenge to the statist model was political. At its most fundamental level, the *dirigiste* project entailed shifting resources from consumers to businesses and from declining sectors to emerging sectors. In both France and Japan, this strategy rested on a political foundation of conservative hegemony (Pempel and Tsunekawa 1979; Zysman 1983; Pempel 1990). The LDP governed Japan without interruption from 1955 to 1993, while in France, the Communist Party was excluded from government from 1947 to 1981 and the Socialists from 1958 to 1981. Conservative parties in both countries slighted the needs of labor, instead favoring core constituencies of business, agriculture, and the liberal professions.

The labor-exclusionary strategy was feasible only as long as the conservative hold on power remained secure, however. In France, a first shock to conservative hegemony occurred with the near-revolution of May 1968. President Charles de Gaulle, who had dominated French politics for a decade, was no longer the unquestioned leader. Indeed, one year later, de Gaulle resigned from office when a referendum designed to relegitimate his rule failed to secure a majority. Conservative hegemony eroded further in 1971, when France's Communist and Socialist parties forged a powerful "Union of the Left." In the 1974 presidential election, center-right candidate Valéry Giscard d'Estaing outpolled his Socialist rival François Mitterrand by a mere 50.8 percent to 49.2 percent. The Left swept nationwide municipal elections in 1977 and was widely expected to triumph in the 1978 parliamentary elections. Although Giscard weathered this challenge, his popularity quickly began to decline, and he was ousted by Mitterrand in the 1981 presidential election. In such a hotly contested political context, conservative parties needed every vote, and the concerns of labor received increasing attention.

The contested political environment of the 1970s transformed *dirigiste* policymaking. More accurately, political pressures diverted *dirigisme* from its postwar modernizing mission (Berger 1981a; E. Cohen 1989). Anxious conservative leaders had no stomach for painful, if much-needed, rationalization of declining or uncompetitive enterprises. Indeed, their initiatives often ran in the opposite direction. While embracing the rhetoric of liberalization and market-driven adjustment, the Giscard administration nationalized the bankrupt French steel industry and created a special agency, the Comité interministériel de l'aménagement des structures industrielles (CIASI), to bail out companies in difficulty.

These problems only intensified under the Mitterrand administration, an alliance of Socialist and Communist parties. Having pledged that *dirigiste* policies would enable industry to create jobs, rather than eliminating them, Mitterrand was trapped by his own campaign rhetoric. Furthermore, job cuts would strike at the core of the Left's electorate—unskilled and semiskilled blue-collar workers in heavy industry. The government, therefore, opted to buy social peace. But this strategy yielded increasingly untenable economic outcomes. By 1983, a number of firms were so heavily subsidized that it would have been far cheaper for the government to pay workers *not to produce*. In shipbuilding, for example, it was estimated that each job paying €15,000 in annual wages cost the government €23,000 to €70,000 in subsidies (E. Cohen 1989: 230–231).[2]

The political pressures that diverted *dirigiste* policymaking in France made themselves felt in Japan in the 1970s (Calder 1990, 1993). The hegemony of the LDP rested on a conservative coalition similar to that of France, encompassing big business, agriculture, and the petty bourgeoisie. As in France, labor was essentially excluded and internally divided. The so-called 1955 system remained relatively stable for over a decade, but beginning in the late 1960s and accelerating in the 1970s, progressives gained support across the country. By the early 1970s, progressives, backed by the Japan Communist Party (JCP) and the Japan Socialist Party (JSP), had taken over the governorships of Tokyo, Osaka, Kyoto, and numerous lower-visibility regions. The results filtered up to the national level as well, with the LDP's margin over other parties declining consistently. The Communists experienced a small boom in electoral support, winning up to 20 percent of the vote in lower house elections in some urban areas in the 1972 elections. Progressives directly challenged many aspects of the developmental state, demanding greater attention to local issues, less heavy-handed central planning, and policies that ameliorated some of the externalities of rapid development.

Rather than succumbing to the opposition, the LDP coopted many of its themes. Successive LDP governments increased spending on programs to improve the quality of life—environment, housing, regional development—and in the process won the support of groups outside the LDP's traditional support base, particularly Japan's growing urban voters. As in France, the institutions of Japan's developmental state came to serve increasingly political aims. Japan's vaunted Fiscal Investment and Loan Program (FILP), which had helped channel funds from the national postal savings system, public pensions, and other sources to developmental projects in the postwar period, was redirected toward political ends. Moreover, the Ministry of International Trade and Industry's (MITI) attentions shifted to managing declining industries, as many of the industries that MITI had nurtured reached maturity, and electoral rather than strategic considerations increasingly guided policy (Boyd and Nagamori 1991; Young 1991).

The transformation of the LDP and its electoral strategy is best symbolized by the rise of Kakuei Tanaka, the LDP leader and prime minister from 1972 to 1974. Unlike nearly every prime minister before him, Tanaka had not been a career bureaucrat and had not even graduated from college. Rather, he had risen through the ranks of the LDP. More than any other politician, Tanaka represented the transformation of the LDP from an elite technocratic party to a catch-all party that would hold on to power by any means necessary, including massively increased patronage.

2. Responding to the Crisis of Statism: Why France and Japan Diverged

If the statist models of France and Japan have confronted many of the same kinds of pressures, the two countries have responded in fundamentally different ways. In France, after a series of failed efforts to reform the *dirigiste* model, governments of the Left and Right moved to dismantle it. Simultaneously, to prevent protest, they extended an array of social protections to the losers of market-led adjustment, notably older workers and the unemployed. Japanese authorities, by contrast, refused to construct an expensive system of social protection. They opted instead to pursue an employment preservation route, introducing liberalization measures in a cautious and limited manner. The divergent evolution of French and Japanese policymaking was rooted in four main factors: (1) economic performance; (2) the international environment; (3) domestic political institutions; (4) a strategic choice about social policy.

Economic Performance

The 1970s and 1980s were the heyday of the Japanese model. Economic growth was rapid and unemployment almost nonexistent. Trade surpluses expanded continuously, as Japanese companies displaced US and European rivals for positions of global leadership. It was a time when scholars, businesspersons, and policymakers flocked to Japan to study a political economy that was rapidly becoming "number one" (E. Vogel 1979).

France's political economy inspired no such reverence. While Japan boomed, France suffered slow growth, double-digit inflation, high unemployment, and chronic balance-of-payments deficits. In this context, it is not surprising that dissatisfaction with the statist model was brewing. In a sense, France began a public reevaluation of statism in the 1970s, a process that would not occur in Japan until well into the 1990s.

Part of the reason for the divergent performance of the French and Japanese economies is that while both countries operated under a statist model, French statism tended to be more insular than its Japanese counterpart (Levy 1999). Both regimes gave short shrift to the interests of labor, but in Japan, state authorities confronted powerful actors on the employer side—*keiretsu* (conglomerates of industry and finance) as well as a number of active business associations (industry associations, chambers of commerce, technology consortia). Policymaking has been a process of "reciprocal consent," in the words of Richard Samuels, with the state and business co-defining economic strategies (Samuels 1987). Postwar French authorities, by contrast, confronted an industrial landscape dominated by small, family-owned companies and weak business organizations that were generally opposed to economic modernization. Policymaking was a much more top-down affair, with French technocrats bypassing traditional elites and creating most of the companies with whom the planners would negotiate (the so-called national champions) through a process of state-sponsored mergers.

The insularity of France's *dirigiste* system created several difficulties. First, state officials experienced difficulty striking a balance between technological ambition and commercial viability. High-tech *grands projets* yielded some commercial successes, but they also generated a number of white elephants, such as the Concorde supersonic aircraft, graphite gas-cooled nuclear reactors, and Diamant rocket launchers.[3] Insularity deprived state officials of checks and feedback mechanisms that might have redirected policy in a more fruitful direction. For this reason, French policymakers continued to pursue certain strategies, notably the commitment to mergers and Fordist mass production, long after these approaches had begun to demonstrate their limits.

The reciprocal, concertational nature of Japanese industrial policy helped avert some of the *dirigiste* excesses that have plagued French policymaking. In the 1960s, MITI officials, like their French counterparts, tended to equate competitiveness with large scale and were taken with the national champions strategy. Unlike the French, however, they were unable to impose their vision on Japanese business. Despite MITI's pleas, powerful *keiretsu* groups refused to sacrifice their autonomy (the "one-set principle") on the altar of "big is better." Not only were mergers blocked, but also in many instances, new entrants joined the fray, such as automakers Honda and Suzuki. As a result, virtually every sector of the Japanese economy continues to have at least five or six producers, corresponding to the major *keiretsu* groups. France's national champions, by contrast, tended to be domestic monopolists, with predictable consequences for innovation, service, and investment.

Powerful business and societal actors in Japan not only provided a check on state intervention or an alternative to state intervention. They also laid the basis for a *different kind* of state intervention in Japan. In the area of technology, for example, state authorities have teamed up with business associations, chambers of commerce, and interfirm research consortia to develop and diffuse technologies widely throughout the economy. In France, by contrast, new technologies were developed primarily in public labs (at great cost) and were rarely disseminated beyond a single national champion. Relatedly, Japanese authorities used their relays in business and local government to implement a variety of policies designed to upgrade small- and medium-sized enterprises (SMEs). Lacking such relays and viewing SMEs with disdain, French authorities focused resources overwhelmingly on the national champions. The benign neglect of SMEs proved especially damaging, as the breakdown of Fordist mass production and intensified international competition placed a growing premium on dynamic, fast-moving SMEs.

The varying performance of France's and Japan's economies shaped the perceived need for economic liberalization. Until the 1990s, Japan's economy was the most successful the world had ever seen, moving from one triumph to the next. Economic success pushed Japan in the direction of the incremental employment preservation strategy in two ways. First, Japan was rich enough and its companies competitive enough to be able to afford to maintain some redundant labor. French firms, by contrast, were floundering and unable to compete with European rivals. Second, given that Japan was the most successful economy the world had ever seen, Japanese authorities were quite confident about their statist model and skeptical of neoliberalism. They perceived the neoliberal methods inferior to their own model. French authorities, by contrast, felt no such sense of superiority vis-à-vis liberal rivals.

International Factors

The second factor behind the divergent trajectories of France and Japan was international. As noted above, international pressures, a

crisis of the French franc within the European Monetary System, precipitated France's repudiation of *dirigisme*. If the agenda of liberalization has often been associated with an external force, that force has
not been the same for France and Japan. In the case of Japan, the
United States has exerted pressure to liberalize, demanding that Japan
open its markets to US exports and roll back arrangements restricting
competition. A political problem for would-be liberalizers is that such
measures are likely to be seen as capitulating to US pressures.

   In France, economic liberalization has been associated with a more
positive external process—the construction of Europe. European integration has provided a handy justification for liberalization: liberalizing reforms are portrayed as a European imperative, the price of
constructing a pan-European entity (that France can hopefully steer),
rather than as a simple policy choice (E. Cohen 1996). In point of
fact, measures like privatization or financial market deregulation went
far beyond the imperatives of membership in good standing in the
EMS, but they could be cloaked in the useful constraint of Europe.
Nor did this process end in 1983. European competition policy is
regularly blamed for preventing France from bailing out lame ducks,
although it is by no means clear that French authorities would wish
to do so if given the opportunity. Likewise, the austerity budgets of
the mid-1990s were necessary to qualify for European Monetary
Union, but they also dovetailed with the desire of French governments
to get their fiscal house in order.

   European integration has further facilitated liberalization by holding
out the promise of Europe-wide common policies to relay the flagging
efforts of French authorities. When President Mitterrand chose European solidarity in 1983, he had a certain vision of Europe in mind:
the Europe of high-tech industrial projects like Airbus and Ariane; the
Europe of generous payments to the "losers" of economic modernization (farmers and backward or ailing regions); the Europe of bold
new ambitions. In short, Europe would enable France to pursue economic and social strategies that were no longer viable at the national
level. Europe would also bolster state sovereignty by allowing France
to regain control over policies that were effectively run by the Germans. The post-1983 strategy of "competitive disinflation," culminating in EMU, was a clear effort to wrest monetary policy from the
control of the Bundesbank. If the practice of European integration has

often disappointed French expectations, these expectations have none-theless lent a positive hue to economic liberalization in a manner that has been largely absent from the Japanese context.

Politico-Institutional Factors

The third feature that pushed French and Japanese policymaking in divergent directions was the political system. Japanese prime ministers face numerous institutional and political constraints that make it difficult to carry out contested liberalization projects. First, until 1994, members of Japan's lower house, the more powerful legislative chamber, were elected according to a single nontransferable vote (SNTV) system. Under SNTV, electoral districts are composed of multiple seats, which leads to intraparty competition, since members of the same party run against each other. The challenge for political parties is to find a way of coordinating candidate selection and campaigning. The LDP's solution was to delegate campaign support to factions, but the growth of factions diffused power and made it difficult to centralize party control.[4] Another important consequence was to make Japanese prime ministers dependent on fragile coalitions of factional support. Only in rare cases, such as Prime Minister Yasuhiro Nakasone, have prime ministers been able to parlay popularity into bold reforms that go against the preferences of backbenchers. Prime Minister Junichiro Koizumi's decision to call early elections in August 2005 and expel a number of LDP members of Parliament was prompted by precisely this inability to enact aggressive liberalizing reforms—in this instance, the privatization of the postal service—in the face of resistance from within his own party.

The difficulty of reform has been exacerbated by the lack of alternation in office from 1955 to 1993. The LDP's long, uninterrupted rule allowed the factional model to evolve into a highly institutionalized system. Cabinet posts were allocated on the basis of the balance of power among factions, which tended to undermine the leadership of the prime ministers. Although cabinet members were formally appointed by the prime minister, in practice, all selections had to be endorsed by the faction leaders. The short tenure of cabinet officials, in turn, allowed bureaucrats to take initiatives in lawmaking, since ministers often did not have the time or resources to learn how to assert control over their ministries.[5] Cabinet members tended to behave as agents of their ministries, rather than exerting political control over the bureaucracy.

The LDP's institutionalized policymaking procedures presented a third obstacle to bold leadership. Groups within the LDP are able to check and block all bills before they are considered by the cabinet. Under this informal yet institutionalized practice, even backbenchers sometimes hold veto power within the LDP. Capitalizing on this practice, *zoku* politicians—that is, politicians with expertise in specific policy areas—are able to influence the policymaking process and outcomes. *Zoku* politicians, bureaucrats, and vested interests lie at the heart of iron triangles that often align against liberalization projects. As a result, even solid majorities in Parliament do not guarantee that reformist prime ministers will be able to carry out reforms. As Aurelia Mulgan notes, in contrast to the Westminster model, the government is subservient to the party and bureaucracy (Mulgan 2002).

The abolition of the SNTV as part of the electoral reform passed in 1994 and the strengthening of the prime minister's office as part of a larger reorganization of government have both contributed to important changes in policymaking and government-party relations. Factions have declined in significance, and policymaking has been centralized. Still, as evidenced by Prime Minister Koizumi's recent showdown with members of his own party over postal privatization, these changes have encountered deep resistance. More than anything, Koizumi's dissolution of the Diet and internal party purge indicate how profoundly difficult it is even now to push through reform measures.

The politico-institutional context in France in the 1980s offered far more favorable terrain for liberalizing reform. President Mitterrand enjoyed a huge parliamentary majority as a result of the 1981 elections. Although his Socialist party governed in alliance with the Communists, Mitterrand had more than enough members of Parliament (MPs) to reform without the Communists and to survive even a pretty substantial defection among the Socialists. In addition, under France's system of "rationalized parliamentarism," many reforms can be enacted without a vote. Mitterrand also held the weapon of calling new parliamentary elections. Thus, however unhappy French leftists may have been about the break with *dirigisme*, they had no way to check Mitterrand's new direction.

Mitterrand held a second valuable trump card not possessed by his Japanese counterparts—that of time. Contemplating his options in 1983, the French president knew that he would have a free hand for the next three years. With or without the support of the Communists, his position was unassailable until 1986, when the next parliamentary elections were scheduled. Indeed, in some respects, Mitterrand's time horizon extended beyond 1986, since his seven-year term as president ran until 1988. Under the dual executive system of the Fifth Republic, a defeat in 1986 would not remove Mitterrand from office. Although the Right would gain control of Parliament, Mitterrand would remain as president. The Left would then get a second chance two years later with the presidential election of 1988. Were Mitterrand to secure re-election, he could repeat the maneuver of 1981, dissolving the conservative-controlled Parliament and appealing to the voters for a leftist majority with which to govern (which is, in fact, what happened).

Thus, in forging economic strategy in 1983, Mitterrand was looking to the political implications for 1986 or even 1988. The president's time horizon was three to five years (not the year or two characteristic of embattled Japanese prime ministers). In the context of the *longue durée* conferred by the Fifth Republic, it was not illogical to take a chance on a strategy that—while unpopular in the short term—might yield significant benefits a few years down the line. The difference with the situation of Japanese leaders could not be more striking.

Contrasting Approaches to Social Policy

The fourth factor differentiating France's and Japan's response to statist crisis was a strategic choice regarding social policy. Welfare policy played a critical role in France's move away from *dirigisme*. In a logic first articulated by Karl Polanyi, the extension of market forces was softened, made politically acceptable through the expansion of social protections for those most affected by liberalization (Polanyi 1944). On the one hand, beginning in 1983, state authorities made a market, imposing liberalization from above. Austerity, privatization, deregulation, and labor market flexibility all heightened the vulnerability of French workers. On the other hand, successive governments, especially those on the Left, expanded the welfare state in number of ways, so as to cushion the blow to the working class and, equally important, to undercut the possibilities for union mobilization (Daley 1996; Levy 1999). Early retirement programs, labor market training, subsidies for low-wage hires, and a guaranteed minimum income were part of a panoply of measures designed to ease the social dislocation prompted by the move to the market—policies that took French state spending to unprecedented heights.

In Japan, by contrast, the LDP leadership opted not to expand the welfare state. Five factors played a role in shaping this strategic choice. The first was the Ministry of Finance's (MOF) preference for restraining public spending. The origins of this preference go back to the postwar period, when proposals surfaced for welfare policies, which MOF easily defeated. MOF's preference for fiscal frugality grew into a larger economic strategy in which the budget would be suppressed to adjust for negative turns in Japan's balance of payments. Even when Japan turned to a surplus, "small government" was seen as a means of encouraging private capital formation. In the 1970s, MOF was able to reassert its preference. Although Prime Minister Tanaka anointed 1973 as the "First Year of the Welfare Era," MOF was able to take advantage of an eroding fiscal situation to slow the growth of welfare spending (Pempel 1990; Gao 2001).

The LDP's ideological orientation also played an important role in blocking the development of Japan's welfare state. In the late 1960s and early 1970s, there was widespread discussion of whether Japan should create a welfare state as it caught up with other Western nations economically. The choice made by the LDP was to create a "welfare society," a notion that was explicitly intended to represent an alternative to a European-style welfare state. LDP leaders feared that generous social programs would foster dependence on the state and weaken the productive drive of Japanese workers.

A third factor behind Japan's limited welfare state was the prevailing treatment of older workers. Whereas France deployed generous early retirement provisions to blunt union and employee resistance to industrial restructuring, the Japanese government used employment maintenance programs to assist employers who retained, retrained, and rehired redundant workers. Such a policy choice was conducive to the widespread Japanese practice of mandatory corporate retirement at age fifty-five or younger. Most workers seek other employment after mandatory corporate retirement, and in many cases, their employers assist in job searches and offer posts in subsidiary companies. Usually, wage levels of postretirement jobs are much lower than preretirement jobs. From the firm's perspective, postretirement workers are relatively cheap, which, in turn, creates job opportunities for these elderly workers. The institutionalization of corporate mandatory retirement made it unnecessary for firms to rely on welfare programs to induce retirement. Instead, corporations called on the government to provide state subsidies for the existing practices of early retirement and reemployment (Miura 2002a, 2002b).

Fourth, the courts played an important role in increasing the level of employment protection in Japan. By the late 1970s, case law limiting the ability of employers to freely dismiss their employees for economic reasons had become a pillar of Japan's system of job protection. Even after the bursting of the bubble economy, dismissals were uncommon.

A fifth reason why Japan's social spending remained limited is that the Left posed a much less serious threat than in France. Japan never experienced anything like France's near-revolution of May 1968. Moreover, Japanese unions in the private sector chose to collaborate with employers in order to secure employment (Kume 1998). They demanded government commitment to employment maintenance programs in exchange for cooperation with industrial restructuring. Such an alliance between employers and unions in the private sector eventually marginalized public sector unions, who opposed liberalization and demanded the construction of the formal welfare state. The marginalization of public sector unions was also the product of conscious government action, with the privatization of the Japanese National Railways and the telecom monopoly decimating the unions' organizational base (Samuels 2003). Because public sector unions lacked mobilizing capacity, the LDP was able to resist calls to reconfigure the state's compensatory strategy.

In sum, the LDP did not choose to expand the welfare state partly because of the preferences of MOF, partly because of the party's ideological orientation, and partly because social demands for welfare programs were contained and defused through a strategy of full employment. The latter was facilitated by the extensive use of public works and an early retirement age in the private sector. Japanese authorities were able to keep social spending well below French levels, but in so doing, they deprived themselves of a potentially valuable social lubricant for accompanying market-led, industrial restructuring.

Although France and Japan have long shared the core features of the developmental-state model, these countries also differed in critical ways. As this section has shown, four sets of differences—in the economy, the international setting, the politico-institutional system, and social policy—pushed France and Japan's responses to statist crisis in divergent directions. France would break with statist industrial policy, while expanding social and labor market measures to pacify and demobilize the victims of market-based restructuring. By contrast, Japan would move cautiously in a market direction, keeping the growth of formal welfare programs in check but multiplying costly policies to preserve employment. In the next two sections, we examine each country's pattern of reform more closely, starting with the French case.

3.   France: Dismantling *Dirigisme*, Redeploying Statism

In France, beginning in 1983, a leftist administration that had been elected on a campaign to intensify *dirigisme* began instead to dismantle *dirigisme*. The 1983 U-turn touched off a range of reforms that struck at the core of the *dirigiste* model (E. Cohen 1989; Hall 1990; Schmidt 1996; Levy 1999, 2000). These changes, inaugurated cautiously by the Socialists from 1983 to 1986, were amplified when the Right returned to power under a neoliberal banner from 1986 to 1988 and confirmed and completed by subsequent governments on both sides of the political spectrum.

Four sets of changes figured most prominently in this transformation of the French political economy. In the realm of macroeconomic policy, French authorities broke with the traditional "inflationary growth" strategy, marked by deficit spending, lax monetary policy, and periodic "aggressive devaluations" that not only compensated for price differentials with France's trading partners but also conferred a temporary advantage on French producers (Hall 1986). The new strategy of "competitive disinflation" sought to keep France's inflation rate below that of its trading partners through a combination of austerity budgets, de-indexation of wages, and especially tight monetary policy.

With respect to France's public enterprises, many of the banks and firms that had been nationalized in the immediate aftermath of World War II and during the Socialists' first years in office were released from their planning targets and instructed to focus instead on profitability. This shift from state dictates to market forces as the governing principle of French industry and finance was accelerated during a wave of privatizations launched by the Right upon its return to power in 1986 and continued by governments of the Left and Right alike since 1993. In the process, the once-vast holdings of the French state were reduced to little more than energy production, public transportation, and some weapons manufactures.

The shrinking of the public sector was accompanied by a third major policy shift—the abandonment of state efforts to steer private industry. The guiding spirit of this change was that firms would receive less government assistance and would, if necessary, be allowed to fail, but they would also be subject to fewer restrictions, so that they could raise the necessary resources by their own means, largely through newly deregulated financial markets and greater freedom to set prices (Hall 1990). The resulting revival of corporate profits was also fueled by a fourth set of developments, the reform of France's system of industrial relations (Groux and Mouriaux 1990; Howell 1992; Labbé and Croisat 1992). State authorities de-indexed wages and lifted restrictions on managerial prerogatives, such as the administrative authorization for layoffs (the requirement that layoffs of ten or more employees for economic reasons receive the approval of an inspector from the Ministry of Labor). They also expanded the scope of workplace bargaining, which enabled employers to introduce significant labor market flexibility in a fairly one-sided manner (as Chris Howell describes in this volume).

The reforms after 1983 left no *dirigiste* stone unturned. Looking across the wealthy democracies, one would be hard-pressed to find any country that shifted so far away from its postwar economic strategy as the France of François Mitterrand and Jacques Chirac. Certainly, compared to other statist political economies, such as Japan and Korea, France moved earlier and more aggressively against its postwar policy model.

If the practices and institutions associated with *dirigisme* have been dismantled with astonishing speed and thoroughness, the same cannot be said of the French state. On the contrary, state spending and tax-

ation have increased somewhat in the post-*dirigiste* period, as new initiatives have been launched, particularly in the areas of labor market
policy, social protection, and the promotion of small business. This
section describes each of these new state activities in turn.

Labor Market Programs

French labor market policy has developed in a number of directions.
State intervention centered initially on early retirement, a strategy designed to square the circle of "job loss without unemployment" (Daley
1996). French authorities recognized the need for companies to be
able to restructure in order to restore profitability and competitiveness
but did not wish such restructuring to come entirely at the expense of
the workforce. Rather, government programs would permit employees
over the age of fifty-five—or, in some cases, fifty—to retire at close
to full pension.

The expansion of early retirement to accommodate and humanize
restructuring began under the Giscard presidency. Between 1974 and
1980, the number of early retirees more than tripled, from 59,000 to
190,400 (DARES 1996: 100). The Left tripled the figure again to over
700,000 workers in 1984. Such measures were expensive, costing as
much as €150,000 per retiree, but they were assumed to be temporary.
Officials expected that once French firms restructured and the
economy recovered, job creation would begin anew, and early retirement programs could be wound down. Employment creation has remained sluggish, however, and the number of participants in early
retirement programs has held relatively steady, ranging from 450,000
to 600,000 since the mid-1980s. Today, fewer than one worker in three
is still employed at age sixty, and France's labor force participation rate
for men aged fifty-five to sixty-four is among the lowest in Western
Europe, at less than 40 percent (Scharpf and Schmidt 2000c: 350).

With the return to recession and rising unemployment in the early
1990s, center-right governments deployed a second labor market
strategy. The right's efforts focused on the reduction of labor costs,
particularly at the low end of the wage spectrum, where a relatively
generous minimum wage (€1,150 per month) and heavy social security
charges (roughly 50 percent of wages) are said to dissuade job creation.
Under Gaullist Prime Minister Edouard Balladur, employers hiring
low-wage workers were exempted from family allowance contribu-

tions, while a program inaugurated in 1995 by Balladur's Gaullist successor, Alain Juppé provided subsidies of €750 to €2,200 for jobs paying less than 1.3 times the minimum wage.

The center-left government of Lionel Jospin added two further labor market initiatives during its tenure from 1997 to 2002. The first was a youth employment program, the Programme Emplois Jeunes (PEJ), which occupied some 350,000 young people. Targeted at youths with no significant work experience, the PEJ provided full-time employment for five years and offered generous subsidies to public sector enterprises who hired young workers, with the aim of enabling participants to acquire the skills and experience necessary to secure permanent employment once the subsidies expired.

Jospin's second high-profile measure was the reduction of the work-week from thirty-nine hours to thirty-five hours. Although conservative critics and the national employer association denounced the reform as a job killer, the government took a number of measures to assuage business concerns. The reform was phased in over a five-year period, giving employers time to adjust and to extract wage concessions from employees as the price for shorter working hours. Employers were also allowed to introduce considerable flexibility into work schedules, and the government tendered significant subsidies to companies that reduced work time.

Figure 3.2 reveals that the number of French workers enrolled in some kind of public labor market program expanded 2.5-fold in the post-*dirigiste* period—rising from slightly under 1.2 million in 1984, at the height of industrial restructuring, to nearly 3 million in 1999 (DARES 1996, 2000).[6] This total is in addition to the 2.5 million French workers formally unemployed. Aggregate spending on labor market policy has shown a similar increase, expanding from slightly over 2 percent of GDP in the mid-1980s to 4.67 percent of GDP in 2003 (INSEE 2005). Today, France spends nearly as much on labor market intervention as Sweden, the mecca of active labor market policy.

Social Protection

The French state has been equally prominent in the social policy arena (Levy 2000). Public social spending rose from 21.1 percent of GDP

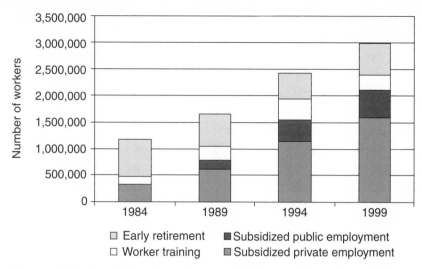

Figure 3.2. Number of French workers in public labor market programs. *Sources:* DARES 1996, 2000.

in 1980 to 26.6 percent in 1990, to 28.5 percent in 2001 (OECD 2004b). Once classified as a "welfare laggard," France has developed the largest welfare state outside Scandinavia, with only Sweden (28.9 percent of GDP) and Denmark (29.2 percent of GDP) exceeding the French outlay in 2001. France's two most expensive social programs, pensions and health care, have both experienced significant growth since the early 1980s. Spending on pensions increased from 7.7 percent of GDP in 1981 to 9.8 percent in 2000 (Ministry of Finance 2001: Statistical Annex, table VII.2). France's pay-as-you-go pension system is among the most generous in the world and, in contrast to most other countries, has experienced only limited retrenchment measures in recent years (Charpin 1999; Myles and Pierson 2001). French health-care spending increased from 7.4 percent of GDP in 1980 to 9.6 percent in 1998, as France passed Austria, Belgium, Denmark, Holland, and Sweden to become the number-two spender in the European Union (EU), behind Germany (OECD 2000b: table A7).

French authorities have not only expanded existing social programs; they have also launched new ones. In 1988, the Socialist government of Michel Rocard established a national social safety net or guaranteed income, the *revenu minimum d'insertion* (RMI). The RMI replaced a patchwork of local and targeted social assistance programs that had left large segments of the population uncovered. Benefits are available on a means-tested basis to all citizens and long-term residents over the age of twenty-five. The RMI provides a monthly allowance of €420 along with the promise of support services to help "insert" (the "I" in "RMI") recipients back into society and, in some cases, into a job. Claimants are also eligible for housing allowances and free health insurance. Although the "insertion" dimension of the RMI remains underdeveloped, the program does provide nonnegligible financial assistance to over 1 million of France's neediest citizens, at an annual cost of some €4 billion.

The Jospin government launched two new social programs. The *couverture maladie universelle* (CMU), introduced in 2000, makes health care available free of charge to low-income groups. The CMU originated with a pledge by the Juppé government in 1995 to extend public health insurance to the 200,000 French citizens (0.3 percent of the population) who lacked coverage. The Jospin government honored Juppé's pledge but also addressed the far greater problem of access among those who actually possess heath insurance. France's public health insurance reimburses just 75 percent of the costs of medical treatment on average (Join-Lambert et al. 1997). Although 85 percent of the population reduces copayments by subscribing to a supplementary insurance, for the remaining 15 percent, low reimbursement rates tended to place all but emergency medical treatment out of reach. The CMU greatly attenuated this problem by providing free supplementary health insurance on a means-tested basis to an estimated 5 million people at a cost of some €1.5 billion annually.

In 2002, the Jospin government created a new welfare entitlement, the *aide personnalisée à l'autonomie* (APA), which helps defray the costs of in-home assistance for the elderly. Like the RMI, the APA replaced a locally variable program, the *prestation spécifique de dépendance* (PSD), which had been established by the Juppé government in 1997. The APA provides up to €1,070 per month, depending on the severity of the incapacity and the financial resources of the claimant, for home-assistance expenses. Around 800,000 elderly citizens benefit from the APA, as against 135,000 for the PSD, at a cost of €3.51 billion per year.

The commitment to expanding France's welfare state crosses partisan lines. The RMI was established by a unanimous vote of the

French Parliament. Although it is true that governments of the Left enacted the CMU and APA, in both cases, the Left built upon earlier initiatives of the Right. Moreover, Gaullist President Jacques Chirac was elected in 1995 thanks to a campaign that stressed the need for heightened state intervention to heal France's "social fracture" and renew the "Republican pact" between state and citizen.

An interesting feature of French political discourse is that the same distrust of market forces and faith in state guidance that animated *dirigiste* industrial policy can now be found in social policy. Chirac would have never dreamed of calling for a new round of nationalizations or a revival of sectoral planning. Yet it was entirely legitimate, even electorally savvy, for him to call for intensified state intervention in the social arena.

Promotion of SMEs

While winding down industrial policy programs for the national champions, state authorities have developed an array of instruments to promote SMEs (Levy 1999). The guiding principle of these programs is to encourage SMEs to "make leaps," to accelerate the pace of their development. State subsidies of up to 50 percent or success-conditional loans are available for a variety of risky ventures, including integrating composite materials or electronics into existing products, developing new products, computerizing production operations, and hiring managers and engineers. All of these actions are designed to usher SMEs to a new stage in their development, whether in the form of new products, new production processes, or new management structures.

The character of SME promotional policies is very different from past *dirigiste* methods. State officials are no longer picking winners and forcing firms to merge; instead, they are trying to create a supportive environment for private managers. They are not imposing competitive strategies or planning targets but, rather, are underwriting the strategies developed by small businesses. Moreover, many of the tools of intervention operate through private consulting companies, as opposed to state technocrats. Thus, the new SME policies are more market conforming and more respectful of private initiatives than traditional state intervention.

For all these changes, the underlying assumption behind the policies toward SMEs is that the heads of small firms do not fully understand their own interests and that the state must encourage (and, in the process, become quite involved in) such desirable practices as investment in risky innovation, improvements in quality-control methods, the introduction of new materials into products, modernization of plant and equipment, use of sophisticated software, and hiring of managers and engineers. Nor is coercion entirely absent from the relationship. If state officials are not telling private managers what to do, they are paying 20 to 50 percent of the costs for them to do certain things. Ironically, it could be argued that at no point in French history has the state meddled in so many firms and in so many prerogatives of management as under today's ostensibly post-*dirigiste* regime.

Economic Liberalization and State Activism

France's break with *dirigisme* eliminated a number of interventionist policies, but it also created pressures for new kinds of state intervention. As described above, the dramatic expansion of early retirement opportunities played a critical role in facilitating market-driven industrial restructuring. Instead of protecting jobs through bailouts of uncompetitive companies, French authorities allowed firms to reorganize, while protecting worker income streams through early retirement. Early retirement helped salve the Left's guilty conscience, but more important, it effectively demobilized France's working class, undercutting the capacity of France's already-anemic trade unions to mount resistance to industrial restructuring. The vast majority of French workers were more than willing to quit smelly, physically taxing, alienating jobs—to receive 90 percent of their previous wages without having to report to work. Thus, the recourse to early retirements was not simply a social strategy but also an economic strategy, a fundamental prerequisite for carrying out much-needed industrial restructuring.

Government policies aimed not only to facilitate the movement away from *dirigisme* but also to palliate the perceived limits or failings of economic liberalization. The restoration of corporate profitability and competitiveness in the mid-1980s did not bring about an appreciable reduction in unemployment. In response, beginning with the Rocard government in 1988, French authorities adopted a much more interventionist approach to labor markets. The Rocard government expanded active labor market policies, notably training programs, public internships, and subsidies for hard-to-place youths and the long-term unemployed. The number of beneficiaries of government measures had already risen from 450,000 in 1984 to 850,000 in 1989 but would more than double during the next five years, reaching 1.9 million in 1994 (DARES 1996: 100). In the 1990s, center-right governments expanded employment subsidies, while the Left multiplied public internships. The thirty-five-hour workweek was also presented as a job-creating measure (although this claim was hotly disputed).

The persistence of mass unemployment has led French authorities to innovate in the area of welfare policy as well as labor market policy. The guaranteed minimum income (RMI) has come to serve as fallback for adults who have exhausted or failed to qualify for unemployment benefits. The CMU provides supplementary health insurance to those not covered by their employers. French authorities have also redirected France's program of family allowances toward poverty relief. The broad trend, since the early 1970s, has been toward the "socialization of family policy": "horizontal redistribution" between childless workers and families with children has given way to "vertical redistribution" between the wealthy and the poor (Lenoir 1990; Commaille 1998). Since the early 1970s, French authorities have added a number of means-tested benefits—including housing allowances, child-care subsidies, and income supplements for single parents—to assist struggling families. As a result, the share of family allowance spending subjected to means testing has risen from 13.6 percent in 1970 to over 60 percent today.

France's break with *dirigisme* in the 1980s provided a dual impetus to state intervention. The *promise* of liberalization induced authorities to commit vast resources to the transition process, to the alleviation of social pain and political resistance, in the expectation that a more flexible labor market would quickly generate enough jobs to make such costly transitional measures unnecessary (or, at least, much less necessary). The *disappointments* of liberalization and the continuing high levels of unemployment not only made it impossible to wind down supposedly transitional early retirement measures but also drove new spending in the form of active labor market programs and social assistance programs. In short, de-*dirigisation* and welfare state expansion were two sides of the same (very expensive) coin. That said, the new statist coin is very different from the pre-1983 specie.

The Social Anesthesia State

If state activism remains a prominent feature of France's political economy, the goals and instruments of that intervention have changed dramatically. Post-*dirigiste* state intervention differs in two important ways from its *dirigiste* antecedents. The first is in the relationship to the private sector. Instead of seeking to impose specific industrial strategies on firms, state initiatives have been geared toward providing an enabling environment, especially for small business: subsidies for innovation, market prospecting, and investment in new technologies; resources for training and low-skill hires; and early retirement programs that permit firms to downsize without provoking worker resistance. All of these state programs have expanded the options available to companies, while leaving the initiative in private managers' hands. They have been market conforming more than market directing.

The other distinctive feature of the new state intervention concerns the losers of economic liberalization. In its original form, the *dirigiste* model shifted resources from consumption to investment, limiting real wages and social spending. By the 1970s, however, the losers of economic modernization had mobilized, and state resources were used increasingly to block change—to bail out uncompetitive firms, thereby preventing layoffs and plant closings (Berger 1981a; E. Cohen 1989). More recent state intervention reflects a strategic shift. The concerns of modernization's losers have been addressed, but not by blocking economic reform. Rather, under what might be termed a "social anesthesia" strategy, public resources are mobilized to pacify and demobilize the victims and opponents of market-led adjustment. Many of the most expensive new policies in France over the past twenty years have reflected this social anesthesia logic: early retirement, guaranteed minimum income, need-based supplementary health insurance, employment subsidies, and public internships. The social anesthesia mission has also bolstered the enabling environment strategy. Whereas the *dirigiste* state sought to steer the market, the social anesthesia state underwrites market-led, privately determined adjustment strategies by pacifying, dividing, and demobilizing potential opponents.

France's social anesthesia state is not without problems and risks. The first is that recurrent state intervention will reinforce the Tocquevillean problem of a demobilized and irresponsible associational landscape. French interest groups have little incentive to organize and bargain with each other if the state is calling all the shots. At one point, the French employer association withdrew from the national health insurance board, arguing that the board's corporatist principles of operation were rendered moot by recurrent government meddling. Moreover, lacking partners and buffers, state authorities often find themselves on the front line, as every aggrieved party in French society—from displaced workers to uncompetitive farmers, to overworked truckers—turns to the state for relief. In an extreme example, workers in a factory slated for shutdown occupied the factory and threatened to dump toxic chemicals into the river unless the state (not the company) dispatched a labor official to negotiate a better severance package!

A second problem of the social anesthesia strategy is that it is very expensive. Many social initiatives, such as generous early retirement programs, were envisaged as temporary. Workers would be pensioned off, companies would restructure, then job creation would resume anew, and early retirement programs could be wound down. Instead of winding down, however, social anesthesia programs have been preserved. What is more, new initiatives—such as a guaranteed minimum income—have been added, as mass unemployment has claimed new victims. Although one can certainly sympathize with the effort to protect the poor and vulnerable, the cost of these programs has pushed the French state to the limits of its taxing capacity and, critics argue, undermined competitiveness and job creation. The persistence of unemployment levels of 9 percent or more, despite the many programs that reduce formal unemployment, attests to the dysfunctions of the French labor market.

A third problem is that social anesthesia is largely passive; it pays people not to work. If this represents an improvement over bailing out uncompetitive companies in order to prevent layoffs, one can imagine better uses for the money. Here a comparative perspective is revealing. Social democratic countries like Sweden spend as much or even more than France on social programs, but the social democratic approach is centered around the so-called work line, the notion that every adult should be employed (Titmuss 1987; Esping-Andersen 1990; Huber and Stephens 2001). As a result, passive measures tend to be limited, with much of the spending concentrated on "active" policies that facilitate employment, such as education and training, relocation assistance, and low-cost public child care. Under the "active" or "social investment" model, there is an economic pay off beyond simply keeping displaced workers from protesting and blocking layoffs. France's social anesthesia strategy offers few such benefits— few, if any, gains in human capital and employment.

The fourth problem of the social anesthesia strategy is that the anesthetic appears to be wearing off. A minimum income of €420 per month may be acceptable as a stopgap but not as a way of life. In the long run, the RMI is no substitute for social integration through a steady job, for upward social mobility. Many of the supposed beneficiaries of social anesthesia policies harbor great bitterness toward a government that offers them meager allowances and a succession of dead-end internships and substandard part-time or temporary jobs. This dissatisfaction probably cost Jospin the presidency in 2002, as leftist voters flocked to three different Trotskyist parties, preventing Jospin from qualifying for the run-off election with President Chirac. It also contributed to the rejection of the EU constitution in a 2005 referendum, with critics portraying the constitution as enshrining a "neoliberal Europe." Frustration with enduring social exclusion and unemployment was a central factor behind the immigrant riots in the Paris suburbs in fall 2005. Finally, and perhaps most ominously, simmering discontent among the disadvantaged has helped fuel the rise of the xenophobic, racist National Front of Jean-Marie Le Pen, which has become the number-one party by far among both blue-collar workers and the unemployed.

French authorities are beginning to tackle some of the problems of the social anesthesia state, albeit with great caution. Both the pension and health-care systems have been the object of cost-cutting reforms during Chirac's second term in office. French labor markets are also being reformed. In 2001, the social partners negotiated an agreement, the Assistance Plan for Returning to Employment (PARE), which increases the pressure on the unemployed to seek and accept a job. A series of tax reforms, including the establishment of a modest version of the US Earned Income Tax Credit (EITC), are designed to increase the returns to paid employment, as opposed to social benefits. Thus, the adaptation and redeployment of the French state remains a work in progress.

For all its limitations and need for further reform, the social anesthesia state has enabled France to jettison dysfunctional *dirigiste* industrial policies, to create a competitive, productive, export-oriented, and reasonably dynamic economy while limiting the social fallout. Seen from a Japanese perspective, this is no small achievement. As the next section relates, the changes in Japan have been less far-ranging, and the absence of a developed welfare state has been a key factor limiting reform.

4. Japan: The Employment Preservation Route

Since the collapse of the bubble economy in the early 1990s, successive Japanese governments have launched a variety of reforms—financial, regulatory, and administrative—intended, at least ostensibly, to circumscribe state intervention in the economy and to create more competitive markets. Deregulation has been on the agenda for over a decade, and the mid-1990s saw the initiation of the Japanese version of the "Big Bang" in financial markets and administrative reform. Virtually every part of the administrative apparatus has been touched by these policies, and calls for liberalization have only increased, as Japan's economic stagnation persisted beyond expectations.

Despite a flurry of activity, however, reforms have been far more circumscribed than in France. Without a way of compensating losers who bear the costs of liberalization, Japanese authorities have acted consistently to block the adverse effects of liberalization, first and foremost unemployment, a pattern that we call the "employment preservation route." Thus, while in France welfare policies have compensated for the employment effects of liberalization, in Japan governments have pursued liberalization, to the extent possible, by attempting to minimize the occurrence of such employment effects in the first place. Liberalization has been both cautious and counterbalanced by expensive policies to preserve employment. We illustrate how the employment preservation route constrains liberalization and invites new state intervention by looking at two cases: job creation policies and financial reform.

Job Creation Policies

Japan's social protection system can be characterized as "welfare through work" (Miura 2002a). The essence of this system is that employment maintenance functionally substitutes for income maintenance programs: unemployment insurance and early retirement programs are not needed in an economy where everyone can find a job. For Japan, the commitment to full employment offered a cheaper alternative to a formal welfare state. The problem, of course, is what to do when the economy falters and employers need fewer workers. One solution is to loosen restrictions on dismissals, while improving social programs to take care of the displaced workers. Japan resisted such a social insurance approach, however.

Facing rising unemployment in the 1990s, the first response of the Japanese government was to increase spending on public works, rather than creating or upgrading the social protection system for the unemployed. Excess labor was to be absorbed by the construction sector, which played a central role in the employment maintenance strategy. In the early 1990s, the share of employees in the construction sector was 10.2 percent in Japan, as opposed to 6.5 percent in France and 6.1 percent in the United States (ILO 1994). The Japanese government then expanded public works spending repeatedly in response to recurrent recessions. From 1992 to 2002, the government launched nine massive public spending packages to boost the economy: ¥10.7 trillion in 1992, ¥13.2 trillion in April and ¥6.2 trillion in September in 1993, ¥9.8 trillion in 1994, ¥14.2 trillion in 1995, ¥12.4 trillion in April and ¥17.9 trillion in November 1998, ¥18 trillion in 1999, and ¥11 trillion in 2000.[7] Public works and special measures to induce housing construction accounted for the lion's share of these fiscal packages. The proportion of public works of total spending was 74.8 percent in 1992, 80.3 percent in April 1993, 16.3 percent in September 1993, 73.5 percent in 1994, 90 percent in 1995, 62.3 percent in April 1998, 45.2 percent in November 1998, 37.8 percent in 1999, and 42.7 percent in 2000.

Over the past five years, Japanese authorities have scaled back spending on public works, largely in response to worsening budget deficits. In 2004, the share of public works in the national budget was the lowest since 1991. Still, the country's outstanding long-term debt reached 157.3 percent of GDP in 2003, the highest figure among the industrialized countries and more than double the level ten years earlier (OECD 2004a). These alarming numbers show how much Japanese authorities have relied on public works to preserve employment, absorbing fiscal resources that might have been used for the construction of a welfare state.

In addition to public works, a number of labor market measures have been taken to preserve Japan's employment model. First, employment protection for regular workers (i.e., full-time employees, with indefinite work contracts) remains secure, if not strengthened. In the late 1990s, the Organization for Economic Cooperation and Development (OECD) ranked Japan first among its member countries in terms of employment security, as measured by the difficulty in dismissing regular workers (OECD 1999a), and Japan has made no major changes since then. Neoliberal scholars persistently call for the legalization of procedures that would make dismissal of Japanese workers easier, but unions and opposition parties have successfully blocked such legislation. Indeed, case law imposing limits on managers' dismissal rights was incorporated into the Labor Standard Act in 2003. This codification did not change the difficulty of dismissing workers in practice, but it formally enshrined state involvement in employment protection. Furthermore, the government has actively supported employment preservation for elderly workers. In 1994, it required employers to set the mandatory retirement age above sixty. (The law became effective in 1998.) As the pension eligibility age is being gradually pushed back to sixty-five years, the government is seeking ways to ensure employment up to that age.

Second, in contrast to the highly protected situation of core workers, employment conditions for irregular workers (i.e., temporary and part-time employees) have been subjected to significant deregulation. The Temporary Staff Work Act in 1999 as well as the revision of the Labor Standards Act in 1998 signaled to employers that they could diversify types of work contracts.[8] As a result, the number of temporary workers more than doubled, from 306,000 in 1998 to 721,000 in 2002 (Statistics Bureau 1998, 2003). While restrictions on the temporary labor market have not been removed completely, irregular workers are mushrooming, even in areas where such contracts are not allowed. The growing number of irregular workers has been accompanied by the contraction of regular workers. As of 2002, the share of regular workers among all employees had fallen to 68 percent, from over 80 percent in the 1980s. The asymmetry between stable employment security and the deregulated temporary labor market shows that the central feature of Japan's social protection model (i.e., employment protection for core workers) remains intact, but at the expense of a large and growing number of unprotected workers. The deregulation of the temporary labor market facilitates job creation, in keeping with Japan's traditional focus on maximizing employment.

Third, the government has intervened to institutionalize the practice of work sharing, which is meant to prevent unemployment and create new jobs. The initiative was taken by Rengo, a peak labor federation, and Keidanren, a peak employers' association. A tripartite agreement, including the government, was signed in 2002, establishing subsidies for firms that undertake work sharing. In the same year, the government budgeted ¥7 billion from the national general account as well as ¥19.7 billion from the Employment Insurance Account to financially support work sharing. In addition, the government, Rengo, and Keidanren agreed to create "Placement Support Centers" in each prefecture run by local organizations of Rengo and Keidanren and financed by the Ministry of Welfare and Labor.

The Japanese government distinguishes between two types of work sharing: "employment preservation" and "multiple work styles." The employment preservation variant of work sharing has been widespread in Japan since the 1970s, allowing a reduction of working hours and thus incomes in order to preserve jobs. What differs is that the government is officially endorsing and subsidizing the process. The multiple work style variant of job sharing is completely new, embracing a concept of part-time regular workers. In practice, it has been difficult to implement, though, since such a concept runs counter to the current distinction and gap between regular workers, who receive full benefits but are expected to work overtime, and irregular workers, who are able to work shorter hours but do not receive full benefits. Work sharing reflects the state's commitment to employment maintenance and its continuing effort to contain the expansion of welfare spending.

Lacking a social safety net, Japanese authorities have approached labor market reform with great caution. Regulations have been loosened for temporary and fixed-term workers, resulting in a significant increase in such employment. Liberalizing reforms have not been extended to core, full-time workers, however, since these workers would have difficulty finding comparable jobs and because existing welfare benefits are inadequate. Indeed, on some dimensions, such as early retirement, the protection of core workers has increased. The government's greatest efforts have focused on fiscal stimulus through massive public works projects—an expensive and unsustainable approach to employment maintenance. Taken together, Japan's labor market policies have combined limited liberalization—confined largely to irregular workers—with expanded protection and especially spending for core employees.

Financial Reform

Like labor market policy, financial reform has been shaped and constrained by the imperatives of employment preservation. On the one hand, finance is clearly one of the areas where there has been a veritable storm of deregulatory activity. Since the 1980s, successive governments have eased market entry, decontrolled prices, and allowed the introduction of a wider array of financial products. Japan's version of the "Big Bang," launched by Prime Minister Ryutaro Hashimoto in the second half of the 1990s, set out to transform Japan's entire financial system and to boost Tokyo's role as a global financial center. On the other hand, the flurry of deregulatory activity has not led to a retreat of the state from financial markets. The government has wielded the instruments of the state to micromanage its financial system, albeit in ways that depart from the developmental model. Rather than leveraging state control over finance to promote developmental ends, successive governments have used existing state instruments and created new ones to minimize bankruptcies and layoffs.

Banking is a case in point. In the wake of the collapse of Japan's asset bubble, Japanese banks suffered from undercapitalization and massive nonperforming loans. These two problems have created a vicious circle. Banks do not want to call in loans because they would be forced to take losses, which would then exacerbate their undercapitalization problem, in some cases driving them into bankruptcy. Instead, banks have covered up their nonperforming loan problems by treating borrowers leniently. In a practice known as "ever-greening"

(Caballero, Hoshi, and Kashyap 2003: 4), banks have rolled over loans, offered interest concessions, and partially forgiven debt in order to avoid having to recognize losses on nonperforming loans. Such actions serve as a life-support system for so-called zombie firms that have little or no prospect of every repaying their loans. These practices, in turn, have widespread negative effects on the economy because they channel capital to inefficient firms. One study found that zombie firms accounted for 30 percent of all publicly traded firms in manufacturing, construction, retail, wholesale (excluding nine general trading companies), and services (Caballero, Hoshi, and Kashyap 2003).

The government has long accommodated these practices by engaging in regulatory forbearance. Banks do not foreclose on zombies because they do not want to take losses, and the government does not force the banks to do so because it does not want to see layoffs and bankruptcies. The government has also refrained from compelling the banks to disclose the true extent of their nonperforming loans. Finally, the government has turned a blind eye to the widely criticized industry accounting practice of allowing deferred tax credits (credits from past losses) to be counted as core capital. Many banks cannot claim these credits because they continue to register losses, so the credits pile up, inflating the banks' core capital figures.

In addition to regulatory forbearance, governments have extended public funds to solve the problem of bank undercapitalization. In some cases, the authorities have intervened in the stock market, using funds from public pensions and the postal saving system to buy shares and prop up prices, a practice that has been dubbed price-keeping operations (PKOs). The purpose of the intervention is to shore up the capital base of banks that own shares.

The state has also recapitalized a number of banks. In 1996, the government bailed out housing loan corporations (jusen), at a cost of ¥685 billion (Maswood 2002: 46). The opposition criticized the bailout and turned public opinion against the use of public funds to save financial institutions, at least temporarily. But as the seriousness of the banking crisis became clearer, more public subsidies were made available. In 1998, the government tendered ¥1.8 trillion to the banks to replenish their capital base, followed by an additional ¥7.5 trillion in 1999 (*Japan Times* 2002). Despite a series of expensive rescue packages, the Japanese banking sector remains undercapitalized, owing to a combination of weak profits, continued slow growth, and the ongoing discovery of extensive nonperforming loans. That said, some of the larger and more competitive banks are beginning to show signs of returning to health.

The undercapitalization of the banks has created a credit crunch, particularly for small and medium-size enterprises. SMEs are highly dependent on bank lending because virtually no bond market exists for these firms. To alleviate the credit crunch, the government has mobilized two financial institutions within the FILP program: the National Life Finance Corporation and the Japanese Corporation for Small Business. These public corporations had been slated to become independent government entities as part of a larger administrative reform. Liberalization was postponed, however, so that they could continue to provide credit to SMEs. Indeed, a cabinet decision in 2000 actually encouraged the National Life Finance Corporation and the Japanese Corporation for Small Business to lend to distressed SMEs. Subsequently, both entities created "safety net loans" designed to forestall bankruptcies among SMEs.

The government's financial rescue efforts have extended to borrowers as well as lenders. The state has micromanaged the nonperforming loan problem by getting directly involved in the business of restructuring firms, rather than letting them go bankrupt. The ruling coalition revised the Financial Revitalization Law to allow the Resolution and Collection Corporation (RCC), which was set up to purchase nonperforming loans and to dispose of them, to rehabilitate companies beginning on January 1, 2002.

At the behest of the LDP, the RCC has focused on small- and medium-sized enterprises. SMEs are a key constituency of the LDP. They account for 99 percent of all business establishments and 67 percent of the country's workforce (National Life Finance Corporation 2003: 4). The LDP has shown a bias toward such firms and has attempted to salvage as many SMEs as possible. The RCC has teamed up with private banks to rehabilitate firms, setting up trust funds to lend to them. The trust funds give banks three to five years to restructure, after which the RCC will call in loans. The RCC has also used public funds from sources such as the Development Bank of Japan to lend to SMEs. In addition, the Financial Services Agency (FSA) has been relatively lenient toward smaller regional banks, refraining from setting any numerical targets for the disposal of bad loans for such banks. Heizo Takenaka, the economy and financial services minister, who is widely viewed as a reformer, has backed this move, commenting, "I don't mind if you criticize this as 'one country, two systems'" (*Nihon Keizai Shimbun* 2003).

The government has not neglected struggling large firms. In fact, another organization, the Industrial Revitalization Corporation of Japan (IRCJ), was created in April 2003 to assist big companies. Like the RCC, the IRCJ links the resolution of the nonperforming loan program with corporate restructuring. While some have viewed the creation of the IRCJ as an indication of dissatisfaction with the RCC's pace of reform, thus far it appears that a division of labor is developing, with the IRCJ focusing on large-scale restructuring efforts and firms that have a relatively high chance of successful corporate rehabilitation.

The government established the IRCJ as part of it 2003 antideflation package. With an infusion of ¥10 trillion allocated from Japan's deposit insurance system, the IRCJ coordinates restructuring plans with corporations and their creditors. Part of this process involves buying debt from non–main bank lenders. Reducing the number of creditors streamlines the process of restructuring, since fewer partners need to be involved. Like the RCC, the IRCJ represents an attempt to address the nonperforming loan problem with a minimum of layoffs and bankruptcies. Indeed, the IRCJ is supposed to serve as an alternative to bankruptcy proceedings, although it is not yet clear how many firms will choose to use the IRCJ to restructure their operations.

If the IRCJ and RCC illustrate how new state capacities have been deployed to avoid more radical change, the FILP illustrates the diversion of established institutions of the developmental state. The FILP system played a critical role in providing funds to finance Japan's economic development. But over time, funds in the FILP system increased exponentially, as deposits to the postal savings system and public pension contributions grew. The system evolved into a massive public financial system and a virtual parallel government. FILP priorities shifted from economic development to politically driven investments, such as housing, the environment, construction, and credit for small- and medium-size business. For the LDP, the public corporations became a useful tool for funneling particularistic benefits to the party's constituencies. Public corporations also provided lucrative second careers for bureaucrats. Retiring bureaucrats could parachute into public corporations under the jurisdiction of their former ministries (a practice known as *amakudari*). This option became even more attractive after regulations were passed forbidding bureaucrats from parachuting into positions in the private sector that are under the jurisdiction of their former ministries for a period of two years. Public corporations came to serve as a useful temporary landing spot for bureaucrats during this period.

The government has pledged to try to abolish the public corporations and financial institutions or to turn them into independent government corporations (dokuritsu hojin) and to privatize postal savings. Because of the credit crunch and the fear of mass bankruptcies among SMEs, however, these reforms have been diluted or delayed. FILP was overhauled in 2001, but contrary to the announced intention of the reform, the government introduced a loophole to allow FILP to continue channeling capital to weak and less competitive sectors of the economy. The government submitted a bill in 2005 to privatize the post office, including the postal savings system, but members of Prime Minister Koizumi's own party rebelled against it, and it failed to pass the Upper House. In retaliation, Koizumi dissolved the Lower House in August 2005, called snap elections as a referendum on the bill, and expelled thirty-seven LDP members who voted against the bill. The episode shows how difficult it has been to reform the system. The actual reform bill contained a number of compromises. Privatization would have been phased in gradually and completed only in 2017. Even so, the bill was rejected. While opposition to privatization stems from many factors, starting with the historic role of postmasters in turning out the LDP vote, an important reason in the current context is the fact that postal savings have become a useful source of finance for the government, including propping up the stock market through price-keeping operations.

The Employment Preservation Route

In contrast to France's social anesthesia path, economic factors, international pressures, domestic political institutions, and strategic choices have led various Japanese governments to prioritize maintaining employment over other objectives. Rather than using the state to buy off or anesthetize opponents of liberalizing measures, Japanese governments have attempted to avoid one of the key consequences of liberalization—layoffs in uncompetitive firms or sectors. Employment maintenance is paramount in Japan. But unlike Sweden, the attempt to maximize employment has not been through active labor market policies that redeploy labor in response to market signals. Rather, state policy has often blocked labor market adjustment, since long-term employment has in essence served as the pillar of social protection.

The Japanese employment preservation strategy has entailed both costs and benefits. The most obvious benefit is employment. Despite prolonged economic stagnation, Japanese unemployment is still very low by comparative standards. Unemployment peaked at 5.4 percent in 2002 and is now below 5 percent. Thus, Japan has been able to steer clear of the kind of structural mass unemployment that has plagued many European political economies, including France.

Additionally, Japan has avoided the permanent expansion of costly social programs, such as the ones that now have exacerbated fiscal problems in France as well as other European welfare states. Of course, Japan's public debt is extremely high, but this is primarily a function of slow economic growth and low taxes, not a large state. Public spending is modest compared to other advanced industrialized countries, and assuming a return to more robust economic growth, Japan still has room to raise taxes in order to draw down its massive public debt.

Third, Japan has retained many elements of its economic model that serve as the basis of its competitive advantage. Economic adjustment has been more at the margins than at the core of Japan's production paradigm. Such incremental adjustment has preserved key economic strengths, such as long-term investment in human resources; management-worker cooperation; and relational contracting among firms, suppliers, and financial institutions.

On the downside, the employment preservation strategy has entailed significant costs. While the cause of Japan's economic stagnation is still debated, the use of state intervention to preserve employment has diverted resources and delayed useful reforms. In finance, the slow response of Japanese governments in disposing of bad loans and the preference for state-led restructuring of banks and corporations have been expensive and have prolonged the effects of the collapse of asset prices. Temporary measures to prop up banks through stock market intervention and the like have sought to forestall disaster, rather than to set Japan's financial system on a sounder footing. Moreover, the FILP, while slightly reformed, continues to be a massive state-controlled finance system that often allocates capital inefficiently and nontransparently.

In industrial relations, the limited liberalization of part-time labor markets, which left the protections of core workers in place, has also reinforced social exclusion and increased income inequality, as the gap between part-time and full-time workers grows. Women and youths tend to populate the part-time and temporary labor markets and bear much of the cost of economic adjustments. Although the overall un-employment rate is low, the high level of joblessness among youths is alarming. In 2002, the unemployment rate was 12.8 percent for those between the ages of fifteen and nineteen, 9.3 percent for those be-tween twenty and twenty-four, and 7.1 percent for those between twenty-five and twenty-nine.

Moreover, the increasing presence of irregular workers poses a new policy challenge because the existing social protection system has been based on the assumption of long-term employment of male workers. Thus, the Japanese system risks leaving irregular workers out of the already frail social safety net. New social policies initiated in the 1990s, such as the creation of long-term care insurance and support for chil-dren, were driven by concerns about the rapid aging of the Japanese population and did not address problems in the labor market. A fun-damental reform of unemployment insurance has not even been on the agenda.

But perhaps the longest-lasting consequences of the employment preservation strategy will be in public finances. Ironically, although the choice to forgo a European-style welfare state was motivated largely by the desire to keep government spending in check, public spending has expanded dramatically, while revenues have shrunk in the wake of the collapse of the bubble. Spending to prop up banks and to fund public works and other activities that essentially acted as a means of maintaining employment have proven very costly and have not been matched by corresponding increases in tax revenues. As a result, public debt has grown to over 150 percent of GDP, exceeding that of traditional fiscal laughingstocks like Italy, Greece, and Belgium. Aggravating matters, the use (or misuse) of this money on public works programs has fueled the perception that government spending is wasteful and inefficient, making it difficult to raise taxes in order to tackle the fiscal problem on the revenue side. Politically, administrative reform to improve public sector efficiency has become a prerequisite to preparing the ground for tax increases, a fact not lost on the MOF, which is trying desperately to push through fiscal reconstruction plans. Revealingly, the platform of the largest opposition party, the Democrats, proposes a sharp reduction in public works, a 20 percent reduction in the number of civil servants, *and* the enhancement of welfare policies.

If the Japanese employment preservation strategy has maintained key features of the vaunted industrial relations and production systems, it has done so by diverting the developmental state. State intervention and public spending have served primarily to avoid market-led adjustment, rather than to nurture emerging industries and services. Japan's political economy still has many strengths, and there are signs of economic recovery. That said, the policies of the past fifteen years have driven up public spending and debt while doing little to assist this recovery.

5. Conclusion: Implications of the French and Japanese Experiences

The experiences of France and Japan over the past twenty years offer four main insights into the transformation of statist political economies. The first is that the road to a more market-centered political economy is paved with new state interventions. Specifically, getting the state out of industrial policy may require getting the state into social and labor market policy. French authorities have paid a very high price to anesthetize the victims and potential opponents of *de-dirigisation*. In recent years, French reformers have begun to grapple with the challenge of reducing social spending and shifting from "passive" labor market expenditures, like early retirement, that pay people not to work to "active" measures that channel people to paid employment. Post-*dirigiste* reform remains a work in progress, and many are unhappy with the contours of the social anesthesia state. For all these qualifications, France has clearly broken with the *dirigiste* industrial policy model and reaped significant benefits from a more market-oriented political economy.

Japan, by contrast, opted not to invest in a European welfare state but to stick with its model of full employment. However, attempting to sustain the employment preservation route while pursuing market reforms has entailed a series of new state interventions that represent a partial diversion of the state apparatus away from developmental goals toward redistributive ones. Economic reform, coupled with policies that neutralize or mitigate its adverse effects, is the typical pattern that has emerged in Japan. Our point is not that Japan has failed to change. Japan has restructured industry, loosened *keiretsu* ties, expanded labor market flexibility, and engaged in far-ranging regulatory reform. Clearly, Japan's political economy today is very different and more market sensitive than in 1990 (S. Vogel 2005, 2006). Still, in comparative perspective, Japan has not moved as far away from the postwar statist developmental model as France.

The second conclusion suggested by the French and Japanese experiences is that there is no "state-free" option for statist political economies. The alternative to the French social anesthesia approach is not necessarily a leaner and meaner neoliberalism. Rather, if the case of Japan is indicative, the alternative to the French approach may be a less liberal political economy. Instead of addressing the concerns of increasingly vulnerable and politically powerful workers through social insurance programs, Japanese authorities have used state instruments to prop up employment. This approach has certainly not held state spending in check. On the contrary, the combination of recurrent bank bailouts and patronage-ridden, Keynesian public works programs has driven Japanese government spending, deficits, and debt to alarming levels. Although the costs of the French social anesthesia approach are widely acknowledged and denounced, Japanese state spending and debt have increased much more sharply over the same period. Thus, the choice in a statist political economy may not be *whether* to increase state spending but, rather, *how*. Whereas French authorities have used state spending to purchase de-*dirigisation*, their Japanese counterparts have used state spending to preserve employment and slow the pace of adjustment.

The third lesson from the French and Japanese experiences is that dismantling specific policies or tools associated with a particular statist framework is not the same thing as dismantling that framework itself. State intervention can morph and migrate. In France, state intervention has migrated. While voluntarist industrial policy has become a thing of the past, labor market and welfare expenditures have grown to near-Scandinavian proportions. In Japan, state intervention has morphed. While formal policy instruments, like FILP, have remained intact, their mode of operation has changed, with support for economic modernization giving way to support for the status quo. If we confine our investigation to existing forms of state intervention, to the question of whether these forms are surviving or being undermined, we may be committing the analytic equivalent of searching for the key under the lamppost. In the French case, such an investigation would yield the erroneous conclusion that the state has become a nonfactor, that it has been scaled back rather than redeployed. In Japan, if we looked only at the structure or size of state policies, we would reach the equally erroneous conclusion that the state's role in the economy has changed very little.

The fourth and final lesson, suggested primarily by the French experience, is that to the extent that globalization or European integration necessitates changes in state intervention, national responses may take the form of a redeployment of the state, as opposed to a shrinking of the state. This vision stands in contrast to strong globalization claims about convergence but also to path-dependent analyses emphasizing the persistence of long-established arrangements. French authorities have not perpetuated postwar *dirigiste* arrangements; they have dismantled these arrangements. There has been real change. At the same time, the French state has not shrunk, as the logic of globalization would anticipate. Between *plus-ça-change* continuity and globalization-driven convergence, France may be on a third path— where old forms of state intervention have been discredited and cleared away, but new forms have emerged in their place. Borrowing from Joseph Schumpeter (1950), we might conceive of this redeployment path as a kind of "institutional creative destruction."

~ II

The State and Social Groups

❧ 4

The State and the Reconstruction of Industrial Relations Institutions after Fordism

Britain and France Compared

CHRIS HOWELL

BY THE END OF THE 1970s, the crisis of the dominant Fordist postwar regime of accumulation had become painfully obvious across the advanced capitalist world, even if the severity and symptoms of that crisis varied from country to country. Within the labor market, Fordism came to be associated above all with a range of *rigidities:* in the ability to hire and fire workers; in the deployment of labor; in work organization; in skill sets; in work time; and in pay and benefits. Unsurprisingly, with that diagnosis of the problems facing capitalist economies, the logical prescription was labor market and workplace flexibility. By the early 1980s, a steady drumbeat of employers, their political allies, and even traditionally social democratic parties were urging a wide-ranging post-Fordist restructuring of work. For employers and parties of the Right, this was usually accompanied by a claim that such a restructuring required an expansion of managerial prerogative and the ability of managers to impose unilateral changes in the workplace, whereas trade unions and their political allies were more likely to urge the collective negotiation of any changes.

Economic growth in capitalist societies is neither a natural nor a spontaneous process. Social conflict and an assortment of crisis tendencies (particularly those resulting from a mismatch of production and consumption and the uneven development of industrial and financial capital) make periods of stable economic growth unlikely in the absence of nonmarket regulation. In practice, it is a set of social institutions operating alongside the market that serve to regulate capitalist growth so as to limit industrial conflict and economic instability. Of particular importance, and the subject of this chapter, are industrial relations institutions, which regulate relations between business and labor—both inside and outside the firm. The role of industrial relations institutions is important not only during periods of relative economic stability but also when one regime of accumulation enters into crisis, and pressure for change appears. At this point, industrial relations institutions play a crucial role in the capacity of economies to restructure. Moreover, when existing industrial relations institutions act as obstacles to economic restructuring, the reform of these institutions becomes an urgent political matter.

This chapter has two central contentions: First, industrial relations reform in Britain and France in the period since the early 1980s has been a precondition for post-Fordist economic restructuring and the introduction of flexibility into the labor market and the workplace; change in the institutions of social regulation had to occur before economic restructuring could take place. Second, the state in these two countries not only played a central role in the process of institutional reform; such reform could not have occurred without the active intervention of the state. This is all the more surprising because the time period during which these transformations took place was one in which it was widely believed that state action was limited and constrained by accelerated international economic integration and resurgent business classes. State action to reconstruct industrial relations took place well after the heyday of statist intervention in France and under an aggressively laissez-faire Conservative government in Britain. Yet in both cases, the state led the process of transformation and business followed, in many cases expressing hostility to important aspects of the reform projects.

For a variety of reasons outlined in the theoretical section of this chapter and the accounts of reform in Britain and France, employers and trade unions are unable to undertake major projects of institutional reform or to create durable industrial relations institutions without state action; indeed, it is often the case that trade unions *and* employers will be hesitant or hostile to industrial relations reform, even where they know that economic restructuring is necessary. In both countries, the state ultimately took on the role of "modernizing" employer practices as part of the reform of industrial relations institutions.

In both the British and French cases, a set of industrial relations institutions had been put in place (again with the state playing a central role, though that is a different story) in the decade or so after the mid-1960s, in response to an earlier perception of economic and industrial crisis. It was these institutions, inherited from the past, that came to be associated by the early 1980s with labor market rigidities and to be perceived as obstacles to post-Fordist economic restructuring. In part, it was the role played by the state in these earlier systems of industrial relations that ensured that the state would have to be a central actor in their reform two decades later.

While the goal of enabling greater labor market and workplace flexibility was similar in the two countries, there were important differences in both the form and the process of industrial relations reform. This was primarily for two reasons. First, the legacies of the industrial relations systems inherited from the past imposed quite different kinds of rigidities. In the British case, the obstacles to flexibility became associated with the decentralized system of workplace collective bargaining and deeply implanted trade union capacities and resources inside the firm that had spread widely through the British economy from the late 1950s onward. The industrial relations reform project of the Thatcher government after 1979 was fundamentally decollectivist, aimed at weakening unions, narrowing the scope of collective regulation, and individualizing employment relations. The New Labour government elected in 1997 has emphasized greater legal protection for workers, but for the most part its industrial relations reform project has complemented rather than conflicted with the earlier Thatcherite project.

In France, by contrast, the rigidities of the Fordist period were associated with the state and its regulation of the labor market. In response to the crisis of May–June 1968, the French state had extended its *dirigisme* from the arena of state planning to the labor market and the system of social welfare. French industrial relations were marked by extremely weak firm-level industrial relations institutions, high levels of class conflict, and a deeply interventionist form of regulation of employment relations, as the French state, in effect, substituted for fragmented and poorly institutionalized trade unions.

The French reform projects of the 1980s and 1990s were aimed not at undermining collective regulation, as in Britain, but rather at enabling deregulation of the labor market by the state. To this end, industrial relations reform sought to create institutions that would permit the negotiation of flexibility through decentralized collective bargaining inside the firm, which would in turn permit the state to withdraw from regulation of the labor market. What has emerged since the mid-1980s is a set of decentralized firm-level institutions and practices that have permitted the negotiation of economic restructuring, while limiting industrial conflict in the private sector. Underlying this process has been constant intervention on the part of the state to encourage and underwrite the negotiation of post-Fordist forms of flexibility in the workplace. Different starting points and sources of labor market rigidity led to different industrial relations reform projects in France and Britain.

The second explanation for differences in the form and manner of institutional reform in Britain and France is more narrowly political. Different governments, with quite distinct ideologies, and different relationships to class actors, led to different understandings of the sources of economic crisis, hence to different reform agendas. It is an important theme of this chapter that states have a discursive power to offer an authoritative narration of crisis, which in turn shapes institutional reform. Furthermore, the discursive element of reform projects created a certain plasticity in the eventual shape of institutional change, which often had unintended consequences for reform efforts undertaken in the context of post-Fordist economic restructuring.

The dominant parties of the Right in the two countries were ideologically quite different: Gaullism did not share Thatcherism's neoliberal ideology nor its hostility to organized labor. It appropriated the language of social solidarity and consensus, with the result that France has seen a high degree of consistency in the direction of industrial relations reform over the past two decades, despite frequent changes of government. Similarly, the British Labour Party—both as "Old" Labour and as "New" Labour—bears little resemblance to the French Parti Socialiste (PS). The latter has been more enamored of the virtues of social dialogue in the workplace and less tied to the fortunes of organized labor. The result was that the PS's industrial relations reform project after 1981 proved quite compatible with the spread of flexibility and the deregulation of the labor market.

This chapter argues that, once triggered by economic restructuring, moments of institutional reconstruction require state action because of a set of unique state capacities not enjoyed by private industrial actors. Periods of institutional stability may permit states to retreat from active regulation of the political economy, but during moments of institutional rupture—even, indeed particularly, in the era of "globalization"—we can anticipate the reemergence of an active state role in the construction of new sets of political-economic institutions. The rest of this chapter is organized as follows. Section 1 offers a brief theoretical discussion of the importance of institutional regulation for capitalist economies and the centrality of state action in institutional change. An equally brief Section 2 contrasts the industrial systems created in the 1960s and 1970s in Britain and France; it points to the different implications they had for post-Fordist restructuring, hence for industrial relations reform from 1980 onward. Sections 3 and 4 outline the major elements of the reform of industrial relations institutions in the 1980s and 1990s for Britain and France, respectively. In each case, the consequences of state reform projects for both industrial relations institutions and the spread of flexibility are examined.

1. States and Industrial Relations Institutions

This chapter has two theoretical interests and explores them through an examination of industrial relations reform in Britain and France. The first interest is in understanding the relationship between economic restructuring and institutional change. The dominant theoretical approaches in contemporary political economy stress institutional durability and continuity in the face of economic change (for an exception, see Streeck and Thelen 2005). Whether the emphasis is on the importance of political culture, the interlocking and self-reinforcing character of sets of institutions, or more conventional notions of path dependence, the expectation is that economic change can be treated largely as an exogenous shock that is mediated and absorbed by national political economic institutions (Dobbin 1994; Steinmo, Thelen, and Longstreth 1992; Kitschelt et al. 1999; Iversen, Pontusson, and Soskice 2000; Hall and Soskice 2001b). It becomes difficult, from this perspective, to explain moments of institutional transformation (as occurred in both British and French industrial relations after 1980), and broad processes of economic restructuring are relegated to the status of background factors, to which existing institutions adapt, rather than as the source of institutional change.

In contrast, this chapter is primarily concerned with those moments of institutional construction and transition when, to paraphrase Antonio Gramsci (1971), one set of institutions is dying while another is struggling to be born. Its focus is on those points at which industrial conflict cannot be contained within existing institutional structures and practices; thus employers, trade unions, and state actors seek alternative arrangements that promise to restore industrial peace, stable accumulation, and the legitimacy of capitalist social relations. In fact, sharp ruptures, in which sets of institutions are rapidly replaced or transformed in function, are every bit as important a feature of institutional development as continuity and path dependence. I argue that it is changes in the pattern and nature of the economic growth regime that trigger these moments of institutional transformation.

The second theoretical interest of this chapter lies in examining the role of the state in institutional change. Again, the main theoretical approaches to understanding institutions anticipate a fairly limited role for the state, one of institutional maintenance rather than institutional construction. In part, this follows from a renewed emphasis on the centrality of business interests and organizations, rather than states or labor organizations, in explaining distinct national patterns of political-economic institutions (Hall and Soskice 2001b: 5). It is also the case that contemporary accounts of political economy are more likely to highlight "cross-class alliances" and shared interests among class actors than conflict (Swenson 2002). The result is that states are assigned a secondary role in coordinating and maintaining institutions, rather than managing class conflict through the construction of alternative institutions. To these factors can be added the more general expectation that national economic autonomy has shrunk, thus limiting the capacity of states to act and contributing to a "hollowing out" of the state.

In contrast, this account assigns a central role to states in explaining institutional development. States have a set of distinctive capacities when it comes to the construction and "embedding" of industrial relations institutions. The argument here is not one of state autonomy or the importance of the distinct interests of state actors but rather that states possess unique capacities to (1) enforce and systematize institutional change; (2) narrate an authoritative interpretation of industrial relations crisis; (3) use the public sector as a laboratory or demonstration effect for new industrial relations practices; (4) solve the collective action problems of employers and unions; (5) create and legitimize new class actors; and (6) anticipate and craft alliances among private industrial actors.

The point, simply put, is that certain forms of economic restructuring require institutional change and that the construction of new institutions requires an active state role. Far from a limited or shrinking role for the state in an era of rapid economic change, heightened competition, and new global pressures, the role of the state becomes more important because of the institutional transformation that accompanies economic change. This process is of particular importance in the sphere of industrial relations, where institutions inherited from the earlier Fordist period have come under challenge, and struggles over institutional change among industrial actors (employers, workers, and their organizations) have generated high levels of conflict.

In offering an explanation of institutional change, this chapter seeks to embed an institutionalist account within the Regulationist tradition of political economy. Regulationist accounts understand capitalist growth to be a profoundly contradictory, unstable, and crisis-ridden process that will not occur "naturally." Left to its own devices, subject only to regulation by invisible hands, capitalism will exhibit a range of crisis tendencies and generate high levels of social conflict. Change within capitalist economies is therefore the product not only of exogenous shocks but more often of a steady accumulation of internal contradictions. It is for this reason that capitalism requires institutions to regulate or stabilize growth. The Regulation approach is, above all, an *institutional* account of capitalism.

Regulation theory goes beyond identifying crisis tendencies to offer a historicization of capitalist development centering on the different growth dynamics (or regimes of accumulation) of different phases of capitalism. While economic restructuring, instability, and crisis are permanent features of capitalist economies, distinct patterns of growth lasting longer than one or two business cycles can be identified. Bob Jessop has suggested that we think of broad growth regimes as families, composed of several (national) variants, differing in many ways and sharing only a basic underlying growth dynamic (Jessop 1991). For Fordism, the common core is the link of wages to productivity and the spread of mass production and mass consumption, whereas for post-Fordism it is the emphasis on supply-side flexibility.

A Regulationist conception of institutional development encourages us to recognize that industrial relations institutions are a congealed form of class power; they reflect a particular moment of class power at the time of their construction. There is nothing necessarily fragile or contingent about class power. What gives institutions in the sphere of industrial relations their stability over time is a rough stability in the balance of class power and the economic interests of workers and employers. This stability rests, in turn, on a stable pattern of economic growth. It is when that form of growth breaks down, and consequently the interests and resources of class actors change, that one would expect the institutions that previously regulated industrial relations to mutate, whether through the creation of entirely new institutions or the investing of new functions and meanings in existing institutions. In this sense, the utility of the Marxist tradition of political economy—with its emphasis on the economic patterning of social relations—is that it points toward a process of institutional construction, deconstruction, and reconstruction, which is not historically contingent, fluid, and open-ended but is instead profoundly structured. A crisis of a particular pattern of economic growth does not cause a new set of regulatory mechanisms to come into being; still less can any new regulatory institutions be guaranteed to ensure stable, orderly economic growth. But the transition from one distinct type of economic growth to another will create a set of problems that are not easily resolvable using existing institutions, and this dilemma will encourage the search for new regulatory mechanisms.

This chapter argues that neither "the economy" nor class actors will spontaneously produce the industrial relations institutions needed for new patterns of economic growth. The state is a site of experimentation, and it is best positioned to select successful regulatory experiments, institutionalize them, and extend them throughout the economy. That process is both one of concrete institution building and a discursive one in which crisis is narrated, and new institutions and practices are discursively constituted and naturalized (Jenson 1990). State actors play a central role in the construction of industrial relations institutions by virtue of a set of unique public capacities, of which I emphasize the ability to solve collective action problems for employers and unions, and a discursive role in the interpretation of crisis, although it is important not to forget the state's overt coercive power. Above all, through its legal authority, the state alone can create a *system* in place of a set of scattered experiments. The role of the state is most significant in the movement from crisis to a new set of institutions designed to manage crisis. Thus, a state role is most visible in the constructive phase of institution building and may be less necessary or visible for the maintenance of existing institutions.

States intervene in the restructuring of industrial relations institutions because they cannot afford not to. The industrial relations system is the collective form, and regulatory mechanism, of the basic unit of the capitalist mode of production: the wage relationship. That relationship is inherently conflictual, as Karl Marx (1999) and Karl Polanyi (1944) (for different reasons) pointed out a long time ago. The social, economic, and political consequences of industrial relations failure—in the form of strikes, unemployment, inflation, political crisis—make it implausible that any state can adopt a noninterventionist stance for long. But states also intervene because business and labor may be unable to construct institutions themselves, even though they may want them and see them as beneficial. States can institutionalize practices, generalize them beyond a few leading sectors of the economy, and solve collective action problems by limiting defection, among both business and labor organizations. States may act against the wishes of industrial actors, for their own reasons. But more often, states will act because other actors cannot—because they are timid, divided, concerned with short-term interests, have sunk costs in existing institutions, or are generally unwilling to challenge existing industrial relations institutions—and because states can perform functions and have capacities unavailable to interest groups. State actors may also *anticipate* potential alliances between segments of business and labor interests (Swenson 1997), crafting policy in such a way as to increase the chances of its eventual acceptance by business interests.

2. Industrial Relations prior to 1980

The character of industrial relations reform in Britain and France in the last two decades has been shaped not only by the imperatives of post-Fordist economic restructuring, but also by the institutional legacy of the industrial relations systems inherited from the past. In both countries, the 1960s saw an upsurge in industrial conflict, as an earlier phase of economic restructuring collided with existing industrial relations institutions. During this period, it was primarily the interests of large, Fordist firms seeking to buy labor peace in return for productivity improvements that drove institutional reconfiguration. Whatever the societal interests in reform, it was the French and British states that played the central role in both narrating crisis and constructing new sets of industrial relations institutions (Howell 1992: chs. 4 & 5, Howell 2005: ch. 4).

Donovan and the Decentralization of Collective Bargaining in Britain

Three distinct systems of industrial relations have been constructed in Britain in the past century. Each one emerged out of a crisis of the last, as changing economic conditions rendered existing industrial relations institutions incapable of containing industrial conflict and permitting economic restructuring. In each case, heightened levels of strikes triggered a public debate about the source of conflict and the shape of future institutions better suited to emerging patterns of economic growth. And in each case, it was the British state that played a central role in the construction, embedding, and legitimization of new industrial relations institutions. This despite the longtime characterization of the British state as abstentionist, and industrial relations as voluntarist, a characterization that has never been adequately reconceptualized, even as evidence of state activism mounted from the late 1960s onward.

The initial system of industrial relations emerged in the early decades of the twentieth century as a response to the first major crisis of Britain's staple industries, those same industries that had powered the second industrial revolution. This system sought to use industry-level collective bargaining as a mechanism for limiting both industrial conflict between trade unions and employers and market competition between firms in highly competitive industries, where the industrial structure made self-regulation by employers extremely difficult.

The second system of industrial relations developed in the early postwar decades, when the center of economic gravity had shifted from the industrial staples to newer industries, for which the central problem was how to reorganize work so as to improve the productivity of more capital-intensive technology and skilled labor. Industry bargaining had sought to regulate wages and hours across each industry, while largely leaving firms without well-developed mechanisms for regulating conflict and managing change. But by the 1960s, there was a widespread perception that the lack of firm-level industrial relations institutions was both generating industrial conflict and contributing to poor productivity performance.

This perception culminated in 1965 in the establishment of a Royal Commission, known colloquially as the Donovan Commission after its chair, with a remit of investigating the state of industrial relations. The Donovan Commission issued its report in 1968 (Royal Commission 1968). The fundamental argument of the Donovan Report was that Britain lacked firm-level institutions of collective regulation. Trade union organizations had limited capacities inside the firm and little control over the actions of unionized workers and lay union officials (shop stewards). Trade unions and employers' associations focused their attention and resources on industry-level bargaining, despite the fact that it was inside the workplace that economic restructuring was being negotiated. In the absence of firm-level industrial relations institutions, restructuring tended to generate high levels of industrial conflict. Workplace bargaining was characterized as "largely informal, largely fragmented and largely autonomous" (Royal Commission 1968: para. 65). Managers, it was famously argued, had lost control of the workplace and could "only regain control by sharing it" with unions (Flanders 1970: 172).

Starting in 1974, a new Labour government introduced legislation that encouraged the emergence of firm-level industrial relations institutions. Collectively, this legislation has "some title to be regarded as a grand plan for the promotion by legal means of the system of collective bargaining" (Davies and Freedland 1993: 386). There were three elements to this grand plan. First, a statutory right to trade union recognition was created for the first time in the history of British industrial relations. Second, workers were granted a set of individual rights designed to encourage and improve collective bargaining. These included funding for shop steward training, time off for shop stewards, and rights to information and consultation. Third, a new form of extension procedure was created that permitted trade unions to use legislation to drive employers to the bargaining table and grant them recognition. This is the sense in which the general secretary of Britain's largest union famously described the legislation as a "shop stewards charter" (J. Jones 1986: 285).

The effect of this legislation was to reduce the cost of decentralizing bargaining for unions and to require employers and the state to subsidize firm-level bargaining. Evidence from an assortment of workplace surveys demonstrates that the next decade saw a remarkable spread in workplace bargaining, the diffusion of trade unionism into new sectors of the economy, and an explosion in the number and formalized role of shop stewards, whose numbers grew 3.5 times between 1961 and 1980 (Millward and Stevens 1986: 85; Terry 1983: 67). Accompanying that growth was the spread of a range of other workplace institutions, including the closed shop and dues checkoff, which had the combined effect of permitting a shift in the role of shop stewards from recruiters and dues collectors to negotiators and grievance officials.

In a fundamental sense, however, this ambitious project of industrial relations reform failed. It did change the face of British industrial relations, creating a new set of workplace institutions, but it did so without bringing about the labor peace that the Donovan Report had anticipated. The decentralizing tendencies of these reforms were both contradicted and undermined by the simultaneous efforts to impose wage restraint through centralized incomes policies. The unsurprising result was industrial action on the part of workers. In response, employer resistance grew, especially after it became clear that the legislation was vulnerable to outright noncompliance on the part of employers. When Margaret Thatcher's Conservative party was elected to power in 1979, following the public sector strike wave known as the "Winter of Discontent," it was plausible to argue that overly strong trade unions, and the system of decentralized bargaining itself, were responsible for economic crisis and that any industrial relations reform project would have to dismantle or sharply circumscribe existing industrial relations institutions.

May 1968 and the Emergence of Statist Labor Regulation in France

France also experienced important efforts to reform the industrial relations system in the late 1960s and 1970s, efforts in which the state took the leading role. The reform of industrial relations was triggered by the massive strike wave of May–June 1968. Paradoxically, the goal of institutional reform was something similar to the decentralized form of collective bargaining that took root in Britain during this same period. Indeed, an influential academic review of the causes of France's wave of industrial conflict elaborated a diagnosis that was almost identical to that of the Donovan Report and a similar prescription (Reynaud et al. 1971)—but the outcome was quite different.

Governments in the 1970s repeatedly sought to encourage regular collective bargaining practices between employers and trade unions at the level of the firm. In 1970, the government of Jacques Chaban-Delmas launched the "New Society," which stressed the need for a reformed set of modern industrial relations as a precondition for economic modernization. It built on the provision of legal protection for unions, won in the heat of the 1968 strikes, by amending the 1950 framework legislation on collective bargaining to make it easier to sign firm-level agreements.

In 1974, newly elected President Giscard d'Estaing set up the Sudreau Commission, charged with reforming firm-level industrial relations. The resulting report recommended a wide range of measures, including a right of worker expression in the firm; new economic powers for works councils; an obligation for firms to present an annual *bilan social* (a report on the company's social responsibilities); a requirement that managers recognize unions and treat them as partners; and an experiment with *co-surveillance* (a watered-down version of German co-determination). It is worth noting that, with the exception of the last element, every one of these recommendations was eventually put in place after 1981 by a Socialist government through the Auroux Laws. In 1978, following the unexpected defeat of the Left in the legislative elections, the new government of Raymond Barre sought to "relaunch" collective bargaining by encouraging employer and union organizations to negotiate over a range of issues. The strategy was one that would become familiar after 1981: to promise employers a withdrawal of the state from regulation of the labor market, hence greater flexibility, in return for agreement to engage in decentralized collective bargaining with trade unions.

State authorities in Britain and France responded to an acceleration in industrial conflict in the 1960s in similar fashion: both sought to encourage the expansion and better implantation of firm-level collective bargaining institutions, in the hope that grievances linked to large-scale economic restructuring would be channeled into peaceful wage bargaining. Yet while this strategy was institutionally successful in Britain (in the sense that decentralized collective bargaining became the norm, even if levels of industrial conflict did not decline), it was an almost total failure in France. The primary difference was the weakness and politicization of French trade unionism. The reforms were predicated upon union organizations that were strong enough to entice employers to the bargaining table and both willing and able to exercise some degree of control over their members, so that collective bargaining would indeed limit industrial conflict. French unions were never up to this task, and it is noteworthy that few of the reforms directly strengthened unions themselves (in contrast to the British legislation of the mid-1970s). The result was that outside the public sector (where the state could mandate collective bargaining and offered quite generous wage contracts in order to keep unions at the table) and a few large Fordist firms, firm-level collective bargaining remained rare.

The failure of the firm-level project did not mean a return to the status quo ante 1968, however. As private industrial actors failed to take the strain of regulating industrial relations through collective bargaining, the French state became more and more directly involved in the regulation of the labor market. In effect, the state came to substitute for the weakness of trade unions and collective bargaining through a more aggressive use of the minimum wage, the requirement that large-scale layoffs receive administrative authorization, and generous unemployment benefits and public sector wage contracts. It was the state, rather than labor organizations, that partially decommodified the labor market in France. All of this was done by governments of the Right, anxious to avoid another social explosion like May–June 1968 and concerned about the electoral danger posed by parties of the Left.

The result in France was that as post-Fordist restructuring gathered pace, and labor market and workplace flexibility moved to the top of employers' agendas, the obstacle to that flexibility was not perceived to be primarily trade unions and collective bargaining, as in Britain, but rather the direct regulative efforts of the French state. All projects of industrial relations reform that sought flexibility had to tackle this problem and to find some route that would permit a withdrawal of the state from industrial relations. In practice, this meant trying to encourage firm-level social dialogue—with independent trade unions or perhaps with alternative institutions representing workers—a strategy that had failed miserably in the 1970s.

3.   Reconstructing British Industrial Relations

For eighteen years after the defeat of the Labour Party in 1979, Conservative governments systematically dismantled the system of decentralized collective bargaining that had come to dominate British industrial relations in the 1960s and 1970s. Seeking labor market flexibility as part of a wide-ranging assault on the postwar settlement and the "British consensus," the Right pursued an aggressive policy of removing the legislative and administrative bulwarks of collective regulation and encouraging the emergence of individualized industrial relations institutions. In this task, the state led, and employers followed; employers' initial caution about disturbing established industrial relations and provoking industrial conflict gave way to acquiescence and enthusiastic support of the Conservative reform project. After eighteen years in office, the Right was replaced by a "New Labour" government whose industrial relations project was broadly compatible with its predecessor in office. Early in the new millennium, a decollectivist industrial relations system, organized around limited individual rights at work and a flexible labor market, has become firmly entrenched.

British Post-Fordism

This section is concerned with the construction of a third system of industrial relations in Britain in the period since 1979. By the 1980s, under conditions of heightened international competition, and as manufacturing shrank to less than a quarter of total employment, employers came to place much greater emphasis on *flexibility* in all its myriad forms. They came to see increasingly individualized relationships between employers and employees as the manner in which productivity gains could be made. Just as different national variants of Fordism appeared in the thirty years after World War II, so a particular "hyperflexibility" came to mark British post-Fordism in the absence of many of the political-economic institutions characteristic of "coordinated market economies" and with the arrival in power of a government that aggressively sought to dismantle those coordinating institutions that did exist. Moreover, employers had become disillusioned with joint regulation of economic change and were more prepared to take unilateral action in the firm. The result was the wholesale collapse of institutions of collective regulation at both the industry and the firm level and the emergence of institutions suited to ensuring employers the maximum flexibility in the deployment of labor.

The main elements of economic restructuring in Britain involved a deepening and acceleration in the processes of internationalization, deindustrialization, and flexibilization. Many of the distinctive institutional features of British capitalism—the absence of employer coordination, of long-term relationships between industrial and financial capital, and of capacity for coordinated wage bargaining—had the effect of encouraging a response to any intensification of international competitive pressure through cost reduction and low-wage/low-skill strategies (S. Wood 2001). This has obvious implications for industrial relations. As Edmund Heery has pointed out, a social partnership model of industrial relations tends to rest on large firms who are dominant in their markets and able to pursue high-quality, high-value-added strategies (Heery 2002). The British economy, characterized by smaller firms in competitive markets, pursuing cost-reduction strategies, was more likely to produce social conflict than social partnership. The role and value of trade unions and collective regulation were less clear under these circumstances.

As the internationalization of the British economy and concern for flexibility increased, employers have sought different relationships with their employees (Boswell and Peters 1997). The ability to respond rapidly to international competition strengthened the existing firm-centric focus of the second industrial relations system. But the greater importance attached to flexibility in this period undermined the collective basis of this system because employers increasingly wanted to differentiate the terms and conditions of their employees.

This made collective bargaining for large groups less attractive to employers, and they were more likely to seek an individualization of their relationship with their employees, rendering collective representation problematic.

Yet despite the shifting interests and practices of employers, the transformation of the institutions of industrial relations required a central role for the state. That was both because employers were unable to change their relations with their employees without the aid of the state (whether through changes in labor law, the demonstration effect of enduring strikes, changes in macroeconomic policy, or the less tangible transformation of the industrial relations "climate") and because employers were, for the most part, significantly more timid and unwilling to challenge established industrial relations institutions and practices than the state. Desmond King and Stewart Wood (1999: 395) have noted the ambivalent relationship between employers and post-1979 Conservative governments, which extended to many areas of economic and social policy. As the Conservatives piled up legislative packages of industrial relations reform in the 1980s and early 1990s, it is striking that the response of employers' organizations to each new consultative document was to be less radical than the government, more willing to take a pause in the reform process, and more cautious about the consequences of further reform. And yet, once the text became law, employers rapidly came to support legislation toward which they had previously demonstrated ambivalence. Employers were won over to the reform project of the state, but they did not instigate or direct it.

The Strong State and Industrial Relations Reform

After 1979, the British state encouraged a sharp break with, and a reversal of, an established set of industrial relations institutions and practices. At a time of historically unrivaled labor movement strength and influence and the deep implantation of collective forms of regulation, state authorities sought to weaken trade unionism and encourage unilateral managerial regulation of the workplace and the individualization of industrial relations. For this reason, the role of the state was more significant, more direct, and more coercive than in earlier periods. Labor law took on a more central role than the administrative measures of previous periods. Despite the much more explicit use of legislation to shape industrial relations practice, it is still necessary to take an expansive view of state action in order to understand the scope of government policy and influence during the period between 1979 and 1997. The state played an important role in both the narration of crisis, which itself permitted the mobilization of state power to restructure industrial relations, and in influencing the manner in which post-Fordist economic pressures were transmitted to the British economy. Higher unemployment, accelerated deindustrialization, and closer international economic integration were encouraged by state macroeconomic policy. In a similar fashion, microeconomic policy reduced the insulation from the market enjoyed by workers, in turn encouraging different behavior on the part of employers, managers, and workers themselves.

The restructuring of the public sector in Britain after 1979 and the collapse of corporatist institutions (and, with them, the direct influence of trade unions on public policy) were also crucial parts of the project of industrial relations reform, which were achieved either through administrative action alone or legislation whose impact on industrial relations was indirect. Nowhere is this truer than in the privatization of the nationalized industries and the decentralization and creation of market surrogates in what remained of the public sector. There was little legislation that sought to directly alter the institutions of public sector industrial relations, but the wider restructuring of the public sector dramatically changed industrial relations practice.

Less tangible, but still important, were such factors as the handling of major strikes and the impact of policing during those strikes. Certainly, a case can be made that the government's victory over the mineworkers' union in the 1984–1985 coal strike—in which the Coal Board was prevented from reaching a compromise settlement by the government, and policing prevented aggressive picketing from spreading the strike—had an important demonstration effect for both trade unions and private sector employers (Adeney and Lloyd 1986; Saville 1986; Kahn 1992). In the same vein, it is difficult to measure the impact of the industrial relations "climate," to which state policy surely contributed, upon the behavior of employers, unions, and workers. Conservative governments made it clear that collective bargaining was no longer considered a public policy good and that it would support employers who sought new relationships with their employees. In some cases (the replacement of collective bargaining with personal contracts, for example), legislation legalized employer practice after courts had ruled against that practice. In short, it seems certain that the climate of industrial relations fostered by the state gave employers the confidence to experiment with new industrial relations institutions and practices of their own.

A distinctive feature of this period of industrial relations reform was the extent to which successive packages of legislation sought to directly restructure industrial relations. When a piece of legislation did not appear to achieve the goals set for it, the response was further legislation, to "add another layer of cement," rather than to seek nonlegislative solutions or to change the goals themselves (Undy et al. 1996: 74). Conservative governments after 1979 had learned a key lesson from the failure of the 1971 Industrial Relations Act, which was to make the legislation facilitative. While Conservative hostility toward trade unions was clear, the main aim of government policy was not to prescribe a particular model or form of industrial relations but rather to remove restrictions (either in the form of legislative obstacles or in the capacity of trade unions to resist) on the right of employers to choose the industrial relations arrangements that they deemed most appropriate. Whereas the 1971 Industrial Relations Act created a set of criminal liabilities for noncompliance—thus focusing attention on the role of the state in the enforcement of the legislation—the legislation of the 1980s and 1990s created only civil liabilities. It was up to employers to choose whether to use the new legislation.

That said, by the end of the 1980s, Conservative policy was less concerned with eliminating abuses of collective bargaining and the collective representation of workers or permitting employers to deal with their employees as they wished. Rather, the goal was an individualization of industrial relations, with trade unions and collective bargaining playing an extremely limited role. Conservative ministers urged unions to get out of the business of collective bargaining and instead offer individual services to their members. Government White Papers called on employers to reconsider their industrial relations practices and stressed the merits of individual contracts, promising to support "the aspirations of individual employees to deal directly with their employer, rather than through the medium of trade union representation or collective bargaining" (*People Jobs Opportunity* 1992: 15).

The permissive nature of industrial relations legislation should not detract from the fact that decollectivization was an explicit state strategy between 1979 and 1997.

The role of legislation after 1979, and the willingness of the police and the judicial branch of the state to enforce that legislation, marked a ratcheting up of the level and nature of state intervention, compared to previous efforts to act as midwife to a new set of industrial relations institutions. That should be no surprise, given the strength of the labor movement and the deep implantation of collective regulation. As Andrew Gamble (1994) so aptly noted, a strong state was indeed a prerequisite for the construction of a "free economy" in this regard.

There were six major pieces of Conservative industrial relations legislation, each one comprising several parts and addressing multiple themes, along with sundry other pieces of legislation that impinged on industrial relations. The main legislative packages came at regular intervals between 1980 and 1993 and were the 1980 Employment Act; the 1982 Employment Act; the 1984 Trade Union Act; the 1988 Employment Act; the 1990 Employment Act; and the 1993 Trade Union Reform and Employment Rights Act. The goals of the legislation were to restrict the freedom to organize industrial action; end the closed shop; provide union members with new rights against their unions; remove legislative support for union recognition; and regulate internal union government, particularly political action. Each piece of legislation had a number of elements, and successive acts frequently returned to the same subject. The net result of this avalanche of legislation has been that secondary industrial action is now practically outlawed, all strikes are now much more difficult to organize (and unions place themselves at great risk when they call strikes), the closed shop is illegal, and union governance is tightly bound up by statutory regulation.

The Transformation of British Industrial Relations after 1979

The period since 1979 has seen the most far-reaching change in British industrial relations since the spread of industry bargaining at the beginning of the twentieth century. John Purcell (1993) has powerfully described the outcome of this period of change as the "end of institutional industrial relations," referring to the collapse of the institutions of collective regulation. It is clear that those institutions, the core elements of the first and second systems of industrial relations, are in tatters; what is less clear is what, if anything, has been put in their place. More profound, though, than institutional restructuring has been the impact of change on the labor movement. There has been a quite fundamental, and potentially irreversible, shift in the balance of class power in Britain, with the shrinking, weakening, and hollowing out of trade unionism. Allan Flanders (1974: 365) famously argued that "the tradition of voluntarism cannot be legislated against," yet the experience of the recent past suggests that indeed it can. The apparently autonomous strength of British trade unionism has been overcome by a combination of the scale and scope of state activism, the willingness of governments to endure industrial conflict, and a raft of industrial relations legislation, alongside a withdrawal of support for collective regulation on the part of many employers and a period of profound economic restructuring.

Since 1979, British trade unions have lost almost 6 million, or 40 percent, of their members, bringing union density below 30 percent. The decline in union density briefly stabilized between 1998 and 2000, before resuming anew (Brook 2002: 343). Turning to evidence from the Workplace Industrial Relations Surveys, a study of the period from 1980 to 1998 detected declines in every measure of union strength and concluded that "falls in union membership were themselves widespread, rather than confined to particular industries or types of workforce or of employer" (Millward, Bryson, and Forth 2000: 89). Trade union recognition fell even faster than union membership, so that recognition in the private sector halved during this period to 25 percent.

This period also saw dramatic changes in the scope and form of collective bargaining. The net result of these changes was that the coverage of institutions of collective pay-setting fell to levels unseen since the 1920s. Overall, the coverage of collective bargaining fell from 70 percent of employees in 1984 to 40 percent in 1998 (Millward, Bryson, and Forth 2000: 221). The decline in coverage was especially precipitous in the private sector, where collective bargaining was replaced with unilateral management determination of pay. Another significant change in collective bargaining has been the dramatic decline of two-tier and industry, or multiemployer, bargaining. The collapse in trade union recognition in engineering was a direct result of the ending of multiemployer bargaining in that industry, as employers picked off poorly implanted unions that had depended on the industry agreement for their survival.

While the coverage of collective bargaining has shrunk, and industry-level bargaining has largely disappeared outside the public sector, the form of bargaining, even where it remains within the firm, has also changed in important ways. The 1960s and 1970s saw an expansion of the scope of collective bargaining beyond basic conditions of work, to include a range of substantive issues of work organization. This followed from the effort to enlist unions in improving productivity. By the end of 1990s, it was "evident that there has been a very substantial decline in union representative involvement in the regulation of employee obligations and work organization," as the scope of bargaining once again shrank, leaving the organization of the workplace as a matter for unilateral managerial prerogative (Brown et al. 2000: 617). Furthermore, collective bargaining itself often took on a less formal character, resembling consultation rather than negotiation. Even where institutions of collective regulation of industrial relations remain, their character has changed.

Overall, the core institutions of collective regulation were systematically dismantled in the two decades after 1979. Decollectivization manifested itself in a number of ways. These included the decline in trade unionism; the decentralization of collective bargaining to the firm and workplace, and its replacement by unilateral managerial determination of terms and conditions (Undy et al. 1996); the weakening of collective decision-making structures within trade unions; and the decline in collective action and its replacement with individual legal cases or complaints directed toward state agencies rather than trade unions (Davies 1999).

Accompanying this transformation of industrial relations has been an increase in both income inequality and poverty. The distribution of household disposable income, after little change in the 1970s, was characterized by rapidly widening inequality in the 1980s and a slowing, but not a reversal, of inequality in the 1990s. For example, between 1981 and 1989, income at the ninetieth percentile jumped 38 percent, whereas income at the tenth percentile rose just 7 percent (*Social Trends* 2004: 81). The proportion of low-income households expanded dramatically from the mid-1980s to the mid-1990s, peaking at 21 percent (National Statistics 2004). These developments should be unsurprising, as the decentralization and decline of collective bargaining and the deregulation of the labor market have both weakened the floor to earnings and permitted wider wage dispersion.

What, then, should one conclude about the restructuring of industrial relations institutions in Britain in the past two decades? The impact of the decline in trade union membership is particularly important for British industrial relations because of the absence of mechanisms for the extension of collective agreements beyond the workplaces where they are negotiated. Without legal extension, or extension by coordinated employer organizations, the decline in trade union coverage leads directly to a decline in collective bargaining coverage, as the exceptionally narrow gap between these two levels at the end of the 1990s demonstrates. As William Brown, Simon Deakin, and Paul Ryan (1997: 75) have put it: "[A]lthough the decline of trade union membership may not have been exceptional in international terms, the implications of it are." What is being created is an economy in which a large majority of workers do not belong to unions and are not covered by any form of collective bargaining. In short, there has been a massive *individualization* of the regulatory mechanisms governing industrial relations.

The period since the Conservative election victory in 1979 has been marked by a sharp break with the past. For all their differences, governments from 1894 until 1979 shared an emphasis on the public policy good of trade unions and collective bargaining. This has now changed. What began in 1979 as an effort to fence in unions, reduce their capacity to damage the economy, and narrow their strategic options, while freeing the hands of employers, has become the embryo of an individualized system of industrial relations. This individualized system is based on the absence of collective representation for workers in the majority of the economy and the collapse of linkages between unions and collective bargaining *inside* the firm and unions and collective bargaining *outside* the firm in what remains of the unionized sector. In the latter case, what is emerging is something close to a de facto enterprise unionism. The result is that even on those scattered islands of collective regulation, overwhelmingly located in older firms, in an ocean of individualized industrial relations, trade unions lack effective sanctions, existing largely at the sufferance of employers. It is an open question as to whether developments in Britain are the harbinger of an industrial relations system appropriate to the twenty-first century or of "a free, unregulated labour market of the sort that predated the birth of collective bargaining 100 years ago" (Purcell 1993:23).

New Labour in Power

In 1997, a Labour government returned to power after eighteen years of Conservative rule and was subsequently reelected in 2001 and 2005. The Labour Party had been transformed during its years of opposition, having embraced the market and price stability as the central macroeconomic goal; distanced itself from the trade union movement, both institutionally and in terms of policy (Shaw 1994; Howell 2000); rejected nationalization as a planning strategy; and rebranded itself as "New Labour," pursuing what its leader, Tony Blair, called "the Third Way." Despite this transformation, New Labour came to power with a different industrial relations agenda from that of the Conservatives, and one might have anticipated reforms that would challenge the trajectory of British industrial relations institutions described in the last section. In fact, while the industrial relations institutions currently being created differ in some respects from those of the government's Conservative predecessor, they are fundamentally convergent with the decollectivist thrust of the third system of industrial relations. The distinctiveness of New Labour's approach to industrial relations lies, first, in the government's emphasis on the creation of individual rights at work, rather than support (legislative or otherwise) for the collective regulation of class relations, and second, on a battery of tax and welfare reforms designed to mitigate the harshest consequences of the flexible, low-wage labor market.

It is worth noting that New Labour is far more explicit than its Thatcherite predecessor in recognizing the importance of the state in the regulation of social relations, arguing that law can operate to deepen, widen, and embed cultural practices. As Blair (Department of Trade and Industry 1998: foreword) put it:

> My ambition . . . is nothing less than to change the culture of relations in and at work—and to reflect a new relationship between work and family life. It is often said that a change of culture cannot be brought about by a change in the framework of law. But a change in law can reflect a new culture, can enhance its understanding and support its development.

New Labour argues that the state cannot evacuate the terrain of work, leaving social regulation to employers and employees alone, because it is possible for employers to organize social relations within their firms in a manner that is not even in their own interests, let alone that of the economy as a whole.

New Labour's approach to the labor market has been to endorse the necessity of a flexible, minimally regulated labor market with a significant low-wage, low-skill sector; there has been no serious effort to reposition Britain within the international division of labor, and indeed any such effort would have been enormously difficult in light of the absence of supporting institutions, as the varieties of capitalism literature makes clear (Hall and Soskice 2001b). In this respect, government policy since 1997 has echoed that of previous Conservative governments. However, New Labour has sought to temper the harshness of this labor market and compensate its main victims: the poor, the unskilled, the long-term unemployed, single parents (categories that often overlap). The tools to accomplish this task have been welfare policy, particularly changes to the tax and benefit system for low-income workers, and a set of industrial relations institutions that provide a minimum level of individual protection at work (H.M. Treasury 1998). The difficult balancing act for New Labour has been how to simultaneously provide protection and compensation, while retaining the labor market flexibility upon which Britain's competitiveness is still believed to rely.

New Labour's Industrial Relations Reforms

New Labour has pursued four main industrial relations reforms. A national statutory minimum wage has been introduced for the first time in British history. Prior to 1993, when they were abolished, Wages Councils set minimum terms and conditions in a set of traditionally low-wage industries as a form of embryonic collective bargaining. Second, Britain signed up to the Social Chapter of the European Union (EU), something its predecessor in government had rejected. This has had an accelerating impact on domestic labor law, as European directives have multiplied, particularly in the areas of "family friendly" policy (maternity and paternity leaves) and the regulation of atypical work. It should be said that the British government has always chosen to interpret these directives in the narrowest possible manner to minimize regulation of the labor market, and it has sought to prevent or limit the impact of directives related to worker consultation. The third element of industrial relations reform was the 1999 Employment Relations Act (ERA). This legislation had a number of features, including a new set of individual rights at work: a legal right for individuals to be accompanied by a fellow employee or union official in grievance hearings; protection from blacklisting for union membership; and more safeguards against unfair dismissals, including during the first eight weeks of a strike. The ERA did contain one major collective right: a right to union recognition if a ballot showed majority support for a union. This right was hedged in important ways, in that it did not apply to small firms and required a turnout threshold on the ballot, but it is nonetheless a significant innovation in British labor law (a somewhat different form of union recognition legislation existed for half of the 1970s). The fourth and final part of the reform agenda appeared in Labour's second term and involved an overhaul of the employment tribunal system to reduce the number of cases being handled. One part of this reform, which was contained in the 2002 Employment Act, created minimum statutory internal procedures covering dismissal and grievances inside firms.

For all the changes since 1997, the overwhelming majority of Conservative industrial relations legislation remains in force and has been endorsed by New Labour. To this basic framework of labor law has been added limited regulation of the labor market. This regulation has taken the form of a set of minimum rights at work, including a minimum wage; limits on working hours; protections against unfair dismissal; expanded rights for working women and parents; and some regulation of precarious, "atypical" forms of labor contract. It is important to emphasize, however, that labor market regulation in Britain remains limited and that the Blair government sought legislation that was compatible with a high degree of labor market flexibility.

Regulation of the labor market has taken the form of individual legal rights, enforceable through labor courts and state agencies, not, for the most part, collective rights designed to strengthen trade unions, which could then take on the role of regulating social relations through collective bargaining. With few exceptions, any benefits likely to accrue to unions will come indirectly, by virtue of a more regulated labor market or a new role as enforcers of legal rights. In several areas, legislation further substitutes for collective regulation, such as the minimum wage and statutory internal procedures. Of the two parallel tracks along which social relations have been regulated in Britain, as elsewhere in the advanced capitalist world—collective regulation by unions and legal regulation by the state—it is the latter that has become the focus of New Labour attention.

Thus, in terms of industrial relations, the current Labour government is best understood as a consolidation, rather than a radical departure, from Thatcherism. It shares a broad acceptance of the current balance of social power in the workplace, a largely unitarist view of industrial relations, and most fundamentally, an emphasis on individual rather than collective regulation of social relations. It is hard to disagree with Colin Crouch's assessment (2001: 104) that, "in the industrial relations field New Labour represents a continuation of the neo-liberalism of the Conservative government, but one required to make more concessions than its predecessor with trade unions and social-democratic policy preferences." The distinction between the two approaches lies, then, in the degree of labor market regulation undertaken by the state, not the agent of that regulation. Both largely reject collective regulation. The institutions for the collective regulation of industrial relations, which were central to both public policy and industrial relations practice in Britain for a century after 1890, are now almost certainly in terminal decline.

4. Reconstructing French Industrial Relations

Like its British counterpart, the system of French industrial relations has been transformed in the last two decades. Firm-level institutions designed to negotiate and facilitate economic restructuring and flexibility have proliferated, and the firm has become the primary locus of collective bargaining (Mériaux 2000). This process has occurred as trade unions continued to weaken, so that those representing workers in these discussions and negotiations are either nonunion workplace representatives or union locals that are functionally indistinguishable from enterprise unions. The result has been the emergence of a microcorporatist system of industrial relations, heavily tilted toward the interests of employers. As in the British case, the state has led the way in this institutional transformation. However, while the spread of firm-level bargaining has permitted some deregulation of the labor market, the weakness of employee representation has prevented a large-scale withdrawal of the state from its regulatory role in the labor market.

The State and Social Actors in France

The emergence of labor market and workplace flexibility in France could not take place without the active role of the French state and a state-led restructuring of industrial relations institutions. First, state regulation and state industrial relations institutions were the primary obstacles to flexibility. Second, private industrial actors, particularly trade unions, were simply too weak to take on the burden of negotiating flexibility. Nevertheless, the role of the French state in industrial relations reform after 1981 cannot be understood within the familiar category of *dirigisme*. As Mark I. Vail (2003a: 3) has pointed out, state action has increasingly involved delicate and careful negotiation with business and labor organizations. The state has tried *both* to encourage class actors to take on more of the regulatory burden of industrial relations *and* "to shore up societal support behind unpopular and often painful reforms." The central problem facing the French state in its efforts to reconstruct industrial relations institutions in a manner appropriate to post-Fordist economic restructuring has been how to withdraw from direct regulation of the labor market in the absence of labor actors at the firm level capable of ensuring that the introduction of flexibility was genuinely negotiated, rather than imposed unilaterally by employers. The core of the state's strategy, under both governments of the Left and the Right, has been to create legal obligations inside the firm that would have the effect of generating *autonomous and self-sustaining* social dialogue that would in turn permit deregulation of the labor market.

The Auroux Laws and the Reform of Firm-Level Industrial Relations

The reform of French industrial relations began with the Auroux Laws of 1982. The Auroux Laws rewrote fully one-third of the French labor code and represented the most thoroughgoing state industrial relations reform project since 1936. There were diverse inspirations for the reforms, and one of the interesting features of the package as a whole is that so many of its elements had been proposed in one form or another in the past. As mentioned above, the Sudreau Commission advocated a right of worker expression in the firm, greater economic powers for the works council, and an annual *bilan social*, all of which found their way into the Auroux Laws. Similarly, in 1978, at the point at which the Raymond Barre government was proposing to relaunch collective bargaining, Jacques Delors set out a reform agenda that involved strengthening trade unions and extending and regularizing collective bargaining inside the firm. Recall that Delors, the first economics and finance minister of the 1981 Socialist government, had also, in an earlier incarnation, been the architect of Chaban-Delmas's New Society project of industrial relations reform. So the Auroux Laws combined some fairly conventional (though nonetheless radical in scope) measures aimed at encouraging decentralized collective bargaining with a series of elements that I have elsewhere characterized as "microcorporatist": strengthening firm-specific industrial relations institutions that are largely autonomous from, and unarticulated with, industry or national institutions of labor regulation.

The central elements introduced by the Auroux Laws were as follows. First, a right of self-expression was established for workers in the form of regular meetings to discuss social relations within the firm. This provision was experimental in the Auroux legislation and limited to firms employing 200 or more workers. Legislation in 1986 made the right of expression permanent and extended it to firms with fifty or more workers. Second, works councils received new rights of mandatory consultation over a wide range of economic issues, greater resources including the right to hire outside experts, and in very large firms, a special economic delegation was created. Third, an annual *bilan social* (a report on the social responsibilities of the firm) was made mandatory. Fourth, trade union delegates received legal protection in all firms, not simply those employing fifty or more workers, as had been the situation since 1968. Unions also gained greater resources (office space, time off for union duties) in firms employing fifty or more workers. Fifth, an obligation to bargain annually (though not to conclude an agreement) at both the firm and branch level was created in firms employing fifty or more workers and having a union delegate. Firm-level agreements could derogate from legislation and higher-level agreements as long as a union or unions receiving a majority of the votes in the last works council election did not veto the agreement.

And the process of state extension of collective agreements was made easier. Sixth, a series of public sector industrial relations reforms decentralized works councils, provided a right of self-expression, and extended a limited form of worker representation on the boards of public companies to firms employing 200 or more workers.

Two main points need to be emphasized about this package of legislation. The first is that it did very little to strengthen French trade unions directly. Union delegates received legal protection in small firms and some additional resources in larger firms (resources were not provided in small firms because of the fear of burdening small firms), but for the most part, the legislation created the obligation to bargain with unions where they were present without encouraging the spread and implantation of unions. The hope was that unions would be strengthened indirectly by the increased powers given to workers councils and the right of worker expression. This was a vain hope at a time when employers were at best ambivalent and often deeply hostile to trade unionism (Coffineau 1993: annex XI).

Second, the Auroux Laws contained within them a whole series of microcorporatist elements, whose logic pointed away from articulated collective bargaining between independent trade unions and employers. The reforms encouraged an assortment of forms of social dialogue inside the firm, involving company-specific institutions of worker representation, unconnected to either outside trade unions or higher levels of collective bargaining. Key microcorporatist provisions within the Auroux Laws included the possibility for firm-level agreements to derogate from legislation and branch agreements; the increased powers of consultation for works councils (which had the effect of blurring the line between consultation and negotiation); and the right of expression inside the firm. In the latter instance, the expression groups were made mandatory at a time when managerial practices that emphasized direct communication with the workforce, unmediated by trade unions, were spreading within French firms, and an assortment of institutions such as quality circles and worker-management groups were appearing (Jenkins 2000: ch. 3). Thus, the legislation had the effect of a forced modernization of managerial practices, extending their reach beyond the leading edge of French firms to the rest of the economy.

The results of the Auroux reforms on the industrial relations institutions of France were made clear by an exhaustive study ten years after their implementation (Coffineau 1993). While branch-level collective bargaining had stagnated, there had been a substantial increase in the scale of firm-level bargaining to the point that it has become "the privileged mode of social regulation" (Coffineau 1993: 93; translation from the French by the author). But at the same time, the weakness of trade unionism had not been reversed and indeed appeared to have accelerated, though the study was ambivalent about the degree of responsibility of the Auroux legislation for trade union decline. The number of union delegates had fallen, especially in smaller firms, and employee representation of all types was limited in these firms. Indeed, one-half of all workers were employed in firms with no employee representation of any kind (Coffineau 1993: 77).

So how to explain the paradox of a dramatic expansion of collective bargaining at a time of growing trade union weakness? In practice, employers were signing agreements with union delegates who represented very few actual members in order to gain dispensation from legislation or branch agreements. At the same time, a blurring of the lines of employee representation was taking place. The distinction between union delegates, negotiating collective agreements, and works councils or worker expression groups, consulting over work reorganization or layoffs, collapsed in the context of an acceleration in the process of economic restructuring. There was instead confusion and competition among forms of employee representation.

New Forms of Worker Representation

A decade after the Auroux Laws were put in place, they had indeed encouraged an assortment of forms of social dialogue inside the firm and a significant expansion of firm-level collective bargaining. But in the absence of strong, independent trade unions, that dialogue and bargaining were of the microcorporatist variety. In the 1990s, the role and form of employee representation inside French firms underwent significant change that had the effect of deepening and broadening the construction of a set of firm-level institutions that regularized social dialogue with largely non–union employee representatives.

The 1990 Belier report (summarized in Coffineau 1993) on employee representation in small- and medium-sized firms, which had identified the paucity of such representation, even in firms where employee delegates or works councils were legally required, recommended a simplification of employee representation to permit a merging of functions. The Five-Year Employment Law (which also had important provisions relating to work-time reduction and flexibility; see below) permitted the merging of the employee delegate and works council function in firms employing fewer than 200 workers. The law also simplified the information that employers were required to provide to works councils.

In October 1995, employers and several of the trade union confederations (but not the Confédération Générale du Travail [CGT] or Force Ouvrière [FO]) issued a general statement about collective bargaining and signed two interprofessional agreements (the other one concerned work-time reduction and flexibility, indicating the linkage between workplace industrial relations institutions and the introduction of flexibility). The general statement (*EIRR* 1995: 6) called for the autonomy of bargaining and decried "social interventionism" on the part of the state. The agreement relating to collective bargaining launched a three-year experiment, during which firm-level agreements on single issues could be signed by either mandated or authorized delegates in firms employing less than fifty workers in which there was no union delegate. This permitted either an elected employee representative or an employee mandated by a national trade union to sign collective agreements. Arguing that levels of collective bargaining should be complementary rather than hierarchical, the accord also permitted firm-level agreements to be signed that contained clauses less favorable than branch or interprofessional agreements, thus breaching the cornerstone of French collective bargaining law since 1950. This accord was sanctioned by legislation in 1996, then extended for another five years in 1999, when the initial experiment expired. As will be discussed below, Martine Aubry's thirty-five-hour workweek legislation also incorporated the principle of agreements signed by non–union employee representatives into the process by which work-time reduction could take place.

However, the most substantial incorporation of these piecemeal reforms of collective bargaining into French labor law took place in the 2004 Fillon Law (Ray 2004; Souriac 2004). The legislation incorporated two sets of changes, mirroring the original 1995 accord by recognizing the clear link between flexibility and worker representation. One set of changes permitted wider recourse to derogatory collective agreements, while the other attempted (much less successfully) to incorporate the so-called majority principle into bargaining. The logic of the linkage was simply that there should be some assurance that derogatory agreements would be signed by organizations or institutions that were genuinely representative of workers. To put it crudely, the employer demand for greater flexibility should be balanced by a trade union demand that labor signatories represent a majority of the relevant group of workers.

The first part of the changes did involve a significant modification of the favorability principle, essentially ending it by permitting derogation unless explicitly denied in collective agreements or legislation. Only in four areas, including the minimum wage, did the legislation prevent derogation. Thus sectoral agreements could now be less favorable to workers than interprofessional agreements, and firm agreements could be less favorable than sectoral agreements. Furthermore, in firms without a union delegate, firm-specific bodies such as the works council could be authorized to sign agreements, and in the absence of any elected employee representative, a union-mandated worker could sign an agreement and the workforce then ratify it.

The second part of the reforms, however, was implemented in much weaker fashion. The French employer association, Mouvement des Enterprises de France (MEDEF), never fully supported the majority principle, for the obvious reason that it limited the ability of employers to sign agreements with weak, nonrepresentative trade unions, and successfully lobbied to undermine the majority principle in the final version of the legislation. Two models were created, one involving ratification by majority unions, the other involving the mere absence of opposition from unions representing a majority. In both, minority unions retained significant power because, at sectoral and interprofessional levels, majority and minority were defined in terms of the number of officially recognized trade union organizations, regardless of the relative size of those unions or the membership they represented. The result, therefore, of the 2004 reform of collective bargaining was to both enhance the autonomy of the firm from the wider industrial relations system and encourage the shift in worker representation from trade unions to nonunion, firm-specific institutions, while doing little to counterbalance this shift with a strong assertion of the need for majority representation where unions existed.

Faced with the weakness of French trade unionism but the need to use collective agreements in order to introduce flexibility, governments of both the Left and the Right, employers, and some of the trade union confederations chose to permit the delegation of trade union responsibilities to employees who had no necessary connection to a trade union, in firms that had no union representative nor any necessary union membership. For the unions that did support this practice (and all the union confederations participated in the mandating process, even if they did not sign the original interprofessional agreement), the hope was that the mandating process would help unions get access to smaller firms and eventually create union delegates out of mandated employees. For employers and the state, these representatives provided an employee interlocutor with whom to negotiate flexibility, and it is no coincidence that legislation and interprofessional agreements on employee representation always went hand in hand with measures encouraging flexibility.

Elsewhere, I have argued (Howell 1998) that French trade unionism can be usefully characterized as "virtual unionism," in which the influence of organized labor rests not on class power (in the sense of control over labor's collective capacities), nor on any of the conventional measures of labor strength, but rather on two functions: as a vehicle representing labor interests to the state (deployed by workers, who are rarely union members, to bargain with the state during moments of social crisis), and as an institution to legitimize state economic policies that cause social dislocation. In this latter function, French governments have tended to seek out trade unions during moments of industrial conflict and social crisis to negotiate the terms of change. That French unions do not represent actual members matters less than that the state be seen to be bargaining with the "labor interest." It is worth noting that, in both cases, the importance of trade unions is a function of their relationship with the state rather than with employers, attesting to the centrality of the French state in labor regulation. With the development of the mandating process, virtual trade unionism is taken to its logical conclusion and endpoint: national trade union confederations without any necessary presence or power in the workplace are called upon to bestow legitimacy on firm-level flexibility agreements.

Flexibility and Work Time

In recent years, the expansion of flexibility has been intertwined with the issue of work time. Despite the derision that greeted the thirty-five-hour workweek legislation of Lionel Jospin's 1997 Socialist government outside France, work-time reduction was a bipartisan strategy. Faced with high levels of unemployment and having handed over control of monetary policy and exchange rate policy to European Union institutions, and with severe external constraints on fiscal policy, creating employment through work-time reduction was one of the few policy options available to French governments (Trumbull 2002). For two decades after 1981, the recipe for modifying work time remained remarkably consistent: greater flexibility in the use of work time was offered to employers in return for a reduction in overall work time and a requirement that collective bargaining be the privileged mode of implementing changes in work time.

The Socialist government elected in 1981 had promised a reduction in the workweek to thirty-nine hours, and bargaining took place between employers and unions on the implementation of that pledge. That bargaining was short-circuited, however, by legislation in 1982 that reduced the workweek, provided a fifth week of vacation time, and required full compensation to workers for reduced working time. It did allow, however, an additional 130 hours over the legal annual limit to be worked without administrative authorization, as long as the outcome was collectively negotiated. After this experience, employers shifted their focus from national bargaining with unions to firm-level bargaining, where unions were weaker (and agreements could be signed with minority unions) and where the 1982 work-time reduction legislation (presaging the later Auroux Laws in this regard) permitted derogation from legislation and branch agreements. The effects were twofold: first a spike in the amount of firm-level bargaining; and second, one-sided agreements that provided far more flexibility to employers than reduced work time or alternative forms of compensation to workers (Howell 1992: 194).

Work-time reduction reappeared on the legislative agenda at the beginning of the 1990s. In fact, as early as 1992, the Socialist government proposed offering reduced social security charges to employers in return for work sharing in the form of part-time work and reduced hours, to be based on a model agreement. But the real impetus came from two pieces of conservative legislation. In 1993, the Five-Year Employment Law of the Edouard Balladur government permitted much greater flexibility in work time, with particular emphasis on encouraging part-time work and the annualization of hours, in return for minimal work-time reduction. Agreements had to be signed at the firm level, and the government offered reduced social security charges to sweeten the deal. The Robien Law of 1996 went further, making it easier to reach agreements on flexible and reduced work time and offering a more generous reduction in social security charges in return for agreements that promised either to create new jobs or save existing jobs. This legislation had a particularly large impact on part-time employment because reductions in social security charges were available for the creation of part-time jobs or the transformation of a full-time job into a part-time job if that led to the creation of a new job. Alan Jenkins (2000:165–166; emphasis in the original) has argued that the Robien Law had a "dynamic role in workplace experimentation and negotiation" and "catalyzed a search for *broader organizational flexibilities.*" As with the Auroux Laws, state action encouraged and subsidized the modernization of employer practices in a manner that promoted post-Fordist restructuring.

This was the backdrop to the more radical proposals of the Socialist government elected in 1997 on a pledge to reduce the workweek to thirty-five hours. What emerged was a three-stage process. The first law (Aubry I), passed in 1998, set out the terms under which voluntary work-time agreements could be reached. A second law (Aubry II), enacted in 2000, made work-time reduction mandatory, where agreements had not already been reached, for firms employing twenty or more workers. The third stage was to have applied the legislation to smaller firms in 2002, but the Left was ousted from power, and that stage of the reform was dropped by the new conservative government.

Aubry I permitted a large assortment of ways in which work-time reduction could be introduced—including annualized hours, a shorter workweek or work day, longer vacation periods, or additional days off—and enormous flexibility in the use of work time as long as the result was the product of collective bargaining (Supiot 2001: 92). The experience of the voluntary agreements reached under Aubry I also demonstrated that employers were less interested in the reduction in social security charges than in flexibility in the implementation of work-time reduction. As a result, Aubry II permitted greater innovation in the forms of flexibility permissible, so long as the outcome was subject to a collective agreement. Indeed, Aubry II provided very strong incentives for reducing work time through collective bargaining.

The legislation also sanctioned the use of the mandating procedure and other alternatives to traditional collective bargaining. In smaller firms where there was no union delegate, firm-level agreements could be signed on behalf of employees by a worker who was mandated to sign by one of the five national trade union confederations; if the worker was not mandated, the resulting agreement had to be approved by a majority vote of employees and approved by a local labor-business commission.

What have been the results of the legislation? First, like the Auroux Laws, the legislation has survived its controversial beginnings. When the Right swept to power in 2002, it blocked the extension of the thirty-five-hour requirement in small firms and gave employers more latitude in meeting the thirty-five-hour requirement in firms where it already existed, notably through the expansion of allowable overtime (*EIRR* 2002). Nonetheless, three years on, with continued concern about unemployment, new legislation continued to endorse the principle of the thirty-five-hour week while offering greater opportunities for employees to work beyond the legal limit and continuing the derogation of smaller firms from the legislation for a further three years (until 2008). Most of the Aubry legislation has been left in place, suggesting that despite the denunciations of the Right and of employers, the legislation has had a less deleterious effect on French firms than commonly claimed.

Second, the impact on firm-level collective bargaining has been undeniable. The number of firm-level agreements signed each year remained stable from 1987 until 1993 (after rapidly rising in the aftermath of the Auroux Laws), then increased steadily between 1993 and 1998, roughly doubling during that period. The number of agreements then accelerated sharply after 1998, increasing from a little under 15,000 to 35,000 in 1999. The number remained roughly at that level in 2000 and 2001 before beginning a rapid decline, to 23,000 in 2002 and 16,000 in 2003 (Ministry of Employment, Labor, and Social Cohesion 2003: 111). Thus the quantity of firm-level bargaining was tied directly to the impact of work-time legislation. Work time was reduced in two phases: prior to 2000, firm-level agreements led to reduction, while in 2000 and 2001, the changeover to thirty-five hours was much more likely to result from the direct application of a branch agreement, in the absence of firm-level bargaining (*EIROnline* 2002).

Third, it is difficult to know who exactly was signing agreements and how representative of employees they were. The mandating procedure was widely used for firm-level work-time agreements; fully 70 percent of such agreements were reached using this procedure in 2001, and unsurprisingly, the smaller the firm, the more likely it was to reach agreement without the signature of a union delegate. The promise that mandating would open nonunion firms to unionization does not appear to have been fulfilled (Trumbull 2002). Even in 2002, when only one-third of agreements dealt with work-time reduction, less than half of firm-level agreements were signed by a union delegate, the rest being the result of mandating, ratification by employees, or signature from a firm-specific body (*EIROnline* 2003). At the branch level, a large number of agreements were signed—112 of 180 bargaining sectors had work-time reduction agreements by October 1999—but they tended to be signed by a small number of unions. By mid-1999, only 22 percent of branch agreements had been signed by either all five confederations or by four of the five. One-third had been signed by only one or two national unions (Jefferys 2000: 50).

Finally, work-time reduction has been accompanied by work-time flexibility and, with it, work reorganization. Firms have taken advantage of the wide range of options for how to introduce reduced work time and how to calculate work time. They have experimented with different kinds of shift work and scheduling that correspond better to demand. In this respect, the widespread introduction of annualized hours—more than one-third of employees saw their work time reduced in this way (*EIROnline* 2002)—offers tremendous flexibility to firms. By creating a greater financial disincentive to use overtime, the thirty-five-hour week legislation forced employers to contemplate a more fundamental reorganization of work.

The Transformation of French Industrial Relations

The last two decades have seen two intimately related developments in French industrial relations: the evolution of a system of decentralized, firm-level microcorporatist bargaining; and the replacement of labor market and workplace rigidities with a high degree of flexibility, accompanying and making possible a post-Fordist restructuring of the French economy. These developments are connected in two ways. First, the former made possible the latter, as the shift in the locus of labor regulation away from direct legislative and administrative rule-making and high-level collective bargaining permitted the spread of flexibility. Second, both developments were dependent on a continuing, activist role for the state.

This has not been a simple story of state withdrawal from industrial relations, with private industrial actors taking over responsibility for regulating the relations between business and labor. Rather, institutional developments have been driven by state actors, and to the extent that firm-level bargaining takes place, it is largely underwritten and guaranteed by the state. Despite its best efforts, the French state has been unable to withdraw from its central role in regulating industrial relations. Autonomous and self-sustaining collective bargaining has never occurred (Lallement and Mériaux 2003); each instance of its invigoration depended on an active role by the state in promoting social dialogue. It is important to emphasize "the roles that French elites have played in stimulating and promoting innovation during the last thirty years" (Jenkins 2000: 206) and to recognize the "extremely important catalytic effect of the law" (Jefferys 2000:142). Paradoxical as it may sound, creating the institutional conditions for post-Fordist economic restructuring has been a state-led process in France.

The core of the state's strategy, under both governments of the Left and the Right, was to create legal obligations inside the firm that would have the effect of generating autonomous and self-sustaining social dialogue that would in turn permit deregulation of the labor market. Opportunities for employers to enjoy greater flexibility in the deployment of labor were tied to a legal obligation to negotiate change at the level of the firm. Given the weakness of trade unions inside the firm, this obligation in turn required a redefinition of who could legally bargain with the employer, or at least formally ratify workplace change. Thus the three consistent elements of industrial relations reform after 1981 were the decentralization of bargaining to the firm, the creation of new institutions of worker representation, and linkage between the use of these microcorporatist institutions and practices and the achievement of flexibility.

Again and again, state actors created legal obligations in the sphere of industrial relations that have the effect of forcing private actors to construct firm-level institutions that permit social dialogue: the Auroux Laws created an obligation to bargain and to enhance communication within the firm through expressions groups and consultation with works councils; social plans required discussion between employers and worker representatives on alternative forms of economic restructuring; the reduction of the workweek "was held out as bait" in the process of "state modernization of industrial relations" (Jefferys 2000: 142). It is not that employers have not been important actors in this process—indeed, employer organizations have become progressively more politicized and radical in their efforts to reshape industrial relations—but institutional reconstruction could not have taken place without the state, and employers were often hostile and resistant to state initiatives that had the effect of forcing them to modernize their industrial relations practices.

Shrinking trade union membership, union dependence on employers, and the process whereby firm-level agreements can be signed by nonunion employees and representatives of firm-specific employee institutions have contributed to the emergence of microcorporatism in which, without access to resources and capacities beyond the walls of the firm, workers are likely to engage in "wildcat cooperation" with their employers (Streeck 1984b). Set alongside the expansion of firm-level bargaining and the ability of local agreements to derogate from legislation and branch agreements, this has been an institutional environment conducive to the negotiation of flexibility.

State authorities have by no means neglected the French working class, however. Whether out of social solidarity or political fear, French governments have combined increased flexibility with various forms of protection and compensation. As Jonah D. Levy, Mari Miura, and Gene Park describe in this volume, France's "social anesthesia" approach has entailed significant new spending commitments to limit the social fallout from a more precarious labor market. These measures include generous early retirement programs; a guaranteed minimum income (*revenu minimum d'insertion* [RMI]) for adults who have exhausted or do not qualify for unemployment insurance; and literally millions of subsidized jobs in both the public and private sectors. The requirement that companies making layoffs negotiate a "social plan" with workplace representatives has also forced French employers to provide some measure of compensation. Finally, in recent reforms, the stick of flexibility has generally been accompanied by the carrot of reduced work time. For a combination of political and institutional reasons, then, French workers appear to have extracted greater protection and compensation for the introduction of flexibility than their British counterparts.

The last twenty years have seen a remarkable "acceleration of changes" in work organization and the labor market (Jenkins 2000: 63), the net effect of which has been to introduce high levels of flexibility. This has been apparent across a range of areas: the diffusion of individualized payment arrangements; the spread of total quality programs of various types; dramatic increases in contractual flexibility that have led to a large expansion in the number of workers on part-time, temporary, or fixed-term contacts; and, of course, the opportunities for reorganizing work made possible by flexible work time (Jenkins 2000: chs. 4–6). In all these areas, state intervention has underwritten change, either by creating the institutional preconditions for negotiating flexibility or by providing strong incentives for firms to introduce flexibility. The common theme to all these developments has been state-led modernization of industrial relations practices.

5. Conclusion

By the end of the 1990s, the political economies of Britain and France had been transformed, in part as a result of radical projects of state institutional reconstruction that began in the early 1980s. This transformation took place along several dimensions, but none was more important than the realm of the labor market and institutions of industrial relations. In both countries, labor markets inherited from the past had exhibited high levels of rigidity, either because of the workplace power of decentralized trade unionism or because of the regulatory role of the state. Yet within two decades, remarkable degrees of labor market and workplace flexibility had appeared.

This chapter has argued that the introduction of flexibility was possible only because of the reconstruction of the institutional architecture of industrial relations in the two countries. Broad shifts in the growth regime put a premium on greater flexibility and made the existing institutions of industrial relations, formed during an earlier period and designed to manage Fordist growth, increasingly dysfunctional. Even as employers in both countries became aware of emerging growth conditions, their ability to introduce flexibility of various kinds into the workplace depended on a fundamental reform of the institutions of industrial relations. Post-Fordist economic restructuring was a hostage to institutional reconstruction.

By virtue of a set of capacities not enjoyed by private industrial actors, transforming the institutions of industrial relations required a central role for the state in these two countries. The reform projects were different in the two countries, primarily by virtue of the legacy of different sets of inherited industrial relations institutions: in the British case, the logic of institutional change was decollectivist, while it was microcorporatist in France. But the British and French states performed a number of analogous tasks in the process of institutional reconstruction. First, they helped to dismantle existing industrial relations institutions by both removing the legislative supports that underpinned them and seeing off challenges from trade unions that sought to defend existing institutions and practices. This was most marked in the British case, where a powerful labor movement was cowed by restrictions put upon its ability to strike, mechanisms to extend the impact of collective bargaining were limited or removed, and major challenges to the state in the form of strikes were defeated, most notably in the case of the 1984–1985 mineworkers strike. In France, where inherited forms of labor market rigidity were largely the product of state regulation, dismantling regulation awaited the construction of new workplace industrial relations.

The second task performed by both states was to create the space and the institutional conditions for the emergence of new industrial relations practices favored by employers. In Britain, this followed naturally from the decollectivist thrust of Conservative policies in the 1980s, and for the most part, legislation was facilitative only, permitting employers to choose how to organize social relations inside the firm. The New Labour government was more proactive in this area, encouraging the emergence of "partnership" in the firm through a combination of persuasion, incentives, and legislation. The strategy was to provide workers with a set of minimum rights and protections at work that would encourage the exercise of voice, though this strategy was often at odds with the priority given to labor market flexibility.

In France, the state played a much more central role in the construction and embedding of new industrial relations institutions and practices. The Auroux legislation and the subsequent linkage between flexibility and decentralized negotiation had an explicitly microcorporatist logic, emphasizing the emergence of institutions within the workplace and encouraging firm-specific negotiation. The effect was a forced modernization of employer industrial relations practices. The Aubry Laws introducing the thirty-five-hour workweek provided an additional impetus to negotiate workplace flexibility. The French state played a role in redefining the very notion of worker representation, in the process bestowing legitimacy on new forms of employee representation. The emergence of decentralized, firm-level bargaining and social dialogue was only possible once the notion of who represented workers and their interests had been redefined, and the microcorporatist logic of French industrial relations followed in part from this process of redefinition as firm-specific forms of representation were privileged. Trade unions are quasi-public actors in France, and the state had to be involved in any change in the legitimacy of labor's representative institutions.

The third state task involved the provision of benefits and compensation to workers and unions, in order to make greater workplace and labor market flexibility more socially acceptable and politically sustainable. In the British case, successive Conservative governments offered little by way of compensation or incentives to trade unions. That said, New Labour has sought to address some of the problems stemming from increased labor market flexibility and insecurity, with a set of legal protections, new rights for union activity, and measures to alleviate poverty among low-income families. These measures were linked rhetorically to the emergence of a modernized, more partnership-oriented labor movement. French authorities have gone even further in compensating employees for flexibility. Key gains for French workers include expanded welfare benefits and labor market programs, shorter working hours, and the requirement that economic layoffs be accompanied by meaningful social plans.

There are obvious dangers in emphasizing the centrality of the state in this process of institutional reconstruction. In neither country did states act alone, nor was the motivation behind reform projects always narrowly economic, in the sense of being driven by the need to bring industrial relations in line with the imperatives of post-Fordist restructuring. States are rarely unitary actors such that competing projects may exist in different state agencies, nor are they omniscient, able to discern economic imperatives that are opaque to private actors. And state autonomy is invariably compromised in capitalist economies.

In both Britain and France, industrial relations reform was driven in part by political and electoral considerations. The French Socialists, while intellectually committed to labor market flexibility from the late 1980s onward, were forced to maintain both a rhetorical and substantive commitment to protecting workers from the social consequences of flexibility. The thirty-five-hour work-time reduction was at least as much a product of a search for a political response to unemployment that was acceptable to its supporters as a desire to encourage post-Fordist restructuring. Similarly, the British Conservatives were prevented from seeking an accommodation with the labor movement that might lead to an alternative form of economic restructuring by the centrality of hostility to unions in the political lexicon of Thatcherism. These political and electoral calculations help to explain why the French state was less successful than its British counterpart in distancing itself from the outcomes of industrial relations reform; why it found itself heavily involved in managing industrial relations throughout the period under review; and why French workers appear to have received more protection, in the form of compensating social programs or continued legislative regulation of the labor market, than British workers.

Nonetheless, the fact that governments are motivated by political considerations should not distract attention from the manner in which industrial relations reforms can develop an economic coherence and point in the direction of a particular economic logic. The way in which the Auroux reforms had a series of unintended consequences that had the effect of encouraging the emergence of microcorporatist elements while limiting the development of articulated collective bargaining illustrates how political projects can be refashioned by the institutional and class context within which they are implemented. Similarly, the more distinctive "Third Way" components of New Labour's industrial relations reforms always lost out when they came into conflict with the imperatives of labor market flexibility. One of the striking aspects

of the two-country comparison contained in this chapter is that differences in the reconstruction of industrial relations between Britain
and France are consistently greater than the difference between the
industrial relations projects of rival governments in the same country.
Thatcherite and Blairite industrial relations are both fundamentally
decollectivist, whereas Socialist and Gaullist industrial relations are
both fundamentally microcorporatist. As the Regulation approach
would suggest, institutional legacies and the imperatives of post-
Fordist restructuring shaped the reform projects of governments in
ways that often overwhelmed political motivations.

In both Britain and France, changing employer interests and the
political mobilization of employers helped to shape the reform projects
of governments. Employer mobilization was most marked in France,
primarily in response to Socialist initiatives in the realm of industrial
relations, and governments found themselves crafting legislation that
provided enough incentives for employers to participate—hence the
importance of the compensating elements noted above. In both the
early 1980s (in response to the Auroux Laws) and the late 1990s (in
response to the thirty-five-hour-week legislation), the national employers' organization mobilized aggressively on behalf of flexibility. It
has been radicalized in the course of the past two decades, though it
is unclear to what extent it represents the views of employers, and has
sought a more active political role in an effort to reduce state intervention on the part of both governments of the Left and the Right.
Indeed, at times it became a kind of de facto liberal opposition party.
British employers have had fewer differences with governments in the
past two decades, in part because of Conservative electoral dominance
and in part because the British Conservative Party is more neoliberal
than its Gaullist counterpart. Nonetheless, governments were responding in part to a shift in employer interests and a growing dissatisfaction with collective bargaining when they designed industrial
relations reform in the 1980s, and the New Labour government has
certainly been highly responsive to its *perception* of employer interests
in maintaining labor market flexibility.

However, while employer pressure played some part in shaping state
action, the state remained the central actor in reconstructing industrial
relations institutions for two reasons. First, employers were by no
means united in a recognition of the need to reform industrial rela-

tions. In both Britain and France, employers were hesitant and often hostile to the reform process, concerned about disrupting established relationships with unions (in the British case) or creating opportunities for the development of independent worker-controlled institutions (in the French case). In both countries, the state led, introducing industrial relations reforms, often over the objections of employers, and only later did employers come to endorse those reforms. The state, in other words, anticipated employer acquiescence. That was the case for the Auroux legislation, for the six major packages of industrial relations legislation between 1980 and 1993 in Britain, for New Labour's introduction of a minimum wage and statutory recognition procedure, and even for the thirty-five-hour legislation: vociferous initial opposition from French employers gave way to wary acceptance after implementation. Indeed, Vail (2005: ch. 5) has noted a "discrepancy between MEDEF's public reaction to the law and its private support for its provisions."

The state has also been central to the reconstruction of industrial relations in both countries simply because these were not changes that employers could bring about without the aid of the state, even had they been aware of their interest in reform. In the British case, union opposition would have made institutional change highly conflictual. In the French case, few employers were willing to see the creation of microcorporatist institutions inside their firms, both because of the challenge such institutions might pose to managerial authority and because of the potential collective action problems had some, but not all, firms experimented with new social relations inside the firm. In neither Britain nor France would existing systems of industrial relations have been transformed, had not the state taken the lead; and in the absence of these state projects of institutional reconstruction, post-Fordist restructuring would have been considerably more difficult and more socially conflictual.

~ 5

Building Finance Capitalism

The Regulatory Politics of Corporate
Governance Reform in the United States
and Germany

JOHN W. CIOFFI

THIS CHAPTER EXAMINES corporate governance reform in the United States and Germany during the past decade. Corporate governance reform illustrates how changing social and economic conditions impose new demands on the state and offer opportunities to expand state capacity, develop instruments of state authority and power, and fashion and implement new policies. The collapse of the bubble economy of the 1990s in the United States and to a lesser extent in Europe led to a wave of corporate finance scandals and stock market crashes around the world. In the aftermath of massive US scandals, such as Enron, Global Crossing, WorldCom, and Adelphia, subsequently joined by European counterparts such as Royal Dutch Ahold and Parmalat, securities market regulation and the internal structure and governance of the corporation have become critical issues of public policy. The fall of the neoliberal American economic and corporate governance model from international grace obscures the most important part of the story: a cross-national trend toward greater protection of shareholder interests within the capital markets and their greater empowerment within the corporate firm. This increasing protection and influence of shareholders are emerging on the foundation of expanded state regulatory authority.

Contemporary reform of corporate governance reflects the rise of what I term "finance capitalism" as an emerging paradigm of capitalism.[1] Finance capitalism is built on an expanding class of private investors, robust international capital markets, and sophisticated financial services. These features of the economy have begun to take precedence over established institutional arrangements and practices that defined the postwar advanced industrial economies. Corporate governance reform is integral to the regulatory framework of finance capitalism. It facilitates the development and integration of securities markets and the formation of large pools of private investment capital by redressing the asymmetries of information and power within the capital markets and the corporation itself to protect shareholders from fraud, abuse, and manipulation by corporate insiders. Accordingly, corporate governance regimes lie at the structural core of the new finance capitalism.

The emergence of finance capitalism presents a paradox, however: the development of financial markets and the increasing prevalence and import of market relations, so often linked to the diminution of state power and authority, have been accompanied by a substantial and ongoing *expansion* of law and prescriptive regulation. Although often neglected in theories of regulation, corporate governance law performs a crucial regulatory function by ordering the authority relationships, decision-making processes, and economic incentives of the most important and ubiquitous economic institution—the corporation. The conduct of parties within the securities markets and the structure and internal functioning of the firm itself are increasingly determined or at least powerfully influenced by the steady centralization of regulatory authority at the national level.

This chapter compares the US experience to that of Germany, which has long embodied a more relational form of market capitalism based, in part, on a bank-centered financial system that supplied firms with relatively cheap, stable, and long-term "patient" debt finance. The development of transparency and disclosure regulation, shareholder rights, and board reform is a leading indicator of the emergence of finance capitalism and a dependent variable in assessing political economic outcomes.[2] A comparison of the developmental trajectories of the American and German national corporate governance regimes clarifies the common pressures favoring the reform of financial markets and corporate governance across national economies and reveals the political and structural features that have propelled the American and German political economies along separate paths.

Corporate governance reform challenges both neoliberal convergence theories and theories of path dependence. Nowhere is the neoliberal rhetoric of globalization, deregulation, and retrenchment of state power more frequently invoked as in relation to the rise of international financial markets and the investors and corporations that utilize them. Indeed, in some ways, the increasing importance of corporate governance as an area of policy and economic practice suggests the devolution of power from the state to the firm and market as the primary mechanisms of economic distribution, innovation, growth, and adjustment. On the other hand, much work in contemporary comparative political economy, particularly that associated with the "varieties of capitalism" literature, maintains that institutional differences among national economies are path dependent and locked into place by the comparative economic advantages that these arrangements confer on domestic firms (Hall and Soskice 2001b).

Neither theory recognizes the intensely political process by which corporate governance regimes are constructed and the state's substantially increased regulatory intervention in the economy that has accompanied corporate governance reform. The past decade has witnessed substantial change in institutional arrangements, policy preferences of important political actors, and economic relationships. Reforms have swept through securities law and regulation, company law, and increasingly corporate practices and organization. Financial regulators and regulations exist where before there were none. Shareholder rights have developed rapidly in an era in which corporate managers were thought to be gaining power and influence over policy. In both the United States and Germany, regulatory authority over corporate finance and governance has become more centralized, hierarchical, and formal, as federal law has superseded state law, selfregulation, and unregulated markets. The changes have been especially dramatic in the German case.

These reforms attest to the capacity of state actors to take advantage of shifting economic conditions, interest group preferences, and public opinion by framing public policy debates and constructing interest group alliances to overcome path dependence. More specifically, they reveal the capacity of state actors to impose significant costs and constraints on a set of actors that is often seen as gaining power—senior corporate managers. Such far-reaching reforms are not the hallmark of a path-dependent equilibrium, as anticipated by the varieties of capitalism literature; nor do they signal the retreat of the state, as presumed by neoliberal convergence theory.

The increasing prominence of the corporate firm and its governance in public policy entails a transformation in the role of the state and regulation in ordering economic relations. In place of state control over finance, public ownership of enterprise, or strong coordinating financial intermediaries, finance capitalism uses law and regulation to structure markets and firms. This is becoming an increasingly important mode of state intervention in the advanced industrial economies.[3] Corporate governance and its reform exemplify this intertwining of public and private whereby the state does not supplant markets but instead restructures both markets and the organizational hierarchies to reallocate economic power and alter economic behavior (Cioffi 2002c: 2).

This chapter describes the changing place of the state as the United States and Germany have moved toward a system of finance capitalism. Section 1 sets out a brief sketch of the legal, institutional, and ideological features of American and German corporate governance regimes prior to the 1990s. These regimes, respectively, embodied distinctive liberal market and coordinated market variants of postwar capitalism, and each contained tensions and flaws that would open the door to the reforms of the past decade. Section 2 discusses the political and juridical responses to economic and corporate governance crises and shows how political and economic institutional structures influenced the course and content of the American and German corporate governance reforms since 1990. Section 3 concludes with a political analysis of these reforms and their implications for the model of finance capitalism and the developmental trajectories of the American and German political economies.

1. The Regulatory State, Public Law, and the Corporate Firm

Corporate governance regimes structure the allocation and exercise of power and decision-making authority among managers, shareholders, and employees—the principal groups involved in corporate affairs.[4] The core of national corporate governance regimes is made up of three legal components: (1) company (or corporate) law; (2) securities regulation; and (3) labor relations law. This core structure varies substantially across different types of political economic organization. The cases of the United States and Germany illustrate this variation. The two countries represent distinctive political economic models defined by neoliberal and neocorporatist institutional arrangements, respectively.[5] (See Table 5.1 for the basic features of the postwar American and German governance models.) Although numerous informal practices are associated with national corporate governance regimes, ranging from managerial compensation to the quality of employee participation in firm decision making and implementation, these practices developed within, and were perpetuated by, formal legal and institutional structures.

The United States

Historically, the structure of American corporate governance has privileged rapidly shifting, arm's-length economic relationships over longer-term relational ties among management, capital, and labor. American law tended to preserve an expansive private sphere of corporate and managerial autonomy bounded by a highly developed framework of formal legal rights, obligations, and regulatory rules. The US approach allowed managers great latitude in structuring intracorporate institutions and relationships. The underdevelopment of representation and bargaining with interest groups inside the firm concentrated power in the hands of the chief executive officer (CEO) and other senior managers.

Company Law. American corporate law is distinctive in that it has been the responsibility of the fifty states, rather than federal authorities. State company laws functioned as general enabling statutes to create the bare minima of the corporate form—limited liability, the "corporate personality" (the capacity to enter into contracts and to sue and be sued), a board of directors, and basic fiduciary duties and shareholder rights. Otherwise, corporate law granted managers and directors wide discretion in how to structure the firm, its finances, and decision-making processes. It offered shareholders comparatively few rights to vote on important corporate decisions. In fact, American corporate law allowed managers to sit on the board of directors— essentially supervising themselves—while federal securities regulations

Table 5.1. Postwar corporate governance models in the United States and Germany, circa 1985

	Law/regulation	Correlated practices
	A. United States: liberal managerial capitalism	
Company law	State law governs internal firm structure and affairs (no uniform federal corporate law).	Broad managerial and board discretion in running firm.
	Hierarchy of fiduciary duties favors shareholder supremacy over other stakeholders.	Corporate law and intrafirm governance favor managerial interests.
	Corporate law statutes and jurisprudence permits wide variety of antitakeover defenses.	Stakeholders receive little legal protection, creating bias in favor of short-term financial interests.
		Fiduciary law weakened—strengthens position of managers and limits protection of shareholders and stakeholders alike.
Securities law	Centralized federal securities regulation in rule making and enforcement by SEC.	Securities markets highly capitalized; substantial use of equity finance and financial innovation.
	Stringent and highly prescriptive transparency and disclosure rules.	Fragmentation of ownership (separation of ownership and control).
	Self-regulation of accounting industry and Financial Accounting Standards Board (FASB).	Weak oversight of accounting industry relies on professionalism and reputational capital.
Labor law	Weak legal protection for labor organizing and bargaining.	Weak, fragmented labor unions and firm-level bargaining.
	Labor law sharply separated from corporate law (no employee representation through codetermination).	Contractual labor relations separate from firm governance; preserves managerial control over corporate decision making.
Enforcement mechanisms	Formal and litigious enforcement of complex prescriptive rules.	High incidence of litigation is potent enforcement method but expensive and encourages strike suits.
	Substantive and procedural law encourages use of private litigation for enforcement.	Less state control through administrative policy and budgets.

	Law/regulation	Correlated practices
B. Germany: organized stakeholder capitalism		
Company law	Federal company law imposes uniformity and prevents regulatory competition. Weak fiduciary duties binding firm directors and officers. Supervisory board codetermination in large public firms.	Stakeholder system of representation and governance is stable. Fiduciary law protects company, not shareholder, interests. Absence of shareholder primacy in law buttresses stakeholder governance and consensual decision making.
Securities law	Weak state (*Länder*) regulation of financial disclosure (transparency) and corporate insiders (e.g., insider trading). No federal regulation or regulator. Law allows banks to wield small shareholders' proxy votes.	Opaque financial reporting and insider-dominated system. Bank-centered financial system and undeveloped securities markets. Concentrated shareholding and networks of stock ownership.
Labor law	Strong legal protection for unions and sectoral bargaining between centralized industrial unions and employer associations. Works council codetermination gives employees voice in firm governance (regarding, e.g., work hours, organization, layoffs).	Cooperative labor relations rest on strong unions within firms, industrial sectors, and political system. Functional split between unions and works councils takes most divisive wage and benefit issues out of firm governance.
Enforcement mechanisms	Procedural and substantive restrictions on private lawsuits reduce use of litigation.	Governance by negotiation among opposing interests tends to replicate neocorporatist patterns within the firm.

have long given *management* control over the nomination and election of directors. In theory, the fiduciary duties of corporate directors and officers partially counterbalanced the resulting weakness of shareholders in corporate governance. These legal duties obligate directors to run the corporation for the benefit of the shareholders in a loyal and reasonably attentive and competent fashion. In practice, however, the "business judgment rule" substantially dilutes fiduciary duties by exempting from liability those decisions taken in good faith in the ordinary course of business.[6]

Securities Law. In contrast to company law, securities law was the responsibility of the federal government, rather than the fifty states. The combination of limited influence over company law and the concentration of power in corporate management increased the incentive for federal policymakers to use market-reinforcing securities regulation as a principal means of constraining managers and protecting shareholders from fraud, misappropriation, and abuse. Accordingly, the United States pioneered modern securities regulation in the 1930s and came to rely on the Securities and Exchange Commission (SEC)—a strong centralized regulatory agency—to relieve information asymmetries and improve the functioning of securities markets. In short, the SEC's mission was to make the markets work.

The SEC was charged with drafting and enforcing elaborate and mandatory registration, disclosure, and securities fraud rules and with overseeing the administration of stock exchanges (and their listing and disclosure rules). As a result of this institutionalization of securities regulation, the United States possessed comparatively strong transparency, disclosure, and insider trading laws and regulations designed to protect minority shareholders, facilitate market transactions, and buttress the perceived legitimacy of the country's securities markets. Within this regulatory framework, the "external" capital markets in the United States became among the most developed and liquid in the world, spawning a high proportion of publicly traded firms, a sophisticated financial services industry, and a wide range of debt and equity financing options. At the same time, the federal Glass-Steagall Act of 1933 had long segmented the financial services industry and *mandated* portfolio diversification. The act curtailed concentrated financial power and investment risk but precluded the use of concentrated equity ownership as a means of checking managerial power.[7]

Although the Gramm-Leach-Bliley Act of 1999 repealed Glass-Steagall, the fragmentation of ownership and corresponding weakness of shareholders in firm governance persist.

Both the emphasis on transparency and disclosure regulation and the weak institutional position of shareholders within the legal structure of the American corporation encouraged individual and institutional investors to respond to governance and management problems through exit by selling their stakes, rather than to participate more actively through voice.[8] There arose a mutually reinforcing relationship between the market-driven American financial system and a legalistic, transparency-based regulatory regime. The weakness of shareholder representation within firm-level structures of corporate governance increased the importance of and reliance on prescriptive disclosure regulation to protect shareholder interests. In fact, consistent with regulatory patterns in the United States, the American corporate governance regime relied to a striking extent on the substantial use of highly formal and prescriptive regulation and litigious enforcement mechanisms.[9]

Labor Law. Managerial dominance over corporate affairs extended to labor as well as finance. While American law limited shareholders within firm governance, it wholly excluded employees. No representational structures ever emerged in US law or labor relations practices to incorporate employees into firm decision making or assure ongoing consultation, such as that provided by board representation or works council structures in Germany (see the discussion of Germany below).[10] By strictly separating labor relations and firm management, American labor law came to protect managerial prerogatives from encroachment by collective bargaining and other forms of employee influence.[11] Matters such as investment, marketing, production, design, and finance were (and are) considered within the "core of entrepreneurial control" and not subject to collective bargaining,[12] although these issues may have decisive importance for the future of the workforce.

Together, corporate law managerialism, strong transparency and disclosure regulation under securities law, and labor's marginalization through comparatively weak labor laws constituted the basic structural features of the American corporate governance regime. These legal-institutional arrangements encouraged risk taking, organizational restructuring, and technological innovation, but at the cost of managerial "short-termism" that elevated immediate financial concerns over long-term growth and stability. The United States came to be seen as the purest incarnation of the neoliberal market economic model. Yet the American legal framework produced a fundamental tension between managerialism and "shareholder primacy" (the principle that the maximization of shareholder value should take precedence over any other stakeholder interests). During the 1980s and 1990s, this tension generated increasingly bitter political conflict and fueled demands for reform.

Germany

The postwar German political economy and corporate governance regime stood in sharp contrast to the neoliberal American model. The German governance regime relied on law and regulation to structure the firm as a largely self-regulating entity, situated within a consensus-based social market economy. The corporatist model was characterized by peak association interest representation, centralized wage bargaining, and networks of relational finance and corporate cross-shareholding. The German regime frequently used law to fashion representational structures and institutional frameworks that channeled opposing interests into negotiation, rather than formal enforcement processes. This ordering of opposing interests into long-term bargaining relationships was replicated at the level of the firm and workplace through the distinctive institutionalization of German finance and labor codetermination. The "microcorporatist" structure of the firm contributed to a stakeholder model of corporate and economic governance that incorporates and protects the interests of nonshareholder constituencies (particularly labor) within the corporation.[13]

Company and Securities Law. Until the 1990s, the framework of German securities and company law was the mirror image of the American model. The American corporate governance regime was defined by centralized federal securities regulation and the dispersion of corporate law among the states. In Germany, the legal framework of corporate governance was defined by uniform federal company law and the fragmentation of securities regulation among the *Länder* (states) and eight local self-regulating exchanges. Disclosure regulations and accounting rules were weak, and company finances remained opaque. Moreover, the law provided few effective avenues for private litigation to enforce shareholder rights.

In place of American-style transparency regulation, Germany's corporate governance regime long relied on mandatory rules to structure the corporation and its governance processes and on the power of large banks to monitor managers. Germany's bank-centered financial system defined a set of stable, interlocking ownership and governance relationships based on concentrated ownership, extensive cross-shareholding networks, and long-term relational finance ties among banks and corporate borrowers. These financial structures reinforced the stakeholder model. Relational finance by banks alleviated pressures for maximizing short-term financial returns and encouraged the adoption of long-term adjustment and growth strategies by industrial enterprises that could balance the competing demands of capital and labor. The major banks' central role in securities underwriting, brokerage, and trading gave them significant power in corporate affairs.

Large German "universal banks" combined the lending and securities services at the core of the financial system. Consequently, these banks were simultaneously important lenders to and major shareholders in publicly traded firms. Further, under German law, the banks could vote "deposited share voting rights" (DSVRs) if authorized by their brokerage clients.[14] Bank representation on the supervisory board frequently cemented the combination of voting power and long-term relational lender and shareholding relationships. The corporate structure organized stakeholder interests into self-regulating relationships within firm governance. In theory, the banks' status as shareholders aligned their interests with those of other shareholders, and the banks' power within firm governance protected these other investors. In practice, banks did not play the active monitoring role assumed by conventional wisdom, and the contradictory status of the banks as lenders first and shareholders second generated conflicts of interest that law and regulation neither policed nor remedied. In the absence of effective shareholder protections or strong incentives for major banks to cultivate equity finance, relatively few German firms were publicly traded, equity was not an important form of finance, and securities markets remained far less developed than in the United States.

Under German company law, public corporations (*Aktiengesellschaft*

[AG]) had a dual board structure, in which the supervisory board (analogous to the American board of directors) was completely separate from the management board (a more collegial version of the CEO and senior management of the American firm), with no overlapping membership between them. The supervisory board *(Aufsichtsrat)* appointed and nominally supervised the managing board *(Vorstand)* and formulated (or at least approved) major corporate policies and strategies. German company law also gave shareholders, through the Annual General Meeting (or AGM), the right to receive relevant information and vote on a broad range of issues, including mergers, significant acquisitions, capital increases, and major changes in business strategies.[15] In the absence of stringent securities regulation designed to improve the efficiency and disciplinary function of stock markets, German company law relied on the internal corporate institutions, the board and AGM, to constrain managerial power. However, these institutional constraints were designed not only to protect shareholders, as in the United States, but also to safeguard the interests of other stakeholders, including creditor banks and employees.

Labor Law. Codetermination integrated employees into the firm's governance processes and embodied the stakeholder vision of the corporation.[16] Company and labor relations law interpenetrated under codetermination to create "microcorporatist"[17] structures conducive to negotiation, compromise, cooperation, and consensus within firm governance. Supervisory board codetermination under the Codetermination Act of 1976, perhaps the most striking feature of German company law, required most corporations with over 2,000 employees to appoint an equal number of shareholder and employee representatives to their supervisory boards.[18] However, the chairman of the supervisory board is elected by the shareholders and wields a second tie-breaking vote (Wiedemann 1980: 79; Charkham 1994: 26). Thus, the structure of the board preserved formal shareholder (or managerial) predominance.[19] Board codetermination became enormously important as a symbol of the country's neocorporatist and social democratic consensus-driven "social market economy," but its practical import has been modest.[20]

By contrast, works council codetermination has provided a second and more important form of employee representation in firm governance.[21] The product of the center-right Konrad Adenauer government's 1952 attempt to break the unions' monopoly over representation of employees, works councils wield substantial influence within the workplace, and often over entire corporate groups, through their ability to use informational, consultation, and codetermination or co-decision rights. Works councils can exert additional influence by using these rights to impede the implementation of managerial decisions. They also have the authority to demand compensation for economic injury caused by changes in corporate policy. Although potentially obstructionist, works council codetermination has also proved highly beneficial to firms as a way of cooperatively coordinating labor relations in workplaces staffed by highly skilled and productive employees.

The German stakeholder system both legitimated the postwar capitalist order and conferred comparative advantages in incremental innovation in industrial production. German industry focused on high-quality and high-value-added market niches that rationalized high wages and investment in skill formation. But these benefits came at an increasingly steep price, raising costs, creating rigidities, and hampering job creation. By the early 1990s, the effects of reunification and declining national economic performance made the need for structural reform more obvious than ever. German politicians then faced the twin questions of what kinds of reforms were needed and whether Germany's well-developed structure of interest representation would permit them.

2. Politics and Policy Reform

Corporate governance reform was launched against a backdrop of systemic crises in both the American and German political economies. Declining national economic performance, the internationalization of financial markets, and fiercer competition within the financial sector spurred the pursuit of higher returns to capital by investors and financial institutions, while policymakers sought ways to encourage corporate restructuring through market pressures. These changes increased the political and economic leverage of capital holders, investment banks, and institutional investors in the United States and of universal banks in Germany. Recurrent corporate financial scandals in both countries also raised serious threats to the legitimacy of established corporate governance regimes and helped mobilize popular support for their reform. Under conditions of crisis and uncertainty, entrepreneurial politicians and political parties seized strategic opportunities to mobilize and cultivate supporters, alter interest group alignments, and take up issues designed to improve their prospects in electoral competition.

In the corporate governance area, the center-left repositioned itself to press for reform. The Democratic Party in the United States used the postbubble scandals and the collapse of share prices to attack the Republican Party with a well-placed appeal to middle-class voters (and investors—many of whom were/are Republicans), who believed in free but *fair* markets. The German Social Democratic Party's (SPD) corporate governance reforms satisfied left-wing and populist constituencies by targeting managerial and (to some extent) banking elites. They also formed part of a strategy to lure political and electoral support from the middle class and financial sector by promoting policies that promised higher returns to savings, greater efficiency in capital allocation, more rapid rates of growth and innovation, and economic restructuring at the corporate level. In each case, economic crisis and scandal weakened the opponents of reform. In both countries, conservative parties were the defenders of the managerial elite and the corporate status quo—but circumstances had brought this status quo into disrepute.

Corporate governance reform fit surprisingly well within the contours of the center-left ideology. The Democratic Party and the SPD have both been committed to the development of the regulatory state as a counterweight to managerial authority, corporate power, and market failure. Both parties had a strategic and ideological interest in shoring up the perceived fairness and equity of markets that absorbed increasing shares of working- and middle-class pension and retirement savings. Governance and securities law reform thus appealed to both the center-left's egalitarian ideology and its welfare state agenda. Conversely, center-right parties were reluctant to endorse an expansion of state regulation that would impose costs and restraints on a key conservative constituency—managerial elites. This depiction is, of course, a highly simplified sketch of complex interparty and intraparty dynamics in both countries. Yet the general point holds: corporate governance reform has been largely a project of the political Left—not the ostensibly pro-business or neoliberal Right.

The American Corporate Governance Crisis: The Politics of Punctuated Reform

The American governance regime contained a set of structural flaws that contributed directly to the systemic corporate governance crisis of recent years. First, the transparency-based system of American securities regulation was weakened by the largely self-regulating character of the accounting industry (the intermediaries responsible for external corporate audits), which had long since treated auditing as a loss leader to sell more lucrative consulting services. The weakness of accounting and auditing as mechanisms of transparency was compounded by highly detailed, prescriptive, but loophole-riddled accounting rules (Generally Agreed Accounting Principles [GAAP]) drafted by the Financial Accounting Standards Board (FASB), a private body composed of accounting industry representatives.

Second, American law virtually ensured management domination of the board of directors. State corporate law and federal proxy voting regulations together gave managers almost complete control over the nomination and election of the directors, who nominally monitored and oversaw the firm's management. Consequently, CEOs and senior managers largely dominated the very governance institutions and processes that were supposed to render them accountable to shareholders.

Third, institutional investors were neither willing nor able to fulfill the active governance monitoring role that many commentators, corporate governance activists, policymakers, and academic theorists envisioned for them. Federal regulation did not substantially depart from the *voluntarist* approach to corporate governance. Institutional investors were largely indifferent to, and often resisted, calls for increased regulatory intervention in corporate governance. Mutual funds prized liquidity of their stock holdings over "voice" in corporate affairs. They also earned substantial fees from managing company pension funds and therefore had a powerful incentive not to antagonize corporate managers through governance activism. Even public defined-benefit pension funds, long the most activist institutional investors, pursued a voluntarist governance agenda in the belief that their market power alone was sufficient to defend shareholder interests.

These structural flaws were well known to commentators and policymakers prior to 2000, and some earnest efforts to address them were attempted but did not succeed. The failure to address these brewing problems grew out of a combination of fragmented governmental institutions imposing multiple veto points on policymaking, political polarization between the parties, and the influence of interest groups hostile to reform. At the same time, protection of shareholder interests remained the chief preoccupation of the SEC during the Clinton administration and was backed by investment funds as well as public opinion. As a result, American corporate governance reform during the 1990s swerved between efforts to safeguard managerial interests and measures increasing shareholder protections. The combination of a Congress closely divided between Democrats and Republicans, established structures of federalism, and fragmented pluralist politics precluded major systemic corporate governance reforms during the 1980s and 1990s, even as problems of balance sheet manipulation, excessive CEO pay, irrational speculation, inflated stock prices, and inefficient and value-destroying merger and acquisition activity were clear to many observers.

The American corporate governance regime entered the 1990s still reeling from the legal and political upheaval caused by the hostile takeover wave of the 1980s. Managers had mobilized an ad hoc cross-class coalition with organized labor and grassroots community groups to fight takeovers and effectively used the courts and state legislatures to erect a wide variety of antitakeover defenses, ranging from judicially sanctioned "poison pill" defenses to antitakeover statutes. American managers took advantage of their strength within the political process at the state level to press for these legal changes and, at the federal level, to block any preemption of protective state law. The relative political weakness of local and labor coalition partners meant that these actors had little influence over the terms of policy, and as a consequence, antitakeover politics reinforced managerialism. Financial interests were too weak to counter this political and legal attack, especially at the state level, where corporate law was made and distant financial institutions and elites were resented by local constituencies. Widespread populist hostility to the dislocation caused by financially driven takeovers and the fragmented and veto-prone structure of politics and policymaking enabled managerial interests to prevent a congressional legislative end-run around state law.[22] By the early 1990s, these legal changes had largely eliminated the market for corporate control and effectively protected incumbent managers from *hostile* takeovers (but not friendly takeovers that often richly rewarded senior managers).[23] The monumental legal and political battles over hostile takeovers gave way to a series of skirmishes over the proper limits of managerial power and how those limits should be imposed.

These conflicts pitted managerialist antiregulation business groups, accountants, corporate lawyers, and antiregulation politicians against pro-shareholder groups, pension funds, unions, regulators, and politicians more favorably disposed toward regulation. The SEC was caught between managerial and pro-shareholder groups during the 1990s. As a consequence, the SEC suffered a series of political defeats in its attempts to protect shareholder interests. It failed in its efforts to address growing conflicts of interest in the accounting industry. Fearing (correctly, as it turned out) that accounting firms acting simultaneously as consultants and auditors would compromise the integrity of their auditing in order to generate and keep lucrative consulting contracts, SEC chairman Arthur Levitt, a Clinton appointee, wanted to prohibit accounting firms from handling both auditing and consulting work for corporations. Accounting firms enlisted allies in Congress to fight on their behalf and bring legislative pressure on the SEC, until the regulatory proposal was withdrawn.[24] Likewise, the SEC under Levitt failed in its attempt to require the expensing of stock options in corporate financial statements. "New economy" technology firms dependent on options enlisted bipartisan congressional and executive branch support to quash the initiative.

The pro-shareholder forces were also split among themselves, with one group favoring expanded disclosure regulation and the other seeking to encourage the monitoring of management and corporate governance activism by institutional investors. Vacillations in SEC policy during the 1990s reflected this political and ideological conflict. From 1992 to 2000, the SEC, under Levitt and his Republican predecessor Richard Breeden, initiated a series of reforms to protect shareholders by improving managerial accountability and financial transparency—with mixed political and practical success. In 1992, the SEC amended its proxy rules to encourage corporate governance activism among large institutional investors by making it easier for them to communicate with each other and with management.[25] These reforms represented an early experiment in "structural regulation," which altered the *institutional* structure of the firm and deliberately modified intra-corporate power relations by design to change behavior and achieve policy goals.

However, in August 2000, the SEC shifted direction with the adoption of Regulation "Fair Disclosure" (Regulation FD). Regulation FD prohibited disclosure of material information by corporate managers to favored analysts, financial institutions, and institutional investors unless that information was also released to the general public. While addressing the problem of informational asymmetries that disadvantage small investors vis-à-vis large institutions, Regulation FD limited the ability of institutional investors to pursue corporate governance activism through their favored approach of private communications with managers and board members and thus ran counter to both the pro-management stance of congressional Republicans and the SEC's own 1992 proxy reforms.[26]

Moreover, in 1995 and 1998, congressional Republicans—strengthened by the 1994 midterm elections—spearheaded "tort reform" legislation designed to reduce the incidence of securities litigation.[27] Securities litigation reform served a dual political purpose. It strengthened the position of managers, a predominantly Republican constituency, while attacking the financial base of a plaintiffs' bar that overwhelmingly supported Democrats. These tort reform measures contained a grave deficiency: they provided for no alternative mechanisms to protect shareholders from fraud and financial abuses. The laws also further centralized securities regulation at the federal level, setting a precedent for the federalization of corporate governance reform. The 1998 law went so far as to preempt state securities fraud laws in order to impose a uniform set of more restrictive federal rules on the filing of securities suits.[28] Unwittingly, the efforts of congressional conservatives to strengthen managers set the stage for a far-reaching reform and expansion of *federal* corporate governance and financial market regulation.

The bursting of the stock market bubble and the collapse of the American equities markets in 2000, along with the postbubble corporate finance scandals of 2001–2002, unveiled the vast corruption and fraud that accompanied the economic and investment boom of the late 1990s. The massive corporate finance scandals at Enron, WorldCom, Global Crossing, Adelphia, and other major corporations, added to the loss of over $7 trillion in stock market valuation, stoked popular resentment of corporate and financial elites. Scandal and the perception of systemic crisis and dysfunction inflamed political support for more wide-ranging reform of the American corporate governance regime. The most severe legitimacy crisis of the American financial and corporate governance systems since the Great Depression disrupted the grip of a conservative coalition that had favored minimal regulation and blocked reform through the 1990s.

By spring 2002, political leaders began to fear that the American securities markets and financial system as a whole might collapse after the successive shocks of the terrorist attacks of September 11, 2001, and the seemingly endless series of corporate finance scandals and bankruptcies. The country that developed modern securities regulation and shareholder capitalism fell victim to an enormously damaging speculative bubble, serious regulatory failures, corporate and accounting fraud on a vast scale, and systemic problems of poor governance and conflicts of interest. However, although the corporate governance crisis that began in 2001 exposed the systemic deficiencies and contradictions of the American model in extravagant fashion, pathbreaking and wide-ranging Sarbanes-Oxley reforms were intended to *reinforce* a faltering market-based financial system and corporate governance model, not supplant it.

The law was the product of a political struggle between Democrats using financial scandals against the Republicans and Republicans seeking to dilute the legislation in keeping with their loyalty to corporate supporters and their antiregulation agenda. Substantial reform was possible only under crisis conditions that weakened interest group influence and made political resistance to reform efforts unpopular. The extraordinary scope, severity, and duration of these financial scandals allowed the Democratic Party to seize the policy agenda of substantial corporate governance reform, despite Republican control of the House of Representatives and White House, while it undermined the legitimacy of managerial and professional elites and their political allies who opposed reform. Under these conditions, the Democratic leadership in the Senate, where the party held a short-lived majority prior to the 2002 midterm elections, outflanked and overrode the resistance to pro-shareholder reforms mounted by congressional Republicans, the George Bush administration, powerful vested managerial and accounting industry interests, and SEC chairman Harvey Pitt (whose tenure did not survive the confrontation). Finally, the multibillion-dollar collapse of WorldCom in the late spring of 2002 broke the resistance of the Bush administration, the Republican-held House of Representatives, and conservative antiregulation Republicans in the Senate.[29] The Bush administration and much of the congressional Republican leadership sought to neutralize the scandals as a potent November 2002 election issue by supporting corporate governance reform and accepting only minor compromises from the Democrats as the price. In the words of one Republican staffer on Capitol Hill, "Congress didn't pass Sarbanes-Oxley, WorldCom did."[30]

The Democrats did face significant constraints, however. In order to ensure quick passage of the legislation, they did not push the Republicans on expanding shareholder rights to litigate. Given the ambivalence over securities litigation among conservative Democrats, the Republicans did not even have to fight for this restriction on corporate governance reforms. Paul Sarbanes never suggested new private rights of action, nor did he seek to roll back the statutory and judicial restrictions on securities suits erected during the 1990s. Likewise, Congress deferred and delegated the resolution of critical governance issues, such as expensing stock options and increasing shareholder power over the nomination and election of directors, to regulatory bodies.

The Sarbanes-Oxley Act of 2002 was an exercise in political opportunism, damage control, pragmatic idealism, and the rehabilitation of systemic legitimacy (usually referred to as "investor confidence"). The political struggle over the Sarbanes-Oxley reforms reveals policy driven by a crisis severe enough to overcome imposing institutional and ideological obstacles to reform. In the absence of these exigent circumstances, reform would have probably foundered on divisive party and interest group politics within a fragmented and veto-prone political structure. This fragmented structure prevents coordination of complex policy and legislative initiatives and empowers interest groups to block legislative and regulatory reforms in pursuit of their own narrow interests. When conditions propitious for legislative reform arrived, it had to be carried out quickly. The process was a sudden, reactive, and episodic response to scandal and popular outcry. Delay would have resulted in the loss of the opportunity. However, the Sarbanes-Oxley Act reflects no elite consensus or coherent long-term policy agenda. Indeed, the reforms are less systematic and more contested by interest groups and political factions than the German reforms of the past decade analyzed below.

Sarbanes-Oxley imposed a host of new regulatory requirements and measures on publicly traded corporations, directors, corporate managers, accountants, and attorneys that reflect trends toward regulatory centralization and structural regulation. The law created the Public Company Accounting Oversight Board (the PCAOB), an entirely new private regulatory body appointed by and under the oversight of the SEC, to enforce a new set of prescriptive regulations governing accounting standards and the activities of accounting firms in auditing and consulting.[31] The creation of the PCAOB, though a private nonprofit entity, represents the federalization of accounting regulation and the displacement of the strictly self-regulatory character of the accounting profession and the FASB as the primary rule-making body in the fields of accounting and auditing. Accordingly, this constitutes a major expansion of federal regulatory authority.

The second pathbreaking aspect of the Sarbanes-Oxley Act is its intervention in the *internal* structure and affairs of the corporation. Sarbanes-Oxley represents the first time that federal law and regulation have directly penetrated the traditional preserve of state corporation law. Similar to recent German reforms (discussed below), Sarbanes-Oxley strengthened the independence of the board and its auditing function. Public firms are now required to appoint an auditing committee composed *entirely* of independent directors, and at least one member must be qualified as a financial expert under new SEC rules. The audit committee has direct responsibility for the appointment, compensation, and oversight of the outside auditors. It must also approve all auditor services. The auditors report directly to the board audit committee, which must resolve any disputes between management and the auditors concerning financial reporting. By encroaching on the traditional subjects of state corporate law, the Sarbanes-Oxley reforms centralized and federalized key aspects of corporate governance. This unprecedented—and underreported—federalization of corporate law represents a sharp break with nearly two centuries of American federalism and suggests the growing policy import of corporate governance issues and the extraordinary political potency of the financial and governance scandals of 2001–2002. Together, these regulatory reforms represent not only a potentially vast expansion of federal regulatory power but also a substantial centralization of regulatory authority, displacing the self-regulating character of the accounting industry and firm governance.

Consistent with this emphasis on government regulation, the Sarbanes-Oxley reforms continued the trend away from private litigation as a mechanism of regulatory enforcement embodied in the securities tort reform laws of the 1990s. The law emphasized increased *governmental* investigation and enforcement actions, rather than the private civil suits that had long characterized securities law. In short, the legislation emphasized the restructuring of the institutional structure and composition of the corporate firm and statist enforcement mechanisms over private rights of action and court-centered enforcement through litigation.

Following the passage of Sarbanes-Oxley, the arena of regulatory politics moved from Congress to the SEC and its troubled ward, the PCAOB. Having resisted calls for reform, the SEC lost influence over the legislative process, and its legitimacy, integrity, and competence were all called into question.[32] In passing the Sarbanes-Oxley Act, Congress substantially expanded the jurisdiction and powers of the SEC but placed the agency in the middle of continuing and intense political conflicts over the future of corporate governance reform. William Donaldson, who succeeded the discredited Harvey Pitt at the helm of the SEC, launched the agency on a historic run of rule making. The SEC tightened financial and proxy vote disclosure, stock exchange regulation, and accounting rules. Agency pressure led the stock exchanges to stiffen their listing rules on board independence and the role of independent board auditing, nomination, and compensation committees (an effort begun under Pitt). In response to a series of mutual fund governance scandals, the SEC also mandated mutual fund board independence from fund advisers (such as Fidelity and Putnam) by requiring a majority of independent directors on fund boards. It ventured gingerly into the largely unregulated world of hedge funds by requiring their registration with the agency. It successfully supported the FASB's and PCAOB's efforts to require the expensing of stock options.

The SEC finally triggered a conservative and managerial backlash when it proposed new board nomination rules in October 2003.[33] The proposal became the single most controversial and bitterly contested initiative in the agency's history. The SEC received over 13,000 comment letters in response to the proposal—a record number (Securities and Exchange Commission 2003; Peterson 2004). The proposed proxy rules would have allowed institutional investors to nominate directors through access to corporate proxies mailed to all shareholders, but only under exceptional conditions and after substantial delays.[34] The proposed rules would have allowed dissident shareholders to elect no more than a minority of three directors in this fashion—a number almost certainly insufficient to reform the functioning of a corporate board as a check on managerial power.

Still, with this rather modest proposed reform of board election rules, the SEC struck the nerve of corporate managerial power and, predictably in retrospect, generated a fierce and gathering managerial backlash. Managers, business groups, and conservative politicians attacked the proposed rules as destructive of corporate efficiency and as opening corporations to "special interest" agendas by public and union pension funds. Business interests, led by the Business Roundtable and the Chamber of Commerce, overwhelmed the institutional investors, unions, shareholder and consumer advocates, and a number of state treasurers who publicly supported the reform. The conflict intensified in the run-up to the 2004 presidential election as the Bush administration reportedly weighed in against the reform behind closed doors. The SEC split over the issue in an increasingly bitter, public, and unseemly divide, with the two Democratic commissioners supporting the change and the two Republicans opposing it. In July 2004, Donaldson conceded that the SEC was hopelessly deadlocked.

The Bush and Republican Party successes in the November 2004 election effectively killed board nomination and election reform. Within two months, the plan was officially dead. With the shift in political winds, the post-Enron era of corporate governance reform ended. Seen by business groups and administration and congressional conservatives as a threat to managerial interests, criticized and stymied by increasingly hostile Republican SEC commissioners, Donaldson found himself in an increasingly untenable political position. The politics of corporate governance claimed a second consecutive SEC chair when he resigned in early June 2005. Within hours of his resignation, President Bush nominated Representative Chris Cox—a well-known pro-business conservative and critic of securities litigation and regulation—to replace him. The post-Enron reform era had drawn to a close.

Even so, no informed observer of American politics expects a reversal of the recent corporate governance reforms. The criteria for political economic legitimacy have been altered by the post-1990s corporate scandals and ensuing reforms. These reforms redefined the normative baseline for corporate and managerial conduct—and the lesson has been repeatedly reinforced by continuing criminal prosecutions stemming for these same scandals. However, to the extent that the fundamental structural flaws of American corporate governance remain in place, notably excessive managerial power, conflict over intracorporate relations will inevitably recur. The American political structure encourages punctuated equilibrium—but equilibrium in the legal and institutional foundations of finance capitalism has not yet been achieved. Reform has redrawn the political battle lines over regulation and corporate power in the United States; it has not brought a lasting peace.

German Corporate Governance Reform and the Logic of Systemic Change

In contrast to the punctuated and contested course of reform in the United States, in Germany, corporate governance reform and the development of finance capitalism have been the product of deliberate governmental policy and sustained party and interest group negotiations. Securities law and corporate governance reform during the 1990s display the trends of regulatory centralization, the steady expansion of formal prescriptive disclosure and transparency regulation, and the adoption of structural regulation even more clearly than in the American case.[35] Since the mid-1990s, the German government created the country's first federal securities regulator and steadily expanded its jurisdiction, increased the stringency of financial disclosure regulation, consolidated all financial regulators within one powerful agency, passed the first major overhaul of federal company law since 1965, eliminated capital gains taxes in certain circumstances to encourage the development of securities markets, and embarked on a comprehensive and complex reform of corporate governance through government-sponsored codes of best practice buttressed by legislation. In short, politics has transformed the legal terrain of German corporate governance since 1990. A central question raised by these developments is why and how a country widely regarded as the model coordinated market economy would embark on a comprehensive and rapid reform of its corporate governance regime that appropriated many (though certainly not all) elements of a more liberal market-centered financial system.

By the 1990s (and especially after the reunification of East and West Germany), Germany's institutional arrangements appeared no longer capable of sustaining a high-growth, high-wage, and high-employment economy. Economic growth slowed to less than 2 percent annually, and unemployment hovered near 10 percent. Germany was widely regarded as a laggard in reforming its financial markets and corporate governance regime, when compared with other advanced industrial countries, such as the United Kingdom and France.[36] Large segments of the political elite and the German electorate began to lose faith in the social market economy, while casting an envious glance at the booming stock market and high-tech sector in the United States.

In Germany, the reforms necessary to develop a more market-based financial system required a thoroughgoing overhaul of corporate governance law. As in the United States, corporate governance reform revealed the political effects of divisions among business interests and elites. Institutional change on the scale of the 1990s corporate governance reforms entailed fierce political and economic conflict among elites and social groups, not to mention *within* the business community itself. As already seen in the American case, "business" is not a homogenous collective entity.[37] Numerous conflicts and cleavages pit segments of business against one another. In Germany, the most fundamental division was between the financial sector and the rest of business. Corporate governance reform generated conflict between these two groups over corporate rents and the autonomy of corporate managers. While managers of financial firms may be ambivalent about rules that enhance their accountability to shareholders, the financial sector benefits from the development of securities markets that these rules are designed to promote. The managers of the German universal banks generally supported corporate governance reform, often over the opposition of other corporate managers.

A second politically salient division within German business was between large public corporations with international operations and smaller, mostly privately held firms that are far more reliant on domestic capital and product markets. The former have an interest in developing securities markets as part of a global financial strategy. In contrast, smaller and family-owned firms, such as the German *Mittelstand*, prefer to maintain a bank-based system of long-term relational lending. The realignment of interests and alliances among large banks and publicly listed industrial firms fundamentally altered the political terrain in favor of reform and the development of an infrastructure for finance capitalism in Germany.

The substantial and comprehensive transformation of the German corporate governance regime began under the government of Helmut Kohl, with a shift in policy preferences and the formation of an enduring and effective political coalition in favor of financial modernization. The European Union's (EU) single market program of unifying capital and financial services markets contributed to this modernization program. The Christian Democratic Union (CDU) leadership accepted some degree of liberalization and regulatory reform as the price of European unity. In the early 1990s, the Kohl government's policy veered sharply in favor of capital market reform as part of the EU integration program to which it was committed. Internationalists overcame the resistance of the more localized domestic interests of the *Länder* governments, the *Länder*-based and -regulated stock exchanges, and small firms and banks.

Corporate governance reform would not have gone nearly as far without substantial domestic support among powerful interest groups and political actors.[38] Declining profit margins caused by oversaturation and excessive domestic competition in traditional bank lending along with increasing domestic market penetration by British and American investment banks in higher-value-added financial services triggered a shift in business strategies and policy preferences of most large German banks.[39]

By the early 1990s, Germany's universal banks began to see financial system liberalization and the cultivation of new financial services capacities as the route to higher profits, returns to equity, and more lucrative international markets. The elements of the new business model functioned together: more sophisticated market-based financial services would boost bank profits; higher profits would increase returns to equity; these higher returns would raise the price of shares that could then be used to make strategic acquisitions; and acquisitions around the world would vault German banks into the "bulge bracket" of top international financial institutions. This shift in business strategies altered the banks' policy preferences and mobilized their peak association, the powerful and well-organized Association of German Banks (Bundesverband deutscher Banken [BDB]), and its political allies in support of securities market and corporate governance reform. The globalization of finance and financial markets also reinforced domestic political pressures for financial and corporate governance reform, as Frankfurt sought to remain competitive in attracting international capital (and retaining German investment capital).

Corporate managers and the leadership of organized labor were divided over corporate governance reform and the development of finance capitalism. Managers of many large German corporations, such as Daimler Benz and Siemens, backed much of the reform agenda. These firms now had global operations and were increasingly interested in tapping foreign credit and securities markets that were out of reach so long as the German financial and corporate governance model remained insular and dominated by domestic insiders. Union leaders, including those of IG Metall, Germany's dominant industrial union, realized that the German economy had slipped into a structural crisis requiring the adoption of reforms to increase growth by increasing restructuring and competitiveness. Despite some skepticism, labor leaders were largely willing to accept financial system and corporate governance reforms so long as they did not disturb codetermination and collective-bargaining arrangements and did not shift the costs of restructuring onto employees, who would lose their jobs.[40] Shareholders, however, played virtually no political role in the reform of securities and company law—even though these reforms were ostensibly undertaken on their behalf. Quite simply, given Germany's historically undeveloped securities markets and lack of an equity culture of mass shareholding, shareholders were too few and too poorly organized to wield significant influence in policy debates. Reforms were almost an entirely top-down process.

The reform of securities law and regulation quickly became a consensual policy among German political and economic elites, and it has proceeded apace since the mid-1990s. The policy agenda was embodied in the increasing scope, stringency, and centralization of securities regulation. The landmark Second Financial Market Promotion Act of 1994 transformed securities regulation.[41] The act replaced Germany's decentralized system of state-level exchange regulators and largely self-regulating stock exchanges with a centralized federal regulator, the German Federal Securities Supervisory Office (Bundesaufsichtsamt für den Wertpapierhandel [BAWe]). It also transformed substantive securities law. The BAWe's creation represented an extraordinary change in the legal and institutional foundations of German finance. Additional legislation and regulatory rule making steadily expanded the agency's powers and jurisdiction and increased the stringency of disclosure rules and other regulatory standards. From late 1997 through 1998, the Third and Fourth Financial Market Promotion Laws, along with other legislative changes, markedly expanded the agency's role in regulating and policing German securities markets (see Cioffi 2002b). In 2002, the German Parliament further centralized financial regulation by consolidating all financial market and services regulation, including the regulation of securities markets, banking, and insurance. The law folded the BAWe within one massive agency, the German Financial Supervisory Authority (Bundesanstalt für Finanzdienstleistungsaufsicht [BAFin]).[42] With this reform, Germany surpassed the United States in the centralization of financial services regulation.

But consensus was far harder to find when policy debate turned to contentious issues of company law and managerial power within the firm. The Kohl government had balked at more substantial corporate governance reform. Corporate managers nestled within the protective network structure of the German economy are a core constituency of the center-right Christian Democrats and were divided over corporate governance reform. Opposition was particularly intense among owners and managers of many small- and medium-sized firms within the *Mittelstand*, often referred to as the backbone of the German economy. *Mittelstand* firms feared that financial system reforms would favor large publicly traded firms over their need for stable sources of credit. The Free Democratic Party (FDP), Germany's sole liberal party, with historically close relations to major banks and the financial sector, was favorably disposed to financial reform but, as a junior partner in Kohl's CDU-dominated coalition, lacked the leverage to push this agenda.

Instead, the center-left Social Democratic Party took up the corporate governance reform agenda, first in opposition in the Bundestag, then as the governing party in coalition with the Greens under Chancellor Gerhard Schröder from 1998 to 2005. The SPD has used corporate governance reform to adopt economic modernization as the centerpiece of its policy agenda and counter the traditional perception of the CDU as the party of business and economic stewardship.[43] The SPD took advantage of the opportunity presented by economic crisis and shifting interest group preferences to claim a strategic centrist policy position on financial system and corporate governance reform. The party's move to include major financial institutions created the political foundation for corporate governance reform. This placed the conservative CDU-CSU and its neoliberal allies in the Free Democratic Party in a difficult position. They have long relied on the support of business and financial elites, but now these elites and interest groups were splitting over financial market and corporate governance reform. The SPD outflanked the CDU-CSU and cast the conservative alliance as the defender of managerial interests and Germany's economic elite, committed to an economic model that had become outmoded and increasingly dysfunctional. The conservative and liberal parties had to follow the SPD lead—but at a distance to avoid alienating prominent managers who were antagonistic toward neoliberal reforms.

Schröder came to appreciate the reform of capital markets, securities law, and ultimately the entire corporate governance regime as a strategy to improve corporate and macroeconomic performance along with the party's electoral fortunes. Centrist SPD and Green Party leaders confronted resistance from more traditional left-wing members, who were suspicious of Anglo-American "casino capitalism." However, Schröder's centrists were able to overcome these objections from segments of organized labor (particularly the rank and file) and traditionalist left-wing factions.[44] In part, the centrists prevailed because the corporate governance policy agenda appealed to the long-standing ideological antagonism of the German Left toward the insularity, hierarchy, and conservatism of Germany's financial and corporate elite.[45] The Greens, the SPD's coalition partners, revealed themselves to be economic liberals in many respects. Corporate governance reform appealed to the Greens' ideological preferences for economic decentralization and devolution—even as this development necessitated regulatory centralization.

The reform process began even before the Schröder government came to power. In 1998, while still in opposition, the SPD took advantage of shifting policy preferences among interest groups to engineer the first major overhaul of company law since 1965. The Social Democrats played on popular resentment of "bank power" among their core constituents, casting themselves as business-friendly economic problem-solvers (Cioffi 2002b). The proposed legislation put the CDU on the defensive and forced the Kohl government to support a compromise version of the Corporate Control and Transparency Act (KonTraG), which moderated the antibank provisions while retaining more important governance reforms.[46] This had been the SPD leadership's strategy from the start: they could claim credit as modernizing reformers; maintain credibility with their left wing, while painting the CDU as beholden to corporate interests; and still continue to cultivate closer relations with the financial sector.

The KonTraG complemented the prior massive overhaul of securities law by addressing issues of bank power, the function of the supervisory board, auditing, share voting rights, stock options, and litigation rules. The law sought to reduce the power of Germany's universal banks in voting shares and supervisory board representation, while strengthening their disclosure and fiduciary obligations to shareholders.[47] However, in the end, the law's restrictions were measures acceptable to the large banks and fit with their emerging business strategies that diverged from the relational banking model of the past. The KonTraG also uses law to shift information and power to the supervisory board as a means of protecting shareholder interests. More than four years *before* the passage of the Sarbanes-Oxley Act, German law required the supervisory boards of listed firms, rather than the management board, to hire and oversee the external auditor.

An equally important regulatory reform introduced by the KonTraG mandated shareholder democracy through a "one share/one vote rule." This rule prohibited unequal voting rights and abolished voting caps among shares of common stock for the first time. Notwithstanding the general principle of one share/one vote, the KonTraG prohibits the voting of cross-shareholding stakes above 25 percent (a blocking minority under German company law) in supervisory board elections. This provision was designed to prevent managers from wresting control from shareholders by engaging in reciprocal voting with the managers of other firms involved in cross-shareholding relationships. However, by weakening their defensive ownership structures, this new structure of voting rights exposes some German firms to unprecedented threats of hostile takeover—a fact underappreciated at the time but one that would soon prove politically contentious.[48]

The reform of securities markets took a further step in July 2000 when the Schröder government pushed through a major tax bill *(Steuerreform)*, over strenuous opposition from the Christian Democrats, that abolished capital gains taxes on the liquidation of cross-shareholdings. By seeking to encourage the unwinding of cross-shareholdings, the Social Democratic government deliberately chose to undermine the network ownership structure of corporate Germany that insulated German corporations from takeovers. The reform further encouraged the German financial sector to replace its bank-centered model with a market-driven corporate finance and financial services system (see, e.g., Holloway 2001). The reform was simultaneously a generous benefit to the financial services sector (which held a disproportionate share of these cross-shareholdings) and a means to improve the liquidity of domestic stock markets (by increasing the proportion of shares actively traded—the "free float"), part of a longer-term strategy to subject firms to capital market pressures to restructure.

The takeover vulnerability created by these reforms, along with the fear instilled in managers by Vodafone's hostile takeover of Mannesmann in early 2000, triggered a backlash against the further liberalization of German corporate governance.[49] The growing domestic political conflict over takeovers spilled into the EU's attempt to adopt an EU Takeover Directive that would have liberalized Europe's market for corporate control. Realizing that the proposed EU directive would render German firms asymmetrically vulnerable to takeover by foreign corporations with stronger antitakeover defenses, German managers, unionists, conservatives, and left-wing Social Democrats together mobilized to block the directive in the European Parliament. They suc-

ceeded in blocking the directive in July 2001—the first major parliamentary defeat ever suffered by the European Commission in its
pursuit of a single EU market.[50] In 2004, the EU finally adopted a
Takeover Directive, but it is weaker than the 2001 version, due to the
political compromises among the member states over takeover defenses necessary to secure consensus on its passage.[51] A week after the
collapse of the 2001 EU Takeover Directive, the German Bundestag
passed the Securities Acquisition and Takeover Act (the "Takeover
Act"), which replaced a voluntary self-regulatory "codex" widely de-
rided as ignored and ineffective.[52]

For the first time in Germany, takeover bids—defined as offers by
one or more parties acting in concert to acquire 30 percent or more
of a public firm's voting stock—are subject to mandatory procedures
and disclosure rules (under BAFin regulation and supervision) to facilitate and ensure the fairness of bids and takeovers.[53] More controversially, the Takeover Act also contains a general "duty of neutrality"—one of the most contested features of the EU Takeover
Directive—that prohibits the management board from taking action
to frustrate a hostile bid. At the same time, however, the statute *expanded* the latitude of management to adopt defenses in advance and
thereafter to deploy defensive tactics against a hostile takeover[54]—similar to the reallocation of legal authority to the boards of American
corporations during the 1980s.[55]

In contrast to the American case, the German government sought
to maintain the balance of stakeholder power within firm governance.
First, rather than enshrining the primacy of shareholder interests in
law, the Takeover Act provides some protection to employee stakeholders. The act obliges both the offeror and the target's management
to disclose to either the works council or directly to the employees
information concerning the terms of the offer and its implications for
the firm, its employees, and their collective representation. Organized
labor is also entitled to two representatives on the government's
thirteen-member "advisory board" on takeovers created under the
act. Thus, the Takeover Act makes use of and may reinforce the institutions of works council codetermination, even as it expands the
supervisory board's power and liberalizes takeover law.[56] Second, codetermination legislation passed with government support in 2001 mar-
ginally expands the competence of works councils and makes them

somewhat easier to form. The legislation also had a political motivation: the Social Democratic government used it to compensate the
unions and left-wing Social Democrats that had supported or acqui-
esced to the far more important and influential pro-business reforms
of securities, company, tax, takeover, and pension laws.

This careful maintenance of stakeholder power, while seeking to
increase shareholder protections, was displayed again, as the government appointed two successive corporate governance commissions.[57]
The first, in 2001, was drawn from representatives of the major interest groups and charged with drafting a comprehensive code of best
practices in German corporate governance. The commission chair,
Professor Theodor Baums, successfully insisted that the politically explosive subject of codetermination be excluded from the commission's
deliberations on the grounds that it would destroy the consensus required on other important issues. The formation of a second government commission on corporate governance followed the release of the
Baums Commission's report.[58] Starting work in 2002, the standing
Government Commission on Corporate Governance was likewise selected from among the peak associations, major interest groups, re-
spected attorneys, and legal academics. Known as the Cromme Commission, after its chairman Gerhard Cromme (the former chairman of
Thyssen-Krupp), the commission made over 150 wide-ranging recommendations (substantially following the Baums Commission's recommendations); many of them proposed legislative changes that have
defined the policy agenda to date. These proposals include expanding
disclosure and transparency; strengthening the role, obligations, and
independence of corporate boards; improving external auditing; and
modernizing corporate finance rules. Most important was a proposed
"comply or explain" rule (since enacted by Parliament)[59] that requires
firms to comply with the Cromme Commission's Code of Best Practice or else explain in a public disclosure why it had not.

Codetermination was the sole major subject conspicuously absent
from the commission report. Once again, the commission's ground
rules had placed supervisory board and works council codetermination
outside the group's purview. The works council reform and the refusal
of the government's corporate governance commissions to alter existing forms of codetermination suggest the importance of organized
labor as a Social Democratic constituency, its continued power within

the German political economy, and the significance of labor relations issues within the politics of the country's corporate governance reforms. These factors protect and have so far ensured the preservation of Germany's stakeholder model.

At the same time, corporate governance reforms under Schröder's SPD-Green government reflect and confirm two fundamentally important trends in the German political economy. First, they indicate the emergence of an alliance among interest groups and political actors on the center-left to foster development of a market-based finance capitalism. Second, they suggest the increased importance of firm-level corporate governance for economic adjustment and the negotiation of conflicts, as postwar neocorporatist arrangements, sectoral collective bargaining, and the political and economic power of unions weaken and decline in significance. Whether this arrangement represents a durable source of comparative advantage in high-end markets or a disruption of established institutional sources of competitiveness and an unsustainable impediment to much-needed "flexibility" remains an open question.

The stability of the political support for continued corporate governance reform and the development of German finance capitalism also remains uncertain. The Schröder government found itself fighting an increasingly tense two-front war against the CDU and FDP opposition parties but also against the left wing of the SPD and industrial unions hostile to further reforms designed to promote the development of German finance capitalism. In the area of takeover law, the perceived threats to German corporate and socioeconomic interests produced both greater unity among managers and political alliances with labor, so that the opponents of neoliberal reform prevailed. Concern over the social and political legitimacy of the emerging corporate governance regime led the Schröder government and the SPD to maintain the balance of power between shareholders and employees within the firm and even buttress the existing institutions of the stakeholder model. In the area of securities regulation, where these conflicts over economic power did not exist, pro-market regulatory expansion and centralization proceeded with astonishing speed, exceeding that of the United States in some respects.

The conflicts generated by the reform agenda and chronic deadlocks within the established bargaining processes led not only to regulatory centralization but to the political centralization of the policymaking process as well. As seen in the case of successive corporate governance commissions, the SPD government relied increasingly on the use of expert commissions to formulate policies and frame legislative initiatives. The Schröder government appropriated (or manipulated) the existing framework of centralized interest representation by hand-picking representatives from peak organizations as well as experts, academics, and professionals, who were likely to reach a consensus on a given policy area close to the government's own position. As a result, party and interest group realignments and extant institutional arrangements permitted sustained systematic reforms. This interest coordination and policy formation by commission allowed the government to increase its control over policy processes and outcomes by circumventing traditional peak association bargaining that tended to produce impasse rather than consensus.[60] However, this style of governance contains a potentially damaging contradiction: it relies on centralized interest group organizations for representational legitimacy while cutting them out of actual policy discussions. The entrenchment of well-institutionalized peak associations made the use of expert commissions possible, but this (arguably parasitic) form of policymaking ultimately may cause these associations to whither (or defect), as their real influence and representational function wane.

Even more damaging to Schröder and the SPD were the tensions over economic and welfare state reform that opened into splits within the party and the reforms' failure to improve economic conditions. Following Schröder's extremely narrow, come-from-behind victory in the 2002 elections, in which the CDU criticized his tax reforms as a giveaway to corporations and banks, Schröder's political position eroded nationally and within the SPD, as growth slumped and unemployment climbed. The SPD continued to lose subsequent *Länder* elections, the upper house of Parliament came under opposition control, and a leftist block quit the SPD and formed a new Left Party in alliance with the largely eastern ex-Communists to oppose further liberalizing reforms. Major corporate governance reform initiatives came to a virtual halt, as German politics entered into a stalemate that destroyed the government's freedom of maneuver and left its more neoliberal policy tendencies vulnerable to attack from both the pro-labor Left and the managerialist Right.

This politics of stasis came just as Germany experienced a pair of corporate scandals that might have returned corporate governance to the center of reform politics under different political conditions. The first, not really a scandal, was the ouster of Jürgen Schrempp as the head of DaimlerChrysler. He stepped down under intense shareholder pressure after his strategy of turning the company into an integrated global giant destroyed vast amounts of shareholder value and threatened to destroy the Mercedes brand, sending manufacturing quality plummeting. The turning point came when the Deutsche Bank, still a large shareholder and controlling even more proxy votes, withdrew its support for Schrempp. In a harbinger of further unwinding of *Hausbank* relations and illiquid shareholding networks, Deutsche Bank then promptly sold a substantial portion of its stake, as shares rose on the news of Schrempp's firing.

The second scandal involved a complex kickback scheme at Volkswagen run by senior managers, which implicated works council members in bribery. It claimed as one of its casualties Peter Hartz, Volkswagen's personnel director, who was also the architect of Schröder's controversial labor market reforms, including steep reductions in unemployment benefits (known as "Hartz IV"). The scandal was attributed to the insulation of management created by German codetermination—displacing primary responsibility for managerial corruption onto employee representation in corporate governance. However, the potential opening for further pro-shareholder corporate governance reform was abruptly closed by a broader political crisis enveloping Germany.

With his reform agenda and capacity to govern effectively blocked by the CDU majority in the Bundesrat and growing divisions within the SPD, Schröder called for the dissolution of Parliament, only the second since World War II, and an early parliamentary election for September 2005. The early election was a final attempt to rescue his reform agenda and political momentum. Instead, the election merely confirmed the divisions and stalemate within German society. Both the SPD and the CDU fared poorly, with neither party able to form a majority governing coalition with its favored partner (the Greens for SPD and the FDP for the CDU), and with the Left Party easily exceeding the 5 percent threshold to enter Parliament. After weeks of public wrangling, the SPD and CDU agreed to form a "grand coalition" under CDU leadership. Whether this coalition will be able to undertake far-reaching reform, thanks to its broad support base, or will bog down in partisan bickering is anyone's guess. What is clear, however, is that Germany's system of corporate governance has been transformed enormously over the past decade.

3. The Regulatory Politics of Corporate Governance

The State and Corporate Governance Reform

Although theories of path dependence and varieties of capitalism predict the stability of political economic structures and institutional arrangements, developments in the law and policy of corporate governance show that regulatory intervention in the structure and operation of firms and financial markets has undergone remarkable change during the past decade. (See Table 5.2). The narrative accounts of corporate governance reform detailed above highlight a number of important common structural trends in the United States and Germany: regulatory centralization and institutionalization; the displacement of self-regulation by formal prescriptive legal rules; the expansion of market facilitating disclosure and transparency regulation; and the restructuring of the corporate firm through structural regulation. These trends demonstrate not stability but, rather, a significant expansion of state power in the economy and its active reshaping of the private sphere.

Market failures within the financial system and institutional failures at the levels of both the corporate firm and the regulatory state generated pressures for structural change of both the American and German corporate governance regimes. In the United States, a sudden and severe crisis of financial market and corporate integrity, accountability, and legitimacy triggered an equally sudden episode of reform politics. In Germany, persistently poor economic performance of a more systemic nature generated a long-term shift in interest group and political party policy preferences and alignments that produced sustained reform of the financial system and corporate governance regime. In each country, economic difficulties and legitimacy crises disrupted long-settled interests and policy preferences within and among powerful interest groups. Significant changes in the interests

Table 5.2. Modified governance models and the effects of reform, circa 2002

	Law/regulation	Correlated practices
	A. United States: managerial finance capitalism	
Company law	Spread of state antitakeover laws.	Weakening of market for control and increased use of side payments to managers to facilitate corporate mergers and acquisitions.
	Federal law partially displaces state corporate law by requiring greater board oversight, independence, and control over auditing.	Too early to tell effect of most recent reforms.
Securities law	Institutional investors' governance role strengthened by proxy rules and tort reform.	Possible increase in informational asymmetries and conflicts of interest between institutional investors and small shareholders.
	Transparency regulation strengthened by more stringent disclosure, risk management, and certification rules.	Too early to tell medium- to long-term effect of other measures.
	Greater regulatory control over accounting rules.	
Labor law	No change.	Continued weakening of unions and employee interests.
Enforcement mechanisms	"Tort reform" limits shareholder fraud suits, empowers institutional investors as "lead plaintiffs."	Modest impact of tort reform as alternative avenues of litigation are developed.
	Increased SEC civil enforcement actions and Justice Department criminal prosecutions.	Medium- to long-term impact unclear; SEC remains understaffed to fulfill enforcement responsibilities.

	Law/regulation	Correlated practices
	B. Germany: organized finance capitalism	
Company law	Restructuring of supervisory board responsibilities for auditing and risk management. Institution of one share/one vote rule. Takeover law allows some antitakeover defenses.	Strengthens transparency and rights of small shareholders. Bars golden and shares and voting caps—empowers both minority and controlling shareholders. Stakeholder system of representation and governance preserved.
Securities law	Centralization and increased stringency of securities regulation in single federal regulatory agency. Creation and steady strengthening of disclosure rules.	Increased transparency and financial reporting by public firms. Banks increasingly focused on securities markets and financial services.
Labor law	Works council codetermination modestly strengthened by making election easier and expanding consultation rights.	Likely to be marginal.
Enforcement mechanisms	Securities regulator given formal investigative powers. Marginal strengthening of private litigation rules.	Increased regulatory enforcement of securities regulation. No significant change in private litigation (though more suits filed after stock market crash of 2000).

of key economic actors, including corporate managers and financiers, who play pivotal roles in domestic politics and economic life, altered the configuration of interest group politics. Division and/or uncertainty over economic interests and policy preferences within interest groups or their loss of legitimacy under conditions of crisis or scandal prevented them from blocking reform. In this context, center-left governments, looking to cement their credentials as economic modernizers and appeal to the rank and file by attacking business elites, pushed through far-reaching reforms.

Economic crisis and corporate governance reform illustrate the vital and unique importance of state actors in restoring systemic legitimacy—a capacity that private institutions, interest groups, and actors do not possess. State actors within state institutions played a leading role in formulating the new institutional and regulatory structures on which sophisticated modern markets depend. This changed political context opened opportunities for entrepreneurial politicians and political parties and triggered realignments in their strategic positioning and policy agendas. These shifts in interest group policy orientations supplied the preconditions for substantial regulatory reforms and institutional change. They gave political actors greater autonomy in articulating and imposing their own policy preferences and opened politics to new regulatory approaches and mechanisms. Under such circumstances, political actors could more easily rearrange interest group alignments and alliances in order to engineer institutional change and regulatory innovation. Together, these changes in interests, political strategies, and institutional structures challenged the institutional coherence and complementarities that had defined distinct national variants of advanced industrial capitalism and their comparative economic advantages. This implies that the development of finance capitalism, of which corporate governance reform is a part, portends an extraordinary period of political economic transition.

Corporate Governance Reform and National Models of Capitalism

Although corporate governance reforms in the United States and Germany display some important convergent tendencies, they also reveal substantial differences in structural and policy outcomes. In part, these trends indicate convergence on a new paradigm of finance capitalism defined by increasingly market-driven national and international financial systems. Yet this broad rubric of finance capitalism has not erased national differences in institutional structures and economic practices. Indeed, reforms and their systemic significance have varied quite substantially across the country cases.[61]

In the United States, reforms have enhanced corporate governance and securities regulation in ways that are intended to increase the scope and accuracy of financial disclosure, strengthen the role and power of the board of directors, and regulate the activities of accounting firms. However, political forces precluded any expansion of private litigation as a means of enforcement and curtailed a substantial increase in shareholder representation and voice in internal corporate decision making. Instead, the reformed American corporate governance regime relies on enhanced transparency and disclosure regulation, governmental regulatory enforcement, private self-regulatory organizations (SROs) to fashion rules, and independent directors on the board to help enforce them.

While the German reforms dramatically increased the level of disclosure regulation and strengthened the supervisory board, they made use of the preexisting capacities of large universal banks and left codetermination intact. The reformed German governance regime also fits within a political economic structure widely divergent from that of the United States. Sectoral coordination of economic policy through networks of corporate and financial relationships remains prevalent, and organized labor retains much more power and influence than in the United States.

If the German model retains many familiar features, it is clear that recent reforms constitute a significant departure. Sarbanes-Oxley does not signal a fundamental break with the established institutional arrangements and power relations of American corporate governance (as did the New Deal reforms of the 1930s). By contrast, the series of securities, company, and tax law reforms in Germany represent a major episode of institution building and structural change that reflects a fundamental realignment of domestic political forces. The prospect of labor market, pension, and social welfare reforms in Germany further reinforces the impression that the German social market economy is now at a critical juncture that will substantially recast the economy and polity. These differences in the significance of reforms in the

United States and Germany stem from the very different political motivations underlying them and the two countries' different starting points. German elites sought a systematic restructuring of financial and company law, in order to address pressing economic problems afflicting the national economy and the financial sector. American politicians had no such systemic reform agenda and merely sought an immediate response to the political and economic threats posed by pervasive corporate scandals. As the politics of reform differed, so did the policy outcomes and their significance.

In Germany, corporate governance reform raises the possibility of far-reaching and potentially destabilizing structural political economic change. The broader repercussions of economic reform have driven Germany to a burgeoning political crisis over the kind of society and political economic order in which the majority of Germans wish to live. State actors' deployment of new modes and mechanisms of regulation alters the institutional environment that defines the institutional complementarities that link financiers, managers, and employees. It follows that alteration of one element of a complex institutionally complementary system without corresponding changes to the other institutional elements will produce systemic dysfunction and intensified political and economic conflict. The vaunted institutional complementarities of the German model—high-skill, high-wage, high-value-added production financed by supplies of "patient capital"—and the comparative economic advantages they confer may be impaired by the reform of the financial system. The empowerment of financial interests and greater protection of shareholders instituted by the corporate governance reforms of the past decade may generate tensions between shareholders demanding higher short-term returns to capital under this new market-driven financial system and the stabilization of economic relationships and labor's governance role under the remaining institutional framework of the stakeholder model. If these tensions cannot be ameliorated through institutionalized negotiations, they could fuel more pervasive and divisive conflict than Germany has witnessed in decades, from the labor relations system to the corporate boardroom, to the shop floor.

Conflicts triggered by reform could come in two general variants. First, intensifying conflicts may arise between interest groups and the state. Legalistic prescriptive regulation encourages more intensive lobbying of state actors and adversarial regulatory relations than self-regulation and consultative or neocorporatist policymaking.[62] Second, regulatory reform may spark greater conflict among interest groups, as more formal and contentious policy processes mediated by legislatures and state agencies displace consensual, cooperative, and negotiated policymaking. Centralized peak association bargaining tends to screen out zero-sum policy outcomes, but at the expense of slowing or preventing reform. The expansion of regulation and the channeling of lobbying directly toward state actors in place of sectoral and peak association bargaining encourage more pluralistic interest group fragmentation, which makes consensus among interest groups harder to achieve. The paradoxical increase in the centrality of the state in neoliberal regulation allows reforms to proceed by striking divisive political bargains during moments of crisis, setting the stage for new rounds of political and economic conflicts. In both the American and German cases, corporate governance reform favors the displacement of relational governance practices by shorter-term contractual arrangements and arm's length economic transactions that sharpen conflict, reduce trust, and increase economic insecurity.

The incorporation of American-style securities regulation and corporate law principles poses a potentially substantial threat to the consensual German neocorporatist system and social market economy. Over the medium to long term, Germany's adoption of transparency regulation and company law rules favoring shareholder interests may sharpen conflicts among managers, shareholders, employees, and other stakeholders that the postwar political economy ameliorated by institutional design. The corporate firm is becoming a more important institutional forum for the negotiated adjustment of economic conflict, as these functions devolve from the levels of sectoral governance and peak associations. Hence, the most striking difference between the American and German corporate governance regimes—the powerful position of labor and employees within politics and firm governance in Germany, in contrast to the virtual exclusion of employees and labor interests from the American structure—has become an even more distinctive institutional feature of the German political economy.

Of course, the demise or substantial erosion of the German model is by no means a foregone conclusion. Just as the broad contours of Fordist mass production admitted numerous institutional and regulatory variants during the postwar era, so contemporary finance capitalism may take on distinctive national variants. Germany could conceivably fashion an innovative and functional institutional fusion of its stakeholder governance and the new finance capitalism to preserve the comparative advantages of its model of organized capitalism, while appropriating some of the benefits (and escaping some of the damaging effects) of a market-based financial system. Much will depend on the capacities of political leaders to recast traditional bargains so as to accommodate both the imperatives of finance capitalism and the concerns and interests of Germany's powerful stakeholders.

In contrast to the German case, the United States is likely to absorb the regulatory innovations of the Sarbanes-Oxley Act without destabilizing the established market-driven corporate governance system. Reform does not entail a fundamental transformation of the financial system and its relationship to the prevailing liberal market model of the American political economy. As a general matter, shareholders historically have been the beneficiaries of federal legislation, as opposed to managers, labor, or other stakeholder interests. The Sarbanes-Oxley reforms fit comfortably within this historical pattern. The new federal politics of corporate governance reinforces the shareholder-centered character of the American model, rather than diluting it, while retaining the basic institutional features of managerialism within the legal framework of the firm and securities regulation.

However, corporate governance reform, initially undertaken with minimal opposition, is entering a phase of intensifying conflict born of resurgent managerial mobilization and power. Managerial interests and parts of the financial sector mobilized against the Sarbanes-Oxley Act's requirement that public firms develop internal risk management practices, the FASB's proposal to require the expensing of stock options on corporate balance sheets, and the SEC's recently proposed rules giving shareholders more power over the nomination and election of directors. They defeated the last, and arguably the most important, of these reforms. These struggles over corporate governance reform suggest the revival of the long-standing political conflict over American managerialism. The intensity of managerial demands for autonomy from government has long been an important aspect of American exceptionalism. Political battles over managerial autonomy have been important episodes in the historical development of the modern American political economy. From the advent of antitrust law in the late nineteenth century to the reform of labor relations and financial markets during the New Deal of the 1930s, to the legal responses to the hostile takeover wave of the 1980s, managers have fought fiercely against encroachments on their autonomous power.

Yet even if a managerial and conservative backlash against corporate governance reform and Sarbanes-Oxley intensifies, as seems likely, the fragmented and veto-ridden American political system will constrain attempts to deregulate corporate governance. In contrast to the institutions of coordinated capitalism that enabled greater policy consensus and coherence in German corporate governance reform, the institutional structures of American politics fostered rapid crisis-driven reform but also will likely lock most of the reforms in place.

Finally, corporate governance and its reform have increasingly clear cross-national repercussions for political economic development. In the wake of the scandals that laid bare the structural flaws of the American corporate governance regime, the American model appears less efficient, less appealing, hence less influential in informing policy overseas than at any time in decades. International and domestic confidence in American capital markets and corporate governance has plummeted along with the public's regard for federal regulatory efficacy. If the 1990s was the decade of speculative booms and faith in neoliberal financial markets, this decade has ushered in a new and more sober era of regulatory politics. Finance capitalism is already a reality in many respects, both at the national and international levels, but it is less likely than ever to take a single homogenizing form. Instead, this new paradigm of capitalism is developing in nationally distinctive ways, driven by varying political forces and embodied in national regulatory structures generated through national political and legal institutions.

~ 6

From Maternalism to "Employment for All"

State Policies to Promote Women's
Employment across the Affluent Democracies

ANN SHOLA ORLOFF

ACROSS THE RICH, DEVELOPED DEMOCRACIES of
Western Europe, North America, and the Antipodes, we are in the
midst of what might be called a series of "farewells to maternalism."
Countries are moving from a "maternalist" policy model, under which
mothers were expected to stay home full-time with their children and
eschew employment, to a model of "employment for all," under which
women are expected to enter the labor force, as are men (but with the
continuing assumption that they will provide or organize household
care). Indeed, housewifery—that is, the full-time, lifelong devotion of
women to caring and household functions—has become all but extinct
within the Nordic states. The majority of women, including mothers
of young children, are employed, and social policy explicitly supports
women (and, to a much lesser extent, men) as (paid) workers who are
also caregivers. In most countries outside Scandinavia, housewifery is
in serious, possibly terminal, decline, even as the political and cultural
changes involved with women's increasing employment are contested.
For example, in the United States, housewifery is upheld as an ideal
by socially conservative political forces, despite its real decline—to an
extent close to that of the Nordic countries.[1] Support for full-time
caregiving, the hallmark of a number of gendered policy regimes, is
diminishing even in some of its former bastions, such as the United
Kingdom and the Netherlands. Other European countries, especially

in southern Europe, are under pressure, including from the European Union (EU), to bring women into their labor forces.[2]

State authorities are playing an important role in structuring the farewell to maternalism. The state has intervened in two critical ways. First, it has been one of the *causes* of the erosion of the maternalist model, encouraging mothers to enter the workplace and failing to sustain men's (relative) wages sufficiently for most men to support families alone. Second, it has shaped the *character* of this shift. Because state policies toward mothers' employment have varied from one country to the next, so, too, has the nature of the farewell to maternalism.

The maternalist model is in decline for a number of reasons. The notion of sharply distinguished activities for men and women—breadwinning and caregiving, respectively—has been challenged by cultural changes and social movements. Women have entered employment for many reasons, including their own professional or material aspirations. Hard economic times have reinforced this cultural shift. Stagnant wages for manual laborers and high levels of unemployment mean that in many households women's salaries are not simply a luxury or supplement to breadwinning men's steady paychecks. Rather, they are essential to household financial well-being. Increasingly, then, women both want and need to work.

Alongside cultural and economic pressures, the farewell to maternalism has been very much encouraged by states. To some extent, state policies reflect the shift in public outlook, the belief that it is normal and appropriate for mothers to be in the labor force. But state authorities are also motivated by more mundane considerations. With birthrates well below replacement levels and the baby-boom generation approaching retirement, the current surplus of labor is slated to turn into a shortage. Workers will be needed not only to staff the factories and offices but also to cover the substantial pension obligations owed to the swelling cohort of retirees. Consequently, new sources of labor will have to be found, and the principal alternative to women, immigrants, elicits considerable political opposition, particularly in Europe.

State authorities are combining carrots and sticks to encourage mothers to enter the labor market. The main stick, epitomized by the US welfare reform of 1996 eliminating the guarantee of support for

(poor) lone mothers, has been the removal of state-sponsored alternatives to employment. The US approach is echoed in Europe (albeit
generally in a somewhat milder fashion) by so-called labor market
activation policies that pressure those outside the labor force—
whether unemployed youths, the long-term unemployed, the disabled,
older workers, or mothers—to take some kind of job. The explicitly
gender-differentiated maternalist logic of politically recognizing, and
financially supporting, mothers' caregiving is being displaced by ostensibly gender-neutral notions of recognizing and supporting only
economically "active" adults, with support to care taking the form of
temporary leaves to workers or public services for the care of their
dependents. "Maternalist" arguments are on the decline among advocates of women's equality, and political claims based on mothering
are meeting less popular and elite approval. This is not to say that
"motherhood" has lost its cultural support and resonances but simply
that making claims on the state for resources and recognition on the
basis of motherhood, or care, is more difficult and, in some cases,
politically impossible.

State authorities are marshalling inducements as well as coercive
measures to increase women's labor market participation. The end of
support for women's full-time caregiving has been accompanied by
new state initiatives to make women's employment more attractive.
Tax and benefit reforms have increased the share of earnings that
employed mothers can retain. Governments in Europe have been
steadily increasing public and subsidized child care, in effect, socializing the costs of care that has traditionally been provided by women
without pay. There has been some movement toward socializing the
costs of elderly care as well. At a time of cutbacks in many social
programs, policies to support women's employment stand out as an
area of new and often expensive state commitments. Thus, it is not
just changing cultural attitudes that are eroding full-time housewifery
but also conscious social engineering. The farewell to maternalism is,
to a considerable extent, state constructed.

It is also state mediated, which points to the second central claim
of this chapter. There is a contentious debate among US feminist
scholars regarding the implications of the farewell to maternalism.
Critics, often seizing on the US welfare reform, see mothers being

deprived of public supports for caregiving and bullied into accepting low-wage, dead-end jobs that fail to lift them out of poverty. Supporters, by contrast, note that paid employment can be an important source of women's autonomy, reducing dependence on the state or a breadwinning man, and can also provide a sense of fulfillment and empowerment (see, e.g., Schultz 2000). They charge that critics too often ignore the experience of other countries, where encouraging women's employment has not been accompanied by the elimination of social rights but rather by expanded public services—in other words, where the "farewell to maternalism" has not been such an unhappy one.

This chapter advances an alternative understanding. Whether the farewell to maternalism and transition to "employment for all" is a development that is "women friendly" depends very much on how state support for caregiving activities and employment is configured. Of course, "women friendliness" is not an uncontested concept; my own preferred understanding rests on an understanding of women's equality movements as advocates of policies that would undergird women's capacity to form and maintain autonomous households (Orloff 1993a), which has sometimes dovetailed with policies that promote women's employment, but not always. The policies deployed across the affluent democracies vary tremendously, meaning that mothers are being integrated into the labor market in very different ways in different countries. Moreover, the implications of public policies are not the same for all categories of women workers.

This chapter focuses on the US and Swedish cases. Sweden has long been celebrated as the archetype "women-friendly" welfare state, to use the term coined by Helga Hernes (1987). The state provides low-cost, quality child care, paid parental leave, and reduced hours for parents, facilitating the reconciliation of family and household duties; women are employed at very high levels, often in the public sector, and paid good wages; and, as Figure 6.1 reveals, child poverty is quite low, even for single-parent households. On the downside, Swedish labor markets are among the most gender segregated in the world, with women finding it difficult to move into more fulfilling and highly paid occupations in the private sector. Although Swedish state authorities have done more to induce men to assume caregiving re-

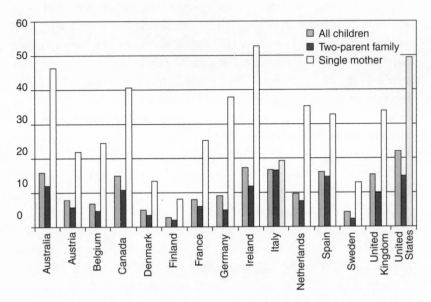

Figure 6.1. Poverty rates for children by family type. *Source:* http://www
.lisproject.org/keyfigures.htm. All figures from 2000, except Australia (1994),
Denmark (1992), France (1994), Netherlands (1999), and United Kingdom
(1999). Estimated data for single mother poverty rates in Austria, Belgium,
Finland, and Ireland. Estimated data for two-parent family in Belgium.

sponsibilities than their counterparts in most other countries, it has
been difficult to induce men to take on substantial caregiving responsibilities, and the gender division of labor remains strong (Hobson
2002).

US social policy lies at the opposite end of the spectrum from
Sweden, and nowhere more so than with regard to working mothers.
The state does not provide child care (except for some of the very
poor) or paid parental leave, nor does the state sector employ large
numbers of women. When it comes to balancing jobs and family,
working mothers are left largely to fend for themselves, and as Figure
6.1 indicates, child poverty rates are among the highest in the developed world. Social policy is not the only state activity that affects
mothers' employment, however. In the judicial arena, far-reaching antidiscrimination laws, affirmative action programs, and hefty jury ver-
dicts against employers convicted of sexual harassment have broken

(or at least begun to crack) glass ceilings. American women occupy professional and managerial positions in much greater numbers than their Swedish (or other European) counterparts. US tax policy, notably the expansion of the Earned Income Tax Credit (EITC), has greatly improved the returns to paid employment at the low end of the labor market. Finally, US immigration and labor market policies have created a large pool of household and child-care workers, making privately provided care affordable for a substantial proportion of the population. The result is a more heterogeneous situation than in Sweden, with some mothers enjoying prestigious, high-paying careers and purchasing the best household help that money can buy, while other women find themselves struggling to get by and relying on unregulated, often marginal child-care arrangements. One can certainly debate the relative merits of the Swedish and American approaches; what is beyond debate is that the farewell to maternalism in both countries has been structured in distinctive ways by state policy, much of it of recent origin.

This chapter analyzes the state-mediated farewell to maternalism across the affluent democracies. Section 1 examines the features of the maternalist model—the predominant gendered divisions of labor and patterns of family and household formation that they depended on and reinforced, for it is against these backdrops that current changes are occurring. In Section 2, I describe the social forces that have eroded the maternalist model. I then take up the policies and politics behind this shift. Section 3 analyzes the Swedish Social Democratic model, emphasizing public services as partially replacing familial care and providing women with employment. Section 4 illuminates the liberal US approach, where civil rights connected to women's employment are joined with market-provided services to partially replace mothers' care. Again, services provide women with employment, but outside the state sector. Section 5 briefly assesses the situation in the "conservative continental" or "Christian Democratic" countries of Western Europe, which have traditionally raised the greatest obstacles to women's employment. Of particular interest is the Netherlands, where women's employment has increased from quite low levels and where politicians have articulated an ideal in which men and women would combine part-time employment and care work, supported by public services. (Dutch realities are less inspiring, as many women but few men combine household duties with part-time jobs.) Finally, I conclude in Section 6 with some reflections on possible future developments, notably the question of whether it might be possible to join higher levels of women's employment with less displacement of family care to either market or state services.

1. Maternalism as Political Configuration

The origins of modern welfare provision are to be found in the late nineteenth and early twentieth centuries, when across most countries in the industrializing West there emerged new forms of social protection for citizens against a range of different problems of income interruption and economic dependency—old age pensions or insurance, unemployment compensation, benefits for widowed mothers, and the like. These replaced (only partially at first) the old systems of poor relief, which had stood as the sole protection against utter destitution, but at the price of citizenship rights and social respectability. During this formative era, alliances of working-class movements and intellectual, political, and reform elites—made up overwhelmingly of men— advocated programs that would give public benefits to breadwinning men, so that they could continue to support their families financially, even when they lost their jobs or wage-earning capacities, in ways that preserved respectability and political rights (Orloff 1993b). Theda Skocpol (1992) has called these programs "paternalist," both because they supported fathers and because they involved paternalistic relations between elites and the recipients of government aid. In addition, in what modern scholars call a "maternalist" strand of welfare politics, reformers (mainly women) helped to establish state support to women in their roles as mothers as well as protective labor legislation for women workers and infant and maternal health programs (see, e.g., Koven and Michel 1993; Pedersen 1993; Skocpol 1992). In some countries, politicians, administrators, employers, or church leaders supported these initiatives because they dovetailed with pro-natalist agendas or their desire to employ mothers. Indeed, all modern systems of social provision and regulation were built upon a gendered division of labor in which women were mothers, wives, caregivers, and domestic workers—even if they also worked for pay—while men supported families economically, almost always through paid labor. If women were not always housewives, they almost always cut back on or in some way made accommodations in formal economic activities in order to carry out their responsibilities for caregiving.

This gendered division of labor and the ideologies of gender difference that accompanied it were accepted by almost all political actors in the early part of the twentieth century, including reform-minded women concerned about women's poverty or the specific needs of mothers who were also employed. Inspired by a maternalist vision, women reformers wanted to offer social support and political valorization to women in their roles as mothers, in some cases as full-time homemakers but in other cases as workers with maternal responsibilities. "Maternalism" may be defined as "ideologies and discourses which exalted women's capacity to mother and applied to society as a whole the values they attached to that role: care, nurturance and morality" (Koven and Michel 1993: 4; see also Bock and Thane 1991; Skocpol 1992).[3] Women reformers—like their male counterparts—almost all shared the view that the gendered division of labor was both natural and good and supported the development of gender-specific legislation and programs. However, this did not necessarily imply agreement about other aspects of gender relations, particularly the family wage for men's and women's economic dependency, or the idea that women should not participate in the public sphere.[4] Maternalists made arguments for gender justice: women should be recognized and compensated by the state for their unique service to society—through maternity and childrearing—as men were for their service in war and industry (Orloff 1991, 1993a). And women did enter the political sphere; indeed, they entered it largely on the basis of "difference," claiming their work as mothers gave them unique capacities for developing state policies that would safeguard mothers and children (Koven and Michel 1993; Lake 1992; Pedersen 1993; Skocpol 1992). Thus, maternalist reformers' claims on the state were for a kind of "equality in difference" and constituted a challenge to patriarchal ideologies and practices that linked women's "difference" to their inequality and their exclusion from politics. In essence, women reformers took part in the discourse of gender difference but attempted (with very limited success) to rearticulate gender difference to equal citizenship claims.

Nowhere did the programs of modern social protection instituted in the late nineteenth and early twentieth centuries, which have, after considerable expansion and restructuring, come to be called "welfare states," embody feminist ideals of women's individuality and independence. Instead, gender difference was linked to gender inequality and women's lack of independence. Policymakers responded to the gendered demands of workingmen to, in essence, secure their core masculine status of breadwinner, either through direct supports to fathers and husbands in the form of "family wage" prerogatives and labor market or tax advantages or through ostensibly more universal support to workers, who were predominantly men. Men's employment sustained a private economy of caregiving, which begat women's economic dependence, echoed in systems of social provision in derived benefits (i.e., benefits that depend on husbands' contributions). The most visionary reformers called for universal motherhood endowments for full-time caregivers or generous family allowances coupled with equal pay for men and women, as proposed by reformers such as Eleanor Rathbone (Pedersen 2004; see also Lake 1992). In the absence of such measures, women's caregiving in a capitalist wage economy created economic dependence on men and their disproportionate vulnerability to poverty when outside marriage (for theoretical discussion of the situation of lone mothers, see, e.g., Hobson 1990, 1994; J. Lewis 1997a). Social provision for women was a "backup" to the family wage system, almost always ungenerous, rather than a system of supports for the economic independence of women and their freedom to make choices about care.

Gender difference and inequality were institutionalized in the systems of all countries, although more deeply in some than others. But everywhere there were different expectations about paid work versus caregiving, rules and benefits for men—wage workers and individuals—and for women—caregivers and family members. At the systemic level, gender relations were reflected in a gendered dualism within all systems of social provision: some programs dealt with risks of income interruption associated with the labor market, such as unemployment and retirement, whereas others targeted the risks of economically dependent family members associated with family dissolution, such as widowhood (Nelson 1990; Fraser 1989; O'Connor, Orloff, and Shaver 1999: ch. 4). The family-related programs were used almost exclusively by women and were usually inferior to programs targeted at paid workers, mainly men. In addition, programs were characterized by what we would now call sex discrimination; for example, women, even when paid workers, did not have the same pension rights as men (Brocas, Cailloux, and Oget 1990). There is nothing novel in the fact that contemporary state policies and practices shape gender relations, although there are clear differences across countries and eras.

I want to call attention to the fact of cross-national policy variation from the very origins of these systems, within an overall gender order that might appear quite similar. These differences stemmed perhaps less from what women reformers, now called "maternalists," demanded, than what they were able to achieve within political fields dominated by generally more powerful organizations of reformist elite men or workingmen. Some systems developed a more maternalist cast than others, which might be better described as "paternalist," the difference turning on whether women could make direct claims on the basis of their caregiving or had to depend on indirect claims as wives in systems geared to the risks and needs of workingmen. Systems also differed in the extent to which women's employment was accommodated within an overall system of support to women's childbearing and caregiving. Some countries—the United Kingdom is a prime example—developed policies that reinforced gender difference and supported breadwinning husband–caregiving mother families. Other countries, such as France—still operating on the principle of gender difference and assuming that women would remain responsible for caregiving and domestic work—developed policies that allowed for some accommodation of women's employment (Jenson 1986; Pedersen 1993; Koven and Michel 1993). As Susan Pedersen (1993: 106) explains in her masterful comparative analysis of interwar family policy, given strong capital and a strong state in France, strong labor and a slightly less powerful state in Britain, "the French state ceded authority over women workers to those who wanted to exploit them, the British state to those who wanted to exclude them [from the labor force]." These institutionalized differences in policy approaches to gender, labor market, and family have been significant in shaping later policy developments, especially in constituting distinctive gendered political groups, identities, and goals.

World War II was critical, of course, in many processes later implicated in the shifts around women's employment, mobilizing women economically, politically, and militarily. And it is perhaps not too obvious to remind ourselves that the defeat of fascism removed from the developed world a reactionary gender program that subordinated women's childbearing and care work to murderous state projects (see, e.g., Bock 1991). In the period following World War II, partially in political repayment for the wartime sacrifices of the popular classes, the programs and policies of the "formative years of the welfare state" were expanded and reformed in the direction of broader coverage. Yet the gendered assumptions and policy arrangements were, if anything, strengthened—even as the gendered division of labor itself was changing, as more and more women entered the labor force. More generous public retirement, disability, unemployment, and health insurance, along with expanded family allowances, improved provision for wage earners and their families. In the United States, while some public programs were expanded, there was also significant provision for working-class men in generous veterans' benefits and "private" fringe benefits negotiated by unions, which have turned out to be more vulnerable to erosion than comparable programs of the welfare state proper (Orloff 2003).

The decades after World War II are now seen, correctly I think, as the heyday of the breadwinner/caregiver family. Working-class men's wages allowed many more to support stay-at-home wives, who provided care to children and others, than ever before. In the 1960s, women's labor force participation levels were considerably lower than today and showed less cross-national variation. Notably, levels in the Nordic countries and North America—now among the highest—did not stand out (Daly 2000). There was something of a consensus across the Western democracies around the need to support mothers' caregiving and to lessen their burden of wage earning, and social policy institutionalized that consensus. State benefits and services provided important supports to these families, on gendered terms—men as individual citizens and workers, women as caregivers and dependents. Many (certainly not all) women received economic protection, and their caregiving was enabled, but at the price of their autonomy. While most women's care was supported indirectly, programs of provision for solo mothers involved some states in directly supporting women's care. An unintended consequence of such "backup" programs, in combination with better employment opportunities, has been to enhance women's bargaining positions within households and to ease women's exit from marriage and allow for the formation of independent households.

2. Transformations of Labor, Family Policy, and Social Politics since the 1960s

"Maternalist" premises, programs, and policies were questioned, although not necessarily repudiated, with women's greater participation in the labor force and the rise of second-wave feminism—the women's movements of the late 1960s and 1970s, called the "second wave" as they built upon the achievements of the "first wave," suffragists and other early women's rights campaigners. Indeed, one important strand of feminist thinking was concerned with valorizing traditionally feminine activities, including care work, and claiming their equivalence— if not superiority—to masculine ones. Among the developed democracies, cross-national differences in policy approaches to women's employment, associated with but not fully determined by different approaches to gender equality among feminists, became more significant in and after the 1960s. Some countries—principally in continental Europe—offered additional supports to the breadwinner-caregiver household and developed more protections for women's caregiving but made little effort to help women work for pay, even as more, particularly among younger cohorts, entered the labor force. At the same time, other countries repealed discriminatory employment, social security, and family laws and explicitly attempted to increase women's employment or to enhance its quality. Both Social Democratic and liberal policy regimes—or Nordic and predominantly Anglophone countries, if you prefer to avoid the terminology of welfare regimes— have moved decisively away from maternalist policy premises. As Figure 6.2 reveals, these countries have relatively high rates of women's employment as compared to other affluent democracies, but are also notable for the levels of employment achieved by mothers. Yet liberal and Social Democratic policy approaches arose from different political circumstances and imply different dilemmas for feminists and others concerned with the quality of care, gender equality, and economic sustainability.

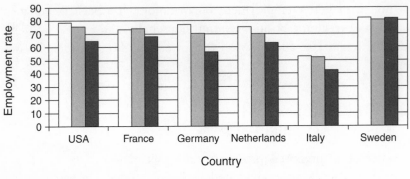

Figure 6.2. Women's employment and children, 2000. *Source:* OECD, Employment Outlook, 2001, Table 2.4, p. 77. Figures from 2000, except USA, from 1999. "Employment" constitutes both full- and part-time employment.

Since the 1990s, mothers' employment is receiving renewed attention, as a confluence of forces—declining fertility, population aging, crises in pension funding, gender equality movements, among others—combine to destabilize earlier gender, family, and work arrangements. The European Union has set new, higher targets for women's employment. It is especially countries with a "strong male breadwinner model," to use the terminology of Jane Lewis (1992, 1997b), and, often, well-developed maternalist policies as well (e.g., in the Netherlands; see Knijn 1994), that have come under pressure. The breadwinner model and major elements of maternalism have been disclaimed in some key political and policy arenas in the Netherlands, and expanding women's employment has been an important part of "the Dutch miracle" (Visser and Hemerijck 1997). Part-time work has been critical here, but so far this presents problems for gender equality in income and employment opportunities (Knijn 1998). In a number of other European countries, employment among younger cohorts of women has risen but is coupled with record-low fertility, for employment remains on the masculine model and is incompatible with childbearing and child rearing. Thus, to the extent that countries cannot break from "strong male breadwinner" patterns, there will be deep problems of social sustainability (very low fertility) or continuing gender inequality. The politics of breaking from maternalism and the breadwinner model are therefore of great interest, both theoretically and practically. In the following pages, I discuss the "adjos" and "farewells" that have already occurred in Sweden and those that are well under way in the United States. In both countries, state authorities have deployed an array of new policies to move mothers into the workplace but have done so in very different ways.

3. Sweden, the "Dual-Earner" Model, and Social Democratic Feminism

The Swedish "dual-earner" or "citizen-worker-carer" policy approach is for many scholars the paradigmatic case of state support for women's and especially mothers' employment, the model to which other states wishing to enhance women's work and gender equality should aspire (see, e.g., discussions of the "women-friendliness" [or lack thereof] of Nordic welfare states in Borchorst 1994 and Borchorst and Siim 2002; Hernes [1987] first coined the term). This dual-earner model has been the product to a considerable extent of conscious social engineering. In the 1960s, Swedish authorities, facing a labor shortage and wanting to limit the inflow of immigrant ("guest") workers, introduced a series of reforms designed to encourage women to enter the labor force. Among the most important such policies were low-cost, quality child care; paid parental leave; flexible, part-time employment rules; and individualized taxation (the elimination of the so-called marriage penalty). Moreover, as the Social Democrats expanded public services, many women found reasonably attractive job opportunities in health care, child care, education, social work, and elderly care.

Today, the vast majority of Swedish women are employed most of their lives, as are men, and these high employment levels are also found among the mothers of young children. Policy explicitly supports mothers' (and, more generally, women's) employment, which is viewed as a cornerstone of gender equality. Housewifery and full-time mothering are all but extinct. As in most countries, leave provisions and other care-linked policies are formally gender neutral, but, more un-

usually, the Swedes have gone beyond formal gender neutrality to actively promote men's care.

While both men and women are earners in Sweden, gender difference has hardly disappeared, and women's caregiving is still central to
social policy. Women manage employment alongside familial activities
by virtue of the extensive state services that take over significant portions of care work and the maternity and parental leaves that allow
"time to care." The policy logic underpinning most state initiatives
assumes a gendered division of labor modified from the breadwinner/
housewife models that predominate elsewhere but that nonetheless
features significant gender differentiation. Women and men have similar (high) rates of participation, but substantial numbers of women
work in part-time jobs. However, these jobs tend to be "good jobs,"
offering reasonable pay; indeed, overall earnings gaps are relatively
low (Borchorst 1994; Borchorst and Siim 2002). Younger women are
increasingly working full-time (Daly 2000: 474), but they continue to
take advantage of maternity and parental leave provisions to a far
greater extent than do men (Jenson 1997; L. Haas 1992). Men are still
principally citizen-workers, whereas women, though employed most
of their lives, remain linked to care.

Women not only bear children but, according to extensive studies
of the domestic division of labor, are still the principal caregivers.
Women are also linked to care in that the overwhelming majority of
public employees in care services are women. Thus, the public-private
employment difference is a gendered one that contributes to Sweden's
relatively high occupational sex segregation (Charles and Grusky
2004). Women are concentrated in public employment, whereas men
have a wider range of jobs and predominate in the private sector. The
fact that women workers are caregivers to a greater extent than are
men means that they face barriers in occupations traditionally held by
men, including positions of authority. There is a greater "authority
gap" between men and women in Sweden than in the United States,
as well as greater difficulties in accessing the highest levels of management (Wright, Baxter, and Birkeland 1995; Baxter and Wright
2000).

To translate into the terms I have been using, Sweden can be seen
as already having bid farewell to "maternalism," if that term is understood as implying that women's political claims are based principally

on motherhood. Things become slightly more complex if we think about policy supports for women's caregiving, for here the Swedish system is certainly directed toward this aim. Jane Lewis and Gertrude Åstrom (1992) argue that Swedish women first established their citizenship claims on the basis of "sameness"—their status as workers— then layered on claims based on "difference," or care. I would put it slightly differently: Sweden succeeded in developing policies that foster women's employment by conceding to gender difference, making women's—but not necessarily men's—employment compatible with parenthood and caregiving. What were the politics that led to the creation of these policies?

Analysts in the power resources or welfare regime traditions understand the patterns and policies that have led to high levels of women's employment as products of the long tenure of the Social Democratic Party. Mary Ruggie's (1984) classic study of Swedish and British policy on women's employment and state policy argued that parties and the state were more significant for women's employment outcomes than specific feminist mobilization: "for the successful achievement of their employment pursuits, women must be incorporated into labor, and labor must be incorporated into the governing coalition" (M. Ruggie 1984: 346). This perspective is more recently echoed in work using a power resources framework, in which the overall configuration of state-labor-capital is the key to the character of gender policy regimes (Korpi 2000; Huber and Stephens 2000, 2001; Esping-Andersen 1999, 2002). Policies supportive of mothers' employment are seen as dependent on left governments willing to use public power to provide "defamilializing" services (that is, state services, such as child care, that substitute for women's household labor), which both allow women to seek employment and directly employ many women (see also Gornick and Meyers 2003).

Sweden may indeed be the best case for making the "Social Democratic" argument, as both organized labor and the Social Democratic Party have been more ambitious with respect to promoting gender equality via women's employment and state services than almost any other such organizations. (Less recognized is the fact that political forces dedicated to promoting women's employment and providing care services have been able to call on well-developed administrative capacities; more noticeable lately, given now-chronic fiscal constraints, is the fact that fiscal capacities during the formative years of the dual-earner regime were extensive.) But far from being a straightforward development on the basis of political commitments to equality "in general," where the Swedish Social Democrats have come to embrace some of the goals of women's equality, including support for women's employment, it has typically been because women's groups within or outside the party organization have pressed such claims (M. Ruggie 1988; Hobson and Lindholm 1997; Hobson 1998).[5] Gender analysts have pushed beyond the "dual-earner" label to reveal the continuation of gender difference and inequality and the gendered patterns of politics. They have investigated women's agency as well as men's gendered interests, often reflected in positions of trade unions and political parties (Bergqvist 1999).

Swedish feminists have generally supported Social Democratic initiatives around women's employment. Indeed, in contrast to some other countries where full-time mothering was exalted above and beyond employment, women's equality advocates have mostly been favorable toward women's employment. Until the 1960s, women's employment was understood as coming in sequence with caregiving activities, but feminists then sought policies, that would allow women, and later men, to combine caregiving activities and employment. Swedish citizenship claims and rights have long been linked politically and discursively to employment, and not only for feminists. For example, we see early feminist efforts to preserve women's right to work and to be mothers during the Depression (Hobson 1993) or later efforts to give substantive support to such rights by expanding childcare services and parental leaves. Swedish women's mobilizing has been a variety of institutional feminism—that is, mobilization within existing organizations, and thus distinct from the autonomous feminist groups seen in the United States or Germany but no less effective or feminist for that (Hobson and Lindholm 1997; Edwards 1991; Siim 1994; Bergqvist 1999). The approach of Scandinavian women has reflected the availability of allies in the labor movement and Social Democratic Party, as well as the way citizenship has been politically constructed.

Policies supporting mothers' employment have a fairly long history in Sweden. In the first decades of the twentieth century, countries such as the United Kingdom, Germany, and the Netherlands established strong social provisions for breadwinning men (and, to a lesser extent, for caregiving women) as well as labor regulations that hindered women's or married mothers' employment in most sectors, while guaranteeing the privileges of (most) men in the workplace. (The United States, as will be discussed below, developed weak provisions for caregiving women, although this was more than what was available for working-aged breadwinning men; in the labor market, however, "maternalism" and the breadwinner ideal translated into "protective" legislation that was a mechanism for excluding women from many kinds of paid work [see, e.g., Hobson 1993; Orloff 2003].) By contrast, Sweden established universal citizenship provisions, that is, entitlements that were not formally based on employment (although, rhetorically, provision was seen to support worthy worker-citizens) and were therefore less structurally favorable to workers, predominantly men. Married women were also guaranteed a right to work, even though a comparably small proportion of women were actually in the labor force (Hobson 1993). Yet one could argue that this was still a variety of maternalism, for an important part of the impulse to give married women the right to work stemmed from concerns about their fertility. Then, as now, there was some concern that if forced to choose between paid work and childbearing, women might opt for employment.

Most students of Swedish (and Nordic) social policy developments agree that the distinctive Social Democratic model emerged only after World War II (even given favorable precedents established in the 1930s). Enjoying an unprecedentedly long tenure, well-developed state administrative and fiscal capacities, and a favorable macroeconomic environment, the Social Democratic Party fashioned extensive, egalitarian, universalistic social provision; active labor market policies; and a commitment to full employment, "solidarity wages," and a labor market regulated by bargains between unions and employers' associations (Swenson 2002; Huber and Stephens 2001). All of these have proved especially beneficial to lower-paid, blue-collar wage earners. This also turned out to be a set of policy orientations quite favorable to women workers, for they tend to cluster at the bottom end of pay scales and occupational hierarchies.

The extensive development of policies supportive of mothers' employment can be dated to the mid-1960s through early 1970s, that is,

on the basis of the universalistic Social Democratic foundation laid
down in the postwar years (for a good overview of these developments,
see Huber and Stephens 2000; Bergqvist 1999; Hobson 1998). First,
decisions were made to expand women's labor supply, rather than
bring in guest workers to cope with labor shortages, as in the continental European countries, or to ease immigration policies, as in the
United States. Shortly afterward, the Swedes developed policies allowing for what would now be called "work-family reconciliation":
publicly provided child-care services, parental leave, and shortened
hours for parents. Also significant in altering economic incentives for
wives' work was the shift from joint to individual taxation. Most recently, concerns about gender equality have moved toward enhancing
men's involvement in parenting, beyond the gender-neutral citizenship
right to take parental leave to positive incentives for men's participation (Hobson 2002; Leira 2002). Exemplary is the so-called daddy
month, a policy in which one month of parental leave is reserved for
fathers and is lost to families if not used by the father.

These policies have become the mainstays of the Swedish dual-
earner model and have been expanded or made more generous several
times since their initiation, with brief setbacks during the economic
crisis of the early 1990s and the short tenure of the bourgeois government (1991–1994). In the former case, the premise of supporting
mothers' employment was not repudiated, but the generosity of policies was, for example, when replacement rates for leaves were reduced. In the latter, there was an attempt to change the premises of
social policy by introducing the notion of "choice" around mothers'
employment, with the government offering cash allowances as a substitute for public services. This initiative was ultimately rolled back by
the succeeding Social Democratic government. The incident is notable for what it says about the political landscape of gender and employment policies in Sweden: opponents of the dual-earner model
have been relatively weak. There is no significant religious antifeminist
political force. To the extent that employers have disagreed with the
Social Democratic approach, it has been mainly in terms of preferring
greater privatization of services and liberalization of labor markets.
This has contributed to gendered partisan differences, as analysts have
noted an increasing advantage for the Social Democrats among
women, who have mobilized to defend and extend the social policies
and public services allowing mothers' employment on favorable terms.

Moreover, within the Social Democratic and union camps, there have been disputes between men and women around care. For example, women's advocates backed a universal six-hour day, conducive to all workers participating in household work, while trade union men preferred to demand extra vacation time—and prevailed. These struggles continue.

One may identify two main challenges to the Swedish model. First, there are ongoing difficulties having to do with government finances and the productivity of the system (Esping-Andersen 1999). The system is expensive, and various forces, including "globalizing" economic trends and developments within the European Union, produce pressures to cut back or keep public expenditures low. Second, there are challenges to further progress toward achieving gender equality (however defined) (Borchorst and Siim 2002). Analysts such as Evelyne Huber and John Stephens (2000) have identified a virtuous circle in Swedish developments, as women's employment has been facilitated by leaves and public services, while these services in turn provide employment to more women, who then demand further policy supports for employment (see Nyberg 2000 for an alternative view of the dynamics by which Swedish social policy supporting mothers' employment emerged). Yet within this circle, one also sees continuing gender differentiation, as women are associated with caregiving, and masculinity may be defined in opposition to care. Some may believe that continuing gender difference and women's "compulsory altruism" with respect to care work are compatible with gender equality, or even with greater occupational opportunities for women in private employment and positions of authority. I am not so sure (see also Fraser 1994).

Can Sweden serve as an example for others? Certainly, many scholars have assumed that the Swedish model is the only one that can lead toward gender equality, even while acknowledging that Sweden has had a particularly favorable political context for the development of policies to support dual-earner households. But even if the lineup of women's movements, their potential allies, and antagonists were to change elsewhere in a more favorable direction—as perhaps it will do, as more younger women gain education and enter employment—one must admit that times have irrevocably changed from the "golden age" of welfare development (prior to fiscal constraint), when the basics of the Swedish model were laid down.

But before we can ask whether there is a model better suited to our era of resurgent liberalism, we must agree that such a model could even exist. And this possibility is blocked for many analysts by what I would call a bad case of Swedophilia, by which I mean the problem of making "distance from Stockholm" (politically and geographically) the measure of policy progressiveness. Applied to the question of women's employment, it is reflected in assumptions that the Social Democratic approach of expanding the public service sector is the only way to increase women's employment and is also the normatively preferable approach to gender equality. In particular, the English-speaking, or "liberal," countries are poorly understood—they are either ignored or seen as simply leaving women's employment to the market, as if women's equality projects have had no impact on policies for enhancing women's employment. This can be seen, for example, in analyses that group Japan or Switzerland with the United States, Canada, the United Kingdom, and Australia as having "market-oriented" gender policies (e.g., Korpi 2000). Anyone familiar with the history of feminist movements and state policies would be shocked to find countries with explicit commitments to equal opportunities, body rights, and civil rights and some record of success—the (mainly) Anglophone countries—equated with countries that have been such all-around laggards on women's rights, simply because none of them has gone the Nordic route of expanding public services. The Swedophile approach leaves us ill-equipped to understand cases where policy instruments other than public services undergird high levels of women's employment, and political actors seek to achieve equality by other means.

4.   The United States, "Employment for All," and Liberal Feminism

The United States is well known for the significant impact feminism has had on popular culture, intellectual trends, political life, access to traditionally masculine occupations, and intimate relationships. However, until fairly recently, the United States was not recognized among scholars of the welfare state as a case of high women's employment levels, nor has the role of state social policies been prominent in studies of US women's employment. This reflects in part the analytic predominance of the Social Democratic approach and the paradigmatic status of the Swedish case. As we all know, "there is no Socialism in America"—or even Social Democrats—and the United States has nothing like the array of services and leaves provided to working parents in Sweden. Meanwhile, flourishing equal opportunity feminisms and their legal and regulatory victories, which have been significant in expanding women's employment, have fallen outside the analytic boundaries of most scholarship on gender and welfare.

Yet of late, the heightened levels of women's and especially mothers' employment in the United States—considerably higher than most European countries (except Scandinavia), as Figure 6.2 reveals, and with relatively little part-time employment—have made the American case harder to ignore. With overall rates of women's labor force participation very similar to the Nordic countries, the United States has lower rates of part-time employment, but with concomitantly lower rates of employment among mothers of young children—the group that takes most advantage of parental leave and provisions, allowing fewer hours of work for the parents of younger children in Scandinavia. (Note that when one examines levels of mothers' actual presence in the work place, rather than just formal participation in the labor force, the proportion of Swedish mothers of preschool children at work shrinks from 85 percent to 66 percent [1990 figures], for many are on parental leave; see Nyberg 2000: 16.) And in a kind of mirror image of the Swedish pattern, the pay gap in the United States is relatively high, but occupational sex segregation is relatively low, and in particular, American women have had relatively good access to traditionally masculine elite and blue-collar occupations (O'Connor, Orloff, and Shaver 1999, ch. 3).

The failure to recognize changed employment patterns among US women may also stem from the fact that in terms of ideology and cultural assumptions about the gendered division of labor the United States until very recently looked similar to countries with a "strong male breadwinner model," such as the Netherlands or the United Kingdom. Moreover, maternalist programs were prominent (if not generous by the second half of the twentieth century), at least relative to the residual US system of social provision (Orloff 1991; Skocpol 1992). Recent policy changes have brought retrenchment but also new forms of governmental action directed at increasing women's employment. The 1996 welfare reform "ended welfare as we knew it," replacing Aid to Families with Dependent Children (AFDC), the policy descendant of early-twentieth-century maternalist programs, with block grants to states for Temporary Assistance to Needy Families (TANF). The law eliminated social rights to assistance ("entitlements") on the basis of economic need and full-time caregiving, which up to that point had been permitted for poor parents of children under the age of seventeen. It included political mandates on state and local governments to increase the employment of those single mothers who depended at least in part on "welfare" (on US welfare reform, see Mink 1998; Weaver 2000; Noble 1997). In other words, the United State has had a very abrupt and uncompromising "farewell to maternalism"! At the same time, a number of programs, most notably the Earned Income Tax Credit, have been expanded, with the goal of incentivizing the paid work of single mothers and others and reducing the poverty of the low paid—and have been somewhat successful. Discursively, government operates under the umbrella of "choice," even as public policy provides no means to allow choice. A better name for the US model (to the extent that there is sufficient systematicity to call it a model at all) would be "employment for all." "Maternalism" has all but disappeared in one of the cradles of its creation.

As yet, few scholars of social provision seem to know how to explain these patterns. (Nor are standard economic models of labor supply and demand adequate to the task—but that's a different set of analytic challenges [see, e.g., England 1992; England and Farkas 1986].) The US case confounds simple versions of the Social Democratic model, for women's employment does not depend on public services to replace family-based care, nor have Social Democratic parties been the principal supporters of women's employment. Many believe that without heavy state spending on public services—ruled out in the United States, it would seem, by strong neoliberal political forces— mothers' employment is difficult if not impossible, at least without a sharp decline in fertility, as has been the case in southern Europe (on southern Europe, see Gonzalez, Jurado, and Naldini 2000). But in the United States, we see relatively high fertility rates—above European levels on average and on a par with Swedish levels among native-born white women—and high employment levels, despite the absence of extensive public services.

The US state encourages women's employment, but not through

the direct provision of social services. While there is explicit talk of the importance of "choice" for women vis-à-vis employment and temporary or lifelong full-time caregiving, there have been no substantive public policies to support such choices outside of the Survivors' Insurance portion of Social Security, which serves a tiny proportion of single mothers who are widows with young children, and an extremely residual entitlement to social assistance for poor (and unemployed) single mothers, which was eliminated in 1996. Instead, the United States features both "carrots"—positive state policies encouraging women's employment—and "sticks," most notably a lack of alternatives to commodification for women as well as men and strict requirements to seek employment or perform worklike activities within remaining social assistance programs. The role of the state has hardly been eclipsed—except perhaps in rhetoric.

In contrast to Sweden, the US government does little to help women enter the paid labor force through provision of public care services or paid leaves that allow workers to attend to family responsibilities (on the history and character of child care in the United States, see Michel 1999). A minority of the very poor receive high-quality public care (Head Start), although this program was not developed to ease women's work-family conflicts but rather to enhance development among underprivileged children. Some states now offer partial child-care subsidies to allow former welfare recipients or low-income workers to enter employment, but demand far outstrips supply. Instead, policy is predominantly in a liberal vein, giving incentives for private service provision in the form of tax deductions for child care. There is a large supply of relatively inexpensive child care in the private sector, supplied by workers whose low pay makes services "affordable" for slightly better-off households but who may themselves have few options for quality care. The quality of care is quite variable, and government does little to encourage better quality. At the federal level, an unpaid family and medical leave entitlement—for employees of large companies—was passed in 1993, but there is little provision for maternity leave, let alone paid parental leave or child sick leave days.[6] A few states are experimenting with using state-level disability insurance for maternity coverage, and in 2004, California became the first state to provide paid family leave, financed through an employee-paid payroll tax. Possibly less noticed—though not by US governmental policymakers—is the fact that the market provision of services has facilitated women's employment. Gøsta Esping-Andersen (1999: 166) presents data suggesting that the cost of child care as a proportion of the average income for a working-class, dual-earner family is about the same for the United States as for Denmark and is less than for France. These data are reproduced in Table 6.1.

The US government is certainly not passive with respect to women's employment and does not simply "leave things to the market." Rather than emphasizing social rights to care services, there is a well-developed apparatus around civil rights relevant for employment (O'Connor, Orloff, and Shaver 1999). While "reconciling" care and work is assumed to be a private choice and responsibility, public policy is committed to enhancing women's employment opportunities, and decades of equal employment legislation, court cases, and affirmative action—though contested (Nelson and Bridges 1999) and uneven in practice—have resulted in decreasing gender wage gaps (McCall 2001) and increased rates of women's entry into some formerly masculine occupations (both professional/managerial and working class) (MacLean 1999; O'Connor, Orloff, and Shaver 1999: ch. 3). In general, gender wage gaps tend to be lower in systems with centralized bargaining structures (such as Sweden) (Whitehouse 1992). However, US women's incomes have increased relative to men's over the past

Table 6.1. The net, posttransfer/tax cost of child care for a family with average income (children under age three, mid-1990s)

Country	Net cost as a percentage of average family income[a]
Denmark	10.9
Sweden	15.7
France[b]	9.4
Germany	19.4
Netherlands	23.2
Italy	39.3
United Kingdom	28.1
United States	10.6

Source: Esping-Andersen, 1999: table 4.4.

a. Average production worker income + 66 percent (wife's assumed income).

b. French data are adjusted for the FF2,000 per month additional subsidy for day care. Note also that the French figures reflect the situation prior to the introduction of an income test.

thirty years by virtue of increased hours worked and rising relative wages, themselves the product of declining occupational sex segregation and declining male wages (McCall 2001; Ellwood 2000). As noted above, the "authority gap" and overall sex segregation are lower in the United States than in Sweden (Charles and Grusky 2004; Baxter and Wright 2000). One might also argue that state regulation and pervasive corporate policies to combat sexual harassment—where the United States has been an international leader (Zippel 2006; Saguy 2003)—reflect the political concerns feminists have raised about creating workplaces open to women.

Because care arrangements are assumed to be "private," some US women may have more scope for choosing *not* to care, by forgoing childbearing or purchasing care services in the market. These women are in a position to take advantage of employment opportunities and affirmative action programs that encourage employers to open formerly male-dominated positions to "qualified" women, which might be interpreted as "women who are like men," that is, without care responsibilities (or whose responsibilities are dealt with "privately," at little or no cost to the employer). One might argue that there are high levels of women's employment in the United States because policy has "conceded to the market," with a political refusal of any public role in providing services or displacing private services and a strong political commitment to the division between public and private spheres, so that care is a private problem or choice. If women are marginalized in Sweden because they care, in the United States, care is marginalized, but some women may not be, because they can make private choices to shed care. Of course, there are striking inequalities in women's capacities to do this, and inequality among women is related partly to the uneven burdens and costs of care.

What are the politics producing this distinctive set of policies?[7] We have already disposed of one set of false narratives—that US gender and employment patterns are simply the result of state withdrawal. Are they the result, rather, of the relative strength of secular right parties, as Korpi (2000) would have it? One would have to concede at least that such parties do more than champion laissez-faire and that there are positive gender equality policies associated with liberalism. Certainly, such partisan patterns have been consequential for gender politics and policies, but, as in the Swedish case, one must also attend to the organization and ideologies of women's equality advocates. However, in contrast to Sweden, especially in the contemporary United States, feminism has had to face powerful opponents as well. In addition to the economic liberals of the Republican Party, the US secular right party, who have often opposed state "intervention" in society to provide services or to regulate labor market practices, there are religiously inspired conservative political forces committed to "traditionalism" in gender relations and therefore opposed to feminism. However, these forces have consistently been quite uninterested in offering substantive support to breadwinner-caregiver families. Their commitment to market liberalism and small (domestic) government trumps their gender ideology.

US feminists have tended to form autonomous organizations, outside the parties, although sometimes in alliance with them, especially the Democrats. The characteristics of the American political system, especially its highly decentralized decision-making structure, the highly decentralized organization of political parties, and the diversity of their policy preferences, frustrate social movement efforts to change policy. The successes achieved by the women's movement have come largely through "sophisticated interest group" behavior (Costain and Costain 1987: 210). In addition, predominant ideologies have shifted quite dramatically between feminism's first and second waves (Freeman 1975). Early-twentieth-century US advocates of women's equality were mainly maternalists, championing women's right to care and claiming political rights on the basis of care; the majority favored protective legislation.

In the contemporary era, feminists have tended to seek to make traditional breadwinner positions in the workforce available to women—partly by repealing the protective laws their foremothers had championed—and have been less interested in championing policies that would support women's full-time caregiving. To use the terms popularized by Nancy Fraser (1994), US feminists have engaged in a "universal breadwinner" strategy, as compared to the "caregiver parity" strategy promoted by Swedish feminists. In terms of available allies and established political discourse, the US political context in the years after World War II has been quite encouraging to liberal feminist civil rights claims—such as equality of employment opportunity—but less open to claims for social rights, such as paid parental leave or public child-care services (O'Connor, Orloff, and Shaver 1999: chs. 2, 6–7; Cobble 2004). Many of the most significant equality achievements by the US women's movement, such as antidiscrimination and equal opportunities decisions, were achieved largely through the courts, although in some instances legislatures and administrative bodies have also been involved. US feminists have supported public child-care services and paid leaves, but with little success. However, they have had much better success with political interventions that encourage the private provision of services, such as tax credits for child care (Michel 1999).

What scholars today call maternalist politics were particularly well developed in the Progressive era United States (Skocpol 1992; Orloff 1991; Koven and Michel 1993). Women reformers made political claims based on women's service to society or the nation in the form of childbearing and rearing. The policy "fruit" of these claims in the United States was rather more meager than the provisions established for mothers and their children in countries such as Germany and France, with less-developed maternalist politics but greater legitimacy for state interventions, stronger state interests in pronatalism, and greater state administrative and fiscal capacities (Koven and Michel 1993). But this era did see the initiation of mothers' pensions, allowances designed to permit full-time caregiving for widowed mothers of young children, which were the forerunners of Survivors' Insurance and AFDC, both initiated in the 1935 Social Security Act. AFDC carried the logic of maternalist provision into the contemporary era, offering a means-tested entitlement to single parents (it was always formally gender neutral, though overwhelmingly used by women) who were caring for children (under seventeen) full-time. On the labor market side, protective legislation designed to safeguard women's reproductive capacities and activities was favored by most women's equality advocates as well as male trade unionists; it often translated into workingmen's privileges and outright discrimination against married women and women in general in employment. Interestingly, the United States never developed the level of state social provision for workers, mostly men, that its European counterparts did, nor was there much in the way of a politically guaranteed economic bonus for breadwinners (Orloff 1993b: chs. 7, 9; 2003).

While Sweden developed a universalistic system of social provision and active labor market policies under Social Democratic hegemony in the 1940s and 1950s, more conservative politics predominated in the United States, eclipsing the policy initiatives of the social liberalism that had flourished in the 1930s, such as universal health insurance or full-employment efforts (Amenta 1998; Weir 1992; Weir, Orloff, and Skocpol 1988). Instead, outside of Social Security for the retired, which was almost continuously extended and made more generous, the US system of social provision for the working-aged population was left to become decidedly residual. Maternalist provision, especially AFDC, stood out as one of the few areas of positive state policy—meager when compared to retirement provision but politically notable when compared to what was available for the general working-aged population, which is to say, not much. This pattern of provision gave rise to what has been called "dualism," as many working-class and middle-class men in the postwar boom years benefited from private "fringe benefits" negotiated by particularly powerful unions or offered through corporate welfare (Stevens 1988)—and their wives benefited indirectly, as long as they stayed married—and only those who had no alternative relied on public provision. Moreover, many men enjoyed relatively high wages, and many also had access to veteran's benefits, all of which helped to support a male breadwinner model "without the state" (Orloff 2003). These benefits, however, began to decline in the post-1973 era (Ellwood 2000), and US breadwinners found themselves more vulnerable than their European counterparts, who continued to enjoy public welfare state provision.

The period from the late 1960s through the early 1970s was in the United States, as it had been in Sweden, the key period for the foundation of the dominant gender policy model, but perhaps more for what was excluded from political possibility than for what was enacted. Defeat was the fate of proposals that resembled scaled-down versions of both the European model of supporting breadwinners—Nixon's so-called Family Assistance Plan, which would have offered economic subsidies to poor breadwinner families in addition to the single-mother families, who were the main clientele of AFDC (Quadagno 1990)—and the Scandinavian model of supporting women's employment through the expansion of public child-care services (Michel 1999). But with the expansion of women's employment and the justifying rhetoric of second-wave feminism, mothers' employment was losing its stigma. And, indeed, despite the failure of more sweeping reforms, work incentives were introduced into AFDC in 1967, so that women could combine employment earnings and welfare benefits while retaining health coverage. Although favorable to beneficiaries in the short run, this line of policy development continued to leave the employed poor and most two-parent families outside the umbrella of social protection, which in turn made AFDC politically vulnerable (Weir, Orloff, and Skocpol 1988; Ellwood 1988). Public provision construed single mothers as unemployable, as full-time caregivers, rather than as potential workers, even as women's labor force participation, particularly among married mothers of children under age six, was accelerating (Reskin and Padavic 1994). Adding to AFDC's political vulnerability, its clientele was expanding to include more women of color.

This era was also significant for current gender patterns because of changes in policy spheres far from the family policy or welfare arena (the usual spots to look). New waves of migrants, especially from Latin America and Asia, expanded the US labor supply as immigration rules were eased, helping to fuel a private service sector expansion that was also encouraged by deregulation of markets. Low-wage workers, many of them immigrants, staff the fast-food restaurants, nursing homes, hospitals, and child-care centers on which the vast majority of Americans, working-class as well as more affluent, rely to care for their families (on the racial and gendered distribution of service work, see Glenn 1992).

The Reagan administration was the leading edge of a harder-right, antigovernmental spending political force that swept over most of the rich democracies, though with greater success in the United States than perhaps anywhere but the United Kingdom and New Zealand (Pierson 1994; M. Rhodes 2000; H. Schwartz 2000; Weir 1998). In terms of supports for caregiving or mothers' employment, little was done. However, new restrictions were enacted in AFDC against combining paid work and welfare, leaving in place a formal model of motherhood based on full-time caregiving, which over the course of the decade was increasingly out of sync with the behavior of most mothers, married or not (Reskin and Padavic 1994: 143–145). With the decline of jobs paying a "breadwinner wage," fewer people could sustain single-earner households, even if they wanted to. At the same time, women's educational levels increased, more women worked for longer periods of their lives, and advocates emphasized legal routes to equal opportunity, with considerable success. Thus, the continuation of the very marginal maternalist program, AFDC, increasingly identified with women of color, as all women's employment levels were increasing, was an explosive combination that was exploited politically by the Republicans, with Reagan's election and after.

Until welfare was "reformed," which is to say, repealed, political struggles raged over the maternalist model enshrined in AFDC and possible state endorsement of mothers' employment. These struggles reflected agendas shaped by concerns about gender and racial relations and about government's spending and regulation. Parallel struggles around work, care, and gender—as embodied in policies such as the Family and Medical Leave Act, child-care subsidies or provision of services, and affirmative action—were also significant, if strangely unlinked to the welfare debates. Yet one can discern some common threads: commitment to "choice" for women with respect to paid work and caregiving (either temporary or longer term) but lack of substantive support to either employed or stay-at-home mothers—which translated into an implicit model of "employment for all."

Government support for increasing poor women's employment is sometimes seen as reflecting a conservative political agenda and the ending of maternalist programs as evidence of racism and patriarchy[8] in denying a "right to care for their children" to poor women.[9] It would be hard to deny the political power of racist and conservative gender ideologies, and President Reagan and other Republicans mobilized these sentiments in the campaign against AFDC—and the "welfare queens" supposedly enjoying its largesse—in the 1980s (see Gilens 1999 on welfare, public opinion, and perceptions of the poor). Still, conservative forces were not hegemonic; the elimination of AFDC was not politically possible under President Reagan, as Democratic control of the House was a bulwark against the most radical retrenchment. However, a Democratic president in 1995–1996 was not a bulwark against the efforts of a Republican Congress to eliminate AFDC. It is not simply a matter of divided government but a question of what deprived AFDC of political protection, even among Democrats in 1996.

Democrats had argued that they needed to move to the right on "wedge issues" (Dawson 1994; Williams 1998), and Bill Clinton was committed to Third Way–like policies with respect to employment and welfare but probably would not have repealed AFDC on his own. Increases in employment among most mothers and the lack of public support to the caregiving needs of most citizens made AFDC politically indefensible at worst, unattractive at best, even among many of those committed to women's equality (or racial justice). Beyond the tiny group of widows of Social Security–covered wage earners with young children, the federal government provides *no one* (woman or man) any sort of *paid* parental leave. Economic self-sufficiency is expected from all, and any kind of time for care must be privately financed.[10] Having lost the commitment of those forces traditionally favorable to social provision, welfare became vulnerable to the Right's campaign for repeal.

By the 1990s, Democrats had joined Republicans in taking advantage of the electoral popularity of welfare "reform." Clinton turned around his party's vulnerability among white voters with his famous 1992 campaign pledge to "end welfare as we know it," while promising to "make work pay." His approach could more easily accommodate EITC expansion than the defense of the existing welfare system. Poverty would be fought not with higher benefits or expanded coverage but by getting everyone—including mothers—into employment, then improving pay and conditions (Ellwood 1988). Clinton Democrats wanted to make AFDC more like unemployment insurance—a short-term benefit to help claimants "get on their feet" but premised on employment. In fact, many women were already using the program in this manner, although the formal rules obscured this practice (Edin and Lein 1997). This suggests that even though women had lost their exemption from the demands of commodification, the "farewell to maternalism" in the United States still might have taken a less harsh form than it ultimately did.

The elimination of AFDC became almost inevitable once Clinton made his famous promise.[11] Although Democrats sought to retain control of the welfare issue, the call to end welfare was seized on mainly by Republicans, who moved the debate in a sharply conservative direction—to outright elimination of a right to assistance. After the Republicans captured the House of Representatives in 1994, President Clinton was challenged by Republicans to sign welfare bills much more restrictive and less generous than his own plan. After vetoing two bills, he ultimately signed the third. Did he have to do it? Critics point out that he could have continued his opposition; the Republicans probably could not have overcome a veto. Yet Clinton apparently worried about losing his healthy margin in the polls in the 1996 race with Bob Dole if he were to come before the electorate having failed in his promise to "end welfare as we know it" (Reich 1999). And at the same time, former defenders of welfare, such as women's organizations and organizations of African Americans, including the Congressional Black Caucus, did not, in the end, make preventing welfare reform a high priority (Williams 1998).

It might be a stretch, but one might consider as analogous to Social Democratic forces those parts of the Democratic Party during the Clinton administration responsible for policies such as the Family and Medical Leave Act and policies that tried to "make work pay" for low-wage workers (especially single mothers) alongside the more celebrated welfare reform. But very much unlike European Social Democrats, even these "progressive" forces had to rely on the market and private provision to a great degree. They very much lacked the political clout of their European counterparts.

The deficiencies of the US model with respect to the vulnerable poor are quite well known among comparativists and students of US social policy. This is a system that treats harshly those who have little training, many care burdens, and limited financial means. And indeed the quality of care for the poor, and even many workers and middle-class people, is uneven, sometimes quite excellent (e.g., Head Start or the child-care centers sponsored by universities), but mediocre or dangerous too often. Given its residualism, this system is not obviously expensive, but we might well argue that the downstream consequences of failing to provide support to care and to families more generally are very costly—here one might think of imprisonment or illiteracy. We are seeing a widening economic gap among women, as has also been observed among men (McCall 2001). Class differences are as salient as gender differences in shaping social politics and policy preferences in the United States.

But perhaps less well articulated are the virtues of the US approach for women's employment. Women with good educations or training are able to take advantage of many employment opportunities and have indeed penetrated the upper echelons of private business and the professions and masculine working-class occupations to a relatively greater degree than their Nordic or European counterparts. A vigorous private service sector has brought both employment and services to many men, women, and families, and clearly not all is of inferior quality (Esping-Andersen 1999). Moreover, the US policy regime does less than the Swedish to link women symbolically to care, precisely because there is little explicit policy around care. Saying "farewell to maternalism" has brought some advances to women in the economy and perhaps in personal life, but surely there are demonstrated needs for providing greater gender-neutral support to workers with caring responsibilities.

5. Other Models?

The US model may be as hard to export as the Swedish—or put differently, the United States and Sweden are both varieties of exceptionalism. If Sweden has been unusually homogenous and solidaristic, the United States is unusually diverse. In some social arenas and localities, such as San Francisco, the United States is unusually tolerant, particularly of different ethnic cultural traditions and styles of living, while other parts of the country are reminiscent of the most isolated and xenophobic villages of old Europe. But both the Swedish and American models can be suggestive of the sorts of things that will have to change if others are to follow them in saying farewell to maternalism.

Where mothers' employment has been promoted, care has shifted to some extent to institutions other than the family, either public or private services.[12] Yet most continental European countries are notable for the "familialism" of their welfare regimes, which has meant that caregiving burdens are borne by families, mostly women; there is little market *or* state provision for young children or the elderly. This creates difficulties for women in reconciling employment and care (given that few fathers step in to bridge the gap), and labor force participation rates are considered lower than optimal by a range of commentators.[13] In some countries, notably where part-time jobs are few and service sector employment is scarce, most mothers drop out of formal employment, but a minority work full-time (Saraceno 1994; Esping-

Andersen 1999). And this points to the other characteristic of these nations that has made increasing women's employment difficult: their labor markets are tightly regulated, and strong interest groups have opposed the expansion of nonstandard employment such as part-time jobs or service sector jobs. In other countries—the Netherlands stands out—services remain scarce, but labor markets have been liberalized sufficiently to allow the extensive growth of part-time and "flexible" employment, which has been taken up by many women (Platenga 1998). Yet this pattern leaves in place a perhaps only slightly weaker version of the problems of the original breadwinner/caregiver model, especially men's and women's unequal access to economic and other resources.

In terms of politics, the continental or Christian Democratic regime faces several problems: the problem of resources, the problem of discourse or public opinion around gender, and the problem of mobilization.[14] Many continental European countries have transfer-heavy welfare states, which means that finding new resources to support an expansion of care services and other programs to increase women's employment would involve difficult politics of rebalancing welfare efforts—taking money from pensions, for example. Sharing the resource of employment, especially through loosening labor market regulation, is also challenging, given political commitments to core workers' organizations. Changing gender relations is quite divisive, given significant investments by many political actors in defending housewifery and breadwinners' prerogatives. There is a sometimes subterranean connection between concerns around women's employment and concerns about fertility and the composition of national populations. However, these worries are increasingly coming to the fore in talk of "birth dearths" and below-replacement fertility, even if there is no agreed-upon solution to the problem. Finally, one can point to something of a "mobilization deficit" in those countries that most need a potent political force to push for strong policies supportive of women's employment.

The Netherlands is an interesting case precisely because it has had such strong policy supports for caregiving mothers and breadwinning men but has moved to encourage and mandate greater employment of all citizens, including mothers. This was part of an overhaul of the welfare state and labor markets in a liberalizing direction but occurred under political auspices also committed to gender equality (Visser and Hemerijck 1997; Bussemaker and Voet 1998). Women's employment has expanded, with the loosening of labor market regulations and the creation of more nonstandard jobs, developments spearheaded by a coalition government with a strong liberal political streak. Moreover, Dutch policy goals present an emergent challenge to the view that women's employment will require extensive "defamilization" of services. Under the rubric of a "combination model," women's employment is definitely being promoted, as is men's care; however, care services have not yet been extensively developed. Instead of a greater development of public services to allow high levels of employment, the Dutch say they will cut back on employment to allow care. Platenga (2002) describes the logic thus:

> The point of departure of the combination model is a balanced combination of paid and unpaid care work, whereas [*sic*] the unpaid care work is equally shared between men and women. The core concept here is that justice is done to both paid and unpaid work. Depending on the life-cycle phase, both men and women should be able to choose a personal mix of paid labour in large part-time (short full-time) jobs, part-time household production of care and part-time outsourcing of care. With some adjustments and with many concrete measures still to be developed, the combination model has been adopted by the Dutch government as the main guideline for policies in the field of labour and care. . . . [F]lexible, non-full-time working hours [i.e., individualised, nonstandard working hours] for both men and women are deemed indispensable to reach gender equality.

In some ways, this is an attractive vision for feminists, as it calls for attention to *sharing* care work between men and women, while valorizing that work. Moreover, regulations about work time are being reformed in ways that allow flexibility from the worker's point of view. But it is far from clear that these Dutch government initiatives will actually lead toward greater gender equality, for women are still scaling back paid employment more than are men. Although Dutch men have the highest levels of part-time work in Europe, few of these part-timers are fathers of young children. Thus, Dutch policies might simply lead to an updated maternalism—if women are still the only ones who care, whose work must be scaled back to accommodate care, and whose political claims are based on care. Much will depend on the evolution of cultural practices and beliefs but also on public policies that make the combination of part-time employment and caregiving more appealing to men as well as women.

6. Conclusion

Depending on each country's starting point, different strategies may be pursued to enhance women's employment, while reducing poverty and economic vulnerability and ensuring that caregiving activities are supported. Where women's employment and employment opportunities are well established, as in North America, it is caregiving that needs attention: supporting parental leaves more generously and assisting more extensively in the provision of services. In addition, there is a need for financially supporting low-wage workers, so that they can in fact provide necessities, including high-quality care, to their families. If all are expected to be (paid) workers, it must be understood that workers have caregiving obligations, which should be supported. In Scandinavia and France, where workers who are caregivers have excellent supports, but employers discriminate on the basis of caregiving responsibilities, it is women's opportunities in employment—rather than simply their participation in the labor force—that must be targeted, while assuring that services and leaves are not cut back. Here, where men are "just" workers, despite the rhetoric encouraging them to take up care, but women are carer-providers, it is women's roles as workers that must be emphasized, while continuing to make clear that men should be carers as well. In the many European systems where women's care work in the family is supported but their paid work is not, the systems of service provision and leave protection that allow women's employment must be built up, even as employment opportunities are expanded. Of course, identifying the way forward is not equivalent to mustering the political resources to undertake the trip.

Supporting mothers' employment presents a challenge not only politically and culturally, but also in terms of state capacities. Support for the breadwinner/caregiver family has been accomplished through "passive" means, such as cash allowances (subject to the caveat that the state's regulatory apparatus has also been significant in policing those who deviated from dominant family models). In contrast, encouraging or mandating mothers' employment brings the state into more "active" modes; to some extent, any employment initiative demands more than a "check in the mail"—training, rehabilitation, job creation, and the like. But "defamilializing" care so that those traditionally responsible for it can take up other activities demands more sophisticated capacities than even "rational" and "modern" states may possess.

The ultimate—though utopian—solution to the problems of reconciliation of employment and care and women's economic dependency in all systems depends on encouraging men's care work to parallel women's move into the world of paid work and redesigning social institutions to allow adults to take part in both care and employment (or other forms of public social participation). This would call upon income security systems to ensure that people can take time to care and have access to care services. And such changes would certainly put unprecedented demands on states. Even if women are to be employed in the new, liberalized economy—with political approval and policy support—we will still see continuing struggles around care and women's independence and individuality. Is women's personal (procedural) autonomy to be pursued in its own right? Or will women's employment and fertility be subordinated to economic or demographic rationales? Can our need for care be reconciled with arrangements in which economically dependent women in families are not available to provide it? Can we find ways to support both autonomy and care, for advantaged as well as less-advantaged women—and, if we are practical, can this be done in the context of straitened state budgets, newly powerful neoliberal ideologies, and globalizing labor and capital markets?

Bidding farewell to maternalism does not in itself solve the core problem it addressed: derived dependency or impaired capacities to participate as individual economic and political citizens, due to caregiving responsibilities for those who are inevitably dependent. Finding solutions to this problem will require changes in social attitudes and workplace organization to facilitate a greater willingness among men to take on unpaid household responsibilities. But it will also necessitate a shift in state policies: having pushed and prodded mothers to become workers, authorities now confront the even more daunting challenge of encouraging fathers to become caregivers.

∼ III

The Market-Making State

∾ 7

The State in the Digital Economy

JOHN ZYSMAN AND ABRAHAM NEWMAN

MOVING BEYOND AN ELECTROMECHANICAL ERA, where machines helped humans manipulate physical objects, the world has entered a digital era, where machines help humans manipulate information in the form of zeros and ones. The digital age rests not only on the ability to express information in binary form but also on the equipment that processes the data and the networks that interlink the multitude of processors. The Internet, as significant as it is, is simply one phase in this technological transformation. The dot-com boom and the crash associated with it do not constitute a self-contained story. Rather, they are one episode in the larger digital revolution.[1]

This digital revolution holds tremendous opportunity for society and the economy as new markets, business models, and means of organization emerge. At the same time, innovation has an intensely destabilizing effect on broad societal bargains, such as the notion of property, and on business positions, as new entrants take advantage of technology to challenge incumbents. Our concern is how the state interacts with this revolution in society and the economy—to consider the role of the state in the political economy of the digital era.

Borrowing from Karl Polanyi, we employ the metaphor of a second great transformation to drive a discussion about the political economy of the digital era (Polanyi 1944). By "great transformation" we mean a fundamental and basic shift in the rules of society that alters the way economy and polity operate. There is one classic example, the great transformation that began in England in the sixteenth century. In this case, the state established a market economy by transforming land, labor, and money into commodities. Before that transformation, markets were more of an adjunct to the society. Peasants were tied to the land, and land was encumbered by its social position in a political order. For landlord, peasant, and burgher, position in a politically defined social community defined access to opportunities and income. When the state forged a market system, it stood these relations on their head. Land and labor became commodities to be bought and sold in the market. Social position could move in relation to what was captured in the market. In the digital era, information rather than land, labor, or capital has become the new object of commodification.

While many argue that the state has little capacity to shape the digital era, it is our contention that the state serves an integral role in the evolution of the digital revolutions transpiring across the globe. Just as in the British example described by Polanyi, the state is actively involved in creating a market for the fictitious commodity of information. The crux of this chapter is to use the metaphor of the great transformation to demonstrate how the state shapes and influences the digital era. The state has performed a number of vital functions: promoting the technological infrastructure necessary for the revolution, establishing the fictitious commodity of information through intellectual property, influencing production processes and business models, and embedding digital markets in social norms. Far from neutral interventions, state actions shape the character of the digital era, including the political effects of the transformation.

This chapter analyzes the role of the state in the emergence and evolution of the digital era in four parts. The first section describes the scope and scale of the technological change. It is followed by a brief presentation of the view that relegates the state to at best a bystander and at worst an enemy of the digital transformation. The third section uses the lens of the great transformation to explore the means by which the state influences the digital revolution. The final section offers some initial insight into how state intervention may vary cross-nationally and thoughts for future research.

1. The Renewable Revolution

Just as the industrial revolution rested on a revolution in tools and power, the core of the information technology sector is the creation and production of a new tool set, which Steve Cohen, Brad DeLong, and John Zysman have termed "tools for thought" (Cohen, DeLong, and Zysman 2000: 7–8). These tools manipulate, organize, transmit, and store information in digital form, thereby creating a set of information services and information products. These services and products allow the application of information to industrial as well as machine processes (Weiner 1954). The digital revolution and the tools for thought can be broken down into three fundamental elements:

- *The concept.* The information revolution begins with the notion of information as something that can be expressed in binary form.[2] Data ranging from supermarket purchases to fingerprints can be represented in digital code.

- *The equipment.* The hardware, the equipment that executes the processing instructions, has evolved from the era of vacuum tubes to individual silicon transistors, to integrated circuits implemented on silicon wafers and may evolve into other physical manifestations. The software consists of written programs, including procedures and rules that guide how the equipment processes information.

- *The networks.* The data networks interlink the processing nodes of individual computers, and the network of networks together create a digital community and society.

The production of the equipment and networks, information technology (IT), has itself become a leading sector in the economy. Tools for thought create the capabilities to process and distribute digital data, multiplying the scale and speed with which thought and information can be applied. IT tools can affect economic activity in which information sensing, organizing, processing, or communication is important—in short, every single economic activity.[3]

The digital transformation began, in part, as a response by American producers to the Japanese production challenge.[4] As the semiconductor industry joined consumer electronics and automobiles as sectors under intense competitive pressure in the late 1980s, it seemed that the fabric of advanced electronics in the United States was coming unraveled. American producers rebounded not by reversing the decline in electromechanical production. Rather, a new sort of consumer electronics product had emerged, defining a new segment of the industry.

This first chapter of the digital production era can be best characterized by two elements: Wintelism and Cross National Production Networks (CNPNs). "Wintelism" is the word Michael Borrus and John Zysman coined to reflect the shift in competition away from final assembly and vertical control of markets by final assemblers (Borrus and Zysman 1997; Zysman 2006).[5] Competition in the Wintelist era is a struggle over setting and evolving de facto product market standards, with market power lodged anywhere in the value chain, including product architectures, components, and software. Much of the value is in the intellectual property (IP), formally in the components, often in partially open but owned standards that create de facto IP-based monopolies or dominant positions. Production becomes modularized as the knowledge about the elements and components they interconnect become codifiable.

CNPN is a label applied to the consequent dis-integration of the industry's value chain into constituent functions that can be contracted out to independent producers, wherever those companies are located in the global economy. This strategic and organizational innovation, what we might now call supply chain management, means that even production of complex products can become a commodity service that can be purchased in the market. The nature of those chains, now often labeled "global value chains," varies with the complexity of the transactions, the codifiability of the knowledge involved, and the competence of the suppliers.[6] The strategic weapon for companies such as Dell moves from the factory to the management of the supply chain. And the supply chain itself is extended both forward into the marketplace and backward into development.

The question remains, Does the IT sector pull harder and represent a larger chunk of new demand than in previous technological transformations? Is a greater portion of the economy influenced as these new tools are taken up?[7] What seems most significant is that information technology represents not one but a sequence of revolutions.

It is a continued and enduring unfolding of digital innovation, sustaining a long process of industrial adaptation and transition. The original innovation, the transistor, really represents an initial step in a sequence of innovations—the functionality of the original transistor being not even a hint of the functionality that would follow. As Cohen, DeLong, and Zysman relate, IT has been a recurrent revolution:

> In the 1960s Intel Corporation co-founder Gordon Moore projected that the density of transistors on a silicon chip—and thus the power of a chip—would double every eighteen months. Moore's law, as it came to be called, has held. Today's chips have 256 times the density of those manufactured in 1987—and 65,000 times the density of those of 1975. This continued and continuing every-eighteen-month doubling of semiconductor capability and productivity underpins the revolution in information technology. The increase in semiconductor density means that today's computers have 66,000 times the processing power, at the same cost, as the computers of 1975. In ten years computers will be more than 10 million times more powerful than those of 1975—at the same cost. We now expect—routinely—that today's $1,000 personal computer ordered over the Internet will have the power of a $20,000 scientific workstation of five years ago. And what was once supercomputing is now run-of-the-mill. The past forty years have seen perhaps a billion-fold increase in the installed base of computing power. (Cohen, DeLong, and Zysman 2000: 13–14)

The conventional economic explanation of a leading sector is that the original innovation creates a set of opportunities, somewhat like distributing money on the ground. Some radically valuable possibilities, the larger bills, are picked up first; the smaller opportunities are captured later. But the original technological revolution loses force as the most valuable opportunities are picked up and implemented. The notion argued in this chapter is, of course, that the revolution is renewed—if not with each cycle of Moore's law, certainly with the radical increases in computing power generated in a very few years. An original transistor, a single bit, bears little relationship to a 16 kilobit (K) integrated memory chip. That 16K chip bears some relationship to a 256K chip that is two Moore cycles further along. Somewhere, along some scale, we could work in a comparison of a Model T to a contemporary car. But that would understate the scale of change. A gigabyte chip with a billion transistors is another thing altogether, and it is five Moore cycles, less than a decade along the road from the 256K. And Moore's law has at least several more cycles to run. The technological revolution is renewed every decade. The currency is redistributed on the ground, as the bills themselves get larger. The fundamental question, then, is to ask how these resources will be distributed.

2.   Putting the State on the Sidelines

At the creation of the Internet, the government effectively laid the foundation for self-regulating groups who established and sustained markets in cyberspace. For those earlier "Net" pioneers, who were forging the system rules, setting the architecture of the early Internet, it seemed like government was an interloper in a system that was run by technologists for technologists. These technological enthusiasts argued that the architecture of the Internet made it impossible to regulate. The famous claim made by early Internet advocate John Gilmore that "the Net interprets censorship as damage and routes around it" epitomized the beliefs of many technologists.[8] They viewed cyberspace as beyond the reach of state controls. National governments would be forced to cede much of their regulatory authority to the cybercommunity, eroding traditional notions of sovereignty.

The digital revolution posed a dual challenge to the state. First, information technologically reduced the costs associated with conducting international business, part of a phenomenon popularly labeled "globalization" (Weber 2001). Firms that took advantage of digital technology to expand their geographic reach in turn limited the efforts of public officials to manage their economies. Stringent domestic regulations, it was believed, encouraged footloose capital to relocate to more hospitable institutional environments, forcing governments around the globe to engage in a race to the bottom in economic intervention (Tonnelson 2000). State autonomy fell victim in the digital era to firm mobility.

Second, the decentralized, nonhierarchical character of digital networks was viewed as incompatible with the rigid, inflexible governance tools available to the state. As Virginia Haufler has argued in the case of information privacy, "The decentralized, open, global character of one of the main transmission sources for personal information—the Internet—makes it difficult to design and implement effective regulations through top-down, government-by-government approaches" (Haufler 2001: 82). The governance problems raised by digital technologies threatened to further erode state autonomy, as nonstate actors were empowered to resolve major societal disputes (Rosenau and Singh 2002). Operating from this perspective, Debora Spar described a cyberworld of state regulation displaced by industry self-regulation:

> Fundamentally, I argue, governments cannot set the rules of cyberspace. That is because cyberspace, unlike governments, slips seamlessly and nearly unavoidably across national boundaries. . . . With governments pushed effectively to the sidelines, firms will have to write and enforce their own rules, creating private networks to facilitate and protect electronic commerce. (Spar 1999: 82)

On a policy level, politicians in the United States relied heavily on the private sector to navigate the first years of the digital revolution. A chorus of business lobbies argued that government regulation would crush this vital infant industry. The role of the government, if any, was to get out of the way of the sector's development. The Clinton administration did not stray far from these concerns, insisting that the government should not interfere with the development of the information technology revolution. The administration believed that private sector self-regulatory mechanisms would guarantee the successful construction of information markets. In the 1997 White House position paper, *Framework for Global Electronic Commerce*, President Clinton and Vice-President Gore asserted that "the Administration . . . will encourage the creation of private fora to take the lead in areas requiring self-regulation such as privacy, content ratings, and consumer protection and in areas such as standards development, commercial code, and fostering interoperability" (White House 1997). Echoing the US view, Europe's then–Commissioner for Telecommunications Martin Bangemann suggested that business should take the lead in developing an "International Charter for Electronic Commerce" that would rely heavily on "market-led, industry-driven self-regulatory models" (Commission 1998).[9]

Of course, the early notions that the Internet should be free of government, like a mythical Wild West community, ignored the fact that western settlements required a local sheriff; they required governments. When the Internet was transferred to the commercial world, those requirements for legal structure in the operation of the network became more evident, more urgent, and the rule making for the Internet became, at least in part, rule making for the economy. The issues were no longer simply technical ones of how to operate the network or communicate across this network of networks. Suddenly, all the questions of an operating marketplace had to be addressed; appropriate rules had to be defined for domains from privacy to taxation. The results of these decisions have real distributional and societal consequences. And states were not about to abdicate this responsibility to private actors. In fact, despite the decentralized, international character of digital networks, governments have played an instrumental role in shaping the character of the emerging digital societies.

The emergence and evolution of the digital era have not been the products of purely neoliberal strategies, on the one hand, nor of purely interventionist strategies, on the other hand. Governments have acted simultaneously to subsidize infrastructure development, extract themselves from direct market control, and forge new rules to promote economic transactions. Framing the role of the state in ideological terms confounds the multitude and seemingly contradictory strategies governments undertook. Like all markets, cybermarkets require definitions of property, exchange, and competitive market structure. And all of this requires rules.[10]

3.   The Role of the State in the Digital Transformation

Borrowing from Polanyi, we use the metaphor of the great transformation to highlight the role of the state in the political economy of the digital era. The drama of the great transformation itself was the shift from a traditional society, in which markets fitted within social order, and economic activity bowed to the confines of social rules, to a market society in which land, labor, and capital became commodities moving in response to price signals from the market. That transition was the product of a series of political battles that redefined England. They included the enclosures, the poor laws, and the repeal of the Corn Laws. The enclosures transformed community public lands into private farming lands, beginning the creation of a market for land. The series of poor laws, culminating in the elimination in 1834 of the Speenhamland system, a primitive welfare system that allowed the rural poor to remain in their parishes, created a labor market. The 1834 Poor Law Reform broke the link for survival between individual and local community, making the individual worker's well-being dependent on wages obtained in the labor market. The repeal of the Corn Laws in 1846 opened British agricultural markets, limiting trade protection, so that lower-cost grain could feed the emerging industrial workforce. That political decision marked a shift in power from the landed classes to the emerging industrial bourgeoisie (Polanyi 1944).

In the contemporary era, as in the industrial revolution, the state has played a vital role in the construction of the digital economy through policies of deregulation, market-making, and reregulation. This effort has focused around two central questions. First, what are the rules that should underpin the new digital markets? As digital technologies diffuse, businesses in industries ranging from financial services to telecommunications search for market advantage. At the same time, these innovations have the potential to disrupt the current distribution of power within a sector and across polities. Incumbents simultaneously see lucrative market potential and economic disruption in digital advances. Market rules, drafted and enforced by the state, fundamentally shape the distribution of economic gains and modulate the extent of the revolution.

The second question confronting state authorities concerns the implications of new market rules for society more generally. As the digital economy is constructed, decisions about market rules inherently structure information flows, thereby influencing the character of the political community. The state must manage the social externalities that arise in parallel to the digital economy. Even without an intentional shift in privacy norms, for example, information technology changes the balance of who can know what about whom. Suddenly, information technology tools for collecting personal information become so powerful that credit card companies can predict divorce from expenditure patterns, and insurance companies can readily access medical records to assess health risks. Legislation that spells out how personal information may be collected and deployed in the economy becomes necessary to address these negative social externalities.

Additionally, in the digital era, quick adjustments to rules or laws often have significant, sometimes unintended, consequences. Old questions are posed in quite fundamentally new ways. Digital innovations have opened the possibility that prior battles could be refought and seemingly settled outcomes could be altered. Rather than a simple addendum to an old deal, the new formulations often require conceptual innovation and political entrepreneurship and may redistribute power and benefits significantly.

The role of the state in the digital debate has a peculiar form in that the rules of digital information, hence of a digital polity, are embedded not only in convention or in the law but in the computer code itself (Lessig 1999). Just as highway architecture dictates where you can get on and off the freeway, the computer architecture and the code implementing applications dictate what is and is not possible in a digital era. In the early years of the Internet, the open and user-controlled architecture led to the sense of cyberspace as a domain outside the control of governments or physical communities. Hence Stewart Brand's infamous remark that "Information wants to be free" reflected the particular architecture of the early Internet. But that early Internet was only one potential architecture; other more controlled or restricted networks are also possible. Digital information wants nothing at all; it flows where the network architecture permits.[11] And the network architecture is a product of the code writers. To say that we must regulate the code, hence the code writers, is not to say that there is a single technologically dictated outcome. While politics is always about values and outcomes, about who gets what, for such choices to have meaning in a digital world, they must inevitably be embedded in code and respect the technological logic of the "tools for thought." Law and code, then, interact to establish the rules of the digital era.

At the dawn of the digital era, governments have played a critical part in the creation of the fictitious commodity of information. In this effort, they have used public policy to build the infrastructure for and remove barriers to the new market. Government legislation has shaped the way that information technology has interacted with production patterns, influencing the success of emerging business models and modes of industrial organization. At the same time, state initiatives have been instrumental in navigating the complex political fights that surround the digital transformation.[12] Government legislation is critical to embed the new markets in social norms and to limit the inevitable pushback by the losers of the new era. In short, the character of the information revolution has been modulated by government interventions. The following section highlights several pathways by which the state has shaped the digital transformation. Chief among these are establishing the infrastructure and removing barriers to market evolution; constructing the commodity of information; shaping production patterns in the digital economy; and embedding new markets in social norms.

Building the Infrastructure and Removing Barriers to New Market Evolution

In the case of Polanyi's England, the government promoted the enclosure at the same time that it repealed protections that hindered the market's development. Similarly, in the case of the digital era, governments have simultaneously developed the infrastructure for and removed barriers to commodified information markets. In the United States, the creation of the Internet was the product of both *purposive intervention*, government action by the Defense Department's Advanced Research Projects Agency (DARPA), and *aggressive deregulation/reregulation*.

In the late 1960s, seeking to promote communication among the scientific community, DARPA funded the creation of the underlying conception and protocols of the Internet in what was called AR-PANET (Advanced Research Project Agency Network) (Hafner and Lyon 1998). This Internet prototype refined the technology necessary to transmit data through packets of information, providing the fundamental architecture of the current Internet. In contrast to telephone lines, which traditionally used switches to directly connect the receiver to the sender, packet switching decomposes information into its components, sends them through the network, before recombining them at their destination. The government managed ARPANET through the National Science Foundation, then prepared it for transfer to commercial use.

The government laid the groundwork for the digital era through regulatory reform as well as infrastructure investment. The aggressive introduction of competition in the telecommunications sector, highlighted by, but not confined to, the break-up of AT&T in 1984, unleashed user-led and consumer-based innovation in data networks. Inexpensive local flat-rate fees, for example, gave consumers the ability to experiment with data networking at relatively minimal cost. That opened the way to user-generated networks and facilitated the radical and rapid spread of Internet technology (Hafner and Lyon 1998).

The European story likewise displays these twin roles of the state. Simplified, one part of the story is the deregulation of the telecommunications system led by the European Commission. The Commission created national coalitions for European-wide rules that would compel the transformation of state administrations responsible for post and telegraph into regulated companies in at least partly competitive markets.[13] The other side of the story is an array of directed state actions intended to develop and diffuse digital technology. The foundations of the World Wide Web (WWW) were developed at CERN, the Center for Nuclear Research in Geneva, Switzerland. A pan-European nuclear physics lab, CERN faced the dilemma of bringing together a highly geographically dispersed European nuclear physics community. An information systems scholar from CERN, in response to this organizational demand, developed the architecture of the World Wide Web based on a language to construct Web pages, the protocol to transmit these pages, and a browser system to read the transmitted information. It was this innovation that resulted in the highly accessible browser system that has facilitated the rapid diffusion of the Web (Gribble 2004).

Government intervention has continued but taken on a different flavor, with the state-sponsored transition to high-speed broadband connectivity. The original consumer use of the Internet could expand so suddenly because it could be deployed over the existing telephone infrastructure. However, new uses of the Internet, such as downloading music or playing videos, require a different infrastructure. That infrastructure is loosely called broadband, with "broadband" typically referring to anything faster than telephone lines, whether a network of fiber or DSL (digital subscriber line) technology. The fact that the next-generation consumer network requires an infrastructure other than the traditional copper-wire phone system has posed new policy problems.

While there is international agreement on the need for rapid deployment of broadband data networks for consumer use, the policies to accomplish that rapid deployment vary radically by country. The question remains whether this build-out should be a purely private decision of local providers or should be encouraged and subsidized by the government. The answers around the world are quite varied. To capture the range, consider Korea and the United States. Korea is a story of stunning penetration of broadband services into the society. Of the 16 million Korean households, 78 percent have broadband access, compared to roughly 20 percent in the United States (Shameen 2004). The broadband build-out was consciously subsidized by redirecting funds from the wireless spectrum auctions. In total, the Korean government has spent nearly $3 billion on broadband diffusion. This effort has been carried out through an aggressive campaign, including direct subsidies, loan programs, and research and development funding. The government has even adjusted its housing ratings system so that units with broadband systems may be priced at a higher rate (T. Richardson 2002). In the United States, we have left the effort to a competition among the cable television companies, generating a cable television infrastructure, phone companies offering DSL services, and potentially even power companies offering access over electricity lines. The result is less overall coverage but more diversity in network forms. In both the United States and Korea, government policy has been instrumental in shaping the technological infrastructure for information markets, albeit in very different ways.

Commodifying Information

Cyber law has for the most part focused on creating a market world in cyberspace.[14] Intellectual property is central to this effort and a critical feature of an information society. We know that property is always a legal fiction, involving the specification of enforceable rules about what a person can have, hold, and dispose of. Hence, in a fundamental way, property and its rules of use are always political creations.

We also know that physical property and intellectual property have different characteristics. In the case of tangible goods with a physical existence, the rules of property set the terms of use and disposition. Since physical property cannot be simultaneously shared, some rules of use and disposal are necessary, whether or not those rules constitute private property. With the great transformation in England, the enclosure movement closed off common public lands, converting them into private holdings. By contrast, intellectual property is a nonexcludable good. In other words, it is not something that one holds, carries about, or physically denies to others. Hence, intellectual property as economic property—that is, something one is willing to buy because one cannot have its use without payment—is an entirely political creation, a fictitious commodity. The very "good" is a product of a rule. The rules of intellectual property in an information society are thus absolutely central.

Digital technology radically changes the logic of control and distribution of intellectual property. Whatever the cost of developing intellectual property, be it a movie or a software product, the marginal cost of precise reproduction and distribution is almost zero. Since media products are so immediately affected, it is evident why media companies have driven the reformulation of intellectual property law to permit them to recreate control over the distribution of their products.

The most blatant example of the effort to recreate traditional notions of property in the digital era is the Digital Millennium Copyright Act (DMCA) of 1998. Faced with the challenge of precise reproduction at zero cost to distribution, content providers ranging from Hollywood to the publishing industry lobbied to rebuild walls around their intellectual property preserves. The DMCA contained two critical provisions. First, it created criminal penalties for the circumvention of encryption programs. These encryption programs hide the underlying software code from the user, preventing the reproduction and distribution of the purchased product. Second, the DMCA outlawed the manufacturing or sale of code-breaking software.

Initiatives like the DMCA do not just recreate past IP protection, however. Regulating code has broader implications for society more generally. The notion of "fair use," which allows the holder of intellectual property to make that information available in a noncommercial manner, has been severely curtailed. A digital recording or book, for example, may be encrypted so that it can never be duplicated, eliminating the consumer's ability to share a purchase with friends or colleagues, even though the practice is fully legal. Digital rights management software may stop the consumer from duplicating downloaded music, preventing the customer from listening to the recording on multiple personal entertainment devices—another legal practice. Implanting intellectual property protection into the product through encryption systems permits the perfect control over use, replication, and distribution.[15]

The digital revolution allows new forms of intellectual property to be created. Expressed in digital form, information becomes a commodity that can be transmitted, manipulated, stored, and sold as an object. As knowledge, including digital instructions for physical control, becomes explicit and explicitly expressible in useful ways, the possibility and importance of protecting that knowledge as property increase. Hence, it is not just the media industry, which turns to copyright for protection, but also semiconductor designers who wish to protect the design and production processes.

Patent law has played a critical role in transforming the intellectual property regime of the digital era. As the patent office recognized the legitimacy of business model patents, processes increasingly expressed in digital form have become property. The patent disputes over the eBay auction or the Amazon checkout strategy provide troubling examples of how previously shared knowledge may become commodifiable through law. The process of establishing a checkout procedure on the Web, rather than the intellectual property behind the book that is being purchased, receives proprietary protection (Preston 2004). The fight over what can and cannot be protected is critical in daily business; for our purposes, the seemingly inexorable expansion of the protectable is the issue.

Intellectual property rules inevitably affect more than just the media industries or the business possibilities of sectors that use digitized information and programs. Intellectual property has always been about balancing the need to reward those who generate knowledge against the desire for widespread distribution and use. Digital technology makes more information more easily accessible; offsetting that, technology and law create new boxes to control that information. The texture of social and political debate is powerfully influenced by who owns and can use content generated by others. The political community is thus influencing and influenced by the rules of intellectual property.

Shaping Production Patterns

In the digital era, the role of the state hinges on how the emerging digital tools and networks alter firm strategies to capture value and market position. Just as the demands on the state during the great transformation were initially defined by the characteristics of the leading sector based on wool production, the digital era is defined by the tools for thought. As the mechanisms that create value in the market change, there is a constant pressure to formulate new rules about markets, intellectual property, and trade. Production matters, if differently, in a digital era. It is increasingly distributed around the globe in supply chains, and new models of production reflect new possibilities of social organization. The state must navigate the shifting production patterns so as to maintain national economic health and guarantee the next round of technological innovation. To understand the governance issues raised, we begin by considering several dimensions of how digital tools affect a firm's core process of creating and sustaining value.

A fundamental feature of the digital era is that analytic tools of database management permit the consumer community to be segmented into subcomponents, attacked with functionally varied products. At an extreme, individuals and their particular needs can be targeted. Early on, the insurance industry moved from using computers exclusively for back-office operations to using them to create customized products for particular consumers (Baran 1986). Thus, collecting consumer information in a variety of forms—credit cards or grocery store purchases are obvious examples—is a critical matter.

Digital tools can create a range of product versions, not only for purely digital products that are themselves principally information but also for traditional products as well. The coffeemaker that automatically turns on at a particular time in the morning depends on simple digital functionality. Versioning is not new; functional variations defined by digital means are new. General Motors transformed the automobile market into a series of segments by using several brands, each aimed at different sets of customers. The variance in underlying technology and cost was often much less than the brand differentiation suggested or the price commanded. What differentiates a fast printer from a slow printer? Often the electromechanical operations are identical, even the fundamental microprocessor controller. The variation is in the instructions built into the controller that tells the printer how to operate. The instructions in the slower, lower-cost printer simply tell it to go more slowly; in other words, it is the same printer forbidden by its makers to go fast (Shapiro and Varian 1999). This is "commercially crippled software," or a sophisticated kind of price discrimination.

Additionally, the digital manipulation of information profoundly blurs the lines between services and goods. Consider the case of IBM. Traditionally, IBM sold a product, mainframe computers, for example, and in the price embedded services that differentiated IBM from the competition. Because IBM controlled such a large percentage of the market, its development costs were spread across such a large product base that no other producer could match the package at the price. Now IBM sells as a service a system solution to company problems, solutions that embed and are often facilitated by distinctive IBM equipment. For the firm, these possibilities pose a strategic question. If what is being sold is a service, then does it matter who produces the product? What changes is which companies are able to capture value and where the activities take place.

The most dramatic evolution comes with newly orchestrated systems of distributed innovation, notably the Open Source movement.[16] It is not simply collaboration across distances by traditional software developers; rather, it is the emergence of entirely new production systems in the open source community. The open source software may be the archetype of the digital era, a system of distributed innovation, where tasks are self-assigned and where even the management of the innovation is voluntary (Weber 2004). It is quite a contrast to the archetype of the industrial era, division of labor, as exemplified by Adam Smith's pin factory, where the production of the classic good, the pin, that had been made by a craftsman is now made by an industrial process. This approach sets the process and the division of labor, assigning tasks that subdivide the process. These two systems of political economy—division of labor and open source—rest, moreover, on quite different notions of property—a factory, with clear title of ownership, versus a computer program, transformed and appropriated by a community—each defined by aspects of its era.

For a government, the immediate development question is, Where are the jobs and the profits? Evidently, this is a corporate strategic problem of what to make and what to outsource. For both governments and companies, attention shifts to the activities that must be retained within the community or within the corporate boundaries to sustain the capacity to generate productivity and innovation within the country, region, or company. Products continue to be made; production does not disappear in a digital era (Kenney and Mayer 2002; Fields 2003). The strategic problem for a firm in a digital era is deciding when actual production is a strategic asset, which may often be kept at home or under direct control, and when it is a commodity that can be purchased in the marketplace, wherever that marketplace leads (Bar 2001). At the other extreme, some products can be entirely digital and exchanged in entirely online marketplaces. These are digital goods in digital markets. Media and finance are examples where the product can be represented digitally *and* the marketplace, even delivery of the product, can be online. What does it mean to make or produce an entertainment or financial product for delivery? There is the creation of the underlying entertainment content or financial instrument, then the digital construction, the programming or development of the digital product. Even pure software products, be it a Windows operating system or the Web structure for delivering an accounting service, are "built." The difficulty is that they can increasingly be built anywhere. The result has been a flow offshore of software development and telephone support services. The basic corporate question of commodity or strategic asset is rarely directly asked in making those decisions: what must be done in-house or at common locations to sustain advantage?

The significance for our story is that competition in the IT sectors often has a winner-take-all flavor. Given the clear possibility of affecting outcomes across industrial segments, states will—whatever the arguments and rules—intervene to help create location advantage and corporate advantage. Those policies run the gamut. Policies aimed at assuring an educated and skilled workforce are essential preconditions and not controversial; outright overt protection of markets with formal trade barriers by any of the advanced countries is not viable now. Somewhere in between, policies for telecommunications infrastructure can quickly become an instrument of industrial and technological development. American telecommunications deregulation created a new customer base, a customer base experimenting with new networks and strategies. New firms emerged that soon dominated the equipment market for digital data networks. Traditional equipment suppliers stumbled in efforts to apply their switched network mentality to an Internet router era. The landscape of the US telecommunications sector shifted from old giants, including Bell Labs and AT&T, to new entrants, such as Cisco. As the United States entered the era of mobile communication, multiple players battled over numerous competing standards, leaving the US market fragmented.

By contrast, in a purposive policy move by government, the Europeans established a single second-generation mobile, cellular, standard for the continent. Through a coordinated effort led by the European Commission, mobile phone standards were harmonized around a single platform known as the Global System for Mobile Communications (GSM). Mobile phone usage took off, stimulating a vast consumer market. The GSM standard created the setting for immense innovation on the platform, giving rise to new equipment and services. As a result, Europe has witnessed tremendous diffusion of wireless technology accompanied by substantial economic success for firms such as Nokia and Ericsson. With competition heating up over the next round of innovation in the telecommunications sector, European firms are well positioned globally because of early government efforts to coordinate technological standards (Bach 2000; Glimstedt 2001).[17]

Since World War II, the affluent democracies have been busy building the institutions to support an open, now global, international economy. The presumption has been that such actions maximize both individual and global welfare, even if the adjustment costs would be real. Alternative views have been marginalized, usually scorned as ignorant. Now, in the digital era, arguably, purposive directed domestic policy for infrastructure and standards, for example, influences broadly the outcomes of competition in IT sectors, creating not only winners but winners with defensible, retainable positions. In our view, the mercantilist tonality will not be denied. The question is the ideological/theoretical tone and institutional form it will take. The final answer, quite evidently, will hinge not on the digital technology sectors themselves but on the broader politics of trade. The breakdown of the recent World Trade Organization (WTO) round hinges on agricultural, not digital, issues. But we must ask whether state actions, and there will be state actions, will be hidden underneath the garb of continued commitment to open trade. Or will the winner-take-all element of digital competition tilt the trade world to a more state-centered, mercantilist structure? It would be an ironic outcome if competition in digital industry, which began in the belief that government hindered development and that information yearned to be free, became a trigger for increased roles for the state at home and abroad.

Embedding Markets in Social Norms

The digital revolution has radically altered the types and amount of information in the economy as well as the ability of actors to transmit and use that information. With data passing cheaply over digital networks, long nourished business dreams become reality. Yet the questions arise: Who will capture the benefits of these innovations? What threats do they pose to society? Government stands at the crossroads of the digital era, constructing the rules that underpin these emerging markets and mitigating negative social externalities. As in the case of the industrial revolution, the immensity of the technological change creates tremendous instability and displacement, which could derail the transformation. The state then steers Polanyi's "self-regulating market" so as to assure its viability. What is "new" about the digital state is less some technologically augmented or vitiated state authority than the ability of the state to influence the resolution of fundamental societal bargains that have been reopened by changes in information technology.

Two debates appear most critical. The first concerns privacy—that which permits us to remain in our personal domains secluded from the view of others. The second debate revolves around free speech— that which we can say and debate in the public arena. These debates began in the *marketplace*—how to use information to economic advantage—and spilled over into *society*—how our communities and political processes will be organized. A failure by the state to address these conflicts risks derailing the transformation and therefore demands government attention. Although the state has long been seen as the primary threat to civil rights, such as privacy and free speech, the digital transformation has ironically positioned the state as a critical defender of these very freedoms. As businesses augment their power to collect data and control the dissemination of information, new private sector threats emerge. While fears concerning potential government abuse persist, the state also has the capacity to construct the rules to mitigate individual exploitation, formulating a consumer protection regime for the digital world.

The rules and norms associated with the collection, processing, and exchange of personal information, which fall under the banner of privacy, are essential to the digital world. With the rise of digital technologies, both the quantity and quality of personally identifiable information have shifted. As each credit card purchase, Web visit, and mobile phone log creates a new bit of data, behavior becomes easily tracked. New moments of personal life become monitorable. From the Webcam in the taxi to emerging genetic tests, these technologies erode the barriers between knowable and unknowable. They also permit the networking of previously discrete data. Information-intensive sectors, such as telecommunications, banking, and health care, are the first to rely on this wealth of personal information to customize products, rationalize costs, and minimize fraud. The supermarket clubcard typifies this line of innovation. With each swipe, the company is better able to target customers and lock in loyalty. There is a shift in a range of service industries, from marketing products to marketing customers.

The opportunities inherent in personal information processing threaten to erode personal privacy, however. As digital technology expands the quantity and quality of personal information available, individuals lose the capacity to control information flows. The boundary between public knowledge and private secrets shifts, leaving less and less room for the private. What worries privacy advocates most is the networking of formally discrete personal information for third-party economic gain. Information privacy deals fundamentally with an individual's ability to control what is known about him or her. And therefore, it addresses at root how individuals construct their identity. If credit data banks cement early risky consumer behavior into a widely distributed consumer report, it is difficult for individuals to be free of the negative data profile. In short, a major concern of the digital age is the inability to forget, a fundament of most healthy societies.

Not only does digital technology shape an individual's ability to construct his or her personal identity, but it risks creating, in turn, new brands of economic discrimination. Credit card firms amassing hundreds of interactions subsorted by purchase types could link their data banks with travel patterns available from electronic toll systems. This might be done innocently to offer a valuable customer an appropriate discount but could easily be used for monitoring purposes. Similarly, one could imagine car insurance firms using mobile phone logs to track commuting patterns and potentially changing rates of individuals traveling through high-risk areas. The flipside to customization and risk reduction is potential discrimination against those who are most vulnerable (Lieber 2003).

As the amount of information held by the private sector rises, the possibility also exists that governments will look to private sector data warehouses to enhance public sector surveillance needs. The recent JetBlue scandal vividly illustrates the potential harm in the linkage between private sector firms collecting information and government bureaucracies hoping to advance security interests. In this case, the airline transferred millions of personal customer files to a Defense Department contractor, who linked the airline data to commercial data banks in order to construct risk profiles.[18] Far from an isolated incident, governments across the globe are looking to private sector data files like telephone or Internet service provider records to monitor citizen behavior. As the line between public and private enforcement breaks down, traditional checks against government abuse are neutralized. The fear of a government-dominated Orwellian world is replaced by the specter of public/private partnerships of control.

If the JetBlue scandal is a case of personal information gathered by a company being made available to the state, public policy has also compelled companies to make private information available to other business actors. For example, in attacking music downloading, the Recording Industry Association of America entered a series of lawsuits. To obtain the information on which the suits were based, the trade associate required access to the records of the Internet service providers (ISPs). The law as now written, the Digital Millennium Copyright Act, compels the ISP to provide access to that information on the basis of suspicion of IP violations, without court authorization or review. This constitutes the creation of a private posse enforcing its will in civil courts.

Such threats have not gone unnoticed by state authorities. Since the 1970s, with the proliferation of computer technology, lawmakers have recognized the danger inherent in the collection and storage of personal information. In response, nations across the industrial world adopted data privacy legislation. These rules have varied considerably, with the United States focusing on public sector data usage and Europe constructing comprehensive regulatory institutions for the public and private sector (Bennett 1992; Regan 1995). As data processing has left the confines of a small number of government agencies in the mainframe era, the comprehensive structure has shown itself better suited at dealing with the explosion of data collection inherent in the digital era. In European countries, for example, it is very difficult for private sector companies to routinely share personal information with government security agencies. Data protection rules often prevent the collection of detailed information by firms, limiting the amount of information available for sharing. Recent disputes between the United States and Europe over data privacy issues, ranging from telecommunications information to passenger flight records, demonstrate the importance of government policy in the development of very distinct information societies (Newman 2005).

Like notions of privacy, questions concerning free speech have been reopened by the emergence of digital technologies. While receiving fewer headlines than the economically more potent cases of property or privacy, speech issues lay at the cornerstone of modern political communities. By defining what can be said to whom, free speech rules shape an individual's ability to express himself or herself, maintain social networks, and organize politically. Free speech is invariably included in the catalog of basic democratic rights as the most critical arrow held by opponents of established power. Yet free speech is far from uncontroversial.

By altering patterns of communication and the capacity to transmit content, digital technology has transformed global debates about free speech. With the rise of international Internet connectivity, a resident in the United States can as easily transmit information to a fellow netizen in Europe as to a local neighbor. As a result, differing cultural norms concerning criminal speech have come into conflict with one another. Most common among these are forms of obscenity, hate speech, and political protests. As digital connectivity permits citizens from one nation easy access to the media of another, jurisdictional conflicts emerge (Kobrin 2001).

Technology has changed not only patterns of communication but also the ability to control content. As previously described, digital goods are naturally nonrival and replicable at no marginal cost. This feature has challenged traditional business models, spurring industry to try to increase the controllability of content. Through legislation and code, content providers have attempted to minimize the amount of IP available in the digital commons. This "second enclosure" restricts the fair use of information and in turn limits the free flow of ideas essential to free speech (Boyle 2003). It becomes much more difficult for activists to circulate news updates, for example, when they have to pay distribution fees to use this digital information. The state is left in the delicate position of determining which types of content individuals should be allowed to share.

Asserting control over content dissemination has been a critical feature of public policy in the digital era. The most famous case concerns the previously described DMCA. By criminalizing decryption technologies used to protect intellectual property, the US government hindered an individual's ability to take advantage of fair use privileges. Many contend that by limiting fair use the law will prevent the circulation of ideas necessary for democratic debate and political freedom (not to mention future rounds of IP innovation).

Potentially equally important for free speech have been policies concerned with harmful content. A distinct feature of modern society is the belief that certain information is dangerous and should be controlled through public policy. European governments, including Germany and France, have applied existing content laws to the digital era, for example, banning the sale of Nazi paraphernalia on the Internet. The firms selling such products are often located in countries with different laws. As a result, the application of content laws can take on an extraterritorial flare (Beeson and Hansen 1997). Far from a technologically driven race to the bottom in standards, firms playing in international markets have been confronted by the projection of national rules through digital networks.

At the same time that governments have moved to control content, they have also actively participated in the dissemination of information technology. Access is no doubt a precursor for communication and participation. In the United States, the E-Rate program was established, which subsidized broadband technology access in schools and rural communities (Newman 2003). Similarly, as discussed previously, the Korean government has been active in subsidizing the rollout of broadband technology. While access is a critical component in overcoming the digital divide, the dissemination of digital technology should not be strictly equated with the promotion of free speech. It is still the case that governments can promote technology diffusion while at the same time controlling (or supporting companies to control) the manner in which it is used (Boas 2006).

4. The Politics of State Regulation of Digital Technologies

The digital revolution has reopened fundamental societal debates and in turn brought a reexamination of the role of the state in the emerging political economy. As firms use digital technologies to create advantage or position in their markets, old political economy bargains are undermined. Often, new entrants see opportunity in the technological disruption, incumbents struggle to hold on to old business models, and public interest groups fight to maintain or expand consumer rights. Amid the commotion, governments begin to formulate policy strategies that inevitably implicate the distribution of business opportunities. Consequently, the digital policy debates are rarely fought over broad principles, such as abstract constitutional claims about the nature of a digital society. Rather, the policy fights tend to emerge as struggles about property or about the rights of sellers in the market to gather and use information. The choices may be technically narrow, but they are socially significant.

The dynamics of these political debates are complex. In addition to the state, business lobbies and public interest groups struggle within a given political institutional environment to construct the emerging rules of the digital economy. In order to understand the variation in policy results across countries, it is vital to identify the roots of business sector and public interest preferences. In short, we contend that the organization of economic and public interest sectors influences their preference formation and their relative stake in digital debates.

Several caveats about business and public interests are important to keep in mind, as we examine the preferences of various political actors. Business interests may be driving the process of reformulating rules for a digital age, but there is no unified business position. There is certainly no "digital sectoral" interest, let alone a class interest. To start, firms have different preferences and positions on the same issues; competitors in networks seek to turn the rules to their advantage; companies building and using different technologies, or at different positions in the market, have quite distinct needs.

But there is more to the story. As Abraham Newman has shown in his work on privacy, the business interests of financial institutions depend not only on the market problems alone but also on the corporate organization of the firms themselves (Newman 2005). This organization is partly a business choice and partly a result of regulation. Integrated financial institutions, as in France, do not depend on information commodity markets to gather the information they need to market to their customers. French financial institutions rely instead on their internal warehouse of information to target customer needs. By contrast, the highly fragmented character of financial services in the United States reinforces demands for a market in commodity information. So interests may be definable, but they are defined as much by nationally distinct politics and regulations as by any self-evident, universal, economic logic.

Similarly, public interest groups have been at the forefront of many digital policy debates across the globe. But their level of engagement, their policy goals, and their lobbying strategies differ dramatically across countries. Compare the work of the most active public interest groups in the United States, such as the Electronic Privacy and Information Center and the Electronic Freedom Foundation, to that of their counterparts in Europe, like data protection or consumer protection bureaus. While the goals appear identical, guaranteeing a social agenda for an information society, the logic of their tactics (e.g., class action suits and media scandals versus negotiated technocratic bargains) vary and are in a very real sense shaped by their institutional settings.

Not only do their tactics differ, but the capacity of players to influence legislative debates varies across policy landscapes. In the United States, broader public interests are represented in only a limited way in the struggles over digital rules. Certainly, the narrow business story of the emergence of electronic commerce and the tools to conduct commerce using networks has become entangled with the broader political struggle over fundamental values, goals, and processes and jurisdiction. But at least in the United States, oversimplified, it is a story of business seeking new rules to implement the digital technologies, with public interest groups seeking to influence the character of those rules.[19] More often than not, groups defending general principles, such as privacy or consumer protection on the network, enter the fights in response to business initiatives and proposed rule changes. No such group has mobilized effectively on a mass basis. The notion of the "environment," as James Boyle (1996) explains, was constructed to unify a diverse set of fights behind a single banner and facilitated mass political organization. No digital equivalent of the notion of the environment has emerged, making it difficult for a diffuse set of interests to join together.

The US debate is driven by markets and market actors, and business appears to be dominating the political debate. Elsewhere, public interest voices are fitted differently into the political system, either through a formal institutional position or through political parties. This positioning may force trade associations to respond to legislative agendas pushed by consumer interests. Two examples prove illustrative. The role of the Green Party in Germany has radically altered the place of consumer groups. This small party, a member of the governing coalition from 1998 to 2005, has successfully raised consumer protection to a cabinet responsibility. At the European Union level, consumer interests have been institutionalized in the consumer protection directorate, elevating public interest demands within European policy debates. As a result, industry is stuck in the position of responding to positions placed on the table by consumer advocates, who at the same time often have the ear of the European Commission or national governments (Young and Wallace 2000).

These differences force us to at least open the basic question of how political groups form and how their interests are defined. Because business now operates globally, because markets and products cross borders, these domestic battles for values and principles, from privacy through the right to expression, will have to be fought again and again—and the terrain of political battlefield will be much more varied, more complex. Political strategies will now involve cross-national coalitions and deals in international institutions to settle what were once exclusively domestic decisions. Indeed, the creation of interests in the whole array of digital cases emphasizes that interest groups are never mechanical functions of markets or institutional structures but rather the product of political struggles.

We can identify three basic strategies that states have adopted in response to the challenges posed by the digital era. First, governments may intervene to promote competition in the new marketplace, as technological change disrupts existing business strategies. States intervene to secure fair ground rules for the fights between dominant players and new entrants. These rules may emphasize equal market access, level regulatory playing fields, and transparency. The European Union convergence effort in the communications regime typifies this policy strategy. As media including telecommunications, radio, cable, and satellite compete head-to-head with one another for core digital products, market disruptions result from regulatory legacies. Telecommunications companies, for example, face very different regulatory burdens when entering new markets than cable companies. Universal service requirements mandate that telephone companies guarantee access to underserved communities, a cost not faced by cable companies looking to compete in broadband markets. The convergence process attempts to smooth over these regulatory differences and create a comprehensive regime for the digital communications industry. This strategy of getting the market rules right prioritizes procedural neutrality and long-term market competition over attempts to shield specific national champions.

In the second policy strategy, governments intervene to reassert incumbent market power. Digital innovations have the potential to upset existing business dynamics in a sector, threatening powerful industry groups. Policies in this strain attempt to shore up the predigital distribution of resources and prevent political coalitions from shifting. The DMCA offers the prototypical example of this form of state intervention. The DMCA criminalized the development and use of devices that may be used to break encryption systems. Technological solutions to intellectual property rights questions received legal support, consolidating the entertainment industry's effort to reassert property rules in the digital environment. Despite intense lobbying efforts by new entrants from the information technology sector to curb the legislation, the government attempted to reassure the entertainment industry as a critical interest group. Potentially viewed as a reactionary strategy, the second approach steers the political character of the digital transformation in favor of existing power centers.

A third strategy likewise attempts to shape the substantive character of emerging digital markets. Instead of bolstering existing interest constellations, however, the state recasts the balance of power in favor of public interests. The citizen-consumer is empowered in the new digital environment, receiving increased control over information resources. Most easily identified with the mission of consumer advocates, this third strategy attempts to promote the public interest more broadly and to prevent digital innovations from further concentrating power in the hands of economic and government elites. Often motivated by political fears that individuals will reject new technologies and thereby stall economic development, this approach emphasizes state safeguards that protect and assure citizens. The European Union data privacy directive provides a clear example. With the explosion of personal information in the digital age, the directive provides individuals with a level of control over industry and government data processing. Before a company or a bureaucracy may transmit personal information to a third party, it must obtain consent from the individual in question. If an organization fails to obtain consent, that organization can be punished by the data protection agency. While not eliminating the commodification of personal information, European regulations reset the default position in favor of consumers. Governments, promoting the third potentially populist or progressive option, channel the transformation so as to rebalance societal relationships prioritizing citizen concerns.

It is clear that new deals are being struck, but the content of these deals is not compelled in any consistent way by the digital tools and networks themselves. Rather, the state finds itself struggling to manage digitally inspired conflicts fueled by business and public interest groups. As technology reopens debates, governments have varying policy instruments at their disposal and confront distinct policy legacies. One should, therefore, expect to see different government approaches to basic digital fights. Not only will proposed government solutions vary, but these proposals will be filtered by each country's unique political configuration. The cross-national diversity of policy debates will reflect market conditions and problems but, more fundamentally, the distinct organization of the public and private sector lobbies involved.

Information, and how it is used, is the very substance of communities, polities, and markets. Communities can be conceived and indeed expressed as the character and flow of communications among members, polities as systems of decisions based on information, and markets as architectures for exchange based on information. Consequently, even the technical rules about digital technology and the digital market are directly and simultaneously decisions about the very nature of the community and the polity.

Far from being debilitated by technological progress, the state has played a fundamental role in the emergence and development of the digital era. As in the case of the great transformation, government policy has created the infrastructure for the fictitious commodity of information. Through a series of deregulation, market-making, and reregulation initiatives, public policy has constructed the rules for the new market and managed conflicts that threatened to derail the digital revolution. These efforts have had important political consequences for the character of the contemporary transformation. And given the differing ways that governments have dealt with the various challenges posed by this digital transformation, several distinct information societies will no doubt emerge.

Building Global Service Markets

Economic Structure and State Capacity

PETER COWHEY AND JOHN RICHARDS

IN AN ERA OF ECONOMIC GLOBALIZATION, a key capacity of states is the ability to restructure global markets to facilitate economic growth and distribute the benefits of economic exchange. This chapter analyzes the transformation of two critical infrastructures of the modern world economy, global telecommunications and aviation, where the hand of governments has gripped the markets firmly. The evolution of these two sectors reflects the effort to restructure the global services economy that now accounts for the majority of the world's economic output. By examining two service industries, we gain insight into how state capacity shapes the reform of global markets (after allowing for the differences among the markets themselves).[1]

Our argument is complicated in its details because the industries and their regulations are Byzantine. But our bottom line is simple. Although both telecoms and aviation went through restructuring in a period favorable to increased competition, they evolved in very different ways. First, the telecoms market was imperfectly but more thoroughly opened to competition globally than was aviation. Second, governments embedded the telecoms industry squarely in a multilateral trade regime, the World Trade Organization (WTO), while aviation remained carved out as a largely separate domain defined by rigid bilateral reciprocity pacts. The form of market restructuring—the degree of global competition and the degree of embedding in multilateral trade institutions—is our dependent variable.[2]

The way that governments change markets is by altering marketplace property rights for participants. By "property rights" we mean the government-defined rights and responsibilities for controlling and using productive assets within a given market, including who may own property and the ancillary rights associated with such ownership (Barzel 1997; Liebcap 1989). Key property rights in the service sector are the right to enter the market (including the right to own and control subsidiaries in a foreign market), freedom of pricing, and the right to interconnect with other domestic networks.

Our explanation focuses on how the major market powers reacted to technological change. We use a combination of market and institutional factors to explain the outcomes. We focus on the United States and the European Union (EU) because they drove the multilateral negotiations through 1998. In terms of market factors, particular aspects of market structure were politically salient. These features can be separated into those common to both industries and those that differ.

Both aviation and telecommunications are network industries with striking economic similarities. The most politically important was that they are both especially prone to problems of commitment and information. These vulnerabilities revolve around the problem of, for example, a country that opens its market to competition but then fails to have rules capable of allowing a new entrant to interconnect with the local network of the dominant incumbent carrier.[3]

There were also at least four politically relevant differences between the aviation and telecommunications markets: (1) the salience of global network entry rights; (2) the salience of reform to key consumers involved in the trade process; (3) the threats to the key incumbents under the status quo; and (4) the ability of new entrants to rapidly expand supply in foreign markets and therefore pose significant risks to incumbents.[4] These differences in politically relevant market structures pushed for more far-reaching and multilateral change in telecommunications as compared to aviation. Historically, both telecommunications and aviation had been structured on the premise that bilateral government agreements would define service flows. In telecommunications, however, new technologies expanded the possibilities for both new entry and cheating on existing rules. The nature of technology and how consumers used the service meant there was the real possibility of significant changes in market dynamics—likely at the expense of incumbents. By contrast, it was much harder for airline traffic to evade rules, since planes are very visible. Moreover, the additional constraints on slots at key airports—and the continued ability of the incumbents to control these slots at critical landing times—mitigated the challenge to the status quo incumbents. Equally critical was the value of reform for the large corporate community. Airline tickets represented a nuisance cost for companies, something that they would like to reduce but that was not critical to their competitiveness. But communications, information, and networking expenses were far more significant—representing as much as 6 percent of total operating costs by the late 1980s (Cowhey 1990a).

In terms of institutional factors, and of prime interest to this volume's enterprise, the institutional competence of national governments and international institutions was equally critical to changing the markets. National (or EU) institutional competence structured global change in two important ways. First, the US and EU market authorities differed in their competence to negotiate new market entry for foreign firms. Second, they differed in their ability to make commitments on implementing their market entry agreements reliably. Global market liberalization in aviation failed because none of the main actors believed that central trade authorities had control over local network access, that is, that they could guarantee the availability of landing slots at the major airports. As a result, grand promises of future liberalization tended to sound hollow and failed to gain adequate support among key players. In telecommunications, by contrast, the major players believed that governments could control market entry and access, due to the development of new state competencies, namely, regulatory powers in the EU and United States designed to ensure the ability for new players to enter telecoms markets. Furthermore, as a matter of European law, the EU possessed negotiating authority in telecommunications but not in aviation.

Our argument unfolds as follows. In Section 1, we briefly set the scene by looking at the transformation of the global services market. Section 2 draws on the literature on institutions and contracting to overview the common challenges of liberalizing telecommunications and aviation on a global basis. Sections 3 and 4 provide cases histories of the two industries. We conclude in Section 5 by examining the explanatory factors for their divergent paths.

1. Transforming the Global Services Economy

Aviation and telecommunications are key examples of the efforts to restructure national and global service industry markets since the late 1970s. Understanding the logic of service markets is crucial for understanding state economic policies because services now account for around 70 percent of economic activity in the developed world and as much as 50 percent in the developing countries.[5] The sheer size of service markets, coupled with their importance as both producers and leading-edge users of advanced technology, makes them an important influence on national economic performance.

Traditionally, service markets were linked closely to the state. Governments often provided services directly (e.g., post, telephones, transport, medical), or they owned the main commercial provider (banking). If there was a private market, governments stringently controlled features like market entry, pricing, and quality of service. Pricing schemes entailed various distributional goals—like having urban consumers cross-subsidize rural areas. Quality of service approvals had consumer protection as one reason, but governments often pursued other purposes, such as technological and industrial development or national autonomy and prestige.

National regulations largely designed to achieve domestic political objectives were buttressed internationally by similarly restrictive arrangements governing entry, competitive behavior, and most aspects of market dynamics. These global rules, unsurprisingly, greatly restricted market entry, pricing, and competitive strategy. In many cases, they were essentially cartel arrangements with government approval.

The introduction of more competition in services at the domestic level raised the question of how to extend this model globally. And, in turn, reorganizing global service markets—whether financial (ranging from banking to insurance and stock trading), communications, aviation, shipping, or architecture and construction (to name just a few)—required a close examination of global market rules for the industries. The largest systematic response and examination of the potential for the global reorganization of service markets in the 1980s and 1990s was the WTO (originally General Agreement on Tariffs and Trade [GATT]) exercise to create authority over, and rules for, trade in services. The creation of a General Agreement on Trade in Services (GATS) in the Uruguay Round was a significant accomplishment. It required, literally, a complete rethinking of what countries meant by international trade and its rules (Hoekman 1996).

In goods, the key to opening markets is to reduce barriers at the border (tariffs and quotas) for imports, then to make sure that there is no discrimination against these goods as they move to the ultimate consumer in the country. Thus, the WTO's national treatment rule states that foreign goods cannot be treated differently from domestic ones, once they enter the market. In services, governments conducted a long fact-finding exercise to identify the common market entry and competition issues (Drake and Nicolaides 1992; Stern 2001). They concluded that the delivery of services in another market sometimes takes place in a manner akin to a traditional export of goods. For example, an architect in New York consults over the phone and Internet with an engineering firm in Paris. But more typically, significant market entry requires the presence of local operations in the foreign market at least to help deliver the main service and often to produce the service as part of a global service network. For instance, a Bank of America automated teller machine (ATM) in London requires both a local operation and integration into a global banking network. This implies that a right to direct foreign investment is critical for entry into many foreign services markets.

In addition, the tradition of strong government control over services in most markets meant that there were extensive licensing systems to authorize provision of services and govern the conduct of service providers, including the freedom to price and to roll out new service products as the market changed. Any firm attempting to operate outside its home market knew that the ability to win a license and be treated in a nondiscriminatory manner was, like love in the lyrics of *Porgy and Bess*, "a sometimes thing." And, just as crucially, local regulatory systems were often designed to restrict the right to compete against the dominant incumbents (often government owned), even after market entry was granted. Stringent rules regarding access to networks on equal terms to incumbents were thus generally considered a weak second best.

This assessment of service issues led the Uruguay Round negotiators to undertake the creation of an entirely new framework for making commitments on liberalizing trade (and investment) in services. There were three parts to the GATS undertaking. First, the negotiators invented a new format for scheduling market access commitments on services. Instead of tariffs, countries could commit on items ranging from entry via creation of a "commercial presence" (that included up to 100 percent foreign ownership) to entry via the movement of peoples (e.g., a commitment to allow foreign professionals to serve the local legal market). Second, it spelled out some GATS principles for competition that purported to respecify existing GATT obligations, such as national treatment, in the context of services. Third, it allowed countries to make commitments on individual service markets (or to take exception to making any commitments).

The shift to services has also increased the importance of property rights for how international markets are organized. Property rights governing foreign investment, national treatment, and competition (e.g., who gets to participate under what rules in a given market) are the key levers for state intervention in the services economy and feature prominently in the current Doha Round of WTO talks. And as in all elements of trade and economic policy, governments seek to use property rights to stimulate growth, create competitive advantages, and redistribute economic rents among political stakeholders.[6]

In both the telecoms and aviation markets, technological innovation in the 1970s created opportunities for dramatic economic efficiency gains through increased competition, including more competition across international borders. The two market leaders globally, the United States and the EU, viewed the liberalization of service markets as important for both narrow interests and structural reform. Liberalization would help specific suppliers of services and equipment that were considered important parts of their economies. Even today, for example, Boeing is one of the largest US manufacturing exporters and has long been considered a national technological asset. The growth of "no frills" airlines in Europe has fueled demand for its 737 jets. And more broadly, liberalization would lower the costs and increase the productivity and innovation potential of "knowledge economies." But the question was how to reorganize the market—how much competition, under what organizing principles, over what time frame, with what ultimate end-state goal?

The next section begins our explanation of liberalization outcomes in aviation and telecoms by focusing on the politics of reforming property rights and the key contracting challenges facing would-be reformers in global telecoms and aviation markets. We tie these issues to the institutional competence of the key market powers.

2. Markets, Institutions, Property Rights, and the Literature on Contracting

There are both a "demand" side and a "supply" side to the granting of property rights, such as the right to entry licenses in foreign markets (including rights to foreign direct investment in the market) and freedom of pricing. On the demand side, constituents "bid" for property rights favorable to their interests, and some are more motivated or have more resources to bid for the rights (e.g., more workers who vote). On the supply side, politicians distribute or modify property rights to ensure their electoral success (Oatley and Nabors 1998; Peltzman 1976). Thus, politicians become entrepreneurs for market reform on some occasions because changing property rights can advance their political prospects.

The Players in Telecommunications and Aviation Reform

As a practical matter in these two markets, the key players on the demand side were the incumbent carriers, the large business users and household users, and the suppliers of equipment to carriers and users. As we shall see, incumbent carriers in the two industries differed in their estimation of the value of the status quo in international markets. In telecoms, most major carriers believed that cheating (rerouting, etc.) would substantially alter competitive dynamics in the market and therefore discounted the future rents from the traditional system. In aviation, by contrast, most carriers believed that they could stem entry (by controlling the limited set of important airport slots at key markets) and that cheating would be limited. This was especially true in international aviation.[7]

The larger users also differed across the two global industries. Large users were more forceful advocates of market restructuring in telecoms than in aviation, at least in part due to the greater costs associated with global telecommunications for multinational corporations. Household users also mattered but were not active proponents for change.

Finally, the equipment supplier industries varied across the industries, due in large part to the special character of the US telecoms industry and the nascent position of Airbus in commercial aircraft. The US electronics industry had long been less concentrated than its European and Japanese counterparts. There was a significant supplier base in the United States that favored market innovations in services, and the efforts of these suppliers produced competition policies that implicitly favored the computer industry over the telephone carriers on data services. In aviation, Airbus then lacked a credible alternative offering to Boeing long-haul aircraft, so Boeing favored opening international long-haul markets.

Political leadership may frame narrow issues in larger political and economic terms, as was the case of Margaret Thatcher making regulatory reform into a leading application for popularizing her political crusade for economic liberalization. In the 1990s, telecoms achieved much higher political status because of its appeal as an instrument and symbol of economic revitalization. Telecoms emerged as a central utility for high tech more broadly and for the restructuring of entire industries. Most observers realized that creating a regulatory framework to drive investment and adoption of robust telecoms network infrastructure was central to competition and efficiency in a wide set of services industries, such as financial services (Petrazinni 1996). This raised the profile of telecoms in the broader policymaking landscape because the efficiency gains from any market restructuring would boost a broad range of the economy. Aviation, on the other hand, had limited impact on the competitiveness and organization of other industries (with the exception of air cargo, which we do not address in this chapter). The liberalized aviation services market promised to offer the same services (a seat in a plane) at a reduced price, whereas telecoms reform promised to usher in a dramatically new set of services with even more dramatic price reductions.

Preexisting international institutions in telecommunications and aviation substantially influenced the solutions available to governments (Zacher and Sutton 1996). The traditional institutions for these markets—the International Telecommunications Union (ITU) in telecoms and the bilateral air treaty agreements and International Air Transport Association (IATA) in aviation—had arrangements at odds with WTO liberalization and the reorganization of property rights. In aviation, expanding beyond bilateral agreements was necessary to fundamentally restructure the market, but major beneficiaries of the bilateral agreements were enfranchised in the political framework of the agreements themselves. In telecoms, ITU rules effectively precluded single ownership of cross-border networks. In short, the existing set of international institutions generally limited flexibility by creating powerful institutional players that benefited from the status quo. However, given the need for extensive state involvement for meaningful reform—particularly in networked service industries like telecoms and aviation services—international institutions are usually required for the conclusion and successful implementation of any deal.

Property Rights, Institutions, and Problems of Commitment and Information

The restructuring of aviation and telecoms markets globally required extensive changes in property rights. For example, an airline only had property rights to a foreign route in conjunction with a bilateral treaty right to that route by its parent government. If a German airline bought a Dutch airline, the Dutch airline might lose its operating rights to a country where the Netherlands, but not Germany, had bilateral air agreements. Similarly, whereas a conventional private market has ownership rights including the right to price freely (subject to constraints such as antitrust rules) in response to market conditions, the telecoms and aviation markets had property rights with limited pricing freedom.

A significant overhaul of property rights was, on the face of it, a major challenge. But it was even more daunting because reformulated property rights were essential to resolving perennial issues of contracting in international markets. And as the discussion in this section will show, establishing strong new property rights almost invariably led to questions of the institutional competence of US and EU market authorities.[8]

The networked structure of telecommunications and aviation services presented important obstacles to market opening. The economics of networks means that the value of the network increases with the

number of users. Firms must be able to access a broad range of geographic markets to compete effectively. Gaining or maintaining pref-
erential access to key markets may provide substantial economic and
competitive advantages. Incumbents may have significant incentives to
deny market access to potential competitors, while potential entrants
have equally large incentives to secure market access on a nondiscriminatory basis. This is particularly true in telecommunications and aviation services, where the traditional arrangements created incumbent
monopolists with strong local positions.[9]

The politicization of these markets raised additional informational
and commitment issues. Historically, governments restricted access to
their domestic service markets and created state-owned enterprises to
serve these markets. State-owned or recently privatized carriers were
thus incumbents in most major markets in the early 1990s.[10] The large
labor force accounted for by these incumbents—coupled with the
legacy of government ownership and various cross-subsidies mandated
by governments and implemented by former monopolists—meant that
governments had significant political incentives to intervene to the
advantage of domestic incumbents, as more extensive competition was
introduced in the 1980s and 1990s. Thus, new liberalization arrangements had not only to satisfy these incumbents and their political
representatives but also to address the potential for domestic political
pressure to provoke subsequent government intervention to the advantage of incumbents. Consequently, any deal needed credible commitment and enforcement mechanisms to resolve the inevitable efforts
to revisit the arrangements—a particularly challenging situation in an
international context, when the credibility of market access commitments depended on persuading other countries that a government
could manage this inevitable political challenge (Levy and Spiller
1996; North and Weingast 1989).

Through the 1990s, negotiators in the two industries defined market
access in strikingly similar terms. One element was *initial market entry*
rights through flexible vehicles for entry, ranging from joint ventures
with local partners to the opportunity to purchase local incumbents,
to classic foreign investment to create directly owned networks in the
market. Equally significant was the emphasis on *extended market entry
rights* (EMERs) through access to "essential facilities" and to "complementary markets."

In regard to initial market entry, two issues concerning the competence of key market centers influenced global negotiations. First, converting global market governance into multilateral trade arrangements meant that the competence of trade officials over these service markets had to be established. This was no small feat, and it fundamentally altered the pathways of reform. Second, in the services industry, the acceptance of entry through foreign investment and control of national service companies was essential to market opening. In most countries, there were prohibitions against foreign control of telecommunications and aviation carriers. The credibility of promises to change these rules influenced the market reform calculations of every player in the private and public arena.

The emphasis on EMERs deserves special comment. Virtually all major players wanted guarantees of access to "essential network facilities" in the national market for new entrants. In a networked industry, a few existing capabilities are indispensable for providing a service, and no new entrant can replicate them in a timely and cost-effective manner. The incumbent(s) controlling these capabilities can foreclose entry into the market simply by denying access to these facilities. Government must create property rights permitting new entrants access to these facilities in a cost-effective and timely manner.

In telecommunications markets, the key essential facility for the traditional wired network is the "last mile network." This is the connection from the main telecoms network to the location of individual customers. The cost, logistical difficulty, and building permit problems involved in duplicating the transmission network to millions of individual customers make this facility hard to replicate, except when serving large office clusters of the biggest corporate customers. In aviation, the most problematic essential facilities have to do with ground service capabilities that are indispensable to operation in another country.[11] Most attention focused on access to takeoff and landing slots and city-center airports, in large part because local incumbents owned and controlled the lion's share of the gates at national airports, particularly at key times when business travelers wish to take off and land.

Any network is inherently more efficient, and often only viable, if it can exchange traffic with other networks freely and competitively. To grow and serve customers, a network must be totally vertically integrated in supplying service markets. Few companies are. Thus, market access requires property rights to interconnect with "complementary markets." Unlike essential facilities, which are easily associated with a few significant functional tasks, access to complementary markets is a classic problem in competition policy. The problem is defined in a very specific market context.

A pair of examples illustrates the challenge. In telecoms, building a large fiber backbone network for data transmission is only feasible if the network can compete for traffic from many other networks that may originate traffic but do not want to transport it over long distances. Level Three, a global backbone network, transports the Internet traffic created by thousands of local Internet service providers around the world. In telecommunications this is known, depending on the context, as the "basic transport" or "resale" market. In aviation, the particularly striking example is the right of a foreign carrier operating on an international route to pick up traffic in a foreign country that originated on a domestic carrier. For example, does regulation prevent American Airlines from freely selling tickets for service from Munich to New York if the customer begins travel with a flight from Berlin to Munich on Lufthansa?

A second set of problems stems from information and enforcement challenges. Informational problems are, in principle, clear. Whether in telecoms or aviation, a foreign competitor wants transparent information about current regulations and enforcement of the rules, not to mention transparency in any processes for changing these rules (Levy and Spiller 1996). Market access also entails timely disclosure about practices of incumbents with significant market power, so that other competitors can monitor the performance of the regulator and the incumbent. This challenge also shows the importance of institutional competence. For example, a key requirement for transparency is the separation of the regulator from the operator providing a service. This was a major issue under International Air Transport Association regulations on international fares, when the airlines themselves (via IATA) were charged with investigating and punishing cheaters on agreed-upon fares. Not surprisingly, cheating was rampant (largely via "bucket shops" that sold vacation tickets directly to consumers) but was rarely discovered or punished. In telecoms, likewise, many countries used to have the government monopoly operator set rules for its conduct, with the unsurprising result that such conduct was rarely found to be anti-competitive.

Enforcement of market rights has two dimensions, both tied to institutional capacity. One is much like information: does the regulator act in a timely, nondiscriminatory, and transparent manner to enforce its own rules? More subtly, governments judge the ability of each major player to handle the inevitable politics of transition from one market regime to another. Can they, for example, manage side payments among market participants without impinging on new international commitments? This is a matter of the institutional competence of the government authorities.

The second dimension of institutional competence concerns local authorities because services are subject to mixed levels of jurisdiction. There are issues of legal authority and of political will. In the United States, for example, the regulation of telecommunications markets is shared between national and state authorities. There are also issues of political will when dealing with conflicts at the very local level. Indeed, the same held true in aviation services—where local bonds issues and tight relationships between incumbent airlines and local governments created not only divided institutional competence but also diverse institutional incentives. Commitments to expand airport facilities thus test even the bravest politician in most countries. This seeming neighborhood matter had huge implications for the competence of governments to make commitments to change aviation markets, as the next section explains.

The following sections review the restructuring of the two global service industries. As we shall show, aviation and telecommunications began with similar starting positions—national monopolies and bilateral cartel agreements operating under a global framework—but they evolved in very different ways. It is important to remember that bilateral liberalization was the default option in both markets. Aviation markets ended up only nominally within the WTO framework and were liberalized piecemeal through bilateral reciprocity deals involving market access. This was also the dominant mode of liberalizing telecoms service markets initially, but then telecoms diverged. In the end, telecoms was more fully opened to international competition and embedded within the WTO multilateral regime in 1998. We now turn to the details of the cases.

3. Aviation Services

The central "institution" of postwar aviation markets was a set of bilateral agreements modeled on the 1946 US-UK Bermuda bilateral.[12] The bilaterals dictated the regulations governing entry, capacity, and some aspects of ancillary services. They were negotiated on the principle of strict reciprocity, that is, each state granted permission to foreign airlines to fly routes of a given economic value in exchange for permission to fly routes of equal economic value. The bilaterals set tight limits on entry and capacity and incorporated very detailed rules on the nature of services, including the size of planes to be flown, the total number of passengers allowed, and even the times of arrival. Many bilaterals predetermined the capacity of each carrier in the marketplace (so-called predetermination bilaterals), and in practice, even bilaterals with less regimented capacity clauses strictly limited the ability of any one carrier to offer much more capacity than the foreign carrier. The bilaterals often included private side agreements between airlines, providing for further capacity restrictions and delineating the terms of revenue sharing ("pooling").[13] Many bilaterals also required that foreign carriers utilize the maintenance, service, and sales staff of the domestic carrier. Finally, almost all bilaterals provided for only a single national carrier to enter any given international route ("single designation").

Generally, bilaterals delegated pricing to IATA,[14] although rates were still subject to the approval of both states ("double approval pricing"). IATA rules dictated that traffic conferences concern themselves with "all international air traffic matters involving passengers, cargo and mail ... particularly the following: ... fares, rates and charges for passengers and cargo."[15] For the purposes of price setting, strict unanimity voting meant that any single airline could veto fares anywhere in the world. IATA also set rules for all aspects of aviation services, notably food service and in-flight entertainment, thereby ensuring that airlines could not accrue advantages by providing additional services. In sum, IATA dictated that airlines provided standardized services at identical prices.

For two decades, the Bermuda regime governed the steady growth of the international aviation marketplace. By the late 1960s, however, improvements in jet technology and changes in the structure of demand for international aviation services raised the political costs of the Bermuda cartel and set the stage for its demise. The introduction of jet technology substantially reduced airline costs and led to consistent declines in the real cost of international air travel vis-à-vis other consumer goods (IATA 1974: 95–98, 231). Real costs per kilometer-ton in 1990, for example, were one-third of what they had been in 1960 (Zacher and Sutton 1996: 82). The decline in costs was especially rapid with the introduction of jumbo jets in the early 1970s (Maillebiau and Hansen 1995). Falling real costs led domestic regulatory agencies to pass some of the savings along to consumers of aviation services,[16] with declining real prices, in turn, leading to a significant increase in the number of international vacation travelers. The fact that jets also dramatically reduced travel time only increased the number of international leisure travelers.[17]

Rising incomes, faster travel times, and cheaper operating costs thus combined to produce an explosion in the number of international leisure travelers and raised the possibility that a more efficient international regulatory system might yield better domestic political results.[18] At the beginning of the jet age in 1960, some 60 to 70 percent of international air travel was accounted for by business; by the late 1970s, this figure had dropped to around 50 percent.[19] Combined with overall traffic growth of about 15 percent per annum (throughout the 1960s and 1970s), the changing composition of total demand translated into increasing numbers of voters who stood to benefit (through lower fares) from more competitive international aviation markets. Most important, given that the price elasticity of demand for leisure travel is significantly higher than for business travel, demands for lower international fares increased, as price-conscious consumers became a significant percentage of international passengers.[20]

Improved jet technology and the changed structure of demand for international aviation services also altered the incentives of incumbent airlines and potential new entrants. Jet technology was important because jets dramatically expanded the potential number of seats available and made new route patterns possible. The introduction of the Boeing 747 in 1970, which effectively doubled the number of seats available on dense international routes, was particularly significant.[21] Many airlines hoped that lower fares would stimulate enough demand to fill the empty seats, and by the late 1960s, cheating on IATA fares was rampant.[22] Jet technology also mattered because it permitted new route patterns, thereby encouraging formerly domestic airlines to add international flights. Indeed, the expanded range of jumbo jets enabled smaller domestic airlines, notably US regional airlines, to provide service in international markets for the first time.[23]

Although would-be entrants were more important in the United States than elsewhere, due to the continental scope of the economy and the absence of a single, government-owned national flag carrier, the maturation of domestic aviation markets in most Organization for Economic Cooperation and Development (OECD) states meant that small domestic carriers in these countries were also poised to enter international markets. This was especially true as the new regulations governing charter operations increasingly blurred the distinction between scheduled and charter carriers—resulting in many international carriers that began as charter operations pressing to enter international scheduled markets.[24]

By the mid-1970s, in sum, significant changes in market dynamics had dramatically increased the political costs of the Bermuda cartel for politicians in most OECD states. Equally important, the inefficiencies associated with the Bermuda cartel were so large that reform promised to generate substantial market efficiencies that could be made available for domestic redistribution. Prodded by US efforts, the period until 1997 witnessed a broad move toward more liberal bilateral agreements and a steady erosion of the role of IATA in setting international fares. Despite the overall trend toward more competitive international markets, however, liberalization has proved neither inevitable nor uniform across markets.

A number of distinct characteristics of aviation markets have driven this pattern of reform. The first is that reforms stemmed primarily from the concerns of consumers and large business users. Second, the inefficiencies of the status quo were so large that politicians had incentive to devise new marketplace rules favorable to both the industry and consumers. A third key factor was how incumbent carriers valued the status quo. The value of the status quo to entrenched carriers was somewhat higher in aviation than in telecoms. Most aviation carriers believed that it was possible to maintain the status quo; they faced limited cheating or arbitrage that would cause them to believe that competition could increase significantly, absent government reform.

The nature of aviation services traffic meant that cheating was limited, implying that discriminatory bilateral arrangements were both possible and sustainable. Aviation traffic (i.e., passengers) is highly sensitive to distance and routing, so the amount of traffic that can be rerouted to arbitrage pricing differences is relatively small. This is especially true of business travelers, who traditionally provided around 50 percent of airline revenues and as much as 80 percent of earnings.[25] Thus, arbitrage opportunities are limited (although the presence of bucket-shops and charter markets demonstrates that there are some opportunities).[26]

These dynamics were accentuated by the fact that the cost of aviation transportation increases with distance, meaning that the potential for arbitrage was limited to geographically close markets that did not require roundabout route patterns. At the same time, most carriers had their traffic concentrated on a few international routes. Their key customers might be satisfied by arrangements to ease booking on an allied airline for travel outside those routes. So the potential of multilateral liberalization to unlock large numbers of global markets simultaneously was not that alluring. Ultimately, the difficulty of rerouting traffic, the increasing costs to distance, the concentration of traffic on a few routes, and the ease of monitoring made bilateral solutions possible in aviation services. Of course, these characteristics of aviation traffic also meant that it was possible to maintain discriminatory bilateral arrangements, even in the face of liberalization in neighboring markets.[27]

The status quo also seemed more viable to major incumbents because of the slower pace of privatization and the less demanding capital requirements of government flag carriers (compared to their telecoms counterparts). In short, compared to telecoms industries in the same period, privatization had advanced much less in aviation markets, the financial demands of modernization were substantially less (although still not insignificant), and the ability of governments to continue to prop up national flag carriers did not threaten to undermine the competitiveness of other major segments of the national economy. Thus, despite the fact that the growing importance of global networks meant an increasing number of airlines had incentives to enter into the global alliance structures (and therefore accept more liberal marketplace rules and marketplace discipline), the potential for governments to intervene to protect their national flag carriers remained a much larger possibility in aviation. An additional facet of the market that both governments and carriers did not understand at the time was how significant an impact the emergence of lower-cost, no-frills airlines offering services from "secondary" airports could have on the market. Although by 2003 EasyJet, Berlin Air, and RyanAir defined much of .intra-EU aviation, the economic logic and subsequent success of these carriers did not shape decision making about liberalization in a way that it might have. Until then, countries still had not concluded that the state subsidy and protection game had come to an end because the financial burdens of the status quo had yet to overwhelm them. This meant that any selective liberalization deal in aviation services had to put in place a much more rigorous set of institutional arrangements to realign incentives.[28]

The movement toward global competition in aviation was hindered by political factors as well as economic factors. Issues of state capacity limited reform in three ways. First, both US and EU negotiating authorities have no legislative authority to liberalize foreign investment and ownership. In the United States, this would have required an act of Congress,[29] and in the EU, it would have required a substantial increase in the delegation of authority to the EU from member states. Fundamentally, this meant that neither the United States nor the EU could overcome the difficulties of making credible commitments, given their weak jurisdiction over local facilities crucial to expanding competition.[30] Second, there never was a liberalization pact with large enough benefits (either politically or economically) near at hand to test the limits of the possible on foreign ownership.[31] Third, and compounding the first, tremendous legal uncertainty surrounds the role of the EU in negotiating aviation agreements.[32] The lack of clear institutional competence for the EU for international aviation made most efforts at broader liberalization a dead letter.

It is worth looking at EU difficulties to see how institutional competence influences options to alter global markets. Most member states have resisted the expansion of EU authority in aviation markets. In particular, the European Commission has only recently obtained the authority to negotiate traffic rights after EU Transport Minister Neil Kinnock launched a series of initiatives to gain control over all aspects of aviation markets, including external aviation negotiations. Kinnock has been supported by a core EU coalition (led by France and Germany) that seeks to consolidate power over external commerce in the hands of Brussels. The coalition has pressed the Commission to use its preexisting authority over competition policy to challenge external initiatives on aviation by member states. Thus, for example, the EU sued member states over their Open Skies bilaterals with the United States. EU competition authorities also launched investigations into the British Airways (BA)–American Airlines (AA) and the Lufthansa-United alliances. The EU was very active in the debate over the landing slot allocation problems arising out of the BA–AA alliance. Although the issue was ultimately resolved in favor of EU competence, throughout the 1990s, the debate over the locus of authority for external aviation agreements (and negotiations) significantly undermined EU-US efforts to restructure the entire transatlantic market.

The limited experience with EU authority and lack of clear ex post authority created uncertainty over the legal basis of aviation markets in EU member states—which in turn undermined contracting for the very simple reason that US actors did not know which set of institutional rules would be used to make decisions on EMERs after formal liberalization. Would EU competition authorities gain jurisdiction over the allocation of airport gate slots—and the public policies associated with airport construction to expand the number of slots—or would member states retain control? What competition restrictions would EU antitrust authorities impose as a condition of approving alliances? Or would member states continue to have jurisdiction over these issues? How would slots be traded—on the open market, subject to extensive EU rules, or (as was the case) in the gray market? Given that the structure and process of decision making directly affect governmental outcomes, these questions were not merely of academic interest; they shaped the future costs and benefits of strategic and regulatory decisions made by firms at the time. So how slots were allocated or the antitrust criteria, which must be met in the future, affected the nature and extent of the concessions that parties were willing to make in current negotiations.[33]

The expected value of future aviation revenues derived under a prospective agreement is directly affected by the perceived likelihood and expense of available slots and airport facilities, along with the potential for alliances. Witness the extensive lobbying and energy that went into

trying to assign specific economic value to slots in the mid-1990s, as
the American Airlines–British Airways alliance debated with the US
and UK regulatory authorities (and other interested airlines) over the
proper number of slots to be given up to competitors and the value
of these slots. And slots are only one piece of the overall regulatory
and market landscape. Uncertainty over the legal jurisdiction of the
EU or individual member nations on key aspects of aviation markets—
hence uncertainty over the institutional arrangements that would define the landscape of the market in these areas ex post—was particularly problematic given the network structure of aviation markets,
where access to key components of markets on a widespread geographic basis is essential for competitiveness. So legal and jurisdictional uncertainties raised commitment problems that contributed to
the failure of efforts to reorganize institutional governance structures
in aviation markets.

In the end, there were no meaningful WTO commitments on
market access for aviation in the 1990s, and most of the efforts to find
a middle road (e.g., regional groups of states liberalizing with trans-
oceanic markets, such as Association of Southeast Asian Nations
[ASEAN] states liberalizing as a group with the United States) failed.
To be sure, significant changes in the marketplace—particularly the
evolution of global mega-alliances composed of multiple airlines—
shifted the industry landscape, but these were individual firms' responses to restrictive marketplace rules, not government initiatives to
establish more competitive markets. Put differently, continued state
intervention in the marketplace drove the creation and evolution of
these mega-alliances as private solutions to the economic incentives
created by network economics.

4.   Telecommunications Services

The post-1945 telecommunications regime focused squarely on the
traditional telephone network and its services. Until the 1970s, it was
assumed that the international regime should support the concept of
monopolistic supply of services and equipment in order to capture
maximum economies of scale and scope. This approach also yielded
economic rents that could be redistributed among countries and
classes of customers. When technology opened the possibility of

change, the speed of change was very different across the major market centers, and the strategic position of the big players in global reform negotiations differed significantly.

The postwar global phone traffic system assumed the logical primacy of monopoly at the national level (usually under the government postal system). The International Telecommunications Union's rules treated international services as a shared undertaking of two monopolies. Prices for providing the service between the two national phone companies were set by a transfer price called an accounting rate. As we explain later in more detail, these accounting rates could remain high because national monopolies were free to charge whatever they wished, and everyone treated international communications services as luxury goods with high margins and low volumes. In short, the norm supported a global cartel with significant rents.[34] For example, many smaller countries typically underpriced local phone services drastically and relied on monopoly profits from international services to make up the difference, thus creating a perverse incentive for building out international phone connections, while penalizing local investment (Braga et al. 1999).

Technological innovations—especially the explosion of cheaper and higher-capacity long-distance transmission technologies (e.g., satellites and modern undersea cables); the rise of the semiconductor, which revolutionized the economics of equipment; and the growth of networked computing (starting with large corporate networks) on a national and global scale—opened the way to new coalitions of large users of communications networks and specialized equipment suppliers (including the computer industry). By the late 1970s, this coalition was challenging traditional monopoly practices. Would-be service providers acquired a strong interest in working the political process to unseat monopolists. MCI, for example, began as an alternative provider of internal long-distance services between corporate offices of individual firms in the Midwest. Computer companies created major computer service networks to allow companies to share mainframe computers.

Unsurprisingly, the United States led the way to market change because it was the most technologically intense economy, had firms operating most extensively on continental and global scaled networks, and had a political economic structure that was most resistant to centralized monopolies. (The US electronics industry, for example, was comparatively free of extensive government guidance and had much greater freedom of entry and exit than other market centers.) Out of this process, large users became politically active advocates for competition in all telecommunications services in order to improve pricing, reliability, and technical innovation. This was a much bigger commitment of political effort than seen in aviation.

The EU and Japan sought to control the amount of competition in their markets much longer than the United States, at least until the mid-1990s. While the formal approach differed, the EU and Japan both tried to shield the bulk of the phone services market from vigorous competition. They reversed course only when most stakeholders in the equipment supplier and large-user communities conceded in the early 1990s that this approach was causing a loss in both the information technology supply markets and the business operations of large users.

For a variety of reasons, the dominant incumbents in the industrial world expected more change in the telecoms market, even without new global rules, than their counterparts in aviation. One reason was that technological innovation was requiring huge new capital expenditures precisely when governments were trying to cut budget deficits. Governments became reluctant to sink the required amounts of new capital into state-owned firms. Indeed, these firms were attractive candidates for partial or full privatization in order to raise money and write down government debts. As a result, firms outside the United States began to brace for big changes.

A related reason was that the US departure from the monopoly model assured that there were going to be problems with maintaining monopolies elsewhere, given the huge place of the United States in the world market (over 25 percent). By 1986, the United Kingdom, Canada, Japan, Australia, and New Zealand had joined the US defection from the monopoly model. If each national experiment with competition could have been hermetically sealed at the border, the old international regime might not have changed. But this was not practical. In addition to the demonstration effect of US success with competition, the diversity of national market structures and extraordinarily high margins on international services encouraged cheating on the sanctioned system of international services and pricing. Put bluntly, international telecoms traffic was increasingly "footloose." A call from Berlin to Mexico could be rerouted secretly through New York to take advantage of the fact that the US carriers offered lower rates to Mexico than did German carriers. Electronic signals did not care, unlike airline passengers, if the routes were convoluted (except in some circumstances where quality assurance required more direct routing). Pricing arbitrage and traffic rerouting meant that the status quo was far less reliable as a guide to the future in telecoms than in aviation.

By the time that the Uruguay Round was launched in 1984, it was clear that telecoms and information service networks would become part of the new trade in services agenda because data networking in the 1980s was of great strategic significance to corporations of every advanced economy and an attractive growth market to suppliers. All major countries had crafted ways to exempt the data networking market in varying degrees from the general monopoly regime. Moreover, the total size of the market was less than 5 percent of the general communications services market globally. Nonetheless, the conventional wisdom held that significant market access commitments on data networking would be hard to obtain because of the general complexity of figuring out how to apply trade liberalization to services (Cowhey 1990b). The problems for negotiators included all of the ones discussed in regard to initial and extended market entry, but the smaller specialized nature of the market made them easier to finesse.[35]

As a result, the key industrial countries crafted an accord on "value-added" data networking as part of the services agreements of the Uruguay Round. Then, in the closing moments of the Uruguay Round, the EU raised the stakes by calling the United States on its long-standing rhetoric in favor of a trade agreement on "basic" communications services and building and ownership of underlying network facilities (voice, fax, and the use of key network functions, such as switching and transport).

As the Uruguay Round came to a conclusion, the EU had decided to introduce general EU competition in basic communications services on January 1, 1998. This decision spurred Europe's interest in a matching WTO agreement. If the EU was going to overhaul the European market, the European carriers wanted access to the US market because US carriers operating in Europe would presumably be treated on a nondiscriminatory basis under internal EU rules; that is, they would be treated as European firms as long as they operated through their EU subsidiaries.[36] Only a WTO agreement could offer European carriers easy access to the United States because, absent a WTO deal, the US policy was to treat European and Japanese carriers on the basis of bilateral reciprocity arrangements.[37]

The US executive branch also saw potential advantages in a WTO agreement. The Clinton administration's top leadership strongly pursued initiatives to show that it could champion an American vision of the information technology future supporting American firms and the "new economics" of the Internet. Sweeping global market change was part of this story (Cairncross 1997). And the large user community gave special points for getting global coverage in a pact due to their business needs. As a complementary political story, a WTO agreement that really liberalized international services would lower consumer prices for global calling radically (Hufbauer and Wada 1997). This consumer benefit would appeal to diverse parts of the Democratic Party—recent immigrants who called to families in home countries, middle-class "knowledge workers," and college students. But this political gain was likely to emerge after market change. It would not win much support for initial approval of a pact. In the meantime, there were still skeptics about a WTO agreement to be overcome politically.

Knowing that there were political obstacles, the Clinton administration still decided to try the WTO route for two key reasons. First, the global nature of advanced networking meant that it was far better to get simultaneous liberalization of all the key world markets quickly. Bilateral reciprocity might have achieved the coverage eventually, but it would have taken many more years. Second, bilateral liberalization required micromanagement of the market through a virtual case-by-case examination of each foreign entrant's request for licensing. It was likely to be subject to the same blatant politicization found in many antidumping cases. But the Clinton administration envisioned the promise of the Internet economy as resting in part on the creation of powerful and very low-cost global networking. Bilateral liberalization would not achieve rapid and dramatic changes in global networks, even it got to some approximation in the long run. So the United States opted for the WTO *if* it could solve the political institutional and economic problems of multilateral liberalization.

Having decided to explore the WTO option, the administration soon ran into the institutional realities of the basic division of powers between Congress and the president. The Clinton administration wanted a WTO agreement on telecoms service that required no new legislation because new legislation is much harder to achieve than tacit acceptance by Congress. But no new legislation also might mean that the United States, unlike Europe or Japan, could not open its local phone services to competition and foreign entry. Moreover, even if it did not need new legislation, the trade pact still required enough industry support to prevent Congress from using its myriad forms of legislative power to kill a trade deal (e.g., by threatening to cut Federal Communications Commission [FCC] budgets radically in retaliation).

By pure luck, as congressional dynamics played out, the 1996 Telecommunications Act enacted a quid pro quo that would allow the Bells to enter long-distance markets if they opened up their local networks to access by competitors in local services. This 1996 act was not driven by trade issues, but it enabled US trade negotiators to commit the United States to allowing foreign firms to compete in local telecommunications services. Thus, the US offer of market access became equal to that of the EU.

The 1934 telecommunications legislation limited foreign companies to a 20 percent stake in US carriers of basic telecommunications services unless the FCC granted an exemption permitted by very convoluted statutory language.[38] The 1996 act left this rule in place. So the office of the US Trade Representative (USTR) had to craft a trade commitment to allow 100 percent foreign ownership of US carriers in a special way that would permit the FCC to create a rule granting a "strong presumption" of the right to invest and control a US carrier for any company from a WTO country. The EU team was much more concerned about how to judge the reliability of this commitment than about any other item.[39] It extensively grilled the American negotiators on the likelihood of congressional action to overturn the FCC.

Even if there were no need for legislative authorization, Congress would listen carefully to the key stakeholders. While large users, equipment suppliers, and the Bells would back a WTO agreement, there were a variety of reasons why it was not their top priority in Congress (Cowhey and Richards 2000). Household consumers could yield political profit if a dramatic deal dropping international prices emerged but were not so valuable in the politics of winning approval.

The key group consisted of the international long-distance carriers, led by AT&T, the dominant carrier.[40]

Understanding the vulnerabilities and interests of long-distance carriers requires careful consideration of the economic realities of the telecommunications markets in the mid-1990s and the political realities of the reform packages for the major domestic markets. The 1996 Telecommunications Act in the United States may have made the US and EU offers equivalent in the markets covered by adding local services to the US WTO offer, but it was far from a perfect policy instrument for liberalizing competition. Much like the EU's program on telecoms liberalization, it was particularly convoluted, and questionable, on its provisions for reliably opening competition in the local telephone market for residential and small- and medium-sized enterprise services.

The 1996 act had at least two glaring problems. First, control over pricing of local phone services remained at the state level. Typically, those prices were set unrealistically low, and as a result, competitive entry for a company building a new network under that pricing was very difficult.[41] Second, duplication of the local network required a massive effort. It would be very expensive and very slow (due to the logistics of construction and the local permitting process), even with strong rights for new entrants, to interconnect with dominant operators' local networks. Together, these issues made it improbable that local services would be an attractive market for foreign entry. With the exceptions of the local market for larger businesses and the wireless phone market (where spectrum licenses for the foreseeable future had already been allocated by auction), the incumbent Bell Operating Companies did not much fear foreign competitors under a WTO pact. The real opportunities produced by a WTO deal in the medium term would be in domestic and international long-distance markets and in the market for providing large corporate networks.

In the mid-1990s, based especially on the example of the US market, would-be entrants around the industrial world were highly confident that they could launch competitive long-distance and global corporate service networks under any regulatory system that matched the one then existing in the United States. The economics and logistics of setting up a new long-distance and corporate service network were more attractive than for local services, and the US regulatory regime had succeeded in showing how to make this competition possible. In this light, a chief attraction of the WTO pact for a new entrant in a foreign country was that its provisions effectively created the right for the entrant to base "make or buy decisions" creating networks in new foreign markets on purely commercial criteria. A new entrant could choose whether to rent facilities on the best available terms from established local networks, form a joint venture for provision of services with an established operator in the market, or—if market conditions demanded—install its own network facilities (an option that enhanced the entrant's bargaining position with incumbent networks).

The "sweet spot" in the entry market included long-distance and corporate services. This meant that the incumbents mainly at risk from a WTO deal were in these market segments. In Europe, the major incumbents were integrated across local and long-distance services, so local services buffered their total exposure to competition. But in the United States, the long-distance and local carriers were (except for a few smaller cases) separated by law and regulation as of 1996. Even the Telecommunications Act's provisions did not promise a swift massive change in that situation.

As the largest operator in the US domestic long-distance market and the entire world market for international services, AT&T had both commercial influence and a strong political interest in market rules. AT&T's highest return on investment came from providing international telephone services under the traditional international regulations. This was a cash cow feeding the rest of the company's ambitious expansion plans. Thus, AT&T's interests in sweeping global change were limited, and it saw many risks to its bottom line from higher settlement payments caused by WTO-enabled tactics like "one way bypass." Nonetheless, AT&T had failed to stop bilateral liberalization, however imperfect, with several big foreign markets, and it knew that "gray market" tactics like "call back" were going to proliferate. Moreover, large corporate networks were being lost steadily to newer entrants because AT&T's marketing was constantly hamstrung by its efforts to protect a complicated set of existing rules and prices, unlike its opportunistic rivals. AT&T knew that an open world market might free it to use the advantages from owning the biggest global infrastructure of any carrier. So AT&T acknowledged that global liberalization might hypothetically serve its interests. But, in the mean-

time, it urged Congress to be skeptical of a WTO deal.[42] The skepticism of long-distance carriers meant that the Clinton administration
had to produce some visible benefit to long-distance carriers to offset
their concerns over risks from a WTO deal—the US government had
to show large potential for new market access (that included EMERs
and enforcement), and it had to address the significant financial risks
created by a transition to competition.

The political challenges in the United States were made both harder
and easier by the EU's institutional structure. In telecoms negotiations,
the EU preferred a more limited scope to the deal than that dictated
by US domestic politics. The EU process of trade negotiation is as
much about negotiations among European states over the organization
of the internal market (and the powers delegated to the EU) as it is
about external commitments. Altering negotiating positions quickly
and on an ad hoc basis thus raises internal problems of renegotiation
and substantially raises the transaction costs of EU bargaining.[43] The
bigger and more complicated the WTO deal, the tougher the process
of internal market negotiation. The EU would have just as happily
not complicated matters by tackling international services or the diplomatic effort to win market access in the major developing countries.
Only after it concluded that these were politically indispensable reforms for the United States did it expand its vision.

All major players wanted assurances on both EMERs and enforcement issues. All concluded that assurances required some form of
WTO competition code to allow new foreign entrants an effective
right to operate against former national monopolists. A competition
policy was a major innovation for the WTO, accomplished (as we
show shortly) by using a "backdoor" in the WTO decision process.
The competition code essentially formalized the new common principles of competition rules found in all countries embracing telecoms
competition (Arena 1997). These rules largely adapted US approaches
to other markets and legal systems, so they shared an underlying architecture. Rightly or wrongly, telecoms regulators told trade negotiators that they had confidence that these competition rules would
work if applied. Perhaps the biggest question was if the national
market access offers were sufficient to allow the competition rules to
operate. After the 1996 Telecommunications Act, the United States
had all of its legal authority clearly in place (except for the investment

question noted above), and the FCC had drafted most of its initial implementing rules. The EU was still cleaning up its legal framework for competition (some key elements were not decided until 2000). But here the internal vetting process of trade offers in the EU eventually bolstered EU credibility. The EU member states have to ratify a tentative trade pact each time they authorize the Commission to make a new WTO negotiating offer. So a US negotiator can be reasonably sure that "what you see is what you get" from the EU, at least in regard to formal legal changes. Whatever the specific decisions of EU Commission and national regulatory authorities, there was a clear political commitment at the European Council to accept these trade implications.

Finally, there was the problem that from the US perspective the politically salient benefits of the agreement (especially lower costs for all classes of consumers) could only arise if trade and investment liberalization led to vigorous competition in pricing and supply of cross-border international services. Simply letting a French firm own Sprint would not end the anticompetitive effects of settlement rates and the US proportionate return rules. The WTO pact had to allow freedom to price and create international networks similar to the dynamics of the US domestic market for long distance. But the United States had by far the largest global traffic flows. Any adjustment of the world market would alter those flows. It was here that the biggest problem for the end stage of the global negotiation arose. The peculiar economics of international phone and fax service meant that there was a big financial risk for US carriers from the transition to global competition, while the institutional rules of the WTO made it hard to craft a response to the risk.

The economics of the problem flowed from the fact that the traditional ITU rules stipulated that the international connection of national monopolies (e.g., a transpacific phone call) should be provided as a "jointly provided service"—that is, two national monopolies would invest jointly in providing the international cable to connect them and would provide the necessary originating and terminating services for an international call jointly. For example, AT&T would originate the call in the United States, and the Korean phone monopoly would terminate it on a cooperative basis. The two monopolists would agree on a transfer price for the call (the accounting rate) and would "settle" up periodically based on a simple formula. Assuming an accounting rate of, say, $0.50 per minute, if one country originated 500 minutes more of calling per quarter than the other country, then it owed $250 per quarter in settlement payments. These "settlement payments" typically transferred funds from richer to poorer countries because the former called more frequently than the latter. As a monopolist that could directly put expenses on its guaranteed rate base under utility regulation, AT&T did not much care if it overpaid for terminating its calls overseas.

All of this changed when the United States switched to competition. AT&T no longer had a monopoly that was guaranteed reimbursement of its settlement payment costs. As the US market for long-distance services became competitive, all consumer prices, including international long distance, began steady declines, and demand proved to be elastic. Consumer demand for international calls increased much more quickly in the United States than in the rest of the world. As a result, US outgoing international long-distance traffic grew much faster than incoming traffic. This trend had major implications because US carriers began to owe the rest of the world soaring settlement payments, profiting other countries at the expense of US carriers. At the same time, foreign monopolists tried to play competitive US carriers off against each other by demanding higher settlement rates from individual carriers in return for access to their markets. As a counter, the FCC intervened to create a de facto cartel of US carriers for bargaining on settlement rates and traffic shares under FCC sanction.[44]

Unsurprisingly, given the economic incentives, experiments with the rerouting of international phone and data traffic in defiance of international rules grew. "Call back" exemplified the changes. In call back, a caller in India dialed a number in the United States, and the receiving number in the United States noted the incoming number, did not "answer" the call, then called back the number in India. US rates were much lower, so the Indian consumer saved money on the call. But this practice had two other effects. First, it denied the profits to the Indian monopolist that would have come from charging for an expensive originating call on its network. Second, it changed the balance of traffic flows between the United States and India—calls that should have been from India to the United States now showed up as being from the United States to India. Because accounting rates used to calculate settlement payments were way above cost, the settlement payments were largely pure rents at the expense of US consumers and carriers. As experience and technology evolved, even more elaborate schemes grew to reroute international traffic.

The FCC rules to create a united bargaining front by US carriers slowed ballooning settlement payments, but these still grew rapidly. The average settlement rate paid by US carriers in 1996 was thirty-nine cents per minute; outside the OECD area and Mexico, the average cost for US carriers was well over sixty cents per minute.[45] In contrast, the FCC believed that the efficient cost of termination (the function paid for by a settlement rate) was no higher than five to ten cents per minute. By 1997, the level of US settlement payments was approaching $700 million per year in the $10 billion US market for international phone calls. Besides driving up rates for US consumers, the FCC calculated that roughly 70 percent of the total net settlement payments represented a subsidy paid by US consumers to foreign carriers.[46]

Given these economics, the US carriers became greatly alarmed that a WTO agreement could make the situation far worse. Routing devices, such as "one-way bypass" could take advantage of asymmetric WTO commitments on market access for international services to transfer large rents to foreign carriers.[47] Ballooning settlement payments due to such routing tricks would also create a perverse incentive system for developing countries to retain monopolies on international services. The United States insisted that any global trade agreement had to provide some way to address these risks during a market transition.

The WTO's institutional rules became vital for solving the three key problems of the size of market access commitments, the credibility of commitments (especially on EMERs), and adjustments to international service problems like one-way bypass. The first two were matters of bargaining over market access among WTO members. That is, it was up to the negotiating countries to decide if the number of countries making offers to liberalize their markets under WTO rules (market access commitments) and the ways in which they liberalized them were adequate. In fact, both the United States and EU had to convince the other that it could deliver foreign investment rights reliably, but they ultimately did so during detailed market access negotiations. Even the desire to have a new competition policy at the WTO could be solved through the market access negotiation. Instead of writing a new WTO competition code, the negotiating parties mutually agreed on an "additional market access commitment" that was a unilateral national agreement to abide by a "reference paper on regulatory principles." Once listed as a national market access commitment, it was binding on the country. It required no general WTO agreement to the code by developing countries because it was a purely voluntary choice by the individual country.[48]

As much as the WTO rules worked in favor of solving the first two problems, they worked against resolving the third. The key obstacle was the nondiscrimination principle embedded in two key WTO rules—most favored nation (MFN) and national treatment. MFN meant that a market access made to one WTO country was automatically extended to all countries. National treatment meant that a country could not treat a foreign firm operating in its market differently from how it treated a domestic firm. If the United States opened its international service markets at the WTO, even monopoly foreign carriers could provide services into and out of the United States. That teed up the one-way bypass problem fully.

In the WTO negotiation, the United States tried to find a way to reconcile nondiscrimination with its worries about international services. In essence, it offered to make its existing rules on the provision of international services in the United States by foreign carriers into the basis of its WTO commitment on international services. By this logic, other fully liberalized countries (in terms of WTO market access commitments) could get a license to provide US international services because they would meet the US competition test. If the United States failed to grant the license, then it could be brought to WTO dispute resolution. Countries in the WTO without liberalized services would be denied a US license. The other OECD countries rejected this offer, arguing that it offered too much of an opportunity for political mischief, in that the United States could delay licenses inordinately. So the United States had a dilemma—it could not agree to a deal covering international services under the WTO nondiscrimination rules without creating a politically untenable situation because its institutions were too weak for rapid enforcement measures.

The solution was to sidestep the WTO altogether through a unilateral regulatory measure by the United States designed to drive down the level of accounting rates dramatically. If accounting rates were low, then the damage that could be done by a variety of measures to manipulate traffic flows (e.g., one-way bypass) would be minimal. Just as crucial, lowering these accounting rates would chop payments from US to foreign carriers, with two benefits. First, it would offer a side payment to US international carriers (lower prospective settlement payments) exposed to more competition as a result of WTO liberalization. Second, it would reduce the profitability of the traditional system of jointly provided services, thus providing a long-term incentive for developing countries to liberalize.

The FCC could reduce accounting rates through an administrative measure that did not limit entry to the US market and had no practical consequence for industrial countries. The measure was effectively a price cap (with a scheduled phase-in) on the amount that US carriers could pay foreign countries for accounting rates. The price caps set maximum rates based on a detailed economic model and used the same model for all countries, so it was a nondiscriminatory regulatory measure in WTO terms (Federal Communications Commission 1997a). And stepped-up competition on routes among the EU, Japan, and the United States would have already driven rates on those routes far below the price caps. So the price caps had no costs for those countries and seemed like a credible administrative instrument in the US context.[49]

The resolution of the transitional problems for managing international traffic flows in and out of the United States permitted a successful conclusion of the WTO agreement. With vigorous lobbying by the EU, the key industrializing countries agreed to make substantial offers on market access, and a number of other developing countries made selective commitments. Thus, the coverage of the agreement, both on current and prospective markets, was strong. In February 1997, the WTO members approved the Agreement on Basic Telecommunications Services. This agreement set a blueprint for liberalization (including foreign investment and EMERs) that was multilateral and anchored in the WTO system.[50]

In sum, telecoms liberalization was much more extensive than aviation, and it became embedded in the multilateral framework of the WTO. Although both aviation and telecommunications are networked service industries, the specialized characteristics of the telecommunications market provided a more favorable political economy for this outcome. Incumbents were less sanguine that they could maintain the status quo, and there were higher returns from having a framework to allow rapid global expansion. The political returns from reform were also higher for government leaders. Large corporate customers cared more about telecommunications reform than they did about aviation, and the Internet boom had turned telecommunications reform into a symbol of governments' commitments to modernizing to take advantage of the "information age." At the same time, the institutional competence of the US and EU governments to make credible commitments on international liberalization was higher in telecommunications than in aviation. The template of domestic long-distance competition in the United States showed that the most salient market segments could be organized to guarantee the rights of new competitors. The negotiating jurisdiction of the EU in telecommunications was clear (unlike the murky situation in aviation). And when faced with a complex issue of competition policy and changing market risks in regard to international services, the US government had the institutional capability to craft a unilateral regulatory solution that relieved the trade negotiations of the burden of solving the problem. Markets, politics, and institutional capacity permitted this pro-competitive restructuring.

5. Comparing the Two Markets

While comprehensive multilateral liberalization occurred in telecommunications in the 1990s, only ad hoc and bilateral arrangements proved possible in aviation services. We argue that these different outcomes stemmed from important differences in the political economy of the two markets, differences involving how market economics shaped political agendas, and differences in the institutional capacity of states and global organizations.

The Political Implications of Differences in Market Economics

Scholars have long recognized that industrial structure shapes preferences on regulation and trade policy and the ability of interests to exercise their preferences through collective action. As networked industries, telecommunications and aviation shared the common challenge of commitment and information problems that influence all dynamics about global liberalization. But there were also important differences between the two sectors.

One difference was financial. There was less financial pressure to end state ownership and protection in aviation than in telecoms. In addition, telecoms were seen as more technologically dynamic and therefore less amenable to state-owned enterprise models because of the need for massive new investment. These factors meant that government negotiators wanted more guarantees about the conduct of state-owned enterprises in aviation than they did in telecoms.

A second distinction was the potential for a "big bang" approach in telecoms versus aviation. In aviation, the inability for any individual bilateral deal in aviation to drive fundamental, global marketplace change meant that the political will and potential gains from restructuring could not be "grouped together" to create benefits large enough to win support for far-reaching market reform. It also limited potential political deal-making. Any given bilateral deal had to stand on its own political and economic merits—slots that went to United and other carriers at Heathrow from approval of the American Airlines–British Airways deal were direct losses to AA and BA that could not be compensated by slots at other airports.

These political and economic realities reflected both market and commitment differences from telecoms (where, as we have seen, a big bang approach proved successful). In aviation, cheating or rerouting was modest and involved mainly adjacent markets or airports. Business travelers did not like indirect routes on long flights, and governments could monitor traffic effectively. Therefore, market participants (e.g., airline carriers) did not discount the value of maintaining the status quo, as they did in telecoms. These forces meant that any given bilateral deal was largely independent of the next—so international pressure or support for a big bang approach was limited.

In telecoms, cheating on traditional international traffic routing was growing rapidly (especially when serving the key corporate customers) and could be truly global (it was possible to reroute traffic very significantly without undue customer harm). This made the value of the status quo to incumbents more problematic. Moreover, the staple of piecemeal change in aviation, a limited bilateral liberalization agreement, posed risks because each bilateral route with more competition increased the avenues for moving traffic surreptitiously. So a global approach (at least covering all of the major market centers) was desirable in telecoms, whereas it was of limited benefit in aviation.[51]

The third and final distinction between telecoms and aviation concerned the economic and political salience of reform. All market reformers tried to emphasize how liberalization would drive down the costs of international services for the average household. But this argument played out differently in the two sectors. Large corporate users, the most easily organized constituency for lobbying during the stage of political approval of a trade pact, cared more about telecoms networking issues as a source of competitive advantage than aviation transportation because telecoms expenses were much more significant. And on a political level, telecoms (and the related information technology industry) became identified with high-profile political platforms to modernize economies around the Internet, computers, and software. Aviation, in contrast, never achieved this status, despite extensive effort and lobbying by airlines to demonstrate the importance of aviation services to tourism and hospitality industries.[52]

The Role of State Institutions and Legal Authority

The competence of state institutions also mattered for our outcomes. We begin with the extreme end points of the problem—the global and the local—and conclude by looking at the institutional competence of the US government and the EU Commission.

Global institutional arrangements matter because they create a reversion point for bargaining under the status quo. This creates predictability in ordinary affairs but also directs the paths for change. Traditionally, both telecoms and aviation had been organized in a cartellike manner. While market advocates could reduce or weaken these restrictions on competition, regime rules meant that efforts at global change had no place to go for easy progress unless reformers could change the venue to the WTO. This in itself was a political hurdle. As we saw in telecoms, it also meant inventing a number of new "tricks" for the WTO on scheduling market access and competition policy. But the WTO carries its own constitutional design, and these rules nearly sank the WTO deal on telecoms when it came to international services.

At the opposite end of the governance spectrum, the ability to control subnational jurisdictions, and thereby offer credible postentry market access rights, was a crucial distinction between the markets. It was a significant problem in aviation. The biggest black hole was the inability of almost all governments to commit to the expansion of airport landing slots (particularly at prime business travel times) that would be required to enable the greatly enlarged numbers of foreign flights that would be created by greater market access. In practice, this meant that a fixed supply of infrastructure had to be redistributed from incumbents to new market entrants, hardly a politically desirable or credible long-term solution to the problem. This problem was exacerbated by the fact that major airports were often dominated by the former state-owned carriers, which promised to make market access difficult.[53] And the very visible and ultimately unsuccessful efforts to reallocate slots at Heathrow or build an additional runway at Narita demonstrated not only the value of incumbency and the difficulty in reallocating a fixed set of assets but also the real commitment challenges faced by all governments. In addition, any effort to allocate landing slots in a way that would facilitate market access—auctions, for example—would run afoul of incumbent airlines claiming (correctly) that the new mechanism for allocating slots would severely disrupt their operations and have significant negative economic consequences. This was particularly sticky for the global marketplace, as a limited set of city-center airports, dominated by former national champions, still accounted for a large percentage of total international traffic flows. Any market liberalization thus required successful negotiations to redistribute small numbers of existing slots from powerful incumbents to new, generally foreign-owned and -operated competitors. Even in centralized parliamentary systems, airport construction was a political powder keg, where local communities had earned quasi-veto rights.[54]

In contrast, telecommunications posed hard but seemingly tractable problems for the credible delivery of market entry, especially interconnection rights. Anyone who has followed battles over access of new entrants to the switching cages of local telephone exchanges or rapid access to customer support systems of incumbents knows that entry is never smooth. But there was a crucial difference with aviation. In telecoms, the US and EU authorities believed that they could deliver these rights to their own competitive entrants, and so they simply were assuring the same to foreign firms. And some dominant facets of wired network entry in the 1990s, such as creating competitive backbone fiber networks, had ample successful precedents in several countries. Moreover, mobile wireless networking had grown up in monopoly environments as the only form of public network competition. So there already seemed to be "proof of principle" of entry prospects based on past experience.[55]

Between the global and the local, the central level of institutional competence displayed significant variation across the market centers that had major implications for regulatory change. For example, the negotiating power of the EU was much less clear-cut in aviation than telecoms, with individual EU states maintaining control over the majority of marketplace rules, even as the EU struggled to assert authority by defining the issues as being ones of trade (where EU institutional competence was well established). A common problem for the two industries was the need for governments to obtain authority to liberalize foreign investment decisions. Both the United States and Europe failed in regard to aviation. (For example, in the United States, any agreement enabling foreign-owned carriers to transport passengers in the United States—say, from New York to Los Angeles—would have required congressional action to change US statues forbidding this exact practice.)[56] In telecoms, while the EU ultimately limited the ability of foreign firms to buy many of its established former monopolists, it had to liberalize all other foreign investment in order to unify its own market. Thus, it was highly credible on investment issues because such internal market liberalization measures are very hard to reverse. The United States had to rely on a very innovative interpretation of its existing law by the FCC, a cause of concern to all trading partners, because the FCC could reverse the decision in the future (although the US obligations at the WTO would not disappear).

Another critical dimension of competence was the ability to manage side payments among domestic market players in a way that would not impinge on international obligations. As we saw, this was crucial to WTO telecoms negotiations in the United States. The FCC had to reduce the worst risks of a market transition for international services by undertaking a bold measure that capped settlement rates paid to foreign carriers. If it had not done so, US agreement to the WTO deal would have been impossible.

This chapter has shown that the globalization of services, which account for 50 to 70 percent of gross domestic product (GDP) among the developed nations, entails more than simply "rolling back the state." Indeed, state capacity, regional (EU) capacity, and international institutional capacity (WTO) are critical to the construction of global service markets. Effective international competition in services requires political authorities to establish two sets of rights. The first is the right of foreign direct investment (FDI), perhaps through the acquisition of a local service provider. The second is the right to interconnect with domestic networks. This second right is especially important in services because there has historically been a dominant, government-supported provider. Even in the wake of privatization and liberalization, the historic provider often enjoys preeminent market position as well as close links to the regulator. Because of the power of these traditional incumbents, some kind of code of competition is needed to facilitate access. The state has an essential role to play because it must check abuses by powerful incumbents. At the same time, because there is a risk that the state will protect the incumbent, instead of controlling it, a code of conduct is needed and must be negotiated. Thus, states are central actors in the construction of global markets. A key reason—along with economic factors—why liberalization proceeded further in telecommunications than in aviation was that federal authorities in the US and the EU in Europe had greater legal authority to negotiate an agreement in this sector. Moreover, United States and EU authorities were better able in telecoms to make credible commitments on future market access, guaranteeing the right of foreign ownership and investment as well as access to the telecoms network. The establishment of a global market for services hinges critically, then, on a new kind of state activism, as opposed to the eclipse of the state.

9

The Transformation of European Trading States

RICHARD H. STEINBERG

MANY HAVE CLAIMED that trade liberalization is weakening the state (Kindleberger 1971; Vernon 1971; Mathews 1997; Alesina and Spolaore 1997). Yet the state is not obviously weakening; it is transforming (Kahler and Lake 2003), as it has been doing throughout modernity (Tilly 1975; Bendix 1978; Skocpol 1979).

This chapter argues that much of the substance and process of contemporary state transformation is driven not by trade liberalization in the abstract but by the particular institutional form of trade liberalization since 1948. At the international level, the "self-regulating market" is not really "self-regulating" (Polanyi 1944). Contemporary trade liberalization has been a product of US (and, later, US-European) power, exercised through the creation and operation of the General Agreement on Tariffs and Trade (GATT) and its successor, the World Trade Organization (WTO), and reflected in the GATT/WTO's substantive rules. The particular form and processes of trade liberalization have entailed not just the abandonment of certain national policies but also shifts of authority within the state, the creation of new kinds of state capacities, and new processes of policymaking.

European state transformation is part of this story. It is generally accepted that European Community (EC) and European Union (EU)[1] institutions have strengthened at the expense of the member states. Intergovernmental theorists explain this development as a result of state-driven interactions, by which the member states agreed at crucial transformative moments (such as conclusion of the Treaty of Rome, the Single European Act, and the Maastricht Treaty) to enhance the economic efficiency or competitiveness of Europe (Hoffmann 1966; Moravcsik 1998). In contrast, neofunctionalists argue that transnational public and private elites have shifted authority from the member states to Brussels for particularistic purposes (E. Haas 1958; Burley and Mattli 1993; Sandholtz and Stone-Sweet 1998). Leadership theorists focus instead on the role of informal politics and the political vision of those who have held the post of Commission president in explaining the Commission's growing role at the expense of the member states (Middlemas 1995; Loth, Wallace, and Wessels 1998; Drake 2000).

The changing organization of Western European states and EU institutions can be more fully understood by considering the exigencies of international engagement, particularly the demands of partnering with the United States to govern the institutions of the global trading system. Effective management of the GATT/WTO system has demanded the transformation of European state institutional authority, capacity, and policymaking processes relating to trade. The United States and the EU have effectively governed the GATT/WTO system since around 1970 and began more actively driving outcomes at the end of the cold war. For the EU to join the United States as a hegemonic duopolist at the GATT/WTO required changes in the organization of the European state: shifting authority upward within states and to the Commission, expanding state capacity within states and at the European level, and changing processes of member state and European trade policymaking. The desirability of playing a leadership role in GATT/WTO governance and other demands for the EC's international engagement (such as enlargement and bilateral trade conflict and cooperation) combined to favor transformation of European states. Europe chose to transform along lines that have enabled it to more effectively cooperate and compete in international trade relations and to co-govern the world trading system.

Section 1 traces and explains the shift from US hegemonic governance of the GATT system to European-US co-governance of the GATT/WTO system. Section 2 describes and explains the transformation of European state institutional structures that enabled the EU to join the United States in governing the GATT/WTO system. Section 3 explains how European-US governance of the world trading system has favored changes in the organization of the state in many third countries toward a Western industrialized model of the state. The chapter concludes with speculation about the political and institutional limits on continued transatlantic governance of the global trading system.

1.   Governance of the Trade Regime: From US Hegemony to Shared Transatlantic Governance

Since its establishment in 1948, the GATT/WTO system has defined the rules and principles that have shaped global trade. By virtue of its enormous market power, the United States set the rules of the system in its early years (1947–1972). The EC was a relatively small market at the time, and it had not yet established its institutional authority, capacity, and internal policymaking processes to co-govern the GATT. Starting in the early 1970s (1973–1989), the United States began sharing power over the development of GATT rules with the EC. By 1973, the EC had both the market power and institutional authority and capacity to help govern the GATT system, but the transatlantic powers were constrained in the exercise of their power by cold war competition with the Soviet Union. With the end of the cold war (1990–present), the EU and the United States have actively cooperated to advance an agenda at the GATT/WTO that reflects their similar interests. The basis of transatlantic power at the GATT/WTO will be discussed first, followed by an analysis of governance in each of the three periods outlined above.

Power at the GATT/WTO

States and customs territories, and no other entities, have legal standing in the GATT/WTO.[2] International institutions are voluntary organizations; states adhere to their mandates out of self-interest. Given a world of sovereign nation–states, decision-making processes either will formally reflect the interests of powerful states or will be supplemented by informal action that allows their expression of power (Krasner 1982).

Operationalizing state "power" poses a central challenge to this line of argument. While there is some consensus that power should be defined as the ability to get others to do what they otherwise would not do, measurement is another problem (Keohane and Nye 1977). Some analysts evaluate state power in the aggregate, considering total military and economic might in order to classify countries as "great powers" or not (Waltz 1979; Gilpin 1981). But in a specific negotiating context, like trade negotiations, in which only some dimensions of power are likely to be brought to bear, the measure of power must be more narrowly tailored.

In analyzing trade relationships, market size—the capacity to open or close a market—may offer the best first approximation of bargaining power (Steinberg 2002). Most political scientists and trade economists agree that governments treat foreign market opening and associated increases in export opportunities as a domestic political benefit and domestic market opening as a cost. Hence, for example, the greater the export opportunities that can be attained, the greater the domestic political benefit to the government of the country attaining them. Market opening and closure have been treated as the currency of trade negotiations in the postwar era (Hirschman 1945; Waltz 1970; Krasner 1976). Whether trade bargaining takes the form of mutual promises of market opening, threats of market closure, or a combination of both, larger, developed markets are better endowed than smaller markets in trade negotiations. The proportionate domestic economic and political impact of a given absolute change in trade access varies inversely with the size of a national economy. An additional value of exports offers proportionately more welfare and net employment gain to smaller countries than larger ones. The political implication is that a given volume of liberalization offers proportionately less domestic political benefit to the government delivering it in the larger country. Conversely, in negotiations entailing threats of trade closure, a threat of losing a given volume of exports is a relatively less potent tactic when used against a large country than when used against a small one. Hence, it is well established that developed economies with big markets have great power in an open trading system by virtue of variance in the relative opportunity costs of closure for trading partners (Krasner 1976).

By this measure, over the course of GATT/WTO history, the

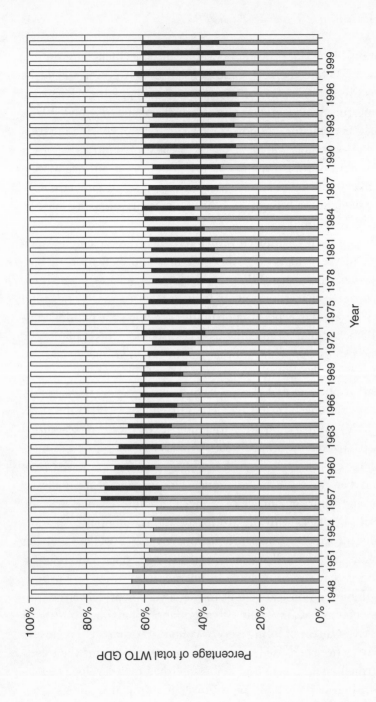

Figure 9.1. US, EC, and all other GATT/WTO shares in total WTO GDP.

United States must be considered the dominant state in shaping GATT and WTO institutions. However, its role waned, and increasingly it has needed to cooperate with the EU in order to govern the system. While the United States may be hegemonic on security matters, for the last three decades, it has shared power with the EU on trade.

Figure 9.1 shows the proportion of gross domestic product (GDP) of GATT/WTO members accounted for by the United States and the EU, respectively, from 1947 to 2001. While such figures are only a best first approximation of power in the trading system (e.g., they do not account for the effects of the fall of the Soviet Union or the increased size and diversity of GATT/WTO membership), the chart illustrates the relative loss of US market power in the GATT/WTO since 1947—and the rise of Europe. In 1948, the first year the GATT was in force, US GDP accounted for about 65 percent of the total GDP of all GATT members, and combined US-UK GDP accounted for about 75 percent of the total.[3] By 1970, US GDP share of the GATT total had fallen to 46 percent, and the EC share was 14 percent.[4] By the 1990s, the US share had continued to fall, while the EC market had become almost as large as that of the United States. In 2000, US GDP accounted for about 33 percent of the total GDP of all WTO members, and EU GDP accounted for about 31 percent. The EU share growth has increased in part as a result of enlargement. Japan accounted for about 10 percent of WTO GDP in 2000, but Japan has always been reluctant to assume a leadership role at the GATT/WTO.[5] Thus, US power at the GATT/WTO has been on the decline, and cooperation with the EU has been increasingly necessary to governing the trading system.

Three Periods of Governance

1947–1972: US Hegemony. The United States, which produced about 45 to 65 percent of GATT GDP throughout this period, dominated the drafting of the original GATT rules and the organization's policies during its first two decades. While the EC was formed in 1958, it never accounted for more than 17 percent of GATT GDP in those early years. Moreover, as discussed below, in the 1960s (which marks the last decade of this broader period), the EC was still building institutional authority, capacity, and processes to speak with a single voice in global trade talks.

Reflecting the size of its enormous market, the United States forged the GATT 1947 system, making some concessions to Britain (the GATT's second biggest market, with about 10 percent of GATT GDP). The GATT established a process for and rules about trade liberalization, but the rules allowed the United States (and all other contracting parties) to maintain specified roles for the state (described below), including those that permit states to engage in nonliberal patterns of behavior. Most of those characteristics mirrored US and British state economic institutions. If the other original contracting parties wanted access to the huge US and UK markets, they had no choice but to accept the rules of liberalization and vision of the state embodied in the agreement drafted by London and Washington. When the United States accepted the GATT 1947 rules, it had to legislate nothing and modify none of its state institutions. (Barton et al. 2006).

1973–1989: EC–US Duopoly Subject to a Cold War Constraint. By the 1970s, Europe was increasingly assertive in GATT negotiations. In 1973, the United Kingdom, Ireland, and Denmark joined the Community, raising the EC share of GATT GDP to about 25 percent. A Community that now included the big three European powers (England, France, and Germany) had to be reckoned with. Moreover, as explained below, the EC now had the institutional authority, capacity, and processes to participate effectively in GATT negotiations. By 1973, Gerard and Victoria Curzon could write that the EC had to be included in any successful initiatives at the GATT (Curzon and Curzon 1973). In the Tokyo Round (1972–1978), the most important multilateral trade roundup to that point, the EC and the United States worked together to set an agenda (i.e., the formation and drafting of texts that would be difficult to amend) that would define the final package of legal undertakings. The developing world obtained significant benefits in that trade round largely because the United States believed it was constrained by cold war competition with the Soviet Union from imposing harsher terms (Steinberg 2002).

1990–Present: Transatlantic Governance. With the collapse of the Soviet Union, cold war competition no longer constrained EC-US dominance of the global trading system. Moreover, the move of European political economies in a liberal direction in the 1980s and 1990s, and the Commission's embrace of a liberal agenda, helped the EC and

United States overcome some of their traditional disagreements over trade policy. The World Trade Organization was established, and its rules were created, by agreements between the EC and the United States that were imposed on the rest of the world. Shortly after conclusion of the Uruguay Round in 1994, both the EC and the United States withdrew from the GATT 1947 system, disengaging from their most favored nation (MFN) commitment to developing countries. In the same period, the EC and United States entered into the Agreement Establishing the World Trade Organization, which included GATT 1994 (and its MFN guarantee) and required adherence to all the WTO multilateral agreements, many of which the developing countries had previously refused to sign—such as the Agreement on Trade-Related Aspects of Intellectual Property Rights (TRIPs), the General Agreement on Trade in Services (GATS), and the Understanding on Balance of Payments. This legal-political maneuver—exercised as the "single undertaking" approach to closing the Uruguay Round—presented the developing countries with a fait accompli: either sign on to the entire WTO package or lose the legal basis for continued access to the enormous European and US markets.[6]

From the time the transatlantic powers agreed to that approach in 1990, they definitively dominated the agenda-setting process. Virtually all of the WTO agreements derived from proposals first formulated and texts first drafted through transatlantic consultations. Subsequent modifications to those texts took into account the preferences of other countries, but the fundamental substance and structure of those texts remained largely EC-US products (Steinberg 2002).

2. International Engagement and the Transformation of European Trading States

While Europe's market is one of the largest in the world, it would not have been able to effectively co-govern—or even participate effectively in—the GATT/WTO without a significant reorganization of the state at both the EC and member-state levels. That reorganization was favored not only by the exigencies of GATT/WTO co-governance but also by other demands of international engagement, such as the desirability of negotiating the terms of EC enlargement and the need to compete and cooperate with the United States, Japan, and other coun-

tries on a bilateral basis. Much of the institutional development necessary for Europe's international engagement occurred in the 1960s
and early 1970s.

Europe's increasingly unified role at the GATT/WTO, and its
emergence as a leader there, parallels the emergence of its broader
geostrategic role. The European Economic Community was established in 1958, most obviously to expand trade within Europe but also
to help embrace and contain Germany within Europe. By the early
1960s, however, it was also clear that the EC was supported to create
Western European unity in opposition to the Soviet Union; it was in
that period that the EC was effectively seated at the GATT and began
to intervene there on behalf of and usually instead of its member states
(Jackson 1969). After the cold war, the challenge was to avoid a resurgence of German dominance by binding it to the rest of Western
Europe, a goal that drove the establishment of the EU and monetary
union; it was in this period that the EU acquired formal membership
status (alongside the EU member states) in the newly created WTO
and fully emerged as a coequal with the United States in governing
the institution. This emergence of the EU as an active GATT/WTO
member and partner with the United States in governing the GATT/
WTO has been made possible by three important transformations of
European state structure.

Shifts of Authority

The first change necessary for European co-governance of the GATT/
WTO was a monumental shift of authority. If the EC were to bargain
effectively at the GATT, it needed a single voice. This demanded a
shift of authority upward, away from the member states to the Community decision-making level; laterally, from the member states acting
through the Council to the Commission; and toward the Commission's trade group within the external affairs directorate from other
groups and directorates. Similar authority shifts also took place within
member states.

Article 113 of the Treaty of Rome gave the Commission exclusive
authority to conduct negotiations with third countries "in consultation
with a special committee appointed by the Council," and in this context, the Council was to act by qualified majority. When the Treaty

of Rome entered into force, a special committee composed of the member states' most senior trade policy officials was established. In February 1959, this became the "113 Committee," but it remained undefined with no guidance as to its working practices, and the Commission did not then recognize the committee as an important institution of trade policy. Indeed, throughout the 1960s, the 113 Committee was reserved mainly for technical questions. Trade policy with third countries was instead coordinated by the Commercial Questions Group, a committee subordinate to the General Affairs Council, which subjected the Commission to precise speaking mandates from the member states and which jealously guarded member state control over Community trade policy. Consistent with this limit on Commission authority, some member states retained bilateral trade arrangements with non-Community countries well into the 1970s (M. Johnson 1998).

In the 1960s and 1970s, as the GATT trade agenda became more complex and as the EC negotiated its enlargement, the Commission developed its authority as the sole spokesperson for the EC. During the Kennedy Round (1964–1967), which was the first round to address trade topics that went beyond tariff reductions, the Commission began to articulate a need for the EC to speak with a single voice. That notion finally went unchallenged in the Tokyo Round (1973–1979), where the growing complexity of trade policy and broader range of topics made it increasingly difficult for Council ministers to understand detail and effectively broker deals with the rest of the world. By the early 1970s, the Commission ran EC trade policy, and the 113 Committee was consulted to help resolve competing member-state interests and priorities (M. Johnson 1998).

Within the Commission, authority over trade-related policy shifted toward the trade section of DG I (now called DG Trade). DG I/DG Trade coordinates European trade policy and takes the lead role in all EC negotiations with third countries. Moreover, the Commission's liaison with the 113/133 Committee[7] has been coordinated since its inception through the international commercial questions directorate of DG I/DG Trade. In discussions with DG I/DG Trade over its central role, other Commission directorates have not always maintained a friendly or collegial stance. Until 1982, DG I acted as Commission spokesperson on all matters that came before the 113 Committee; since then Commission officials with responsibility for policy that is of domestic and trade-related interest (e.g., agriculture, competition policy, and intellectual property protection) speak directly to the committee when those policies are raised, but DG I/DG Trade still coordinates the liaison (M. Johnson 1998; Nugent 2001).

These formal shifts of authority have had a big impact on who controls trade-related policy in Europe, for the effect has been to shift agenda-setting on trade-related issues from the member states toward the Commission, and toward DG I/DG Trade from other Commission directorates. As the scope of trade policy has expanded over the decades, from exclusively addressing tariff matters to now including such topics as agricultural subsidization, trade remedies laws, health and safety measures, environmental regulation, and services regulation, so has the scope of DG I/DG Trade's authority and influence over policy. Michael Bailey, Judith Goldstein, and Barry Weingast have shown how analogous shifts in the US trade policymaking process have shifted agenda-setting authority from Congress to the Office of the United States Trade Representative (Bailey, Goldstein, and Weingast 1997). Indeed, the establishment of congressional-executive trade agreements with ex post congressional approval is regarded by most legal scholars as a "silent" US constitutional amendment (Ackerman and Golove 1995; Tribe 1996).

A parallel upward shift has occurred within the member states. The member states retain influence over trade-related policy through their representatives on the 113/133 Committee. The 113/133 Committee now operates on three levels, that of the Principals, the Deputies, and the Titulaires. The member-state representatives at each committee level are from the central governments—not from member-state parliaments or subfederal levels of government—and usually from member-state trade or finance ministries (M. Johnson 1998; Murphy 2000). As the Commission often uses the 113/133 Committee to broker package deals on trade-related policy among the member states, the 113/133 Committee itself sometimes acts as an agenda-setter, which has the effect of shifting authority within member states toward the central government's trade or finance ministry and away from other ministries, parliament, and subnational levels of government.

For example, in Germany, there has not been a consistent trend in *formal* shifts of the balance of authority between the federal government and the *Länder*, but *informal* government practices have expanded the federal government's authority. Since enactment of the Basic Law of 1949, the federal government has been entrusted exclusively with the conduct of foreign relations, but treaties that regulate the overall political relations of the Federal Republic with other states or international organizations, or treaties that concern specified matters of legislation, require an Act of Consent by the two houses of the Parliament—including the Bundesrat, which represents the *Länder*. As a German constitutional matter, *Länder* governments have explicit authority over regional economic development (among other things), and most administrative matters (except defense, postal service, and foreign affairs), many of which have been delegated to local governments (e.g., economic public services, such as water and power supply).

The formal federal balance of authority in Germany has shifted back and forth over the last twenty-five years. The period of divided government that began in 1969 precipitated a 1974 decision by the Federal Constitutional Court. The ruling limited the Bundesrat's jurisdiction by denying its veto authority over bills that only revised existing programs. But in 1993, *Länder* politicians gamely managed to reverse their fortunes: in return for their support for two constitutional amendments needed to implement the Maastricht Treaty, they secured a veto over all future transfers of sovereignty that affected them and gained representation at the EU Council of Ministers meetings that addressed specified issues.

While these seesaw shifts in formal federal authority have been driven more by German and EC politics than by GATT/WTO pressures, the German state has taken action related to trade politics that has helped the federal government increase its authority over economic matters and the content of trade negotiations. Fears that the *Länder* were not able to respond to lost economic competitiveness, or to economic shocks associated with the free movement of goods, services, and labor, led to a substantial upward shift in governmental authority in the late 1960s and 1970s (Katzenstein 1987; Fukui et al. 1993). Moreover, as a practical matter, as the breadth of international trade topics has expanded to include such matters as subsidization, government procurement, and police affairs, the breadth of the federal government's authority has expanded as well. Perhaps most significantly, during the Uruguay Round, the federal government agreed with the European Commission to a "Code of Conduct," which allowed the Commission to negotiate at the GATT in strict coordination with the Council and the member states via the 113 Committee. In this committee—as well as in the Council—Germany was represented exclusively by the Economics Department and the Foreign Office, without any direct participation by representatives of the *Länder* (Hilf 1997). Hence, the international negotiating process had included participation by the federal government to the exclusion of the *Länder*.

By retaining control over international negotiations and the package of outcomes contained in each international trade agreement, the German federal government has placed itself in the position of agenda-setter on substantive undertakings, able to logroll trade agreements that have a good chance of success in Parliament. The *Länder* are relegated to a position of after-the-fact veto players operating through the Bundesrat. As the topics of regulation considered at both the European and GATT/WTO levels have broadened, so has the effective authority of the federal government.

Development of New State Capacities

The second implication of the EC's international engagement—including its emergence as an active participant in GATT/WTO trade negotiations—has been the development of new state capacities at both the European and member-state levels. Not only has the Commission developed great expertise on external trade relations in DG I/DG Trade; it has also built its capacity to use a host of policy levers to protect European industry.

The development of antidumping and countervailing duty law and associated Commission activity constitutes one such area of increased EC capacity. In 1968, based on the vague Article 113 mandate to establish a common commercial policy, the Community established through Regulation No. 459/68 that its institutions would have the exclusive capacity to erect "protection against dumping or the granting of bounties or subsidies by the countries which are not members of the European Economic Community." Antidumping measures quickly became the most frequently adopted trade policy instrument after tariffs in the EC. The EC has targeted over forty-eight countries through over 1,000 proceedings since 1970 (Bael and Bellis 1990). In their regression analysis of Commission antidumping and countervailing duty cases in the 1980–1987 period, P. K. M. Tharakan and J. Waelbroeck found that the larger the size and cohesion of the affected EC industry, the greater the chance that the Commission imposed an antidumping or countervailing duty, suggesting that these EC "trade remedy" policies serve to protect the strongest and most vocal EC economic interests. The same study also found that countries with which the EC had a short-term bilateral trade deficit were less likely than countries with which the EC had a short-term bilateral trade surplus to obtain a "softer" undertakings resolution of antidumping cases, suggesting that EC antidumping policy perhaps has been used partly for mercantilist purposes (Tharakan and Waelbroeck 1994).

EC competition law has also been implemented in a way that is intended to protect European industry or advance its competitiveness. Treaty of Rome Articles 85 through 90 (now Articles 81–89 in the EC Treaty, as amended) provide a basis for regulating activities that interfere with free market competition, a policy that could be consistent with the Treaty of Rome's objective of ensuring the free movement of goods, persons, services, and capital throughout the Community. The operational basis for Commission regulation of alleged anticompetitive practices rests in Regulation 17, which was approved by the council in 1962. This gave DG Competition a firm procedural foundation to make inquiries and carry out investigations of alleged anticompetitive practices (Goyder 2003). In 1989, DG Competition's competence was enhanced by Council Regulation 4064/89, the Merger Regulation, which was significantly revised in 2004 and established clear guidelines for the regulation of firm mergers and acquisitions that might threaten to create excessive market concentration in Europe (Rivas 1999; Cook and Kerse 1991). However, unlike US antitrust law, which is now generally interpreted in line with the Chicago School's objective of promoting free market efficiency, DG Competition implements its policy to advance both consumer welfare and "the competitiveness of European industry"[8] (Wolff and Howell 1999). It may be difficult to show empirically how this latter policy objective affects Commission activity (Gerber 1998), but it suggests the possibility that the Commission may use its competition policy regulatory capacity for protectionist or mercantilist ends.

The Commission has also developed a capacity to protect or grow particular sectors that might otherwise suffer from the Community's exercise in global trade liberalization through the GATT/WTO. The Common Agricultural Policy (CAP), which was inaugurated in 1962, has maintained farm income through price supports. While initially intended to appease French interests, the CAP has favored not only intra-EC agricultural trade but also expanded EC agricultural exports (Hurwitz 1987; Marsh and Swanney 1983; Steinberg and Josling 2003). Likewise, while the Airbus project was not launched under EC auspices, by the mid-1990s, it had become clear that the EU provided the only available political, legal, and financial framework in which all of the project's needs could be addressed. Consequently, the Commission created the Aeronautics Task Force, which coordinates the European aeronautics policy that supports Airbus (McGuire 1997; Hickie 1998).

State capacity at the European and member-state levels has also increased in ways intended to enhance the political palatability of European participation in the global trade liberalization exercise. Member states have long engaged in strategies of "domestic compensation," tendering generous early retirement benefits or retraining programs to workers displaced by international competition (Katzenstein 1985). Indeed, the expansion of Europe's massive welfare states has tended to go hand in glove with increased exposure to international trade (D. Cameron 1978; Rodrik 1997, 1998; Garrett 1998a).

An analogous development has been taking place at the European level. The EU deploys significant regional and structural funds to help alleviate the hardship of backward or struggling regions facing intensified competition. For example, European regional funds were doubled as part of the 1992 Single Market project. Today, they represent nearly 25 percent of the EU budget, the second biggest program after agriculture (which itself originated as a kind of compensation to France for accepting greater competition in industry). The capacity to offer such protection and side payments has helped make EU participation in GATT/WTO trade liberalization politically viable at home.

Processes of Policymaking

A third implication of EU international engagement has been the development of new processes of policymaking within the EU and the member states. Some of these changes have been described above, but a few others deserve mentioning.

At the Commission level, global and bilateral trade bargaining have required increased consultation and coordination across directorates. Two reorganizations of intra-Commission policy consultation are particularly notable, the first in 1993 and the second in 1999. In the Uruguay Round of trade negotiations (1986–1995), there was so much intra-Commission conflict and difficulty in reconciling positions among the DGs (particularly DG I–External Affairs and DG XIII–Agriculture) that in 1993 the Commission adopted Rules of Procedure (hereafter the "1993 Rules") to ensure cooperative efforts in policymaking. The Commission's Manual of Operational procedures already specified that only one directorate should be the lead department on any proposal. The 1993 Rules noted that consulting directorates have no authority to insist that changes be made to a proposal prepared by the lead DG but established a formal mechanism for consultation among directorates over the formulation of trade policy and other policy. In 1999, Commission President Romano Prodi reorganized the constituent parts of DG I (the directorate responsible for external affairs) into four directorates (subsequently known collectively as RELEX), investing DG Trade with responsibility over trade policy, and provided for new mechanisms of coordination. These mechanisms included meetings of the four RELEX directors general (at least monthly); establishment of the Commissioners' Standing Group on External Relations, which may be attended by non-RELEX commissioners when agenda items cover matters within their portfolios; and regular bilateral meetings between trade-relevant commissioners. While these procedural reforms have enhanced coordination, tensions still exist between DG Trade and other DGs, such as Agriculture (Bermann 1996; Nugent 2001; Pedler 2002).

Commission representation of Europe at the GATT/WTO and in bilateral negotiations has also necessitated the development of new nodes of direct interest articulation to the Commission. For example, the Trade Barriers Regulation, adopted in 1994, provides detailed

rights and procedures by which industries and member states can require the Commission to investigate allegations of damaging barriers
in third countries. This regulation is similar to the US Section 301
statute in that it formalizes the channels of complaint that are open
to industry in the EU, empowers the Commission to decide whether
there are grounds for the EU to take action (particularly legal action
at the WTO), and requires the Commission to refer information
about investigations to the 113/133 Committee, so that it can consider
any wider implications for the common commercial policy (Murphy
2000; Shaffer 2003). Others have identified a myriad of means by
which civil society may articulate its interests to the Commission in
the process of developing Community trade policy (Moravcsik 1997).

EC international engagement has demanded clarification of the responsibilities of the Commission and the member states, respectively,
in third-country trade talks. As explained above, in the EC's first decade, the political tension between Commission and member-state
control over such trade negotiations focused on which negotiating role
would be performed by various EC institutions—the Commission, the
Council, the Commercial Questions Group, or the 113 Committee.
By the 1970s, it had become settled that the Commission would have
the lead, but by that time, the breadth of "trade" negotiations began
to expand, and the Commission–member-state tension began repeatedly reemerging and resolving through European Court of Justice
(ECJ) decisions about the extent of the Commission's legal competence to act. In a string of decisions starting in 1971,[9] the ECJ created
and elaborated three categories of Commission competence to represent the EC area in trade talks. The Commission has *exclusive competence* to represent the EC area in negotiations over trade in goods,
trade in services that are electronically transmitted, and trade rules
that may affect an internal regime of the Community. The Commission has *no competence* to represent any of the member states on topics
that are not within the competence of the Community to act, such as
defense policy. And the Commission has *mixed competence* (and so must
permit member-state diplomats to participate alongside it) on trade
topics that raise issues both within and outside its exclusive competence, such as services trade (which raises, inter alia, extra-Community
immigration issues) or member-state–financed commodity trading

schemes (as direct member-state financing of such schemes is not within the Community's competence). In two of these decisions,[10] the ECJ suggested a process for Commission–member-state coordination in mixed competence negotiations. Thus, not only has the process of EC–member-state coordination evolved in negotiations with third countries, but the ECJ has also offered a process for resolving questions about process.

Finally, EC participation in international trade negotiations has offered opportunities and incentives for change in the trade policymaking process within member states. For example, in France, as the scope of trade liberalization has expanded and its implications for the French economy have deepened, the trade policymaking process has changed. Since the 1970s, French trade policy has been coordinated by an interministerial team created under the direction of the prime minister, led by the Ministry of Economics, Finance, and Industry (in which the Foreign Trade Ministry is housed), and including the Treasury and the Ministry of Foreign Affairs. In more recent years, as the impact of trade negotiations on the French economy became obvious, the Direction des Relations Economiques Extérieures (DREE) was established within the Foreign Trade Ministry, and the head of the DREE has become the official French representative on the Article 113/133 Committee. In 2001, members of the National Assembly began demanding input into trade negotiations before they are concluded, and the National Assembly now maintains a committee that tries to watch over EC trade negotiations with third countries.

3. The Formation of Trading States on the Western, Industrialized Model

Once the EC had emerged as a substantial trading power, with the institutional capacity to wield that power, it was able to join the United States in co-governing the GATT/WTO system. The GATT/WTO rules promulgated by Europe and the United States may be seen as a cast of the Western, industrialized trading state (J. Ruggie 1983), which has molded the state in third countries in the image of that model.[11] Of course, the extent to which particular states have converged on the Western, industrialized model has varied.

Casting the Western, Industrialized Trading State

What do GATT/WTO rules and principles, which were shaped by EC-US trade bargaining power, suggest about the state and the structure of the national political economy of each GATT/WTO member? Not surprisingly, they assume national political economies and state structures similar to those of the United States and Western Europe. GATT 1947 rules and principles presumed that the political economy of each contracting party would be fundamentally market oriented. The GATT was built on four cornerstones—MFN treatment,[12] national treatment,[13] bound tariffs,[14] and the elimination of quotas[15]— each of which could be undermined by the activities of state enterprises or state trading enterprises (Jackson 1989). For example, a state trading enterprise with a monopoly on all imports of a particular product could undermine the tariff binding on that product in the country where the enterprise operates: it could simply import the product, pay the tariff rate bound in that country's schedule of concessions, then internally resell all units of the product at a markup that exceeded the tariff paid for each unit. Hence, while GATT 1947 negotiators expected that some contracting parties might maintain state enterprises, Article XVII was written to severely constrain their activities, so that decisions would be taken according to purely commercial considerations (Wilcox 1972). Yet that solution has not always been considered sufficient, and the accession of some countries has been delayed or denied until there was convincing evidence of a trend and commitment toward drastic reduction in the role of the state in the economy (Steinberg 1998; Clarke 1993).

GATT contracting parties were also expected to have relatively few monopolies or oligopolies engaging in anticompetitive practices. Just as large monopoly state enterprises could undermine the four cornerstones, so could sizable private monopolies. For example, anticompetitive distribution networks could behave in ways that created a barrier to trade, with effects similar to tariffs, quotas, or denial of national treatment. Such arguments have frequently been leveled at the Japanese *keiretsu* and the Korean *chaebol* systems (Tyson 1992). The Havana Charter, an expanded form of what became the GATT, included express provisions against "restrictive business practices," and while the Havana Charter never came into being, a shared European-US norm against anticompetitive practices sufficed to limit political friction over the issue until Japan emerged as a significant economic power in the 1980s. Since then, the United States, the EC, and other GATT/WTO members have used GATT-legal national laws and agencies aimed at "unfair trade practices"—such as antidumping law—to offset and pressure countries that tolerate anticompetitive business practices.

In addition to capacity to act against anticompetitive practices, constituent states have been permitted by the GATT 1947 to maintain other capacities—regardless of their trade-limiting effects. GATT Article XXI permits the state to perform military security functions without constraint. Article VI, Article XVI, and related rules contemplate that the state may maintain simultaneously agencies that actively subsidize certain sectors (e.g., agriculture and commercial aircraft)—and agencies that monitor and act against other excessive subsidies by foreign governments. Moreover, in requiring "specificity" in order to challenge foreign subsidies, GATT negotiators have carefully permitted states to pursue broad social welfare and social safety net programs, which are presumed to be common to GATT/WTO members and crucial to their domestic politics. Article X, requiring transparent publication and adjudication of disputes over trade regulations within each contracting party, demands in effect that constituent states maintain an operational judicial system. And the Article XX exceptions show that constituent states are expected and permitted to maintain agencies to protect consumers, the domestic environment, public morality, and intellectual property. The Tokyo and Uruguay Rounds further defined GATT/WTO rules and principles and expressly acknowledge the role of constituent states in regulating various service sectors, including telecommunications and financial services.

Not every GATT/WTO member state was expected to be structured precisely along the lines suggested by the regime's rules and principles. For example, derogations have applied to the least developed countries. And some countries, such as France and Japan, were able to conduct significant state economic intervention without substantial foreign complaint until their economies became large enough to threaten the interests of other powerful contracting parties (S. Cohen 1998). These exceptions aside, GATT/WTO rules and procedures have been drafted with a particular range of permissible state structures in mind, structures that reflect those of the United States and Western Europe.

Molding the State in Third Countries: State Change Favored by GATT/WTO Rules

GATT/WTO rules and principles have provided opportunities and incentives for the transformation of the state, particularly in newly industrializing countries. As suggested above, the agenda-setting that led to the GATT 1947 and the 1995 WTO agreements was dominated by the United States and Europe, establishing agreements that demanded relatively little immediate legal or institutional change in either territory. Yet for most other countries, particularly midlevel developing countries, the procedural and substantive requirements of joining and participating in the GATT/WTO, and the incentives and opportunities created by the regime, have required or favored substantial change in state institutions.

There have been powerful economic incentives to accede to the GATT/WTO system. Nonmembers suffer trade and investment diversion (Viner 1950) and risk losing access to the world's largest markets (Steinberg 2002). As the GATT/WTO started to grow and integration among its members deepened, so did these costs of nonmembership, creating a bandwagon effect (Barton et al. 2006). Accession also promised to buttress the domestic political position of liberal-minded reformers in developing countries that had embraced import-substitution–industrialization policies and transitional economies that had pursued central planning (Goldstein 1996). Hence, the regime grew from 22 members in 1948 to nearly 150 members by 2005.

For most states with significant internal markets, GATT/WTO accession necessitates not only policy changes, sometimes referred to as "paying the price of admission" (Jackson 1969), but also institutional changes in the acceding state. For example, consider the substantive and institutional demands of implementing just one of the GATT/WTO agreements—the TRIPs agreement. TRIPs requires each WTO member to enact substantive laws guaranteeing protection for patents, copyrights, trademarks, and know-how. It also mandates the establishment or maintenance of various state institutions, such as a patent office. Moreover, by requiring that each WTO member offer "effective means" of enforcing intellectual property protection through injunctive relief, civil actions, and other enforcement mechanisms, the agreement demands that states maintain court systems that operate according to the rule of law. Institutional form follows function. Failure to adhere to TRIPs on substance or form makes non-adherent members susceptible to the WTO dispute settlement system, which can ultimately subject such states to trade sanctions for non-compliance.

As GATT/WTO liberalization has deepened, so has the scope of the demand for state institutional change among members. Over time, the scope and scale of GATT/WTO obligations have increased. This increase is reflected in the size of GATT/WTO accession protocols: in 1951, the Model Protocol of Accession to the GATT was 4 pages and required adherence to the GATT and the acceding country's schedule of tariff concessions; in 2001, China's Protocol of Accession was over 50 pages and required adherence to the GATT, China's schedule of tariff concessions, its schedule for services liberalization, approximately 300 pages of additional WTO agreements, and de facto adherence to the rules and principles established in GATT/WTO dispute settlement decisions. The GATT 1947 and subsequent multilateral trade negotiations prior to the Tokyo Round addressed largely border measures, such as tariffs and quotas. Since the 1970s, however, GATT/WTO agreements have concentrated increasingly on behind-the-border issues, such as services regulation, health regulations and industrial standards, and intellectual property rights. The Doha Round of negotiations initially added investment regulations, competition policy, and environmental regulation to the agenda, suggesting a host of new issues for the future trade agenda. As multilateral integration has deepened, the demands on GATT/WTO member states have increased.

In third countries, the extent of state change to comply with the GATT/WTO terms of integration depends on the starting point. The trade regime's pressure on states to adapt in a functional manner is mediated by particular national histories and strategic choices. However, empirically, in third countries, a country's level of economic development is the most important determinant of the extent of state institutional change associated with GATT/WTO membership. Such change has been least extensive in the least-developed countries (LDCs), such as the Democratic Republic of Congo and Lesotho; in these countries, most of the demands of the GATT/WTO system have been formally suspended or simply not enforced, largely because their markets are too small to matter to US and European business interests. Moreover, in most LDCs, state institutional capacity and political authority structures have not reached a threshold at which trade regime demands would have any meaning. In some of the poorer developing countries, such as Ghana, there has been significant change in the form of the state, but it is not clear to what extent such change may be hollow in the sense that many state institutions may be unable to perform the functions for which they were organized (Meyer et al. 1997).

The opportunities and incentives embodied in the GATT/WTO agreements have precipitated the most state change in developing countries. In these countries, GATT/WTO rules have favored a bounded convergence toward some aspects of the US/Western European and GATT/WTO model of the state along five dimensions:

1. *Reduced role for state-led and central planning institutions.* GATT/WTO trade liberalization and the trade and investment diversion suffered or feared by those countries outside the GATT/WTO system have favored reducing the state's direct role in domestic economic planning—central planning, state trading enterprise systems, state-owned enterprises, and state-led capitalism.

2. *Elements of new state capacity.* At the same time, the GATT/WTO (a) expressly permits, employs, and disciplines increased regulatory capacity over sectors once controlled by—and fallout from—dismantled state trading and state-owned enterprises (especially over competition, financial services, telecoms, labor policies, etc.) (S. Vogel 1996); (b) provides opportunities (that combine with strategic trade goals to become incentives) for strategic trade institutions that can administer antidumping, countervailing duty, and safeguards laws, technology policy (but not industrial policy), export promotion capacity, and technical standards and testing; (c) requires (or is moving toward requiring) the establishment and maintenance of state institutions supporting intellectual property rights, environmental protection, and labor rights; and (d) favors the establishment of capacity for addressing internal spillovers from liberalization—internal revenue generation (to replace revenue previously generated from duties), a social safety net that can address dislocations associated with liberali-

zation, and more technical standards and testing (to protect consumers, workers, and the internal environment from damage from imported goods).

3. *Shifts of authority.* The GATT/WTO has required or created incentives for shifts of authority within the state. While formerly state-led and central planning systems have experienced diminished state authority over the economy, in other countries, authority over the economy has in some ways become more concentrated in the state: (a) in federal systems, from subfederal levels to the central government (so that the state can negotiate with a single voice and comply with international obligations); (b) in presidential systems, from the legislative to the executive branch (so that the executive can bargain credibly and secretly); and (c) to trade ministries from other ministries—or to the external affairs division of trade and industry ministries—as previous domestic topics, such as intellectual property, environment, and labor, have become objects of trade negotiations.

4. *Changes in national policymaking processes.* Shifts in state capacity and the concentration of authority demand new processes of policymaking. For example, if authority over a particular policy shifts from one agency to another, then the processes of policymaking must also shift, so that nonstate actors can articulate their interests to the new authoritative policymakers. Similarly, if authority over a particular policy becomes shared by two domestic institutions when it was previously controlled by one, policymaking processes must shift, so that the institution previously at the center of a policymaking processes can participate in the new and expanded process. As the range of issues that are the subject of GATT/WTO negotiations has expanded, the domestic institutions of trade policymaking have adapted, so that broader sets of interests can feed into the trade policymaking process.

5. *National legal system changes.* The process and outcomes of GATT/WTO trade liberalization have favored and been accompanied by (a) an expansion in constitutionally acceptable forms of international agreements (e.g., in the United States, from treaties and executive agreements to congressional-executive agreements); and (b) marginal increased rule of law along some dimensions—formalization, transparency, and independent judicial review (e.g., all are required by GATT articles, TRIPs, and accession agreements).

4. Conclusion: The Prospects for Continued Transatlantic Duopoly and the Future of European State Structure

The international system has shaped national political economic structures in ways that are historically contextual (Gourevitch 1978; Tilly 1975; Gerschenkron 1962). Global trade liberalization in the postwar period has assumed a distinct institutional form embodied in GATT/ WTO law and characterized by a process of lawmaking that has depended crucially on EC-US cooperation and power (Steinberg 2002, 2004).

For the last thirty years, no single GATT/WTO member has had the power to unilaterally dictate outcomes. Without EC-US cooperation and power, change in GATT/WTO law would have required cooperation and a convergence of interests among dozens of countries with highly varied demographics, histories, and levels of economic development. Even if such cooperation could have taken place, the resulting growth of global trade would likely have been more modest than we have seen. A successful conclusion of the Uruguay Round, the establishment of the WTO, and the launching of the Doha Round would have been hard to imagine. Development of the GATT/WTO multilateral system would have been stunted.

The transformation of European state institutional authority, capacity, and processes has been necessary for the EC to cooperate effectively with the United States in GATT/WTO negotiations. This chapter has identified the main elements of that state transformation in Europe. Monumental shifts of authority were necessary before the EC could speak with a single voice at the GATT. New EC and member-state capacities were developed to provide policy tools that could make regional and global liberalization more politically palatable at home. And those shifts in authority and capacity required changes in policymaking processes. As suggested by the battle in the 1960s and 1970s over EC authority for negotiating third-country trade agreements, many alternative institutional arrangements were imaginable. The outcome we have witnessed was not foreordained. The Commission and the member states have made, and continued to make, choices to transform the organization of the trading state in Europe.

Will the EU and United States continue to dominate bargaining and outcomes at the GATT/WTO? The EU and US markets are the source of their dominant power at the WTO. Chinese and Indian economic growth, along with expansion of WTO membership, will likely erode that dominance. But the historically slow pace of change in the relative size of EU and US markets, indicated in Figure 9.1, suggests that power will shift slowly at the WTO—barring an unforeseeable catastrophic shock. In the short term, the bigger challenges to EU-US dominance at the WTO would seem to be from a potential divergence of EU and US interests, which Sylvia Ostry has identified as a basis for a possible "New Geography" at the WTO (Ostry 2004). Another risk is that the EU fails to continue transforming itself in ways that make its central governmental institutions effective (Tsebelis and Yataganas 2002), thereby reducing Europe's ability to contract credibly at the global level.

The State after Statism

From Market Direction to Market Support

JONAH D. LEVY

ANDREW SHONFIELD'S PIONEERING WORK gave rise to a rich literature on the various national forms that "modern capitalism" could take (Shonfield 1965).[1] Although the features emphasized and terminology varied from one study to the next, the comparative capitalism school identified three main ideal types: a liberal, market-driven model; a corporatist, negotiated model; and a statist, technocratic model (Katzenstein 1978; Zysman 1983; Hall 1986). These national models were portrayed as deeply rooted in culture and institutions, making them exceedingly difficult to change. International or economic shocks would not overwhelm national models but, rather, would be refracted in distinctive ways by the liberal, corporatist, and statist systems, respectively.

If the economic disruptions and turbulence of the past thirty years have challenged all of the advanced industrial democracies, the effects have seemed especially disruptive to the statist countries. As noted in the introduction, the archetype statist political economies, France and Japan, have experienced profound difficulties, with French authorities repudiating and dismantling the *dirigiste* industrial policy and Japanese authorities probably wishing they could do the same. The collapse of communism, the strong improvements in the US and British economies, the East Asian financial crisis, and the spread of globalization have all fueled the notion that state activism does not work and that even if it did, it is increasingly impracticable in the contemporary environment. Statism, in Shonfield's sense of faith in planners and technocrats to steer capitalist economies more effectively than market signals ever could, has lost its following. Today, few would equate "modern capitalism" with statism.

The central question animating this book is, What has become of the state's economic role among the affluent democracies in this post-statist era? How should we understand the state after statism? The chapters in this volume paint a very different picture from the images of state eclipse, common to the international political economy literature, and of displacement by employers suggested by *Varieties of Capitalism*. The state after statism remains an activist state. Its missions are evolving, rather than eroding. At the most general level, the state is moving from a market-directing to a market-supporting orientation.

This concluding chapter examines the new missions of the market-supporting state after statism. Section 1 describes a first, *corrective* vocation. State authorities are repairing elements of traditional national models that—for a variety of reasons—are no longer operating effectively. Relatedly, they are shifting the logic of labor markets away from an emphasis on worker protection or "decommodification" in favor of promoting employment. Section 2 analyzes the second state vocation, this one *constructive* in nature. Seeking to lay the foundations for future economic growth, state authorities are erecting institutional frameworks to help usher political economies across economic and technological divides. They are also striving to enhance and expand market competition. Section 3 considers the kinds of capacities that the market-supporting state needs to carry out its new missions. Finally, Section 4 ponders the implications of the analysis in this book for states beyond the affluent democracies.

1.   Correcting the Old: Repairing Varieties of Capitalism and Expanding Employment

Shonfield's use of the phrase "modern capitalism" suggested that the advanced economies had reached a stable resting point, a happy terminus. In contrast to traditional capitalism, with its depressions and unemployment, "modern capitalism" had achieved steady, rapid growth, of benefit to all groups in society, thanks to Keynesian demand management and planning. Different national models—liberalism, statism, corporatism—may have met the challenges of "modern capitalism" in different ways, but each represented a lasting solution.

The return to recession and mass unemployment in the mid-1970s cast the practices and institutions of the golden age in a more fragile light. Indeed, a central task for state authorities everywhere has become to reform their respective national models of capitalism. The pressures of mass unemployment have also led state authorities to reconfigure labor market policies.

Repairing the Varieties of Capitalism

The agenda of reforming the statist, liberal, and corporatist varieties of capitalism is, to a large extent, a product of hard times, of the general inclination to tinker with the economic machine when it is perceived to no longer be delivering the goods. But there are at least three factors driving reform beyond the ebb and flow of the economic conjuncture. First, certain institutions and practices that were adapted to a particular context—whether Fordist mass production or sheltered national economies—have become dysfunctional as that context has shifted. Second, the goals and values of society have changed, so that arrangements that seemed perfectly legitimate in the past—such as the exclusion of most mothers from the labor market—may appear anachronistic or even offensive in the contemporary context. Third, a number of policies have eroded and degenerated over time, as political or economic pressures have taken them in unintended directions. For example, in France, industrial policies designed to accelerate modernization evolved into mechanisms for sheltering uncompetitive enterprises, while in many European countries, social policies established to protect the sick and disabled became vehicles for mass early retirement. Thus, rather than a fixed end point, "modern capitalism" is perhaps best understood as a perpetual work in progress.

If policymakers everywhere are seeking to repair and revitalize inherited economic and social institutions, the agenda of reform has tended to diverge across the three principal varieties of capitalism. The statist variety, represented by France and Japan, has confronted two main challenges. The first challenge is to shift from highly directive to more light-handed and market-conforming modes of economic promotion. The combination of less sheltered national markets and increasingly innovation- and quality-based competition has made it much more difficult for governments to "pick" and build winners simply by showering them with resources and imparting a clear direction. As the chapter by Jonah D. Levy, Mari Miura, and Gene Park relates, Japan has long held an edge over France in conducting market-conforming intervention, thanks to a more organized and structured business sector, which has been able to resist and redirect some of the *dirigiste* excesses of state technocrats. Recently, French authorities have sought to cultivate less heavy-handed policy instruments. While successive governments have wound down the highly voluntarist core of their industrial policies—nationalized companies, sectoral industrial policy, *grands projets*, and the like—they have poured considerable resources into providing an enabling environment for innovation among small- and medium-sized enterprises (SMEs). These policies provide financial support for technological and managerial "leaps" by SMEs. In contrast to traditional *dirigiste* methods, the strategies are initiated by the employers and are drafted and implemented by private consulting companies, rather than the state.[2]

The second critical challenge for the statist political economies has been to move from a system of labor exclusion to one of labor inclusion without undercutting the mechanisms of rapid growth. Historically, developmental state models have been associated with conservative governments that squeezed consumption in order to channel resources to business investment. As labor and parties of the Left grew stronger, however, it became less feasible to ignore the interests of vulnerable and low-income workers. The chapter by Levy, Miura, and Park shows how this pressure diverted French industrial policy away from its modernizing mission in the 1970s and early 1980s, leading state authorities to favor employment preservation at almost any cost. A similar dynamic has also been at work in Japan over the past fifteen years.

Since the mid-1980s, French authorities have partially resolved the problem through a "social anesthesia" strategy that has allowed them to curtail dysfunctional industrial policies and permitted companies to restructure, while expanding state spending to divide and pacify the victims of restructuring. The dilemma is that this strategy is very expensive, pays people not to work, and generates considerable social exclusion. French authorities are trying very hard to "activate" labor market policy—that is, to reorient spending toward policies that promote employment—but progress is slow and contested. Japanese authorities, for their part, are seeking to combine cautious, gradual liberalization with employment maintenance. This strategy, too, is extremely expensive, and the jury is still out on whether it will revitalize the Japanese economy. While the ultimate success of the French and Japanese strategies remains uncertain, one point is undeniable: moving from labor exclusion to some kind of effort at incorporation has greatly expanded the social responsibilities and spending of state authorities in both countries.

That the state continues to play a prominent role in the statist political economies of France and Japan is perhaps not so surprising. After all, state authorities amassed vast power in the postwar period, which they were not necessarily eager to cede. No less important, popular expectations, shaped by decades of proclamations from above that the state would assure the nation's economic destiny, continue to pressure national authorities to show that the state still matters. As Levy, Miura, and Park relate, this set of expectations has helped drive the migration of the *dirigiste* impulse in France from industrial policy to social and labor market policy. French politicians no longer promise to nationalize companies or to "reconquer domestic markets" through aggressive industrial policy, but even center-right leaders like President Jacques Chirac pledge to mobilize the state on behalf of "preserving social cohesion" and "healing the social fracture."

What is perhaps more surprising than the behavior of French and Japanese elites is that the state seems to be playing a central role in adapting the liberal and corporatist models of political economy as well. Among the liberal political economies, state authorities have developed two main lines of activity. The first has been to intensify the historic market orientation of their political economies through programs of tax relief, budget cuts, privatization, union weakening, and pro-competitive regulatory reform. As the chapters by Michael Moran, Chris Howell, and John W. Cioffi reveal, this liberalizing agenda has kept state authorities very busy. The irony of an intrusive, activist state recasting liberal political economies from top to bottom in the name of individualism and free market competition is not lost on scholars of Thatcherism, who title their works with such phrases as "the free economy and the strong state" (Gamble 1994), "doing less by doing more" (J. Richardson 1994), and "freer markets, more rules" (S. Vogel 1996).

The second agenda of state authorities among the liberal political economies has been to address two sets of externalities or social pathologies stemming from the liberal, market-based strategy of economic adjustment. One such pathology is insider self-dealing: the weakening of state controls and the privatization of state enterprises have opened the door to abuses by privileged market players. Cioffi sees corporate governance reform as a response to this challenge, imposing significant costs and restrictions on insider groups. Such regulations go against the traditional liberal (and contemporary Republican Party) preference for economic laissez-faire, but in the United States, public outcry over corporate scandals like those at Enron and WorldCom has forced the state into action. Thus, as neoliberal reform has expanded market forces, state authorities—even in recalcitrant polities like the United States of George W. Bush—have felt tremendous pressure to expand their regulatory capacities to match. Increasingly, self-regulation, with its pervasive conflicts of interest, has been displaced by state regulation. Moran tells a similar tale in the case of Britain. The British state has dismantled the system of "club government" and self-regulation by incompetent amateurs that Moran believes led the country to economic decline. In its place, British authorities have established a system of intrusive state regulation, powerful independent regulatory organizations, and clear performance standards, which he describes only slightly tongue-in-cheek as a "high modernist" project.

Howell's chapter speaks to the other significant cost or pathology arising from the liberal course of adjustment—poverty and social exclusion. State authorities have played a dual role in British industrial relations, according to Howell. On the one hand, they have taken the lead in demolishing Britain's problematic Fordist industrial relations system and laying the foundations for a decentralized, flexible, and somewhat brutal post-Fordist system. On the other hand, the shocking increases in poverty and inequality that have accompanied this transformation have led British authorities to construct new forms of social protection, particularly since Labour's return to power in 1997. Government officials are proceeding gingerly, for fear of undermining the flexibility and low labor costs that have become a central component of British comparative advantage. They have avoided strengthening the trade unions or conferring new collective rights. That said, they have sought to reduce poverty and inequality, particularly among working families, through a combination of individual workplace protections, a higher minimum wage, and an array of targeted tax credits. Interestingly, whereas in an earlier era state authorities delegated considerable responsibility for combating low wages and poverty among workers to British trade unions and the collective-bargaining process, they are now increasingly pursuing this objective by direct means, via legislation.

State authorities are also playing a critical role in repairing the corporatist or coordinated market economies, as Anton C. Hemerijck and Mark I. Vail describe. Corporatist political economies have tended to suffer from rigid divides between a core of well-paid and highly protected "insiders" and a growing mass of "outsiders"—composed disproportionately of women, young people, ethnic minorities, and the unskilled—who are unable to find steady employment or to qualify for decent social insurance benefits. Reforming these systems has entailed two main challenges for state authorities. The first has been to induce the insiders to internalize some of the social costs of their behavior—to moderate wage demands, so that jobs can be created for all, and to reduce reliance on disability and early retirement programs that shelter displaced workers at tremendous cost to the collectivity.

Invariably, such reforms have rested on the projection of state power. In their chapter on economic adjustment in Holland and Germany, Hemerijck and Vail show that the transformation of the "Dutch disease" into the "Dutch model" or "Dutch miracle" was triggered by "the shadow of hierarchy." Put more prosaically, in 1982, a newly elected, center-right prime minister threatened to emulate the industrial relations practices of Margaret Thatcher if the unions did not accept wage restraint, and out of this "shadow," the Wassenaar accords were born. Other Dutch and German outcomes have been less felicitous but certainly not less statist. In response to the inability or unwillingness of Dutch social partners to manage social programs in a reasonably responsible manner, exemplified by the fact that one adult in seven came to draw a disability pension, state authorities have begun evicting the social partners from the main social programs by either privatizing these programs or taking them under direct state control. Hemerijck and Vail observe that in Germany, state authorities have been unsuccessful in inducing the social partners to embark on a course of Dutch-style wage restraint. As a fallback position, to try to limit the unemployment generated by a dysfunctional labor market, successive German governments have multiplied labor market programs, from activation to subsidies for unskilled hires, sending state spending skyward in the process.

The second critical challenge for state authorities in corporatist countries is to expand the employment opportunities for outsiders without unduly eroding existing social protections within the labor market. The Dutch "flexicurity" approach (flexibility + security) has sought to tread this fine line by expanding the rights of part-time and fixed-term workers in exchange for slightly weakened protections of permanent, full-time workers. Dutch authorities have been especially attentive to the situation of part-time workers, who constitute over one-third of total employment and who are overwhelmingly female. Successive reforms have essentially equalized the hourly wages and fringe benefits for full-time and part-time workers. In this way, total employment has expanded, Dutch employers have been able to hire part-time workers in response to genuine needs for flexibility, and Dutch women (and occasionally men) are better able to reconcile childrearing and paid employment. At the same time, employers are not able to use part-time employment as a vehicle for evading or undercutting the wages and benefits of full-time workers.

Scholars since Karl Polanyi (1944) have noted that state intervention is critical to the establishment of a liberal market economy. Leading theorists of corporatism, such as Philippe Schmitter and Wolfgang Streeck, have likewise acknowledged a key role for the state in providing social partners with the power, resources, and sometimes monopoly of representation that they need to carry out their quasi-public functions (Schmitter 1979; Streeck and Schmitter 1985). This section has shown that state intervention in liberal or corporatist political economies is not just a one-shot deal. The state does not simply set up liberal or corporatist regimes; it also helps them to adapt. Inevitably, over time, new problems and challenges arise, which established institutions are ill-equipped to handle. The functioning of liberal and corporatist institutions can also degenerate, becoming sclerotic and change resistant. These problems are rarely self-correcting; in most instances, the impetus for reform has come from the state.

Across the three varieties of capitalisms, we see state authorities engaging in new economic and social missions. For the statist model, the economic challenge has been to recast business promotion strategies on a more market-conforming basis, while the social challenge has been to incorporate the working class without fundamentally disrupting the developmental growth process. For the liberal regime, the economic challenge has been to reinforce the traditional comparative advantage in rapid, market-based competition, while the social challenge has been to attenuate sharp increases in poverty and inequality that have often accompanied liberalization. (The reform of corporate governance to rein in managerial insiders reflects both an economic and social logic.) Finally, for the corporatist variety of capitalism, the economic challenge has been to make wage bargaining and welfare policies more conducive to employment, while the social challenge has been to upgrade the opportunities and protections of labor market outsiders without undercutting the insiders. Reforms across all three varieties of capitalism evoke the "double movement" or expansion of the state first described by Polanyi: on the one hand, state authorities are extending market forces and making policy more market friendly; on the other hand, they are enhancing the social protection that shelters the most vulnerable citizens from the market.

Reconfiguring Labor Markets

Closely related to the mission of repairing the varieties of capitalism is that of promoting employment. During the postwar golden age, policymakers sought to bolster the security of a historically vulnerable working class (Marshall 1963; Castel 1995). Welfare policy disconnected the enjoyment of certain rights and consumption opportunities (education, health care, pensions, and income in times of trouble) from performance in the marketplace. Labor was thereby "decommodified," in the terminology of Gøsta Esping-Andersen (1985, 1990), meaning that workers ceased to be wholly dependent on the sale of their labor ("commodification") for survival. Thanks to the welfare state, workers were no longer a mishap or a layoff away from destitution.

The onset of mass unemployment in the 1970s called these postwar welfare and labor market arrangements into question. Unemployment stemmed from many causes, including Organization of the Petroleum Exporting Countries (OPEC) oil shocks, the changing character of economic competition, dysfunctional industrial policy and government regulation, and the breakdown of Keynesian demand management. Still, it was perhaps inevitable that state authorities would turn their attention to the impact of social and labor market protections. However well intended, these protections have in some cases produced perverse effects, fueling unemployment. Thus, the repair and adaptation of labor markets has become a central new mission of the state after statism. The chapters in this volume, notably those of Hemerijck and Vail, Howell, and Ann Shola Orloff, point to four main lines of labor market reform.

The first is what Paul Pierson has termed "recommodification" (Pierson 2001). State authorities are seeking to partially reverse the process of "decommodification" described by Esping-Andersen by intensifying employee dependence on the market. This recommodification agenda has led the state to mobilize both carrots and sticks. The main stick has been to close off or at least make less attractive alternatives to paid employment. One of the first initiatives of the Thatcher government was to slash unemployment benefits, and the strategy was repeated on a more modest scale in 2005 through Germany's so-called Hartz IV reforms. In many countries, though, the main vehicle for labor market exit is not unemployment insurance but rather early retirement, disability programs, or sickness insurance. Reform in these cases has generally entailed a tighter definition of sickness or disability, the introduction of waiting periods, lower benefits, closer monitoring, and repeated medical examinations. Finally, under the rubric of "welfare to work," "New Deals," or "labor market activation," state authorities have increased job search requirements among the nonemployed. State authorities are deploying carrots as well as sticks to recommodify workers. In particular, they are striving to "make work pay" through a combination of higher minimum wages, targeted tax credits, and subsidies to offset certain work-related costs, such as transportation and child care.

A second line of reform has been to make labor markets regulations more supportive of employment. In Holland, the state-impelled Wassenaar agreement was designed to set wages at closer to market-clearing levels. The emphasis on maximizing employment was further bolstered by the creation of the "dependency ratio," which conditioned the annual indexing of the minimum wage and social benefits on a minimum ratio of employed to inactive adults. The "flexicurity" reforms, combining enhanced protections of labor market outsiders with slightly weakened guarantees for insiders, also sought to expand employment opportunities, particularly for parents with child-rearing responsibilities, who are unlikely to accept full-time jobs. These reforms have generally been negotiated by the social partners, before being enacted into law by the government, but in several instances, the negotiations have been conducted under the threat of state-imposed solutions, should they fail.

A third line of reform, emphasized by Howell, has been to encourage labor market flexibility and productivity. Howell traces this reorientation to the exhaustion of the Fordist model of mass production. In today's fast-changing, highly competitive context, employers voice the need to shed some of the restrictions on workplace organization, individual wage setting, and hiring and firing established in the more stable Fordist age. Still, Howell notes that it is not the employers in Britain or France who have spearheaded industrial relations reform. Rather, state authorities opened the door to post-Fordist arrangements by weakening union power and creating opportunities for decentralized bargaining. Thus, British and French employers may have negotiated many of the specific reforms, but they did so under singularly favorable conditions established by the state.

The fourth line of labor market reform, analyzed by Orloff, is a revival of the traditional "reserve army" vocation. Governments have been actively promoting a "farewell to maternalism" or mass entry of women into the labor market. This policy reflects changing understandings of gender roles across the affluent democracies. Increasing numbers of women expect and need to be employed during their child-rearing years. Governments are motivated by more than concern for gender equity, however. As the baby-boom generation begins to retire, today's glut of labor is forecast to become a shortage. Keeping the economy going, not to mention the pension system, will require an alternative source of labor. Given the sensitivity of the immigration issue, boosting female employment is the obvious solution. In this spirit, the European Union's (EU) "European Employment Strategy," approved by the member states, has enshrined a formal target of 60 percent female labor force participation by the year 2010.

As Orloff relates, the state is playing a critical role in moving women into the labor force. Part of that role is coercive. The 1996 welfare reform in the United States and, to a lesser degree, various labor market activation programs in Europe have dried up public support for full-time motherhood. But state authorities have been tendering rewards as well as punishments. Tax and benefit reforms have increased the share of their earnings that employed mothers can retain. Of central importance, governments in Europe have been steadily increasing public and subsidized child care, in effect, socializing the costs of care that has traditionally been provided by women for free. There has been some movement toward socializing the costs of elderly care as well, although the programs in this area are less developed. The bottom line is that if female labor represents a formidable potential resource for aging Organization for Economic Cooperation and Development (OECD) nations, changing social norms alone will not fully mobilize that labor. The "farewell to maternalism" is, to a considerable extent, an exercise in social engineering.

2.   Constructing the New: Crossing Divides and Building Markets

The state after statism is more than a corrective state, overhauling varieties of capitalism or labor markets that have gone awry. In addition to repairing the old, it is laying the foundations for the new. State authorities are playing a critical role in establishing new bases for economic growth. They have been especially active in two areas: (1) helping usher societies across economic and technological divides; (2) expanding and building new markets.

Moving Societies across Economic and Technological Divides

Several of the chapters in this book posit that the affluent democracies are entering a new economic and technological era. For Howell, the transition is from Fordism to post-Fordism. For Cioffi, insulated,

enterprise-centered capitalism is being supplanted by a more internationalized and impersonal "finance capitalism." And for John
Zysman and Abraham Newman, the digital revolution creates possibilities for a contemporary "great transformation."

Economic and technological divides offer tremendous opportunities
for innovation and growth. But as Polanyi instructs us, society does
not generally cross such divides on its own. New divides redistribute
resources and opportunities, benefiting some groups at the expense of
others. Such divides also tend to require fundamental changes in economic practices or even lifestyles. For all these reasons, the paths from
one era to the next described by the contributors to this volume tend
to be paved with new state interventions.

According to Howell, the exhaustion of the Fordist mass production
model triggered a dramatic upsurge in industrial relations conflicts
that was too significant for state authorities to ignore. State authorities
played a central role in extinguishing the old industrial relations
system—and, in some cases, weakening the unions that went with it—
and laying the foundations for the new system. They also enacted a
series of social and labor market reforms designed to take some of the
harsh edges off the flexible, post-Fordist system: tax breaks and hikes
in the minimum wage to limit poverty; some minimal legal rights for
workers and, less frequently, their representatives; and in France, a
guaranteed minimum income for adults over twenty-five and improved
social assistance benefits for those whose employment records do not
qualify them for social insurance.

Cioffi's analysis of the rise of "finance capitalism" attributes pride
of place to the state as well. Finance capitalism requires a corporate
governance regime that allows international investors, who lack local
knowledge—let alone insider knowledge—to invest with confidence.
In both Germany and the United States, state authorities have responded with an array of new regulations and institutions to police
markets, prevent insider trading, standardize accounting practices, and
enhance transparency and disclosure. These reforms have extended
the regulatory hand of the state into some of the most private, discrete,
financial affairs of powerful multinationals. They have also imposed
significant restrictions and costs on managers. Thus, the movement
toward finance capitalism has entailed more intrusive, formalized, and
adversarial regulation by the state.

Zysman and Newman's chapter on the emerging digital economy is more speculative, by definition, as this economic and social transformation is only beginning. The authors do not know where the digital revolution will ultimately take us, but they do have an idea of what it will take for this revolution to go far. At a minimum, information technologies and the Internet will be a significant growth sector, adding businesses and jobs to the economy. But for the digital revolution to become a Polanyian "great transformation," a range of delicate issues will have to be resolved, from intellectual property to privacy, to free speech. If the next great transformation is anything like the one described by Polanyi, state authorities will have a lot on their plate.

Expanding Market Competition

The title of this book, *The State after Statism*, is meant to convey the notion that statist direction of market outcomes has fallen out of favor. It would be hard to imagine a book today with a title like Esping-Andersen's *Politics against Markets* (1985). The market referent has supplanted the state as the primary mechanism for steering the advanced industrial economies. The role of politics is to serve the market, not direct it. As many scholars have noted, however, the state does not serve the market by simply retreating. Rather, market construction is an active undertaking.

Three of the chapters in *The State after Statism* are devoted explicitly to the market-making activities of the state. Richard Steinberg shows that international trade liberalization has historically been a vehicle by which rich and strong countries impose their rules on weak and poor countries, an asymmetric exchange rooted in power politics. Steinberg also observes that what he terms the "trading state" is an increasingly capacitous state, with a slew of agencies to administer antidumping provisions, enforce intellectual property rights, expand environmental protection and labor rights, and address the spillovers from liberalization (lost jobs and lost tax revenues).

The chapter by Peter Cowhey and John Richards argues that the construction of global markets in services like airline traffic and telecommunications entails more than simply rolling back existing state regulations. In addition, it requires a credible commitment by state authorities to guarantee access to the network infrastructure and a right of foreign ownership to nonnational companies. These commitments are critically dependent on state capacity. One of the main reasons why the liberalization of telecommunications services outpaced that of aviation is that trade negotiators in Washington and Brussels possessed wider jurisdiction and authority in the former sector than in the latter. In other words, market-making in services is an inherently political and state-constructed operation, necessitating the projection of state power, as opposed to mere state withdrawal.

Finally, Zysman and Newman explore the emerging digital economy. Like the "fictitious commodification" of land, labor, and capital described by Polanyi, the creation of a market in digital technologies rests on the establishment of new kinds of property rights by the state. The state is creating a fictitious commodity of digital information, which can be individually appropriated, bought, sold, and denied to others. Nor is this the only state contribution to the digital economy. State authorities have both built the infrastructure (Advanced Research Projects Agency Network [ARPANET], Center for Nuclear Research [CERN]) and removed the barriers to the circulation of commodified information. They are also coming under pressure to embed the new information markets in social norms, notably by introducing protections of personal privacy and free speech. Because the character of these political decisions and social compromises tends to vary from the United States to Europe to East Asia, Zysman and Newman suggest that the digital economy will likely take on regionally differentiated forms as well. Thus, state policies shape not only *whether* there will be digital markets but also *what kinds* of markets these will be.

If the chapters by Steinberg, Cowhey and Richards, and Zysman and Newman focus explicitly on the state's market-making activities, this theme is present throughout the volume. Levy, Miura, and Park demonstrate that dismantling a dysfunctional *dirigiste* state requires new kinds of state intervention in the social and labor market arenas. The chapters by Moran and Hemerijck, Howell, and Vail point to the role of the state in either reforming or displacing troubled corporatist systems of self-regulation. Cioffi demonstrates that such intervention is no less important in establishing a market-based system of corporate governance. Finally, Orloff shows that creating something like a "free market" for labor requires state intervention, not only to coerce or bait women to enter the labor force but also to replace some of the child and elderly care that mothers provided previously outside the marketplace. In short, the move to the market is both widespread and state supported. The next section considers the kinds of state capacities that are helping to drive and shape this move to the market.

3.   State Capacity after Statism

Traditionally, state capacity has been understood in one of two ways (Katzenstein 1978; Evans, Rueschemeyer, and Skocpol 1985; Hall 1986). The first is the capacity of authorities to formulate an agenda and act independently, with little constraint, even in the face of substantial societal opposition. From this perspective, a country like France represents the ideal capacitous or "strong" state. The second understanding is the capacity of the state to forge partnerships with powerful groups in society, to harness the capital and resources of the people on behalf of a jointly defined project. From this perspective, corporatist polities like Germany appear most effective. The same duality can be identified in the initial period of state building, with countries like Prussia and France corresponding to the first conception, while Britain evoked the second. Analyzing this earlier period, Michael Mann has labeled the first form of state capacity as "despotic power" and the second as "infrastructural power" (Mann 1986). In order to avoid the appearance of endorsing authoritarian, antidemocratic governance, I choose to substitute the phrase "authoritative power" for "despotic power."[3]

During the postwar golden age, both the authoritative power of the French state and the infrastructural power of the German state seemed capable of sustaining "modern capitalism." In the current context, however, many scholars, borrowing explicitly from Mann, argue that "what it takes to be a strong, effective state has evolved" from authoritative to infrastructural power (Mann 1986; Ikenberry 2003; Weiss 2003b).[4] Top-down, directive state intervention is less effective in today's more uncertain competitive environment. What is more, the dispersion of power from the national level to the international/European and local levels ("glocalization") and from the public sector to the private sector means that the strategies of state officials are more and more dependent on enlisting the participation and resources of nonstate actors. States lack both the know-how and resources to go it alone. Consequently, authoritative power is of marginal use, while infrastructural power is increasingly valuable.

Without denying the need for state officials to work with groups in society, the chapters in this volume suggest that authoritative power remains critical to the adjustment capacities of affluent democracies. Three reasons stand out. First, as the case of the corporatist countries reveals, the threat of authoritative power can be essential to the exercise of infrastructural power. In Holland, the government's threat to regulate wages unilaterally and weaken the power of the trade unions drove the social partners to the bargaining table, resulting in the path-shifting Wassenaar accords. By contrast, in Germany, where the combination of more fragmented political power and the constitutional principle of *Tarifautonomie* barred the government from intervening in wage setting, the high-wage, insider-outsider problem persists. Thus, if societal or infrastructural capacity has helped turn Holland's political economy around, the Holland-Germany comparison suggests that tapping infrastructural capacity depends critically on state capacity to act (or threaten to act) in a unilateral, impositional manner.

One can identify a similar development regarding the external face of the state. On the one hand, infrastructural capacity in the sense of the state's ability to work with other actors—in this case, with other states—is becoming increasingly important as more and more decisions are made in international arenas, like the EU and World Trade Organization (WTO). On the other hand, as the chapters by Steinberg and Cowhey and Richards reveal, for states to play this infrastructural role, they need to enhance their authoritative capacity to act rapidly and speak with one voice. For Steinberg, the essence of the "trading state" is a concentration of power and autonomy, with authority shifting vertically, from the local to the national level, and laterally, from the legislature to the executive. Cowhey and Richards argue that the outcome of negotiations to liberalize international services depends very much on the ability of the EU to capture jurisdiction from national authorities and of both Brussels and Washington to make commitments on behalf of a number of government agencies, not just trade missions. In short, forging authoritative power in the domestic arena is a prerequisite for exercising infrastructural power in the international arena.

A second reason why authoritative power remains essential is that, as noted on several occasions, the social partners are often part of the economic problem that needs to be fixed. The case of corporatist wage setting in Holland and Germany, with insiders pricing outsiders out of jobs, is one such instance. Another is corporate governance reform, as noted by Cioffi, where the key challenge is to rein in and regulate the power of managers and other privileged market players. Moran's analysis of Britain's dysfunctional model of "club government" by incompetent amateurs is a third case. In contexts such as these, relying on infrastructural power to address pressing problems is somewhat like asking the fox to repair the henhouse. The solution runs instead through the deployment of authoritative power. The state must either induce the actors to fix the problem themselves through the threat of something worse or else displace the insiders through a shift to direct state regulation.[5]

A third, related reason for the continued reliance on authoritative capacities is that many contemporary reforms entail hotly contested withdrawals of benefits and protections. Managerial insiders have not exactly welcomed the transparency and accountability associated with corporate governance reform. Nor have the French and British workers analyzed by Howell embraced labor market "flexibility" in the form of lower wages, weaker job protections, and enhanced managerial control. Although some changes have been negotiated, in many instances, state officials have needed to stare down (or even crush) substantial societal opposition.

Contrary to the image in much of the literature, authoritative state power is not being supplanted by infrastructural power. Even among the corporatist and liberal varieties of capitalism, state imposition and leadership remain essential to economic adjustment. Yet contemporary state activism looks quite different from the postwar variant. The missions of the state have changed. State officials are no longer dictating to and steering markets but, rather, are supporting and enabling them. What is more, state missions seem to vary far less across the three varieties of capitalism than during the postwar golden age.

Figure C.1 (page 386) summarizes the changing place of the state among the affluent political economies. It draws two main distinctions. The first relates to the *mode or form* of state intervention: authoritative on the left side of the figure; infrastructural on the right. The second distinction relates to the *purposes* of state intervention: directing markets in the top half; supporting markets in the bottom half.

During the postwar golden age (top of Figure C.1), state intervention was geared toward directing or steering markets. This direction took two main forms. The *developmental state* (quadrant 1), embodied by France and Japan, sought to direct the market primarily through the exercise of authoritative power. Characteristic policies included economic planning, sectoral industrial policy, nationalizations, and selective protectionism. The *corporatist state* (quadrant 2), incarnated by Germany or Sweden, sought to steer the market primarily through the exercise of infrastructural power, that is, by working with the societal partners on behalf of public objectives. Characteristic policies included centralized wage bargaining, bank-led development, and codetermination, apprenticeships, and skill certification. Both systems tended to expand social protection to shelter workers from the market, but the corporatist polities, where labor was a pillar of policymaking, did so with considerably greater alacrity than the developmental states, particularly during the initial postwar period, when organized labor was weak. For this reason, the label "expanded social protection" straddles the vertical axis, with somewhat more text located on the right (infrastructural) side of the axis than the left (authoritative) side.

In the current period (bottom of Figure C.1), state intervention has centered on supporting rather than directing market forces. This supportive vocation likewise tends to take two main forms. The *corrective state* (quadrant 3) seeks to repair the three varieties of capitalism and restructure labor markets primarily through the exercise of authoritative power. State action often displays a unilateral character, imposing unpopular reforms designed to enhance the operation of the economy and labor markets. Characteristic policies include reduced subsidies to industry, privatization, pro-competitive regulatory reform, increased labor market flexibility, and labor market activation. Finally, the *constructive state* (quadrant 4 or, more accurately, the intersection of quadrants 3 and 4) seeks to cross technological and economic divides and build new markets through the exercise of a combination of authoritative and infrastructural power. (Again, the labels of these vocations are placed close to or straddling the vertical axis, with left-right positioning meant to convey the relative salience of authoritative and infrastructural power, respectively.) In laying the foundation for new forms of economic accumulation, state officials tend to ally with one class or economic interest at the expense of another, thereby both working against (authoritative power) and working with (infrastruc-

PURPOSE OF STATE POWER (ERA)	FORM OF STATE POWER	
	AUTHORITATIVE	INFRASTRUCTURAL

MARKET DIRECTION (Postwar golden age)	*DEVELOPMENTAL STATE*
	 • Keynesianism
	 • Planning, industrial policy, nationalizations
	 • Selective protectionism
	                • Expanded
	      1
		CORPORATIST STATE
		 • Centralized wage bargaining
		 • Bank-led development
		 • Codetermination, apprenticeships, skill formation & certification
		 social protection
		 2

MARKET SUPPORT (State after statism)	*CORRECTIVE STATE*
	 • Repair varieties of capitalism
	 • Restructure labor markets
	            • Cross
	             and
		3 4
		 CONSTRUCTIVE STATE
		   economic
		 technological divides
		 • Build markets

Figure C.1. From market direction to market support: changing state intervention among the affluent democracies.

tural power) groups in society. Characteristic policies include industrial relations reform (generally favoring business over labor), more transparent and accountable corporate governance (favoring outside investors over managers), the establishment of new property rights, such as digital information (owners over users), and trade opening (competitive companies and sectors over uncompetitive).

Obviously, Figure C.1 represents an abstraction, a simplification of a much more complex reality. Each of the four ideal types (developmental state, corporatist state, corrective state, constructive state) is associated with a constellation of policies, some of which correspond more closely to the ideal type than others. The classification of particular state activities is not always self-evident. For example, the introduction of labor market flexibility is depicted as a form of labor market restructuring by the corrective state (quadrant 3), but this activity could conceivably be placed in quadrant 4, as an instance of market-making by the constructive state. Moreover, as noted on several occasions, the distinction between authoritative and infrastructural power is not always cut and dried. In some cases, authoritative power is a means to infrastructural power, rather than an alternative. Notwithstanding these limitations, Figure C.1 conveys the broad-brush strokes of changing state intervention among the affluent democracies. It points both to the changing purposes of state activism (from market direction to market support) and to the enduring need for authoritative capacity. Three additional insights about the changing character of state intervention follow from Figure C.1.

The first insight concerns patterns of variation in state activism and capacity. During the postwar golden age, the principal source of variation was cross-national. Developmental states directed the market, whereas corporatist states steered the social partners. States tended to be good at one kind of activity or the other, but not both. There was something of a trade-off between authoritative and infrastructural capacity. In the current context, the principal form of variation is cross-policy rather than cross-national. Corrective activities tend to draw on authoritative capacity, whereas constructive activities rely more on infrastructural capacity. Individual states or countries do not fall clearly into one category or the other. Rather, the challenge is for state officials to mobilize different combinations of authoritative and infrastructural capacity, depending on the task at hand.

The second insight suggested by Figure C.1 relates to the revival of liberal political economies. During the golden age of market direction, the liberal state was defined primarily by what it *could not* do. It could not steer the market in the manner of developmental technocrats, nor could it mobilize societal actors to take on parapublic responsibilities in the manner of corporatist polities. In the current, market-supporting context, by contrast, the main state activities are essentially liberal in nature: turning the varieties of capitalism in a more market-conforming direction, recommodifying labor, crossing economic and technological divides, and building new markets. Continental European and Japanese officials are trying to pursue these liberal objectives in what might be viewed as a nonneoliberal way. In other words, they are trying to tap the benefits of market forces while seeking to avoid the poverty, inequality, and crime associated with the harsh Anglo-American approach through reformed and expanded social protection. Whether they can achieve this delicate balancing act is an open question. Less disputable is that the liberal Anglo-American polities no longer seem deficient in what it takes to promote "modern capitalism."

Part of the reason, perhaps, is that several of the leading liberal countries (most notably, the United States, United Kingdom, and New Zealand) have overhauled their political economies on the basis of what appears to be a latent authoritative capacity. The case of Britain under Margaret Thatcher is the most well known example. Britain's vaunted postwar consensus was rooted in the shared beliefs of Conservative and Labour party elites more than institutional features of the British state. Under Thatcher's "conviction politics," the combination of few veto points, no written constitution, a first-past-the-post electoral system that generated large parliamentary majorities, disciplined political parties, and extremely limited judicial review opened the door to far-reaching neoliberal reform spearheaded by an activist state. New Zealand experienced a similar pattern of reform, prompting voters to go so far as to replace the first-past-the-post electoral system with proportional representation in an effort to rein in neoliberal adventurism. In the United States, with its Madisonian system of checks and balances, neoliberal reform through legislative channels has been halting, albeit still significant. But much change has been initiated outside the legislative arena, through the courts and independent regulatory agencies (Securities and Exchange Commission [SEC], Federal Communications Commission [FCC], Federal Reserve Bank, etc.). As any executive at AT&T would attest, there has been no shortage of authoritative capacity in the US regime. Foreign governments have also felt the whip of US authoritative capacity, with Congress and the executive branch using the threat of reduced access to the giant US market to force market opening on other countries. Liberal polities were probably never as "weak" and incapacitous as the golden age literature suggested. In any case, the strengths and resources that they did possess have become especially valuable in today's market-supporting policy environment.

The third insight from Figure C.1 concerns the implications of European integration for the market-supporting state after statism. Historically, the European Union has embraced four main vocations: (1) market-making (the original Common Market, the 1992 project, the commission's aggressive competition policy, and arguably European Monetary Union); (2) social cohesion (the biggest budget items, the Common Agricultural Policy and the Structural or Regional funds); (3) industrial policy (Airbus, Ariane, European Strategic Programme for Research and Development in Information Technology [ESPRIT], European Research Coordination Agency [EUREKA]); (4) regulation (regulatory harmonization for market-making but also the protection of worker rights, environmental standards, and social norms). In constructing Europe, state officials did not just abandon sovereignty; they pooled it. As British historian Alan Milward has argued, Europe "rescued the nation–state" by enabling authorities to pursue policies at the European level that they could no longer afford or that were no longer practicable at the national level (Milward 1992).

In recent years, however, the center of gravity of the EU, like that of national policy, has shifted from the top of Figure C.1 to the bottom. Market-making by the EU has flourished, aided by the shift to qualified majority voting on most decisions and by the aggressive, pro-competitive orientation of the Commission. At the same time, industrial policy has fallen out of favor, while budgets for social cohesion and industrial policy have been squeezed by rival priorities and by the accession of a number of low-income countries. As a result, many contend that European integration is no longer "rescuing" the nation–state but rather is narrowing its room to maneuver. Figure C.1

suggests two qualifications to this vision of the EU as annihilator of state sovereignty.

First, market-making can itself drive and underwrite new social and regulatory safeguards. Within the EU, the extension of the market is generally a package deal. New countries are admitted in return for expanded social funds for those countries most threatened by the competition; regulatory barriers are phased out but subject to minimum standards that often raise the level of safeguards across the integrated market (D. Vogel 1995). Beyond the EU, several of the chapters in this volume show that the market-making project has been essential to the extension of European regulations and norms to third parties. In Steinberg's account, Western Europe could not join the United States in co-managing the global trading order until it had created a large market and, no less important, a single institutional actor to negotiate the terms of access to that market. Cowhey and Richards tell a similar tale regarding service liberalization: for Europe to negotiate effectively, the EU needed to speak with one voice. In a separate work, Newman demonstrates that Europe has been able to export its data privacy norms, which are far more restrictive than those of the United States, the world over, including to US multinationals, by denying market access to countries and companies with laxer standards (Newman 2005). Thus, both within the EU and outside the EU, the market-making face of European integration is often a complement to the social or regulatory face of European integration, rather than an alternative.

The second qualification suggested by Figure C.1 is that while the European Union has shifted from the top to the bottom of the figure, it is less clear whether policymaking operates on the left side (authoritative power) or the right side (infrastructural power). Critics of "neoliberal Europe" and of the Commission see the EU as operating primarily on the left side, in quadrant 3. Unelected Brussels technocrats are pursuing a radical, free-market agenda with no regard for popular opinion or social cohesion (the so-called democratic deficit). This sentiment fueled the French rejection of the EU constitution in a May 2005 referendum. Others counter that the Commission is less neoliberal and impositional than portrayed and that, in any case, it must act in concert with national governments and the European Parliament. Market-making takes place through negotiated, infrastructural means, not despotic Brussels *diktats*. Consequently, the EU may be building markets, but these are not Anglo-American, neoliberal markets. Rather, they are embedded in European social and regulatory norms. Without attempting to forecast the future direction of European integration, we can see that many of the most contentious issues about the EU's impact on national sovereignty—the role of the Commission, the alleged "democratic deficit," the proposed constitution— revolve around the changing purposes of state intervention (from market direction to market support) and associated modes of intervention (authoritative versus infrastructural) that this volume has analyzed in the national context.

4.   Beyond the Affluent Democracies

For a combination of theoretical and practical-logistical reasons, this book has focused on the affluent democracies. The developing and postcommunist countries present a very different situation for the state. For starters, these countries are poorer than the affluent democracies, so that state officials possess fewer resources. They also tend to be more dependent on foreign investment and lending, hence more subject to the antistatist "Washington consensus" of the actors that wield these resources. Finally, with the exception of a few East Asian polities, state activism has a more problematic history, which may block or impede the effective pursuit of new state missions.

For all these differences between the affluent democracies and developing countries, however, we can observe one important similarity. The developing countries are likewise moving from the top of Figure C.1 to the bottom, from market direction to market support. The main statist models of economic promotion—import-substitution industrialization, communism, and to a lesser extent, the East Asian developmental state—have all fallen out of favor. The market referent is supplanting the state referent as the pathway to prosperity. Yet as among the affluent democracies, this shift is not necessarily synonymous with the eclipse of the state. It also opens the door to new state missions—both economic and social, corrective and constructive.

A further parallel is that the character of these new missions and challenges is by no means uniform across the developing world. Just as the chapters in this volume have identified distinctive challenges to the statist, liberal, and corporatist varieties of capitalism, so the developing world displays considerable diversity in the emerging missions of the state after statism. For East Asian developmental states, the main challenges resemble those confronting France and Japan: in the economic arena, making strategies of industrial promotion more light-handed and market conforming; in the social arena, incorporating labor without undermining the mechanisms of economic accumulation (Woo-Cumings 1999; Doner and Ramsay 2003; Ramesh 2003; Weiss 2003a). For countries exiting from import-substitution industrialization (ISI), notably in Latin America, state officials have been pressed to bolster the capacities of domestic firms to confront intensified international competition and to forge new modes of regulation to govern the increasing presence of privatized and foreign companies (Etchemendy 2004). Latin American authorities also tend to confront a more extreme form of the Germanic, insider-outsider problem: they face the difficult task of both making welfare and industrial relations regulations more employment friendly and finding new resources to address devastating problems of poverty and social exclusion among the mass of outsiders (Weyland 2004; Garay forthcoming). In the postcommunist world, state authorities need to build an effective infrastructure for a market economy, with clear property rights, accounting standards, and effective regulation, notably of financial markets (Ekiert 2003; A. Schwartz 2006). In the welfare sphere, the central challenge is to shift the locus of social protection away from firms, which are increasingly reluctant to continue this mission inherited from the communist era, to the state through formal, national welfare policies.

Of course, these generalizations represent a crude simplification, underplaying significant variation both within and across regions and neglecting certain areas of the world altogether. Still, it is clear that the developing countries confront significant demands for new kinds of state intervention. On the economic front, state officials are striving to cultivate light-handed, market-conforming methods for encouraging industrial development and upgrading. They are also seeking to establish or enhance their regulatory capacities in a context of reduced state ownership and heightened exposure to private and international investors. On the social front, state authorities are seeking to extend formal social protection to the mass of neglected citizens, while curtailing some of the benefits of labor market insiders. These challenges are more pressing and on a larger scale than anything seen among the affluent democracies.

If state officials in developing countries have as much or more to do than their counterparts in affluent democracies, their capacity to carry out these responsibilities is significantly constrained. Put crudely, developing states are often being called upon to do more than affluent states with less—less money, less autonomy from both domestic and international capital, and less professional bureaucracy. The extreme cases, of course, are the so-called failed states of Africa (Herbst 2003), but few if any developing states approach the reach and resources of the affluent democracies. These limitations can potentially derail pressing new economic and social missions. Corruption and capture by powerful business interests (from postcommunist "oligarchs" to Korean *chaebol* to Latin American elite families) can prevent the establishment of effective, independent regulation; international financial constraints can check the expansion of social protection. Thus, many developing countries confront an additional challenge beyond those faced by affluent democracies: they not only must reform and redeploy state *policy* but also must rebuild, refinance, and professionalize *the state* itself (World Bank 1997; Schneider and Heredia 2003). The challenge of the state after statism in the developing world is often to redirect the state while simultaneously reconstructing it.

This book has shown that the contemporary shift from market direction to market support has entailed a redeployment of state initiatives, rather than the retreat of the state. State intervention is more than a fixed and eroding historical legacy. Changes in the economy, technology, society, and ideology invariably encourage the state to launch new activities as well as repudiate (some of) the old activities. Thus, if the purposes of the state after statism are evolving in the age of liberalization, the necessity of that intervention shows no sign of abating, whether among affluent or developing countries. To put it in Shonfield's (1965) language, modernizing "modern capitalism" is a state-mediated, not state-eclipsing, process. Capitalist development and state development are—and for the foreseeable future will continue to be—inextricably intertwined.

Notes

The State Also Rises

1. I wish to thank the following people for their comments on the project as a whole and on earlier drafts of this chapter: Suzanne Berger, Stephen Cohen, Peter Gourevitch, Yong-Chool Ha, Peter Hall, Yohei Nakayama, T. J. Pempel, Richard Samuels, Steven Vogel, J. Nicholas Ziegler, and an anonymous reviewer for Harvard University Press. I also benefited from the suggestions of all the contributors to *The State after Statism*, especially Chris Howell and John Zysman.

2. The phrase "finance capitalism" was coined in the early twentieth century by the German Social Democrat, Rudolph Hilferding. Hilferding used the term to describe what he saw as trustified "monopoly capitalism" in Germany, marked by tight linkages between banking and industry. Cioffi employs "finance capitalism" in almost the opposite way, to denote an increasingly fluid and internationally open set of economic relationships. For a discussion of the concept of finance capitalism, see Cioffi's chapter in this volume, notably note 1.

3. In a subsequent paper, Peter Hall and Daniel Gingerich array the affluent democracies along a variety of indices of coordination, including industrial relations, social protection, labor market flexibility, firm structure, corporate governance, and earnings (Hall and Gingerich 2001).

1. The Transformation of the British State

The chapter derives from a Berkeley Roundtable on International Economy (BRIE) series of workshops on "The State after Statism," held at the University of California, Berkeley, in 2002 and 2003. Previous versions have been presented to the American Political Science Association (APSA) (2003) and to research seminars at the University of Warwick and the University of Manchester in 2003. I am grateful for the many helpful comments offered—in particular, to Jonah D.

Levy and to Peter Gourevitch, for his comments on the APSA version. I also thank three anonymous Harvard University Press referees for helpful comments. The research that this chapter reports was supported by a Leverhulme Major Research Fellowship grant, for which grateful acknowledgment is also made. The research is reported more fully in Michael Moran's *The British Regulatory State: High Modernism and Hyper-Innovation* (2003).

1. The assertions here are implicitly comparative, but I think the assertions are easy to ground.

2. Since Scott's great book is in the main a hostile study of authoritarian high modernism, I should emphasize two things: I am not equating modernism with its authoritarian variant; and, therefore, unlike Scott, I am rather a fan of high modernism. I return to this issue at the end of the chapter.

3. In Scott's study there is a disapproving illustration of an afforestation scheme, with its regimented lines of trees. Cycling through the pine forests of Aquitaine in the summer when I was drafting this chapter, I suddenly realized that I was in precisely such a project and was enjoying the benefits of high modernism: the afforestation scheme begun in the Second Empire arrested the march of sand, cleared diseased swamp, and endowed the French in the twenty-first century with an economic asset and a vast resource for tourism.

2. The Forgotten Center

1. Emphasis added.

2. For a more critical reading, see Becker 2001.

3. Despite its effectiveness at creating economic and employment growth, the magic of governing without confessionals and the novelty of social liberalism in Dutch politics faded rapidly in the election year 2002. With unemployment closing in on 3 percent, tight labor market conditions reduced the willingness of the trade unions to moderate wages. While other countries have begun to follow the Dutch example of wage moderation, Dutch labor costs have been rising faster than the European Union average since 1997. In the wake of the economic downturn of 2001, these developments spurred an increase in unemployment, the first since 1994. Under such strained economic conditions, "September 11" made many Dutch voters increasingly wary of EU enlargement and globalization more generally. Hidden frustrations and anxieties were then mobilized against the purple government by the right-populist, Islamophobic politician Pim Fortuyn. Fortuyn's murder by a radical environmental activist nine days before the election led to a dramatic breakthrough of the List Pim Fortuyn (LPF), which entered Parliament with twenty-six seats. In July 2002, the VVD agreed to became the third coalition partner in a center-right coalition with the CDA and the LPF, led by Christian Democrat Jan-Peter Balkenende, whose short-lived first government was unable to make much of an impact. After new elections in early 2003, the second conservative-liberal Balkenende government proposed a rather statist austerity package, thereby setting the scene for confrontation with the social partners. Though some social pacts were concluded after widespread protest in the autumn of 2004, these were based more on organized distrust than on the joint-problem-solving approach that had developed under the Lubbers and Kok administrations.

4. In the words of Ludwig Erhard, economics minister in the 1950s and one of the conceptual "fathers" of the *soziale Marktwirtschaft*, "The restructuring of our economic order must thus create conditions such that the purchasing power associated with rapid economic growth can overcome obstacles and finally end the resentment between 'poor' and 'rich.'" See Erhard 1957: 7; translation the authors'.

5. Some observers went so far as to portray the Bündnis as a cartel, in which unions and employers defended established interests rather than addressing unemployment and which the government used to create a veneer of social dialogue.

6. Quickly dropping to 60 percent after reunification, eastern industrial output had recovered to only 68 percent of western levels by 1993, resulting in the elimination of 3.9 million jobs. By February 1996, unemployment in the East had reached 17 percent, with an additional 800,000 people participating in make-work schemes (Flockton 1996: 214–215).

7. These policies have resulted in one of the lowest labor market participation rates in the Organization for Economic Cooperation and Development (OECD) for workers aged fifty-five and older (52.9 percent in 1995) (Manow 1997: 39).

8. In 1999, another 800,000 were participating in various training and subsidized job schemes managed by the BA (OECD 2001: 37).

9. There are two categories of German early retirement programs, those for workers with "reduced capacity" to work (claims that are often specious) and benefits for those unable to find part-time work but who wish to retire from their full-time positions. Early retirees often base their claims on reduced capacity, even as they continue to work part-time.

10. Joblessness among workers under age twenty-five rose significantly in the 1990s, reaching 10.4 percent in 1998. Equally alarming, between 1991 and 1998 the number of young applicants registered for apprenticeship slots increased from 541,790 to 796,400, whereas the number of available positions decreased from 830,940 to 603,900 (Bundesanstalt für Arbeit 1999: 69, 72).

11. The law was intended to last twelve months but has been extended each year by agreement between the BA and the government (Bundesanstalt für Arbeit 2000b).

12. The law also introduced new instruments to train and retrain workers, increased subsidies to employers to reduce non–wage labor costs and encourage hiring, and instituted additional job creation schemes (SPD und Bündnis 90/Die Grünen Bundestagsfraktionen 2001).

13. Previously, the government was obligated to cover the BA's deficits but had no authority to set its budget.

14. The highest German administrative regulatory agency concluded that as many as 70 percent of cases had been incorrectly reported and that it was doubtful whether the statistics issued by the BA "can at all be used as the basis for the lawmaking and budgetary decisions of the Bundestag and the government" (*Frankfurter Allgemeine Zeitung* 2002a). Labor Minister Walter Riester admitted that "it cannot be excluded that workers in the labor office had an interest in falsely reporting statistics on successful job placement" (*Frankfurter Allgemeine Zeitung* 2002b). The scandal led to the resignation of BA President Bernhard Jagoda and proposals for major reforms of the BA.

15. The qualified character of the commission's tripartism could be seen in the

selection of Peter Hartz, the personnel director at Volkswagen, as its head. Rather than compose a board of union and employer association representatives, Schröder turned to Hartz, with whom he had a long-standing business association, dating back to when Schröder was president of the Niedersachsen region (Lower Saxony). Lower Saxony is Volkswagen's largest shareholder.

16. Many of the October 2003 labor market reforms were devised in response to the Hartz Commission's recommendations. The "Agenda 2010" program also involved proposals for health insurance, pensions, and income support.

17. In order to secure the passage of the package's labor market measures, the government was forced to make concessions on its tax reform proposals that significantly reduced the total size of the tax reduction. It also made some concessions on some of its labor market measures, including an obligation for the long-term unemployed to accept any legal job, as opposed to those that are "appropriate" with respect to their employment history. Other parts of the package, which did not require the Bundesrat's approval, had been passed unchanged by the Bundestag in October.

18. The reforms incorporated and extended a measure passed by the Christian Democrats in 1997 but quashed by the incoming administration in 1998, suggesting that the pattern of increased state intervention in the pension system crosses partisan lines.

19. This actuarial figure is deceptive, since it represents the benefits of a notional worker having contributed for forty-five years. Most workers' benefits would thus actually be lower.

20. This provision meant that each cohort's benefits would be 0.3 percent lower than those of the previous year's retirees, with each individual retiree's benefits remaining constant.

21. Interview, Ludger Loop, Gesellschaft für Innovation, Beratung und Service, IG Metall, March 13, 2001.

22. In the words of one union leader, "[T]he welfare state has the task of holding society together." Accordingly, unions feared that the partial exit of employers from pension financing would jeopardize the integrity of German society. Interview, Michael Guggemos, IG Metall Vorstand, January 19, 2001.

23. In one famous incident during a congress of the moderate public service union, the chancellor declared in response to heckling from the audience, "It is necessary, and we are going to do it. *Basta*" (*Frankfurter Allgemeine Zeitung* 2000).

24. Much has been made of the Bundesrat's ability to block legislation. As the pension reform demonstrates, however, the government's control over the ways that laws are drafted and gray areas in the Constitution provide flexibility in determining which measures will be subject to the upper house's approval.

25. In part, the incoherence of these objections reflected competition among various CDU constituencies, but it also mirrored internal disorganization resulting from a major party financing scandal that broke in 1999. One CDU member actually admitted privately that his party had no coherent positions on social policy reform. Interview, member of CDU/CSU Arbeitsgruppe Arbeit und Soziales, March 15, 2001.

26. The additional money was required because the *Länder* were already suffering decreased revenues as a result of the 2000 tax reform. This DM1 billion supplement was provided in addition to existing subsidies to the pension system, which by 2001 had risen sharply to an annual DM114 billion.

27. The government used a similar strategy to see through the 2000 tax reform, securing Bundesrat approval by granting federal money for infrastructure projects in *Länder* whose votes were needed.

28. State intervention has also involved efforts to control spiraling health-care costs by rebalancing corporatist arrangements. In 1989, for example, the Kohl government passed a measure that limited physicians' autonomy and introduced elements of competition and patient choice, while working within the existing corporatist framework. For details, see Giaimo and Manow 1997.

3. *Exiting* Etatisme?

The authors wish to thank the following individuals for their comments and suggestions on earlier drafts of this chapter: Robert Boyer, Stephen Cohen, Yong-Chool Ha, Peter Hall, Ellen Immergut, Yohei Nakayama, Bruno Palier, T.J. Pempel, Richard Samuels, Wolfgang Streeck, Kathleen Thelen, Nicolas Véron, Steven Vogel, and John Zysman. We also thank Mark I. Vail for his help in collecting figures, putting together tables, and editing the chapter.

1. In addition to coordinated market economies and liberal market economies, Hall and Soskice evoke the possibility of a third "Mediterranean" type of capitalism, characterized by a large agrarian sector and a recent history of extensive state intervention. The countries in the Mediterranean category include France, Italy, Spain, Portugal, Greece, and Turkey. This Mediterranean variant of capitalism is mentioned only in passing, however, in a single paragraph. Its features are not elaborated in any kind of systematic way, like the CME and LME ideal types.

2. The euro replaced the French franc in 2000. For purposes of simplicity, this chapter presents all French figures in euros, even for the period before 2000. The figures have been converted into euros at the rate of 6.56 French francs per euro.

3. Geopolitical ambitions were also part of the problem, particularly under President Charles de Gaulle (1958–1969). In the name of national autonomy, de Gaulle insisted on developing technologies distinct from existing American ones. This costly policy was reversed by de Gaulle's successor as president, Georges Pompidou. In nuclear power, for example, Pompidou abandoned France's graphite gas-cooling process in favor of a water-cooled technology licensed from the American firm Westinghouse.

4. In 1994, a new electoral system was created that combines single-member constituencies and proportional representation. The new system aims to reduce intraparty competition and enhance interparty policy competition. It is still too early to tell whether the electoral reforms will produce the desired effects.

5. Junichiro Koizumi is the first prime minister to break with the practice of faction-based ministerial appointments.

6. Figure 3.2 also suggests that French labor market expenditures have become more "active" over the years, encouraging recipients to work ("active"), rather than to withdraw from the labor market ("passive"). Whereas the number of employees in passive early retirement programs declined slightly from just over 700,000 in 1984 to less than 600,000 in 1999, subsidized jobs in the private sector expanded from 320,000 to 1.6 million, subsidized jobs in the public sector from 8,000 to 509,000, and positions in training programs from 143,000 to 298,000.

7. These data exclude tax cuts.

8. Both the Temporary Staff Work Act and the Labor Standards Act were revised again in 2003, with the goal of creating more flexibility in labor markets.

4. The State and the Reconstruction of Industrial Relations Institutions after Fordism

This chapter has enormously benefited from comments on earlier drafts by numerous people. I would like to particularly thank Colin Hay, Dave Marsh, Jonah D. Levy, Mark I. Vail, David Coates, Kathy Thelen, Peter Swenson, Peter Gourevitch, John Kelly, Bruno Palier, and Joel Krieger.

5. Building Finance Capitalism

I am grateful for comments received following presentations at the workshop "The State after Statism: New State Activities in the Age of Globalization and Liberalization," University of California Berkeley, May 2–3, 2003; at the Max Planck Institute for the Study of Societies, Cologne, Germany, July 2003; and at the American Political Science Association Annual Meeting, Philadelphia, PA, August 2003. In particular, I would like to thank Peter Gourevitch, Martin Höpner, Jonah D. Levy, Wolfgang Streeck, Nick Ziegler, and John Zysman for their comments and advice. Any remaining errors are, of course, my own.

1. The term "finance capitalism" was coined in the early twentieth century by German Socialist Rudolph Hilferding. Hilferding used the phrase to denote a German economy dominated by monopolistic enterprises with strong financial linkages to major banks (and often to each other). He imagined a form of monopoly capitalism that verged on socialism in its concentration of industrial and financial organization and power. As conceived here, "finance capitalism" designates economic conditions that are increasingly competitive and a loosening of ties between financial and industrial capital, hence between investors and managers. Contemporary finance capitalism entails the expansion and deepening of markets through more extensive regulation of the corporate firm's financial and governance practices. In many ways, it is the antithesis of Hilferding's original conception.

2. One should note that the political and structural transformation to finance capitalism is assessed here by reference to legal and formal institutional change, not to observable changes in corporate financial structures, patterns of saving and investment, public stock ownership, and market capitalization. Corporate governance reforms are adopted either to maintain a market-driven financial system (in the United States) or to create the preconditions to allow it to take root and flourish. The question of whether these reforms will prove effective in Germany and much of Europe will not be answerable for years.

3. For an extended discussion of this change in state intervention in the economy, see Cioffi 2002c.

4. Cioffi 2002a: 1; cf. Gerke 1998 (quoting Schmidt 1997). This definition of the term "corporate governance" goes well beyond the narrow confines of the shareholder-manager (principal-agent) relationship that preoccupies the vast ma-

jority of scholarship in law and economics. This broader definition more accurately describes the function of corporate governance and its relationship to the broader political economy.

5. For a classic typology of national financial systems, see Zysman 1983. An updated analysis of national corporate governance regimes from this typological perspective is presented in Cioffi 2000 and Cioffi and Cohen 2000.

6. American law endows shareholders with comparatively well developed substantive rights. For a leading treatise on the subject, see Block, Barton, and Radin 1993. This rights-based approach encourages litigation and has made courts and attorneys important actors in corporate governance. Shareholders may enforce rights through private lawsuits brought under a set of favorable procedural rules, including derivative suits, class actions, and contingency fee retainers. However, the business judgment rule reveals the structural weakness of fiduciary duties as a mechanism of regulation. The potential liabilities of corporate fiduciaries are so enormous that no rational individual would agree to act as a director if not granted a very broad safe harbor from personal liability. Likewise, in the absence of a business judgment rule, insurers would refuse to write "directors' and officers' " insurance policies at acceptable rates.

7. The Glass-Steagall Act severed investment banking from commercial banking and traditional lending. The Investment Company Act of 1940 and the Employee Retirement Income Security Act of 1974 limited the size of the stakes that investment firms and funds could hold as a percentage of their own capital and of outstanding corporate equity. Under these deliberately fragmented ownership conditions, it was all but impossible for shareholders to solve the collective action problem of coordinating and compensating the monitoring of managers. These rules thus inadvertently strengthened managers. See generally Roe 1998, 1994, 1993a, 1991, 1990.

8. See, e.g., Roe 1991; Coffee 1991. For the classic analysis of the use of exit and voice in governance relationships, see Hirschman 1970.

9. For a comprehensive analysis of the structural forces inducing this reliance on formal regulation and litigious enforcement of legal rules, see Kagan 2001.

10. Labor law, as interpreted by the National Labor Relations Board and the federal courts, impedes the formation of *alternative* forms of employee representation. A broad legal prohibition of company unions protects employee organization at the expense of organizational experiments, such as workplace committees dealing with safety and productivity issues. See *Electromation, Inc.*, 309 N.L.R.B. 990 (1992), *enforced* sub nom, *Electromation, Inc. v. NLRB*, 35 F.3d 1148 (7th Cir. 1994); *E. I. du Pont de Nemours & Co.*, 311 N.L.R.B. 893 (1993); see also Estreicher 1993; Hyde 1993; Summers 1993. These rulings reinforced the sharp distinction between the spheres of state corporate law and federal labor law.

11. American labor law maintains this strict separation by limiting "mandatory subjects" of collective bargaining to a highly circumscribed range of "bread and butter" issues concerning the terms and conditions of employment. *NLRB v. Borg-Warner Corp.*, 356 US 342 (1958); *Fibreboard Paper Prods. Corp. v. NLRB*, 379 US 203 (1964); see also *First National Maintenance Corp. v. NLRB*, 452 US 666 (1981).

12. *Fibreboard Paper Prods. Corp. v. NLRB*, 379 US 203, 223 (1964) (Stewart, J., concurring); see also *Ford Motor Co. v. NLRB*, 441 US 488, 498 (1979) (quoting *Fibreboard*).

13. For a classic article comparing the legal and political histories of the German and American corporate governance regimes, see Vagts 1966. For more recent comparative treatments, see, e.g., O'Sullivan 2000; Roe 2003, 1994, 1993a; Charkham 1994.

14. Thus, in addition to their own equity holdings, the banks wielded disproportionate voting strength and substantial leverage when it came to board nominations or key strategic decisions. Charkham 1994: 37–38; Vagts 1966: 53–58. Even when German management attempted to maintain autonomy by diversifying sources of bank debt, banks adopted a practice of designating a "lead bank" to monitor the corporation, vote their aggregate DSVRs, and maintain supervisory board representation. Deeg 1999; Vitols 1995: 6.

15. Shareholders may bring a private action to nullify any corporate decision taken in violation of their informational and procedural rights. Because these decisions often concern important and time-sensitive strategic issues, managers usually seek to settle such suits quickly. In effect, German company law created a disclosure and transparency regime outside of securities regulation—although it functions only when an AGM is held, rather than continuously, as under securities law. This provision has also created the problem of allegedly frivolous lawsuits that afflict the far more litigation-prone American governance regime.

16. For discussions, see Katzenstein 1987: ch. 3; Wiedemann 1980.

17. Assmann 1990; Streeck 1984a (use of the term "microcorporatism" in relation to firm structure and organization).

18. Wiedemann 1980: 79. Firms with 500 to 2,000 employees must set aside only one-third of the board seats for employee representatives. Wiedemann 1980: 80. "Montan" codetermination, the third (and original) variant, only applies to firms in the coal, mining, and steel sectors employing more than 1,000 workers. It provides for full parity of shareholder and employee representation. The decline of the mining and steel sectors in Germany has reduced the importance of Montan codetermination.

19. It does so, however, at the expense of well-defined fiduciary duties. Fiduciary duties under German company law protect the corporation's interests, rather than the interests of shareholders alone. Codetermination institutionalizes the recognition of the "interests of the corporation" as the interests of multiple stakeholder groups, including labor.

20. The effects of board codetermination are debated perennially. For a discussion of the difficulties of empirically assessing the impact of board codetermination, see Prigge 1998: 1006–1011 (tentatively concluding that board codetermination weakens the governance role of the supervisory board but finding no compelling evidence of a significant economic impact on the firm); see also Baums and Frick 1999 (event study showing no negative impact of pro-labor codetermination decisions by German courts); compare Roe 2003: 32–33, n. 9 (arguing that board codetermination has a substantial negative impact on corporate share values).

21. Wiedemann 1980: 80–82 (discussing the Works Constitution Act of 1972). Although the law only creates works councils at the plant level, many large firms voluntarily instituted enterprise (or *Konzern*) works councils covering an entire corporate group to ensure stable and cooperative labor relations. For general discussions of the political origins and impact of codetermination, see, e.g., Vagts

1966: 64–78; Streeck 1984a; Katzenstein 1987: ch. 3; Muller-Jentsch 1995. For the role of works councils in German labor relations, see Thelen 1991; cf. Turner 1991.

22. For a good account of the politics surrounding hostile takeovers and the managerial counterattack, see Roe 1993b.

23. There continued to be an extraordinarily vibrant market for companies—which reached its apogee during the 1990s boom and stock market bubble. The overwhelming majorities of mergers and acquisitions during the 1990s were friendly deals that tended to be highly lucrative for senior managers in the acquired company. See, *for example*, Cioffi 2002a, ch. 4.

24. The regulation of accounting firms and their conflicts of interest became an especially important issue following a 1994 Supreme Court decision that largely abolished "aiding and abetting" liability, under which third-party accounting and law firms could be held liable for fraudulent statements and omissions by publicly traded corporate clients. *Central Bank of Denver v. First Interstate Bank of Denver,* 114 S.Ct. 1439 (1994). Without the threat of private litigation, SEC regulation was the only enforcement option remaining. Tort reform legislation in 1995 authorized aiding and abetting suits brought by the SEC but not by private plaintiffs.

25. The 1992 proxy rule changes appear to have encouraged greater governance activism by institutional investors, but at the expense of transparency. Institutional investors, with some notable exceptions, preferred to voice their concerns and criticisms to management in private communications that would not become public. These communications thus became occasions for managers to disclose significant information to the representatives of institutional investors and analysts associated with investment banks and brokerages.

26. Transparency regulation and institutional activism have always been in tension. By the end of 2000, these two paradigms of corporate governance regulation and reform had collided on the levels of politics, law, and investor relations. The 1992 proxy rule amendments presumed that more intensive communications between institutional investors and managers would benefit all shareholders. Regulation FD presumed the opposite. Another noteworthy feature of Regulation FD is that it expressly failed to create a private cause of action for its enforcement by shareholders. The 1992 proxy rule reforms are structural regulations that were undermined by the prescriptive (or prohibitive) rule of Regulation FD. In contrast, Regulation FD is a prescriptive rule without the established effective enforcement mechanism of private litigation.

27. See Private Securities Litigation Reform Act of 1995 (PSLRA), Public Law 104–67 (December 22, 1995), amending Title I of the Securities Act of 1933, 15 U.S.C. 77a et seq., Pub. L. No. 104–67, 109 Stat. 737 (1995). Passed over President Clinton's veto, the PSLRA raised the pleading requirements and authorized the appointment of a "lead plaintiff" in securities fraud suits to curb the power of plaintiffs' attorneys to bring frivolous and allegedly extortionate class actions.

28. See Securities Law Uniform Standards Act of 1998 (SLUSA), Pub. L. No. 105–353, 112 Stat. 3227 (codified as interspersed subsections of 15 U.S.C. §§ 77–78). At a time when federalism formed a core part of the Republican Party platform, Republicans—with some Democratic allies—pushed through the SLUSA's preemption provisions, which dramatically limited state authority and increased

federal control over securities regulation. This legislation had the strong support of some core Republican constituencies, such as corporate executives, the corporate bar, and financial services firms. Its passage belies the notion that economic conservatives in the United States are ideologically wed to doctrines of devolution and decentralization of government authority.

29. Although named for both Democratic Senator Paul Sarbanes and Republican Representative Michael Oxley, Sarbanes was the law's chief architect and congressional proponent. Oxley took the lead in advocating the Bush administration's much narrower and limited reform program and *opposed* the more sweeping reforms pressed by congressional Democrats. Oxley only signed on to the Sarbanes bill once the White House chose to support passage of the Senate bill in order to control the political damage that the Republican Party was beginning to incur as the November 2002 midterm elections approached and the corporate scandals continued to spread. Anonymous interviews, Washington, DC, March 2003 and 2004. Both Democratic and Republican interviewees recounted this version of events.

30. Anonymous interview, Washington, DC, March 2004. Interviewees inside and outside government unanimously agreed that the WorldCom collapse broke Republican resistance to the Sarbanes bill and made substantial corporate governance reform politically inevitable.

31. The act also required the SEC, inter alia, to draft new regulations requiring heightened corporate disclosures, including off-balance sheet transactions, codes of ethics (and their waiver by the board), the reconciliation of "pro forma" financial results with generally accepted accounting standards, disclosure of and limitations on nonaudit services performed by the firm's auditor, and real-time disclosure of material financial information and business developments. Sarbanes-Oxley also increased civil and criminal penalties for a host of securities law violations and required CEOs and chief financial officers (CFOs) to certify the accuracy of the corporate balance sheet as reported to the SEC and the public.

32. SEC chairman Harvey Pitt, President Bush's appointee to head the SEC, had been a prominent securities lawyer on behalf of major accounting firms in private practice, and his efforts to minimize the significance of the corporate scandals and to derail legislative reforms were regarded as suspicious and illegitimate by reformers and, increasingly, by the public at large. The struggle over corporate governance reform, accounting regulation, and PCAOB appointments ultimately prompted Pitt's resignation. The first chairman of the PCAOB, former Federal Bureau of Investigation (FBI) and Central Intelligence Agency (CIA) director William Webster, was also forced to resign when he was found to have been a director of a corporation charged with financial improprieties.

33. Securities and Exchange Commission, 2003. For a more thorough analysis of the post-Enron American corporate governance reforms and ensuing business backlash, see Cioffi 2005.

34. The amendments proposed a two-step, multiyear process to place shareholder board nominations on the corporation's proxy ballots. In step one, access would only be triggered if at least 35 percent of voting shareholders withheld their support for a company's director candidate in an annual board election. Upon satisfaction of this criterion, step two would have allowed a group representing at least 5 percent of shares to nominate and run its own candidate(s) on the corporate proxy the following year.

35. For a more detailed description and analysis of the German reforms, see Cioffi 2002b.

36. In many contemporary accounts, Germany is still regarded as lagging other countries in modernizing its financial and corporate governance systems. These criticisms neglect the substantial legal reforms that have changed the foundations of Germany's financial system. They also tend to focus on the perpetuation of codetermination and the low level of equity financing. Although codetermination has remained untouched, largely for political reasons, this has not appeared to affect investment behavior to a significant extent. Hostility to codetermination seems more rooted in ideology than practical economic considerations.

37. Nor does the business community necessarily have a political or ideological "center of gravity" that represents its aggregate political positions and policy preferences.

38. Prior to the breakthrough of the Second Financial Market Promotion Act in 1994, the German government and financial elites were notorious for resisting EU directives requiring increased transparency, restrictions on insider trading, and other regulatory reforms. With the exception of the fight against the EU's neo-liberal Takeover Directive, this resistance has largely evaporated.

39. For a more detailed discussion of the shift in the business strategies and policy preferences of large German banks, see Cioffi 2002b. Numerous interviews conducted in Germany in July 2000 and July 2003 confirmed the SPD's political strategy of allying with the banks in support of financial system reform in order to strengthen business support for the party and weaken support for the CDU.

40. German welfare state policy has played a critical role in facilitating corporate restructuring in the face of powerful unions. Organized labor has been accommodated by the extension of generous unemployment and early retirement pension benefits to ease the impact of restructuring on the workforce. Germany has effectively socialized the risk and costs of restructuring, but at increasingly enormous costs in terms of pension outlays and structural unemployment. See Streeck 2003.

41. Second Financial Market Promotion Act (Gesetz über den Wertpapier-handel und zur Änderung börsenrechtlicher und wertpapierrechtlicher Vorschriften, Zweites Finanzmarktförderungsgesetz) of July 26, 1994, Federal Law Gazette, Part I, p. 1749.

42. Law on Integrated Financial Services Supervision (Gesetz über die integrierte Finanzaufsicht [FinDAG]), April 22, 2002 (effective May 1, 2002).

43. See Cioffi 2002b; Höpner 2003. For an excellent account and analysis of the ways in which the Schröder government sought to create a shareholding culture in Germany during the late 1990s, see Ziegler 2000.

44. Indeed, Schröder's rise within the SPD and his victory in this policy debate attest to the decline of these traditional powers within German social democracy. That said, they remain a force with which to be reckoned. In the 2005 parliamentary elections, the defection of left-wing Social Democrats and union leaders to a newly created "Left party" hurt Schröder badly, arguably costing him the chancellorship.

45. For a fine historical account of this ideological aspect of German social democracy in historical perspective, see Höpner 2003; see also Cioffi 2002b.

46. Corporate Control and Transparency Act (Gesetz zur Kontrolle und Transparenz im Unternehmensbereich [KonTraG] of April 27, 1998, Federal Law

Gazette, Part I, p. 786 (Gesetz vom 27.4.1998, BGBl. I, S. 786 vom 30.4.1998). For a political analysis of the KonTraG, see Cioffi 2002b.

47. The KonTraG actually preserved much of the traditional bank-centered proxy voting system to ensure that reform did not inadvertently empower managers. The law also imposes limited prescriptive rules on banks that require them to disclose all board mandates held by their representatives, their ownership stakes in firms, and alternative ways for their share depositors to exercise their votes. For a detailed discussion of these complex provisions, see Cioffi 2002b.

48. The KonTraG also partially embraced Anglo-American financial practices and litigious enforcement mechanisms. The law allowed stock repurchases and the use of stock options as executive compensation for the first time (though with stricter limitations than in the United States to prevent excessive executive compensation and abuse). In the area of shareholder rights and enforcement mechanisms, the KonTraG contained modest reforms of shareholder litigation rules. However, the KonTraG did not alter the *substance* of fiduciary duties, nor did it otherwise alter the mechanisms and procedures for enforcing shareholder rights to make them more effective in practice (e.g., by authorizing class actions, contingency fees). The German ambivalence toward Anglo-American capitalism and litigation continues.

49. One curious aspect of this backlash against takeovers is that the Mannesmann takeover *preceded* the enactment of the July 2000 tax reform law. At the time of the Mannesmann takeover, corporate Germany appeared relatively unconcerned. Interviews conducted by the author, as well as journalistic accounts, indicate that the fears of German managers grew when they considered the combined effects of the KonTraG and the tax reform, the unequal playing field that these changes might create against firms from countries that allowed more potent antitakeover defenses—including, ironically, the United States. For an excellent analysis of the Mannesmann takeover, see Höpner and Jackson 2001.

50. For an extended discussion of the relation between the politics of German corporate governance and the failure of the EU Takeover Directive, see Cioffi 2002b.

51. See Maul and Kouloridas 2004. In particular, the 2004 Directive contains an "opt-in/out" provision that permits member states and companies to opt into or out of the Directive's restrictions on takeover defenses. It also includes a "reciprocity" provision that allows a target to employ takeover defenses that would be legal for the bidder to use. The text of the Directive is available at: http://register.consilium.eu.int/pdf/en/03/st15/st15476.en03.pdf.

52. See Ashurst 2005 (translation); Strelow and Wildberger 2002; Osborne and Clarke 2002; Rissel 2002; Zehetmeier-Mueller and Ufland 2002; H. Williamson 2001; BBC 2001; R. Wood 2001.

53. The Takeover Act does not transform the core of the stakeholder corporate governance scheme. Codetermination and fiduciary obligations remain undisturbed. The law imposes a mandatory bid rule, which is triggered when an ownership stake reaches a 30 percent threshold. The details of takeover bids and the offeror's business plans must be fully disclosed in a filing with the BAFin.

54. Securities Acquisition and Takeover Act, § 33.1 & .2; see also Braude 2000a.

55. However, "poison pill" defenses common in the United States, whereby

(for example) a hostile takeover attempt triggers the issuance of stock or stock options that would dramatically dilute the would-be acquirer's stake, remain illegal under German company law.

56. Codetermination actually may have served a crucial legitimation function that made the pro-shareholder liberalizing elements of the Takeover Act palatable enough for passage. This hypothesis, however, remains speculative without further research.

57. This narrative of the German corporate governance commissions is indebted to an interview with Theodor Baums, July 9, 2003, Frankfurt.

58. See Baums Commission Report 2001; also Cromme Commission 2003.

59. See Transparency and Disclosure Act (TraPuG) (Gesetz zur weiteren Reform des Aktien- und Bilanzrechts, zu Transparenz und Publizität [Transparenz- und Publizitätsgesetz]), v. July 19, 2002, BGBl. I S. 2681.

60. For discussions of the German government's increasing use of commissions as a means of formulating policy, forging consensus, and avoiding deadlock among interest group and peak associations, see *The Economist* 2003; Baums 2001; Zumbansen 2002; cf. Heinze and Strünck 2003. Some critics have accused the government of using expert commissions to circumvent Parliament. Government defenders counter that Parliament still must pass all legislation and that the commissions have not impaired democratic lawmaking. See *The Economist* 2003; Baums 2003. In contrast to corporate governance policy, the German Constitution circumscribes governmental intrusion into negotiations among the "social partners" in the area of labor relations. Accordingly, the government could not circumvent neocorporatist gridlock through commissions or the tripartite negotiations under the Alliance for Jobs (Bündis für Arbeit. See Streeck 2003; Hemerijck and Vail, this volume).

61. For an analysis of the influence of labor relations institutions on corporate governance reform that reaches similar conclusions, see Goyer 2003.

62. See generally Kagan 2001, 1997.

6. From Maternalism to "Employment for All"

1. The cultural currency of stay-at-home motherhood has helped to obscure how similar many American practices are to Scandinavian ones. The most notable example is that when mostly educated and affluent married mothers drop out of employment temporarily to care for infants and young children, this is heralded as an embrace of "traditional" values, even when it is clear that the retreat from the labor market is meant to be temporary. I would argue that these withdrawals from the labor force ought to be understood as privately financed parental leaves.

2. That said, in southern Europe, political debates feature greater reluctance to give up on housewifery, or even its defense, as, for example, the arguments of the Italian housewives' association (Federcasalinghe).

3. Koven and Michel (1993) emphasize the ambiguous and competing meanings and uses of maternalist ideas. By their definition, maternalist thinking encompassed pro-natalists who were more concerned with population increase than women's subordination, women who accepted the ideal of a family wage for men as the source of support for mothers, and feminists who called for an independent state-supplied income for mothers ("the endowment of motherhood"). Other his-

torians (e.g., Ladd-Taylor 1994: 5) have preferred a more restricted definition that contrasts maternalism to feminism, particularly in terms of their positions on the desirability of the family wage and women's economic dependence (maternalists supported them; feminists opposed them). In an earlier article (Orloff 1999), I tried to map out the dimensions of gender ideology—sameness/difference, autonomy/dependence, equality/inequality, inclusion/exclusion—that characterize maternalism.

4. Feminist maternalists also fought for the "endowment of motherhood" for all, conferring political recognition on mothering and providing an income that would free women from economic dependence on husbands, even as it confirmed their status as caregivers. However, the calls for endowing all motherhood did not succeed, at least partly because of men's opposition. See Pedersen (1993) and Lake (1992) for analysis of these episodes.

5. Mary Ruggie (1988) qualified her earlier views, arguing that even given general agreement around a dual-earner model, men and women might have different gendered interests. These differences have been expressed by women's caucuses and other bodies around questions of hours of work (the six-hour day was championed by Swedish women trade unionists, whereas men preferred more vacation time), affirmative action, access to jobs with authority, and the like. Such an understanding has been difficult to come by, given the predominant discourse of Swedish equality politics, which has construed gender equality as subsumed in class equality (Jenson and Mahon 1993).

6. In this context, it is striking that the bulk of the "crisis of care" literature emanates from the United States. Arlie Hochschild (1997), Juliet Schor (1991), Sylvia Hewlett (1991), and Theda Skocpol (2000) have all bewailed a culture of long working hours, paucity of time to care, and resulting family stress. My thanks to Jane Lewis for raising this point.

7. See O'Connor, Orloff, and Shaver 1999: ch. 6 for a more developed version of this argument.

8. While women exhibit more generous attitudes than do men vis-à-vis social spending, they did not defend "welfare as we knew it." Rather, public opinion data showed that their predominant sentiment was for helping those who tried to work for pay (Gilens 1999). Women's interests were not politically united around welfare, and AFDC did not capture the pro-caregiving sentiments that many women express. Few women or women's equality organizations mobilized to protest against welfare reform. Why did the proposed or actual elimination of AFDC not call forth popular protests similar to those that followed the 1989 Supreme Court *Webster* decision, when hundreds of thousands of women turned out to defend abortion rights? The Women's Committee of One Hundred, one of the few pro-welfare, feminist lobbying groups to appear when welfare was being debated, tried to mobilize under the slogan "A war against poor women is a war against all women" (Mink 1998). But it drew only hundreds in several demonstrations. In the case of abortion rights, women across the social spectrum saw an issue that engaged their interests; in the case of welfare reform, most women were not directly concerned.

9. The situation of poor women is rhetorically contrasted with that of affluent women, who, unlike poor women, are said to have "choices" about employment and full-time care and to be targets of popular cultural encouragement to stay at

home with their children. Of course, it is not direct state welfare policy that makes such choices possible but rather private resources, such as affluent women's own savings or their partners' salaries. This is certainly undergirded by an unequal earnings and wealth distribution, which is not devoid of political support. Still, it would be a stretch to argue that the principal aim of sustaining these economic inequalities is to allow better-off women to stay at home with their young children. Note that better-educated women across racial and ethnic groups have higher levels of employment than less-educated women (England, Garcia-Beaulieu, and Ross 2004.)

10. Consider the overall shape of the US welfare regime, with the large share of private provision for working-aged people. Before they reach retirement age, the majority of women, like most men, must rely on employer-provided or privately financed services and benefits—or do without. This includes the vast majority of single mothers, 84 percent of whom were in the labor force in 1997 (Meyer and Rosenbaum 1998). Women, particularly mothers of young children, sometimes depend at least partially on male partners' income, but labor force participation has become the norm for women as well as men. In 2004, among mothers of children aged six through seventeen, 74 percent of married women were in the labor force, almost the same level as for single mothers, with 77 percent (US Bureau of Labor Statistics 2005: 8). Even among mothers of children under age one, in 2003, half of married women were in the labor force, and 45 percent of other mothers (US Bureau of Labor Statistics 2005: 10).

11. I make this argument at greater length in Orloff 2001.

12. This phenomenon has been called "defamilization" by various analysts, but this usage—which focuses on the locus of care—may obscure its initial feminist use to get at gendered questions about power and dependency within families.

13. While almost all European countries provide care for children from ages three to six in the course of fulfilling an educational mission, care for children under the age of three, essential for mothers' employment, is much less developed outside the Nordic countries and France. Care for school-aged children is de facto provided by elementary schools, but there is less provision for after-school hours, and school days in many continental European countries are irregular.

14. Thanks to Maurizio Ferrara for suggestions on these points.

7. The State in the Digital Economy

This chapter is drawn from a larger project that is presented in Zysman and Newman 2006.

1. Some argue that in its sheer scale relative to an existing economy, the IT revolution is greater than the textile boom of the first industrial revolution. And the telecom collapse that followed the dot-com collapse opened real possibilities. Brad DeLong notes that it was the collapse of the railroad bubble that set the stage for the transportation revolution, facilitating the applications and uses that depended on lower-price shipping (DeLong 2004). When excess rail capacity drove down transport prices in the late nineteenth century, the result was innovative and transformative businesses, such as mail-order retailing. Similarly, today, telecom network providers have overbuilt, creating excess network capacity that

is, at this writing, available at pennies on the dollar, generating new innovations in delivery.

2. The work of Claude Shannon and Norbert Wiener in a real sense defines the information age (Weiner 1954, 1965; Shannon 1993).

3. The use and application of transformative technologies alter the array of activities in the economy as a whole. The diffusion of these transformative technologies is undoubtedly the critical step. It is not just the fortunes made as the leading sector expands but also the industrial development that transformative technologies engender, as Brad DeLong points out (see note 1).

4. The innovators were the core auto and electronics firms who, in a hierarchical manner, dominated tiers of suppliers and subsystem assemblers. The production innovation was the orchestration and reorganization of the assembly and component development process. The core Japanese assembly companies of the lean variety have been less vertically integrated than their American counterparts. That said, they have been at the center of vertical *Keiretsu*, loosely speaking, a Japanese conglomerate conventionally understood to be headed by a major bank or consisting of companies with a common supply chain that tightly links the supplier companies to their clients (Johnson, Tyson, and Zysman 1989).

5. By "vertical control" we mean both vertical integration from inputs, through assembly, to distribution, as in the case of American auto producers, and the "virtual" integration of Asian enterprise groups, as when Japanese producers of consumer durables effectively dominate market relations with semi-independent suppliers through the *Keiretsu* group structure (Aoki 1988, 1993; Gerlach 1992; Aoki and Dore 1994).

6. See Global Value Chain Initiative at http://www.globalvaluechains.org.

7. According to the Department of Commerce Bureau of Economic Analysis, in 1998, US trade in IT was $314 billion. The total volume of American trade—imports and exports—in information technology is now doubling in less than seven years.

8. See John Gilmore as quoted in Peter Lewis 1996. See also Barlow 1996. Manuel Castells makes a more nuanced argument that the rise of complex networks has limited the power of the state (Castells 1996).

9. For a more general discussion of the role of self-regulation in the early years of the Internet, see Marsden 2000. For the role of the state in shaping the character of self-regulatory efforts, see Newman and Bach 2004.

10. Steven Vogel titled his excellent comparative study of telecommunications and financial deregulation in Britain and Japan *Freer Markets, More Rules* (S. Vogel 1996).

11. Thanks to Steve Weber for the reference to Stewart Brand.

12. For the important role states have played in resolving international challenges posed by digital technologies, see Drezner 2004.

13. For a discussion of the political development of telecommunications liberalization, see Cowhey 1990a.

14. Our thanks to Jonathan Sallet for this point.

15. For a discussion of the DMCA as well as its implications for fair use, see Samuelson 1999; Nimmer 2000.

16. The Open Source system, the rules of community and property, rests on three principles: (1) the source code must be distributed or made available with

the software for no more than the cost of distribution; (2) anyone may redistribute the software, but they may not charge royalties or licensing fees; and (3) anyone may modify the software or derive other software from it, then distribute the modified software under the same terms. Open Source is not a challenge to property or capitalism but rather a challenge to particular business models. Interestingly, the entire open software project rests on contract law and the legal system that enforces those commitments. In essence, the rules of property have been shifted from rules of exclusion to rules of distribution. See Weber 2004.

17. It is interesting to note that another policy, spectrum allocation, has in many instances erased the lead that Europe enjoyed because of standards harmonization. See Cowhey, Aronson, and Richards 2006.

18. See *New York Times* 2003.

19. There are exceptions, of course. One is the present debate about the effort to restrict telemarketing calls in the United States, which has mobilized a broad constituency. But even this issue, which receives almost universal popular support, has faced a harrowing road to implementation, including multiple court injunctions that threaten to derail a consumer-friendly outcome.

8. Building Global Service Markets

1. Unlike many analyses of state capacity, our emphasis is not on the ability of states to manage national economic adjustment or create competitive advantage. We focus on the impact of institutional capacity at the national and global levels on the restructuring of international markets.

2. Only recently have changes in the locus of control over aviation markets within the EU opened the potential for more dramatic restructuring of the market. The rise of low-cost carriers serving second-tier (or outlying) airports has reshaped the market, absent fundamental changes in the regulatory regime. Although important, these changes have not fundamentally altered the structure of international markets, and most observers expect real change to evolve slowly and be largely shaped by the interests of incumbent airlines on individual bilateral routes.

3. Section 2 examines these issues in detail.

4. In telecoms, the need to build out networks (in particular, local networks that served major multinational corportation [MNC] customers) meant that new entry would likely take time to alter local market competition and therefore incumbent positioning. In aviation, by contrast, access to airport landing slots and gate capacity was all that was required for new entrants to dramatically alter competitive dynamics. Incumbent airlines thus faced more significant near-term adjustment challenges to new competition rules than did their telecoms counterparts.

5. Services include aviation, telecommunication, banking, insurance, health care, transportation, accounting, and so on.

6. The manipulation of property rights is one of the oldest and most powerful tools for state intervention in the economy. While reforms in property rights in recent years predominantly attempted to create more competitive markets, tinkering with property rights is as much an instrument of strategic economic policy as more traditional forms of intervention, such as government subsidies. Indeed,

assigning property rights to private owners as an incentive for building networks is a classic strategy, dating back at least to the construction of railroads in the nineteenth century.

7. However, the emergence of the Southwest Airlines model (low-cost travel between "second-tier" airports) in both the US domestic market and intra-EU market has substantially altered the competitive landscape.

8. There is a large literature on the role international institutions play in monitoring actor behavior and sanctioning cheaters, thereby facilitating international economic exchange. For the classic statement, see Keohane 1984.

9. Economists devote enormous effort to modeling the precise mix of incentives that will lead incumbents to follow the temptation to deny access to their networks (e.g., Noam 2001; Tirole and Laffont 1993). This is the correct efficiency question for competition policy. As a political matter, companies routinely assume that the potential for discriminatory conduct exists and, accordingly, treat this as a contracting risk requiring caution on their part.

10. The United States is the exception, although even the American market was dominated by entrenched privately owned incumbents.

11. Obviously, new entrants in aviation needed access to such safety resources as navigation and approach landing systems. But these facilities were collective goods that were not traditionally supplied by any one carrier, even the national airline. So they were not contentious. A similar point applied to telecoms issues like access to the national numbering plan for area codes. In addition, traditional global institutions (e.g., the ITU) remained relevant to global harmonization in these areas.

12. The US-UK bilateral formed the "model" bilateral upon which all other bilateral, state-to-state agreements were built. However, it is important to note that there were important differences between individual bilateral agreements (Richards 1999).

13. The United States was the exception, as antitrust laws precluded US carriers from concluding side agreements with their foreign counterparts. The Civil Aeronautics Board did, however, occasionally grant permission for US carriers to collude with foreign airlines.

14. It is worth noting that IATA did not "capture" fare-setting authority. Rather, the Bermuda bilateral contained explicit language granting IATA authority to set fares. In the United States, IATA authority was dependent on a grant of antitrust immunity from the Justice Department, which was renewed annually until 1955, when antitrust was granted indefinitely. For a discussion of airline motivations regarding IATA, see Sochor 1991: 13.

15. On IATA traffic conferences, see Lowenfeld 1981: 455–476. The discussion of IATA rules draws heavily from this source unless otherwise noted.

16. In 1951, for example, the average cost of a New York–London round-trip ticket was $611, or 39.6 percent of US per capita income. By 1965, the fare had dropped to $375, or 17 percent of per capita income (*Aviation Week and Space Technology*, January 23, 1967, 49–50).

17. On US-Japan routes, for example, the introduction of commercial jets reduced travel time from eighteen to eight hours. See Hansen and Kanafani 1990.

18. The number of passengers on scheduled international airline flights increased from 14 million in 1956 to 23 million in 1960, and international traffic

doubled between 1959 and 1965. By 1970, there were 74 million international passengers. The data are for IATA members only and do not include charter carriers. Data supplied to the authors by IATA officials and available on request.

19. In the immediate postwar years, business accounted for about 80 percent of travel, whereas leisure constituted some 20 percent. Today, those figures are reversed. See Tallon 1979: 1030–1032; Hanlon 1996: 18.

20. For a detailed discussion of demand elasticities for international aviation services, see Oum, Waters, and Yong 1992.

21. The three jets that flew international routes before the 747 carried 140 to 180 passengers, depending on seating configurations. The first 747s carried 350 to 420 passengers.

22. Although Pan Am did not take delivery of the first 747 until 1969, the range and cost structure of the 747 were known as early as 1966. In the 1968 transpacific proceeding, for example, all of the major US airlines applied for permission to enter US-Asia markets and planned to serve these markets with 747s. Interview with Bill Kutzke, Washington, DC, October 24 and 30, 1996.

23. The limited range of aircraft in the immediate postwar period meant that the market was organized around coastal cities. As the range of jets increased, it offered the potential for international travel from interior domestic cities.

24. See *Aviation Week and Space Technology*, May 8, 1967, 33–47; and December 25, 1967, 26–27.

25. See *New York Times* 2003. Of course, this has changed dramatically in the wake of September 11 and the ensuing shifts in the industry (demand patterns, competition from low-cost carriers, etc.).

26. The potential for arbitrage is greater in cargo markets, given the decreased importance of routing and the lower increase in costs with distance.

27. Our point is not that there was no potential for traffic diversion in aviation markets, just that these effects were much less significant than in telecommunications markets. Traffic diversion in geographically close markets for passengers who were less time or route sensitive was important in aviation markets, especially if price differences were particularly large. For a discussion of these dynamics, see Kasper 1988. The potential for monitoring traffic and the limited potential for rerouting have also made possible private governance solutions (international strategic alliances) to market access problems in aviation services.

28. The incumbents had much to fear if somehow governments shifted in favor of more competition because there is ample elasticity of supply in aircraft market. Large stocks of aircraft are available for lease on attractive terms for new entrants seeking to build capacity quickly. The privatization of airlines removed some obstacles to bilateral liberalization. Consider, for example, the conclusion of US-France negotiations shortly after the announcement that France would sell off a major stake in Air France. See *Financial Times* 1998 and *New York Times* 1998b.

29. The act setting up the Civil Aeronautics Board explicitly prohibited foreign airlines from carrying intra-US traffic and placed a cap of 25 percent on foreign ownership. In the 1990s, KLM and Northwest tested the political will behind the legislation and ultimately failed to create a complex yet legal solution to the problem. In the late 1990s and early 2000s, off-and-on discussions between American Airlines and British Airways resulted in a similar legal impasse.

30. The rise of low-cost carriers may ease the problem because they use smaller airports with available gates as part of their cost-cutting model.

31. This was in marked contrast to the potential political benefits of a "big bang" liberalization for telecoms markets.

32. Only in 2003 did uncertainties regarding EU competencies and jurisdictions in negotiating aviation services agreements resolve. Interviews with EU officials, October 2003.

33. The economic value of any bargain will depend, in part, on the extent of real market access available under the new agreement, and this market access will depend on the decision-making process used to determine particular features of market access.

34. The ITU also organized the "global commons" of radio spectrum and communications satellites' orbital slots around practices that assured national control, while seeking to assure noninterference among national plans. This coordination function has remained even in an era of competition, although the implementing mechanisms have slowly adapted to more diverse market participants and market uses. The global regime also included expectations and rules for equipment markets. This chapter omits these factors.

35. Given the smaller specialized nature of the market, incumbents were more open to ad hoc accommodations. The new trade rules essentially reinforced the bargaining power of large multinational corporate customers. One solution was really remarkable. Rather than figure out how to assure meaningful market entry in the agreement, which was hard to do as long as the underlying network was controlled by a local monopolist, the negotiators effectively acknowledged the right of corporations to procure data networking competitively (including the use of self-supply of computer networks). Guaranteeing the right of the consumer substituted for guaranteeing the rights of competitive entrants fully.

36. The EU was creating cross-market competition within the EU, so it did not want national rules that could discriminate against other EU companies. Under long-established trade rules, US firms operating in Europe are treated as EU firms.

37. Using its administrative discretion under the controlling 1934 statute on communications, the FCC had created special competition rules to govern foreign carrier entry into the United States on a country-by-country basis. The United States only allowed foreign corporate control of a US carrier if its market was competitive and open to equivalent US investment. In the 1995 G-7 Summit on the Global Information Society, Vice President Al Gore delivered a blunt message to the G-7: the United States would liberalize its markets under a new bilateral reciprocity rule (called the Effective Competitive Opportunities formula at the FCC) unless the WTO found an acceptable formula for multilateral liberalization (Cowhey and Richards 2000; Federal Communications Commission 1997b).

38. The 1996 Telecommunications Act nearly had a foreign investment liberalization clause inserted by House Republicans. But this clause disappeared in light of resistance by some key Democrats.

39. The EU, based on prior experience, believed the US promise that compliance by its state regulatory commissions would not be a major problem, especially after the passage of the 1996 Telecommunications Act, which mandated competition in local telephone services.

40. The Bells' indifference or support meant that most Republicans had no major objection to a WTO deal as long as it did not interfere with ending restrictions on the Bells. The competitors to AT&T in international services (MCI, Sprint, and a host of smaller long-distance operators, such as WorldCom, the subsequent buyer of MCI) traditionally operated under the umbrella of AT&T in the world market, following AT&T's lead on negotiating settlement rates and the rest, then discounting prices and offering service innovations to win market share. They officially supported AT&T in all of its reservations about the risks of a WTO agreement, but some showed great flexibility on details.

41. We thank Howard Shelanski for emphasizing this point.

42. The senior Democrat on the Senate Commerce Committee (which had jurisdiction over the FCC) was Senator Ernst Hollings, a strong ally of AT&T on domestic policy and long a critic of multilateral trade policy. Hollings had made it known that he was highly suspicious of any WTO deal on basic telecommunications services.

43. Put comparatively, the EU member states ratify a tentative trade pact each time they authorize the Commission to make a new negotiating offer in a WTO negotiation. The Congress ratifies the US trade offer only at the conclusion of a negotiation, although, of course, the executive branch tries to anticipate congressional preferences.

44. First, it imposed uniform settlement rates for all US carriers. Second, it declared "proportionate return," a rule saying that a carrier was entitled to the same percentage of incoming traffic from India, for example, as it sent from the United States to India.

45. These figures were calculated by the staff of the International Bureau of the FCC based on settlement rate data published by the Commission (Blake and Lande 1999).

46. At the same time, FCC bargaining rules effectively reduced competition among US carriers on international long distance. After twelve years of competition in international services, margins remained huge. Prices for consumers were even higher than those demanded by settlement rate effects. There were very large markups by carriers even in the most competitive national market, the United States. In August 1997, for example, the FCC estimated that the average price of an international phone call from the United States was eighty-eight cents per minute, compared to thirteen cents for domestic long distance (Federal Communications Commission 1997a). These price differences existed despite negligible differences in the costs of transmission between the two types of calls. Even after the effects of settlement payments on costs for US carriers were calculated, margins for US carriers remained very high, despite the fact that US rates for international service were generally by far the lowest in the world.

47. For example, if the United States opened its market to competition on international phone services under the WTO deal, while India did not, Indian carriers would still have free access to the US market. Under "one-way bypass," the United States would have a WTO commitment to permit market access for the provision of international services in and out of the United States by a variety of methods, including the resale of international transport services (or "international simple resale" in regulatory parlance). Thus, the Indian international carrier, as a company in a WTO country, could lease a transmission circuit from US

companies to deliver India's phone traffic to the United States. This transport circuit would be exempt from the settlement rate system, so that all of the Indian phone calls to the United States would result in no settlement payments to US carriers. But since India had not opened its international services markets through WTO commitments, US carriers would still have to deliver all American calls to India at inflated settlement rates. This would drive up the net settlement payment of the United States to India. Under WTO MFN rules, the United States could not deny a market access benefit offered to the EU to an Indian carrier even if the Indian market was not open to competition in international services.

48. If all market commitments on competition had needed to be ratified in a WTO code by all states, dissenters would have scuttled the code. It was much easier to agree to a prototype of the language on competition and leave it up to the individual state to decide if it would accept the language. On the WTO rules and logic, see K. Cameron 2004.

49. For an explanation of why the United States believed that it could enforce its unilateral caps on a negotiated accounting rate, see Cowhey 1998.

50. See Sherman 1998 for a detailed discussion of the specific outcomes of the agreement.

51. It is important to note that a very limited set of point-to-point routes accounted for the vast majority of international aviation traffic.

52. See the US-Japan Connect analysis of the potential economic impact of improved US-Japan air traffic flows. Data available from the authors.

53. Access to US airports was governed by somewhat more transparent and clear regulatory rules, which promised to be easier for foreign airlines to negotiate. Access to US airports and landing slots fell under the jurisdiction of local authorities (traditionally, the city government or municipal government where the airport is located). However, one or two large US carriers usually dominated each major international airport and were major co-investors with the airport. So foreign entrants still had much to worry about.

54. The problem was not the legal competence of the central government. It was politics. The Commerce Clause of the US Constitution gave the US government authority to intervene at the local level in regard to airport conduct if it impeded interstate commerce. The EU's authority was far more limited unless it could redefine aviation services as a trade issue. Even if this jurisdictional issue could be resolved, the political problems remained.

55. The satellite services industry did undergo a bout of skepticism in 1996 but later concluded that nothing about a WTO agreement made it worse off. Its problems focused not on interconnection but rather on spectrum allocation, equipment reliability certification, and initial licensing issues.

56. The right to fly internal passengers is known as "cabotage" in the industry.

9. The Transformation of European Trading States

Parts of this chapter are excerpted from Barton et al. 2006 and Steinberg forthcoming 2007.

1. "EC" is used herein to refer to the European Community, the European Communities, and the European Economic Community. "EU" is used here in all contexts where reference is made to either the EU exclusively or the EC and the

EU, over the course of their respective histories. These acronyms are used for purposes of simplicity and in accordance with convention in this book, despite the fact that the European Union did not exist before 1992 and the EU is not a member of the WTO. The European Economic Community was seated at GATT meetings from about 1960 (Jackson 1969). The European Communities became a member of the WTO at its inception.

2. For a more detailed account of these arguments, see Barton et al. 2006.

3. Calculated from International Monetary Fund 1977.

4. Calculated from World Bank 1972.

5. Many have speculated why Japan has not assumed a leadership role at the GATT/WTO. Perhaps the Japanese government is reluctant to lead global market liberalization efforts because Japan's own market has been relatively closed. It is also possible that Japan's ultimately unsuccessful effort at exercising global power in the first half of the twentieth century has left it with a cultural legacy biased against reassertion of leadership.

6. At that time, the combined EU and US markets accounted for approximately two-thirds of GATT/WTO GDP (World Bank 2001).

7. The articles of the EC Treaty have been renumbered so that Article 113 of the Treaty of Rome is now Article 133 of the EC Treaty, as amended. Accordingly, the relevant committee has been renamed the 133 Committee. References to the "113/133 Committee" refer to either the 113 Committee or its successor.

8. This statement appears on the EU's official Web site, in "Citizen's Guide to Competition Policy": http://europa.eu.int/comm./competition/index-en.html#5.

9. *Commission of the European Communities v. Council of the European Communities*, Case No. 22/70 (decided March 31, 1971) (where the Community has adopted internal rules in a given field of activity, external negotiations that may affect that internal regime are within the exclusive competence of the Commission); Case No. 1/76 (decided April 26, 1977) (where a power exists for the Community to adopt internal rules, relevant external negotiations are within the exclusive competence of the Commission, even though the Council may not have yet exercised the initial internal rule-making); *International Rubber Case*, Case No. 1/78 (decided October 4, 1979) (the Commission has exclusive competence to negotiate agreements that are essentially commercial in nature but only "mixed competence" to negotiate agreements that commit member states to directly finance it); and Case No. 1/94 (decided November 15, 1994) (placing each of several trade negotiating topics into one of three categories, Commission exclusive competence, mixed competence, and no competence).

10. *International Rubber Case*, Case No. 1/78; Case No. 1/94.

11. The "cast" and "mold" terms are used here as metaphors. Neither the cast nor the mold is perfect. As stated elsewhere herein, there is merely bounded convergence in the form of the state, suggesting that there is variance in the extent to which the trading state is converging on the Western model.

12. The MFN principle generally prohibits measures that discriminate against imports from one GATT/WTO member in favor of like products imported from another member.

13. The national treatment principle generally prohibits measures that discriminate against imports in favor of domestically produced like products.

14. The GATT generally limits the tariffs that may be charged on a product

to the level established for that product in each country's schedule of concessions. Tariffs so limited are said to be "bound tariffs."

15. GATT Article XI generally prohibits GATT/WTO members from maintaining quantitative restrictions on the importation of any good.

The State after Statism

1. I wish to thank the following people for their comments on the project as a whole and on earlier drafts of this chapter: Suzanne Berger, Stephen Cohen, Peter Gourevitch, Yong-Chool Ha, Peter Hall, Yohei Nakayama, T. J. Pempel, Richard Samuels, Steven Vogel, J. Nicholas Ziegler, and an anonymous reviewer for Harvard University Press. I also benefited from the suggestions of all the contributors to *The State after Statism*, notably Chris Howell and John Zysman.

2. Scholars of Finland, a political economy that has traditionally combined statist industrial policy with corporatist industrial relations and social protection, describe a similar shift toward more market-conforming industrial promotion. The success of Finnish information technology companies, notably Nokia, was greatly abetted by massive public investments in the late 1980s and early 1990s in research and development, technology sharing, and technical education (Ornston and Rehn 2006; Rouvinen et al. 2006).

3. I am thankful to Peter Gourevitch for suggesting the phrase "authoritative power."

4. All of these authors use the phrase "despotic power." Again, in analyzing the policies of democratic countries, the label "authoritative power" seems more appropriate.

5. In some cases, market regulation may offer a third alternative, but this alternative, too, requires the deployment of authoritative state power. As Hemerijck and Vail recount, Dutch officials attempted to curb excessive use of the sickness and disability schemes by introducing private insurers, who would vary premiums according to usage ("experience rating"). Such a shift from corporatist to market regulation entailed the exercise of authoritative power by the Dutch state, with officials rewriting the rules governing sickness and disability insurance—often over the objections of the social partners.

References

Ackerman, Bruce, and David Golove (1995). "Is NAFTA Constitutional?" *Harvard Law Review* 108: 799–929.

Adeney, Martin, and John Lloyd (1986). *The Miners' Strike 1984–85: Loss without Limit*. London: Routledge and Kegan Paul.

Alesina, Alberto, and Enrico Spolaore (1997). "On the Number and Size of Nations." *Quarterly Journal of Economics* 112: 1027–1056.

Amenta, Edwin (1998). *Bold Relief: Institutional Politics and the Origins of Modern American Social Policy*. Princeton, NJ: Princeton University Press.

Aoki, Masahiko (1988). *Information, Incentives, and Bargaining in the Japanese Economy*. New York: Cambridge University Press.

—— (1993). *The Japanese Firm as a System of Attributes: A Survey and Research Agenda*. Stanford, CA: Center for Economic Policy Research, Stanford University.

Aoki, Masahiko, and Ronald Dore, eds. (1994). *The Japanese Firm: The Sources of Competitive Strength*. New York: Oxford University Press.

Arena, Alex (1997). "The WTO Telecommunications Agreement: Some Personal Reflections." *In TeleGeography 1997*. Washington, DC: TeleGeography.

Ashurst, Morris Crisp (August 2000). "Act on the Regulation of Public Offers for the Acquisition of Securities and Corporate Take-overs: German Take-over Code—Adopted Bill, unofficial translation produced by Ashurst Morris Crisp." http://www.ashursts.com/pubs/approvedtakeover.htm.

Assmann, Heinz-Dieter (1990). "Microcorporatist Structures in German Law on Groups of Companies." In David Sugarman and Gunther Teubner, eds., *Regulating Corporate Groups in Europe*, 317–534. Baden-Baden: Nomos Verlagsgesellschaft.

Aviation Week and Space Technologies. Various issues.

Bach, David (2000). "International Cooperation and the Logic of Networks: Europe and the GSM." BRIE Working Paper 139, University of California, Berkeley.

Bael, Ivo Van, and Jean-François Bellis (1990). *Anti-Dumping and Other Trade Protection Laws of the EEC.* 2d ed. Bicester, Oxfordshire: CCH Editions.

Baglioni, Guido, and Colin Crouch, eds. (1990). *European Industrial Relations: The Challenge of Flexibility.* London: Sage.

Bailey, Michael, Judith Goldstein, and Barry Weingast (1997). "The Origins of American Trade Policy: Rules, Coalitions, and International Politics." *World Politics* 49, no. 3: 309–338.

Bar, François (2001). "The Construction of Marketplace Architecture." In BRIE-IGCC E-conomy Task Force, ed., *Tracking a Transformation: E-commerce and the Terms of Competition in Industries,* 27–49. Washington, DC: Brookings Institution Press.

Baran, Barbara (1986). "The Technological Transformation of White Collar Work: A Case Study of the Insurance Industry." Ph.D. diss., University of California, Berkeley.

Barlow, John Perry (1996). "A Declaration of the Independence of Cyberspace." February 8. http://www.eff.org/barlow/Declaration-Final.html.

Barton, John, Judith Goldstein, Timothy Josling, and Richard H. Steinberg (2006). *The Evolution of the Trade Regime: Politics, Law, and Economics of the GATT/WTO.* Princeton, NJ: Princeton University Press.

Barzel, Yoram (1997). *Economic Analysis of Property Rights.* Cambridge: Cambridge University Press.

Bauchard, Pierre (1986). *La guerre des deux roses: Du rêve à la réalité, 1981–1985.* Paris: Bernard Grasset.

Baums, Theodor (2001). "Reforming German Corporate Governance: Inside a Law-Making Process of a Very New Nature, Interview with Professor Dr. Theodor Baums." *German Law Journal* 2, no. 12.

Baums, Theodor, and Bernd Frick (1999). "The Market Value of the Codetermined Firm." In Margaret M. Blair and Mark J. Roe, eds., *Employees and Corporate Governance,* 206–235. Washington, DC: Brookings Institution Press.

Baums Commission Report (2001). *Bericht der Regierungskommission Corporate Governance.* July 10. Complete official German version: http://www.otto-schmidt.de/corporate_governance.htm. English summary: http://www.shearman.com/publications/cm_pubs.html.

Baxter, Janeen, and Erik Olin Wright (2000). "The Glass Ceiling Hypothesis: A Comparative Study of the United States, Sweden, and Australia." *Gender and Society* 14: 275–294.

BBC (2001). "Germany to Curb Hostile Takeovers." July 11. http://news.bbc.co.uk/1/hi/business/1433380.stm.

Bebchuk, Lucian Arye, and Jesse M. Fried (2004). *Pay without Performance: The Unfulfilled Promise of Executive Compensation.* Cambridge, MA: Harvard University Press.

Becker, Uwe (2001). "Miracle by Consensus? Consensualism and Dominance in Dutch Employment Development." *Economic and Industrial Democracy* 22: 453–483.

Beer, Samuel (1982). *Britain against Itself.* London: Faber.

Beeson, Ann, and Chris Hansen (1997). "Fahrenheit 451.2: Is Cyberspace Burning?" American Civil Liberties Union White paper, Wye Mills, MD.

Bendix, Reinhard (1978). *Kings or People: Power and the Mandate to Rule*. Berkeley: University of California Press.

Bennett, Colin (1992). *Regulating Privacy*. Ithaca, NY: Cornell University Press.

Berger, Suzanne (1981a). "Lame Ducks and National Champions: Industrial Policy in the Fifth Republic." In William Andrews and Stanley Hoffmann, eds., *The Fifth Republic at Twenty*, 160–178. Albany: State University of New York Press.

———, ed. (1981b). *Organizing Interests in Western Europe: Pluralism, Corporatism, and the Transformation of Politics*. Cambridge: Cambridge University Press.

Berger, Suzanne, and Ronald Dore, eds. (1996). *Convergence or Diversity? National Models of Production and Distribution in a Global Economy*. Ithaca, NY: Cornell University Press.

Bergqvist, Christina, ed. (1999). *Equal Democracies? Gender and Politics in the Nordic Countries*. Oslo: Scandinavian University Press.

Bermann, George A. (1996). "Regulatory Cooperation between the European Commission and US Administrative Agencies." *Administrative Law Journal of American University* 9: 933–983.

Birley, Derek (1995a). *Land of Sport and Glory: Sport and British Society, 1887–1910*. Manchester: Manchester University Press.

——— (1995b). *Playing the Game: Sport and British Society, 1910–45*. Manchester: Manchester University Press.

Blair, Margaret (1995). *Ownership and Control: Rethinking Corporate Governance for the Twenty-first Century*. Washington, DC: Brookings Institution Press.

Blake, Linda, and Jim Lande (1999). *Trends in the US International Telecommunications Industry*. Washington, DC: FCC, Common Carrier Bureau's Industry Analysis Division. http://www.fcc.gov/Bureaus/Common_Carrier/Reports/FCC-State_Link/Intl/itltrd99.zip.

Blien, Uwe, Ulrich Walwei, and Heinz Werner (2002). "Labour Market Policy in Germany." IAB Labour Market Topics No. 49, Bundesanstalt für Arbeit, Nürnberg.

Block, Dennis J., Nancey E. Barton, and Stephen A. Radin (1993). *The Business Judgment Rule: The Fiduciary Duties of Corporate Directors*. Englewood Cliffs, NJ: Prentice-Hall.

Block, Fred (1982). "The Ruling Class Does Not Rule: Notes on the Marxist Theory of the State." In Thomas Ferguson and Joel Rogers, eds., *The Political Economy: Readings in the Politics and Economics of American Public Policy*, 32–46. Armonk, NY: M. E. Sharpe.

Blunkett, David (2001). "The Challenge of Improving Schools: Lessons for Public Sector Reform." Speech to IPPR seminar, May 1. http://www.dfee.gov.uk/dfee_speeches.

Boas, Taylor (2006). "Weaving the Authoritarian Web: The Control of Internet Use in Non-Democratic Regimes." In John Zysman and Abraham Newman, eds., *How Revolutionary Was the Digital Revolution? National Responses, Market Transitions, and Global Technology*. Palo Alto, CA: Stanford University Press.

Bock, Gisela (1991). "Antinatalism, Maternity and Paternity in National Socialist Racism." In Gisela Bock and Pat Thane, eds., *Maternity and Gender Politics:*

Women and the Rise of the European Welfare States, 1880s–1950s, 233–255. New York: Routledge.

Bock, Gisela, and Pat Thane, eds. (1991). *Maternity and Gender Policies: Women and the Rise of the European Welfare States. 1880s–1950s.* New York: Routledge.

Borchorst, Anette (1994). "The Scandinavian Welfare States—Patriarchal, Gender Neutral, or Woman-Friendly?" *International Journal of Contemporary Sociology* 31: 1–23.

Borchorst, Anette, and Birte Siim (2002). "The Women-Friendly Welfare States Revisited." *Nora* 10: 90–98.

Borrus, Michael, and John Zysman (1997). "Globalization with Borders: The Rise of Wintelism as the Future of Industrial Competition." *Industry and Innovation* 4, no. 2: 141–166.

Boswell, Jonathan, and James Peters (1997). *Capitalism in Contention: Business Leaders and Political Economy in Modern Britain.* New York: Cambridge University Press.

Boyd, Richard, and Seichii Nagamori (1991). "Industrial Policy-Making in Practice: Electoral, Diplomatic, and Other Adjustments to Crisis in the Japanese Shipbuilding Industry." In Stephen Wilks and Maurice Wright, eds., *The Promotion and Regulation of Industry in Japan*, 167–204. London: Macmillan.

Boyle, James (1996). *Shamans, Software, and Spleens: Law and the Construction of the Information Society.* Cambridge, MA: Harvard University Press.

——— (2003). "The Second Enclosure Movement and the Construction of the Public Domain." *Law and Contemporary Problems* 66: 33–74.

Braga, Carlos, A. Prinzo, Emmanuel Forestier, and Peter A. Stern (1999). "Developing Countries and the Accounting Rate Regime." In *Private Sector: Viewpoint 167.* Washington, DC: World Bank. http://www.worldbank.org/html/fpd/notes.

Braude, Jonathan (2000a). "German Panel Offers Proposed Takeover Rules," *Daily Deal*, May 17.

——— (2000b). "Germany Seems Ready to Accept Hostile Takeovers." *Daily Deal*, May 23.

Brocas, Anne-Marie, Anne-Marie Cailloux, and Virginie Oget (1990). *Women and Social Security.* Geneva: International Labor Office.

Brook, Keith (2002). "Trade Union Membership: An Analysis of Data from the Autumn 2001 LFS." *Labour Market Trends* (July): 343–354.

Brown, William, Simon Deakin, David Nash, and Sarah Oxenbridge (2000). "The Employment Contract: From Collective Procedures to Individual Rights." *British Journal of Industrial Relations* 38, no. 4: 611–629.

Brown, William, Simon Deakin, and Paul Ryan (1997). "The Effects of British Industrial Relations Legislation, 1979–97." *National Institute Economic Review* 161 (July): 69–83.

Bruno, Michael, and Jeffrey D. Sachs (1985). *Economics of Worldwide Stagflation.* Cambridge, MA: Harvard University Press.

Bundesanstalt für Arbeit (1999). "Ausbildung, Qualifizierung und Beschäftigung Jugendlicher." Informationen für die Beratungs- und Vermittlungsdieste der Bundesanstalt für Arbeit, 2/99. January 13.

——— (2000a). "JUMP: Das Sofortprogramm zum Abbau der Jugendarbeitlosigkeit." *Direkt: Fördern und Qualifizieren* 10 (April).

——— (2000b). "Sofortprogramm zum Abbau der Jugendarbeitlosigkeit: Zwischenergebnisse aus der Begleitforschung." Informationen für die Beratungs- und Vermittlungsdieste der Bundesanstalt für Arbeit, 20/00. May 17.

——— (2003). *2002 Annual Report*. Nürnberg: BA.

Bundesministerium für Arbeit und Sozialordnung (2000). "Die Rentenreform 2000: Ein mutiger Schritt zu mehr Sicherheit." Bonn: Bundesministerium für Arbeit und Sozialordnung. August.

——— (2002). "Jump ist ein voller Erfolg." Press release, February 15.

Burley, Anne-Marie, and Walter Mattli (1993). "Europe before the Court: A Political Theory of Legal Integration." *International Organization* 47: 41–76.

Bussemaker, Jet, and Rian Voet, eds. (1998). *Gender, Participation, and Citizenship in the Netherlands*. Brookfield, VT: Ashgate.

Caballero, Ricardo, Takeo Hoshi, and Anil Kashyap (2003). "Zombie Lending and Depressed Restructuring in Japan." http://gsbwww.uchicago.edu/fac/anil.kashyap/research/zombie.pdf.

Cable, Vincent (1995). "The Diminished Nation–State: A Study in the Loss of Economic Power." *Daedalus* 124, no. 2: 23–53.

Cairncross, Frances (1997). *The Death of Distance*. Cambridge, MA: Harvard Business School Press.

Calder, Kent (1990). "Linking Welfare and the Developmental State: Postal Savings in Japan." *Journal of Japanese Studies* 16, no. 1: 31–59.

——— (1993). *Crisis and Compensation: Public Policy and Political Stability in Japan*. Princeton, NJ: Princeton University Press.

Cameron, David (1978). "The Expansion of the Public Economy." *American Political Science Review* 72: 1243–1261.

——— (1996). "Exchange Rate Politics in France, 1981–1983: The Regime-Defining Choices of the Mitterrand Presidency." In Anthony Daley, ed., *The Mitterrand Era: Policy Alternatives and Political Mobilization in France*, 56–82. New York: NYU Press.

——— (2001). "Unemployment, Job Creation, and Economic and Monetary Union." In Nancy Bermeo, ed., *Unemployment in the New Europe*, 7–51. Cambridge: Cambridge University Press.

Cameron, Kelly (2004). "Telecommunications and Audio-visual Services in the Context of the WTO: Today and Tomorrow." In Damien Geradin and David Luff, eds., *The WTO and Global Convergence in Telecommunications and Audio—Visual Services*, 21–33. Cambridge: Cambridge University Press.

Cannadine, David (2002). *Ornamentalism: How the British Saw Their Empire*. London: Penguin.

Caporaso, James (1996). "The European Union and Forms of State: Westphalian, Regulatory, or Post-Modern?" *Journal of Common Market Studies* 34, no. 1: 29–52.

Carson, W. G. (1970). "White-Collar Crime and the Enforcement of Factory Legislation." *British Journal of Criminology* 10, no. 4: 383–398.

——— (1974). "Symbolic and Instrumental Dimensions of Early Factory Legislation: A Case Study in the Social Origins of Criminal Law." In Roger Hood, ed., *Crime, Criminology and Public Policy: Essays in Honour of Sir Leon Radzinowicz*, 107–138. London: Heinemann.

——— (1979). "The Conventionalization of Early Factory Crime." *International Journal for the Sociology of Law* 7, no. 1: 37–60.

Castel, Robert (1995). *Les métamorphoses de la question sociale: Une chronique du salariat.* Paris: Arthème Fayard.

Castells, Manuel (1996). *The Rise of the Network Society.* Cambridge: Blackwell Publishers.

Central Planning Bureau (1991). "De Werkgelegenheid in de Jaren Tachtig." Werkdocument No. 41, The Hague, Netherlands.

Cerny, Philip (1990). *The Changing Architecture of Politics: Structure, Agency, and the Future of the State.* London: Sage.

——— (1997). "Paradoxes of the Competition State: The Dynamics of Political Globalization." *Government and Opposition* 32, no. 2: 251–274.

Charkham, Jonathan P. (1994). *Keeping Good Company: A Study of Corporate Governance in Five Countries.* Oxford: Clarendon Press.

Charles, Maria, and David Grusky (2004). *Occupational Ghettoes: The Worldwide Segregation of Women and Men.* Palo Alto, CA: Stanford University Press.

Charpin, Jean-Michel (1999). *L'avenir de nos retraites.* Paris: La Documentation Française.

Cioffi, John W. (2000). "Governing Globalization? The State, Law, and Structural Change in Corporate Governance." *Journal of Law and Society* 27, no. 4: 572–600.

——— (2002a). "Public Law and Private Power: The Comparative Political Economy of Corporate Governance in the United States and Germany." Ph.D. diss., Department of Political Science, University of California, Berkeley.

——— (2002b). "Restructuring 'Germany, Inc.': The Politics of Company and Takeover Law Reform in Germany and the European Union." *Law and Policy* 24, no. 4: 355–402.

——— (2004). "The State of the Corporation: State Power, Politics, Policy-Making and Corporate Governance in the United States, Germany, and France." In Martin Shapiro and Martin Levin, eds., *Trans-Atlantic Policy-Making in an Age of Austerity,* 253–297. Washington, DC: Georgetown University Press.

——— (2005). "Irresistible Forces and Political Obstacles: Securities Litigation Reform and the Structural Regulation of Corporate Governance." Unpublished manuscript. September.

Cioffi, John W., and Stephen S. Cohen (2000). "The Advantages of Forwardness: The Interdependence of the State, Law, and Corporate Governance in an Age of Globalization." In Stephen S. Cohen and Gavin Boyd, eds., *Corporate Governance and Globalization,* 307–349. Cheltenham, UK: Edward Elgar.

Clarke, Donald C. (1993). "GATT Membership for China?" *University of Puget Sound Law Review* 17, no. 3: 517–531.

Cobble, Dorothy Sue (2004). *The Other Women's Movement: Workplace Justice and Social Rights in Modern America.* Princeton, NJ: Princeton University Press.

Coffee, John C., Jr. (1991). "Liquidity versus Control: The Institutional Investor as Corporate Monitor." *Columbia Law Review* 91: 1277–1366.

Coffineau, Michel (1993). *Les lois Auroux, dix ans après.* Paris: La Documentation Française.

Coghlan, John, and Ida Webb (1990). *Sport and British Politics since 1960*. Basingstoke: Falmer Press.

Cohen, Elie (1989). *L'Etat brancardier: Politiques du déclin industriel (1974–1984)*. Paris: Calmann-Lévy.

—— (1996). *La tentation hexagonale: La souveraineté à l'épreuve de la mondialisation*. Paris: Fayard.

Cohen, Elie, and Michel Bauer (1985). *Les grandes manoeuvres industrielles*. Paris: Belfond.

Cohen, Stephen S. (1977). *Modern Capitalist Planning: The French Model*. Berkeley: University of California Press.

—— (1998). "Form, Scale, and Limits in China's Trade and Development." *Journal of Asian Economics* 8, no. 4: 615–618.

Cohen, Steve, Brad DeLong, and John Zysman (2000). *Tools for Thought: What Is New and Important about the "E-conomy."* Berkeley, CA: BRIE.

Commaille, Jacques (1998). "La politique française à l'égard de la famille." *Regards sur l'actualité* (January): 12–24.

Commission of the European Communities (1998). *Globalization and the Information Society: The Need for Strengthened International Co-ordination*. Brussels: European Communities.

Committee on Standards in Public Life (1995). *Standards in Public Life*. Vol. 1, *Report*. Cm 2850–1. London: HMSO.

—— (1996). *Local Public Spending Bodies*. Vol. 1, *Report*. Cm 3270–1. London: HMSO.

—— (1997a). *Review of the Standards of Conduct in Executive NDPBs, NHS Trusts, and Local Public Spending Bodies*. Cm 3270–1. London: HMSO.

—— (1997b). *Standards of Conduct in Local Government*. Vol. 1, *Report*. Cm 3702–1. London: HMSO.

—— (1998). *The Funding of Political Parties in the United Kingdom*. Vol. 1, *Report*. Cm 4057–1. London: HMSO.

—— (2000a). *Reinforcing Standards: Review of the First Report of the Committee on Standards in Public Life*. Vol. 1, *Report*. Cm 4557. London: HMSO.

—— (2000b). *Standards of Conduct in the House of Lords*. Vol. 1, *Report*. Cm 4903–1. London: HMSO.

Cook, John, and Chris Kerse (1991). *EEC Merger Control*. London: Sweet and Maxwell.

Costain, Anne, and W. Douglas Costain (1987). "Strategies and Tactics of the Women's Movement in the United States: The Role of Political Parties." In Mary Katzenstein and Carol Mueller, eds., *The Women's Movements of the United States and Western Europe*, 196–214. Philadelphia: Temple University Press.

Courpasson, David (2000). "Managerial Strategies of Domination: Power in Soft Bureaucracies." *Organization Studies* 21, no. 1: 141–161.

Cowhey, Peter (1990a). "The International Telecommunications Regime: The Political Roots of Regimes for High Technology." *International Organization* 44: 169–199.

—— (1990b). "Telecommunications." In Gary C. Hufbauer, ed., *Europe 1992: An American Perspective*, 159–224. Washington DC: Brookings Institution Press.

———— (1998). "FCC Benchmarks and the Reform of the International Telecommunications Market." *Telecommunications Policy* 22, no. 11: 899–911.

Cowhey, Peter, Jonathan Aronson, and John Richards (2006). "The Peculiar Evolution of 3G Wireless Networks: Political Institutions, Property Rights, and the Politics of Technological Transitions." In John Zysman and Abraham Newman, eds., *How Revolutionary Was the Digital Revolution? National Responses, Market Transitions, and Global Technology*. Palo Alto, CA: Stanford University Press.

Cowhey, Peter, and John Richards (2000). "Dialing for Dollars: The Revolution in Communications Markets." In Jeffrey Hart and Akheem Prasash, eds., *Coping with Globalization*, 148–167. New York: Routledge.

Cowling, Maurice (1971). *The Impact of Labour, 1920–1924: The Beginning of Modern British Politics*. Cambridge: Cambridge University Press.

Cromme Commission (2003). (Government Commission of the German Corporate Governance Code), *German Corporate Governance Code*, adopted February 26, 2002, as amended May 21, 2003. Information and official German version and English translation: http://www.corporate-governance-code.de/index-e.html.

Crouch, Colin (1993). *Industrial Relations and European State Traditions*. Oxford: Clarendon Press.

———— (2001). "A Third Way in Industrial Relations?" In Stuart White, ed., *New Labour: The Progressive Future?*, 93–109 New York: Palgrave.

Curzon, Gerard, and Victoria Curzon (1973). "GATT: Traders' Club." In Robert W. Cox and Harold K. Jacobson, eds., *The Anatomy of Influence*, 298–333. New Haven, CT: Yale University Press.

Daley, Anthony (1996). *Steel, State, and Labor: Mobilization and Adjustment in France*. Pittsburgh, PA: University of Pittsburgh Press.

Daly, Mary (2000). "A Fine Balance: Women's Labor Market Participation in International Comparison." In Fritz W. Scharpf and Vivien Schmidt, eds., *Welfare and Work in the Open Economy*. Vol. 2, *Diverse Responses to Common Challenges*, 467–510. Oxford: Oxford University Press.

DARES (1996). *Quarante ans de politique de l'emploi*. Paris: Direction de l'Animation de la Recherche, des Etudes et des Statistiques.

———— (2000). *La politique de l'emploi en 1999*. Paris: Direction de l'Animation de la Recherche, des Etudes et des Statistiques. 52.2. December.

Davies, Jackie (1999). "Labour Disputes in 1998." *Labour Market Trends* 107, no. 6: 299–312.

Davies, Paul, and Mark Freedland (1993). *Labour Legislation and Public Policy*. Oxford: Clarendon Press.

Dawson, Michael (1994). *Behind the Mule: Race and Class in African-American Politics*. Princeton, NJ: Princeton University Press.

Deeg, Richard E. (1999). *Finance Capitalism Unveiled: Banks and the German Political Economy*. Ann Arbor: University of Michigan Press.

DeLong, Brad (2004). "The Economics of the New Economy." Lecture to the Governance of the E-conomy, Berkeley, CA, Spring.

Department for Culture, Media and Sport (2000). *A Sporting Future for All*. London: DCMS.

———— (2001). *The Government's Plan for Sport*. London: DCMS.

———— (2002). "World Class Sports: World Class Performance Programme." http://www.culture.gov.uk/sport/performance.

Department for Education and Skills (2002). *Education and Skills: Delivering Results. A Strategy for 2006*. London: Department for Education and Skills.

Department of National Heritage (1995). *Sport: Raising the Game*. London: Department of National Heritage.

———— (1996). *Sport: Raising the Game: The First Year Report*. London: Department of National Heritage.

Department of Trade and Industry (1998). *Fairness at Work*. Cm 3968. London: HMSO. http://www.dti.gov.uk/er/fairness/index.htm.

Die Zeit. Various issues.

Dobbin, Frank (1994). *Forging Industrial Policy*. New York: Cambridge University Press.

Doner, Richard F., and Ansil Ramsay (2003). "The Challenge of Economic Upgrading in Liberalising Thailand." In Linda Weiss, ed., *States in the Global Economy: Bringing Democratic Institutions Back In*, 121–141. Cambridge: Cambridge University Press.

Drake, Helen (2000). *Perspectives on a European Leader: Jacques Delors*. London: Routledge.

Drake, William, and Kalypso Nicolaides (1992). "Ideas, Interests, and Institutionalization: Trade in Services and the Uruguay Round." *International Organization* 46 (Winter): 37–100.

Drezner, Daniel (2004). "The Global Governance of the Internet: Bringing the State Back In." *Political Science Quarterly* 119: 477–498.

Dunleavy, Patrick (1995). "Policy Disasters: Explaining the UK's Record." *Public Policy and Administration* 10, no. 2: 52–70.

Ebbinghaus, Bernhard (2000). "Any Way Out of 'Exit from Work'? Reversing the Entrenched Pathways of Early Retirement." In Fritz W. Scharpf and Vivien Schmidt, eds., *Welfare and Work in the Open Economy*. Vol. 2, *Diverse Responses to Common Challenges*, 511–553. Oxford: Oxford University Press.

The Economist (2003). "German Reform and Democracy: The Exhausting Grind of Consensus." August 28.

Edin, Kathryn, and Laura Lein (1997). *Making Ends Meet: How Single Mothers Survive Welfare and Low-Wage Work*. New York: Russell Sage Foundation.

Edwards, Maud (1991). "Toward a Third Way: Women's Politics and Welfare Policies in Sweden." *Social Research* 58: 677–705.

EIROnline (2002). "Government Issues Assessment of 35-Hour Week Legislation." October 24. http://www.eiro.eurofound.eu.int/2002/10/feature/fr0210106f.html.

———— (2003). "Collective Bargaining in 2002 Examined." September 25. http://www.eiro.eurofound.eu.int/2003/09/feature/fr0309101f.html.

EIRR (1995). "Joint Employer/Union Declaration." *European Industrial Relations Review* 255 (April): 6.

———— (2002). "New Law Relaxes Implementation of 35-Hour Week." *European Industrial Relations Review* 346 (November): 15–18.

Ekiert, Grzegorz (2003). "The State after Socialism: Poland in Comparative Perspective." In T. V. Paul, G. John Ikenberry, and John A. Hall, eds., *The Nation–State in Question*, 291–320. Princeton, NJ: Princeton University Press.

Ellwood, David (1988). *Poor Support*. New York: Basic Books.

———— (2000). "Winner and Losers in America: Taking the Measure of New Economic Realities." In David Ellwood, ed., *A Working Nation: Workers, Work, and Government in the New Economy*, 1–41. New York: Russell Sage Foundation.

England, Paula (1992). *Comparable Worth: Theories and Evidence*. New York: Aldine.

England, Paula, and George Farkas (1986). *Households, Employment, and Gender: A Social, Economic, and Demographic View*. New York: Aldine.

England, Paula, Carmen Garcia-Beaulieu, and Mary Ross (2004). "Women's Employment among Blacks, Whites, and Three Groups of Latinas: Do Privileged Women Have Higher Employment?" *Gender and Society* 18: 494–509.

Erhard, Ludwig (1957). *Wohlstand für Alle*. Ed. Wolfram Langer. Düsseldorf: Econ-Verlag.

Esping-Andersen, Gøsta (1985). *Politics against Markets: The Social Democratic Road to Power*. Princeton, NJ: Princeton University Press.

———— (1990). *The Three Worlds of Welfare Capitalism*. Princeton, NJ: Princeton University Press.

———— (1999). *Social Foundations of Postindustrial Economies*. New York: Oxford University Press.

————, ed. (2002). *Why We Need a New Welfare State*. New York: Oxford University Press.

Estreicher, Samuel (1993). "Labor Law Reform in a World of Competitive Product Markets." *Chicago-Kent Law Review* 69: 3–46.

Etchemendy, Sebastian (2004). "Models of Economic Liberalization: Compensating the 'Losers' in Argentina, Spain, and Chile." Ph.D. diss., Department of Political Science, University of California, Berkeley.

Evans, Peter B. (1994). *Embedded Autonomy: States and Industrial Transformation*. Princeton, NJ: Princeton University Press.

———— (1997). "The Eclipse of the State: Reflections on Stateness in an Era of Globalization." *World Politics* 50, no. 1: 62–87.

Evans, Peter B., Dietrich Rueschemeyer, and Theda Skocpol, eds. (1985). *Bringing the State Back In*. Cambridge: Cambridge University Press.

Fajertag, Giuseppe, and Philippe Pochet, eds. (2000). *Social Pacts in Europe*. Brussels: ETUI.

Favier, Pierre, and Michel Martin-Roland (1996). *La décennie Mitterrand*. Paris: Seuil.

Federal Communications Commission (1997a). *In the Matter of International Settlement Rates*. Report and Order, IB Docket No. 96–261.

———— (1997b). *Rules and Policies on Foreign Participation in the US Telecommunications Market*. Report and Order, IB Docket Nos. 95–22 and 97–142.

Feigenbaum, Harvey, Jeffrey Henig, and Chris Hamnett (1999). *Shrinking the State: The Political Underpinnings of Privatization*. Cambridge: Cambridge University Press.

Ferrera, Maurizio, Anton C. Hemerijck, and Martin Rhodes (2000). *The Future of Social Europe: Recasting Work and Welfare in the New Economy*. Oeiras, Portugal: Celta Editoria.

Fields, Gary (2003). "From Communications and Innovation to Business Organization and Territory: The Production Networks of Swift Meat Packing and

Dell Computer." BRIE Working Paper 149, University of California, Berkeley.

Financial Services Authority (2001). *Introduction to the Financial Services Authority.* London: Financial Services Authority.

—— (2002). *Annual Report 2001/02.* London: Financial Services Authority.

Financial Times (1998). "Air France: State to Sell Off up to 47 Percent of National Carrier." February 24.

Flanders, Allan (1970). *Management and Unions.* London: Faber and Faber.

—— (1974). "The Tradition of Voluntarism." *British Journal of Industrial Relations* 12 (November): 352–370.

Flockton, Christopher (1996). "Economic Management and the Challenge of Reunification." In Gordon Smith, William E. Patterson, and Stephen Padgett, eds., *Developments in German Politics 2,* 211–232. Durham, NC: Duke University Press.

Frankfurter Allgemeine Zeitung (2000). "Schröder bleibt bei der Renternreform hart: 'Wir werden es machen. Basta.' " November 6: 1.

—— (2002a). "Bundesanstalt gerät immer Starker ius Kreuzfeuer der Kritik." February 6: 13.

—— (2002b). "Jagoda weist Rücktrittsforderungen Zurück." February 7: 13.

Fraser, Nancy (1989). *Unruly Practices.* Minneapolis: University of Minnesota Press.

—— (1994). "After the Family Wage: Gender Equality and the Welfare State." *Political Theory* 22: 591–618.

Freeman, Jo (1975). *The Politics of Women's Liberation.* New York: McKay.

Friedman, David (1988). *The Misunderstood Miracle: Industrial Development and Political Change in Japan.* Ithaca, NY: Cornell University Press.

Friedman, Thomas (1999). *The Lexus and the Olive Tree.* New York: Farrar Straus Giroux.

Fukui, Haruhiro, Peter H. Merkl, Hubertus Muller-Groeling, and Akio Watanabe, eds. (1993). *The Politics of Economic Change in Postwar Japan and West Germany.* New York: Saint Martin's Press.

Gamble, Andrew (1994). *The Free Economy and the Strong State.* Houndmills, UK: Macmillan.

Ganghof, Steffen (2000). "Adjusting National Tax Policy to Economic Internationalization: Strategies and Outcomes." In Fritz W. Scharpf and Vivien Schmidt, eds., *Welfare and Work in the Open Economy.* Vol. 2, *Diverse Responses to Common Challenges,* 597–645. Oxford: Oxford University Press.

Gao, Bai (2001). *Japan's Economic Dilemma: The Institutional Origins of Prosperity and Stagnation.* Cambridge: Cambridge University Press.

Garay, Candalaria (forthcoming). "Social Policy Regimes in Newly Liberalized Economies: Argentina, Brazil, Chile, Mexico." Ph.D. diss., Department of Political Science, University of California, Berkeley.

Garrett, Geoffrey (1998a). *Partisan Politics in the Global Economy.* Cambridge: Cambridge University Press.

—— (1998b). "Shrinking States? Globalization and National Autonomy in the OECD." *Oxford Development Studies* 26, no. 1: 71–97.

Gerber, David (1998). *Law and Competition in Twentieth Century Europe: Protecting Prometheus.* New York: Oxford University Press.

Gerke, Wolfgang (1998). "Market Failure in Venture Capital Markets for New Medium and Small Enterprises." In Klaus J. Hopt, Hideki Kanda, Mark J. Roe, Eddy Wymeersch, and Stefan Prigge, eds., *Comparative Corporate Governance: The State of the Art and Current Research*, 607–635. Oxford: Oxford University Press, 1998.

Gerlach, Michael L. (1992). *Alliance Capitalism: The Social Organization of Japanese Business.* Berkeley: University of California Press.

Gerschenkron, Alexander (1962). *Economic Backwardness in Historical Perspective.* Cambridge, MA: Harvard University Press.

Giaimo, Susan, and Philip Manow (1997). "Welfare State Adaptation or Erosion? The Case of Health Care Reform in Britain, Germany, and the United States." Paper presented at the American Political Science Association Annual Meeting, Washington, DC, August 28–31.

Gilens, Martin (1999). *Why Americans Hate Welfare.* Chicago: University of Chicago Press.

Gilpin, Robert (1981). *War and Change in International Politics.* Princeton, NJ: Princeton University Press.

Glenn, Evelyn Nakano (1992). "From Servitude to Service Work: Historical Continuities in the Racial Division of Paid Reproductive Labor." *Signs* 18: 1–43.

Glimstedt, Henrik (2001). "Competitive Dynamics of Technological Standardization: The Case of Third Generation Cellular Communications." *Industry and Innovation* 8: 49–78.

Glyn, Andrew, Alan Hughes, Alain Lipietz, and Ajit Singh (1990). "The Rise and Fall of the Golden Age." In Stephen Marglin and Juliet Schor, eds., *The Golden Age of Capitalism: Reinterpreting Postwar Experience*, 39–125. Oxford: Clarendon Press.

Goldstein, Judith (1996). "International Law and Domestic Institutions: Reconciling North American 'Unfair' Trade Laws." *International Organization* 50: 641–664.

Goldthorpe, John H. (1968). *The Affluent Worker.* Cambridge: Cambridge University Press.

——— (1978). "The Current Inflation: Towards a Sociological Account." In Fred Hirsch and John H. Goldthorpe, eds., *The Political Economy of Inflation*, 186–214. London: Martin Robertson.

———, ed. (1984). *Order and Conflict in Contemporary Capitalism.* Oxford: Clarendon Press.

Gonzalez, Maria Jose, Teresa Jurado, and Manuela Naldini (2000). *Gender Inequalities in Southern Europe: Women, Work, and Welfare in the 1990s.* London: Frank Cass.

Gornick, Janet C., and Marcia K. Meyers (2003). *Families that Work: Policies for Reconciling Parenthood and Employment.* New York: Russell Sage Foundation.

Gourevitch, Peter (1978). "The Second Image Reversed: The International Sources of Domestic Politics." *International Organization* 32, no. 4: 881–912.

Goyder, Daniel G. (2003). *EC Competition Law.* 4th ed. New York: Oxford University Press.

Goyer, Michel (2003). "Corporate Governance, Employees, and the Focus on Core Competencies in France and Germany." In Curtis Milhaupt, ed., *Global Markets, Domestic Institutions: Corporate Law and Governance in an Era of Cross-Border Deals*, 183–213. New York: Columbia University Press.

Gramsci, Antonio (1971). *Selections from the Prison Notebooks.* New York: International Publishers.

Gray, John, and Brian Wilcox (1995). *"Good School, Bad School": Evaluating Performance and Encouraging Improvement.* Buckingham, UK: Open University Press.

Greider, William (1997). *One World, Ready or Not: The Manic Logic of Global Capitalism.* New York: Simon and Schuster.

Gribble, Cheryl (2004). "History of the Web Beginning at CERN." July 13. http://www.hitmill.com/internet/web_history.asp.

Groux, Guy, and René Mouriaux (1990). "Le cas français." In Geneviève Bibes and René Mouriaux, eds., *Les syndicats européens à l'épreuve*, 49–68. Paris: Fondation Nationale des Sciences Politiques.

Haas, Ernst (1958). *The Uniting of Europe.* Palo Alto, CA: Stanford University Press.

Haas, Linda (1992). *Equal Parenthood and Social Policy: A Study of Parental Leave in Sweden.* Albany: State University of New York Press.

Hafner, Katie, and Matthew Lyon (1998). *Where Wizards Stay Up Late: The Origins of the Internet.* New York: Touchstone.

Hall, Peter A. (1986). *Governing the Economy: The Politics of State Intervention in Britain and France.* Oxford: Oxford University Press.

——— (1990). "The State and the Market." In Peter A. Hall, Jack Hayward, and Howard Machin, eds., *Developments in French Politics*, 171–187. London: Macmillan.

Hall, Peter A., and Daniel Gingerich (2001). "Varieties of Capitalism and Institutional Complementarities in the Macroeconomy: An Empirical Analysis." Paper presented to the annual meeting of the American Political Science Association, San Francisco, CA. August 30, 2001.

Hall, Peter A., and David Soskice (2001a). "An Introduction to Varieties of Capitalism." In Peter A. Hall and David Soskice, eds., *Varieties of Capitalism: The Institutional Foundations of Comparative Advantage*, 1–68. Oxford: Oxford University Press.

———, eds. (2001b). *Varieties of Capitalism: The Institutional Foundations of Comparative Advantage.* Oxford: Oxford University Press.

Hanlon, Pat (1996). *Global Airlines: Competition in a Transnational Industry.* Oxford: Butterworth-Heinemann.

Hansen, Mark, and Adib Kanafani (1990). "Airline Hubbing and Airport Economics in the Pacific Market." *Transportation Research* 24, no. 3: 217–230.

Hartog, Joop (1999). *Country Employment Policy Review: The Netherlands.* Report for symposium on "Social Dialogue and Employment Success." Geneva: ILO.

Hartz Commission (2002). "Moderne Dienstleistungen am Arbeitsmarkt: Vorschläge der Kommission zum Abbau der Arbeitslosigkeit und zur Umstrukturierung der Bundesanstalt für Arbeit." Berlin, August.

Haufler, Virginia (2001). *Public Role for the Private Sector: Industry Self-Regulation in a Global Economy.* Washington, DC: Carnegie Endowment for International Peace.

Heery, Edmund (2002). "Partnership versus Organising: Alternative Futures for British Trade Unionism." *Industrial Relations Journal* 33, no. 1: 20–35.

Heinze, Rolf G., and Christoph Strünck (2003). "Contracting out Corporatism: The Making of a Sustainable Social Model in Germany." Paper delivered at the Progressive Governance Conference, Hilton London Metropole. July 11–13.

Hemerijck, Anton C., Marc van de Meer, and Jelle Visser (2000). "Innovation through Coordination: Two Decades of Social Pacts in the Netherlands." In Giuseppe Fajertag and Philippe Pochet, eds., *Social Pacts in Europe: New Dynamics*, 257–278. Brussels: ETUI.

Hemerijck, Anton C., and Jelle Visser (1999). "The Dutch Model: An Obvious Candidate for the Third Way?" *Archives Européennes de Sociologie* 1, Vol. 40: 102–121.

Herbst, J. (2003). "States and War in Africa." In T. V. Paul, G. John Ikenberry, and John A. Hall, eds., *The Nation–State in Question*, 166–180. Princeton, NJ: Princeton University Press.

Hernes, Helga (1987). *Welfare State and Woman Power.* Oslo: Norwegian University Press.

Hewlett, Sylvia (1991). *When the Bough Breaks: The Cost of Neglecting Our Children.* New York: Basic Books.

Hickie, Desmond (1998). "The Aeronautics Task Force and the Industry Interface." In M. P. C. M. Van Schendelen, ed., *EU Committees as Influential Policymakers*, 89–108. Brookfield, VT: Ashfield.

Hilf, Meinhard (1997). "Negotiating and Implementing the Uruguay Round: The Role of EC Member States—the Case of Germany." In John H. Jackson and Alan O. Sykes, eds., *Implementing the Uruguay Round*, 12–136. Oxford: Clarendon Press.

Hirschman, Albert O. (1945). *National Power and the Structure of Foreign Trade.* Berkeley: University of California Press.

——— (1970). *Exit, Voice, and Loyalty: Responses to Decline in Firms, Organizations, and States.* Cambridge, MA: Harvard University Press.

Hirst, Paul, and Grahame Thompson (1996). *Globalization in Question: The International Economy and the Possibilities for Governance.* Cambridge, MA: Polity.

H. M. Treasury (1998). *The Modernization of Britain's Tax and Benefit System: No. 1, Employment Opportunity in a Changing Labour Market.* http://www.hm -treasury.gov.uk/media//63FB1/fpp.pdf.

Hobson, Barbara (1990). "No Exit, No Voice: Women's Economic Dependency and the Welfare State." *Acta Sociologica* 33: 235–250.

——— (1993). "Feminist Strategies and Gendered Discourses in Welfare States: Married Women's Right to Work in the US and Sweden during the 1930s." In Seth Koven and Sonya Michel, eds., *Mothers of a New World: Maternalist Politics and the Origins of Welfare States*, 396–430. New York: Routledge.

——— (1994). "Solo Mothers, Social Policy Regimes, and the Logics of Gender." In Diane Sainsbury, ed., *Gendering Welfare Regimes*, 170–187. Newbury Park, CA: Sage.

——— (1998). "Between Identities and Institutions: The Centrality of Paid Work and Swedish Women's Mobilization in Periods of Welfare State Expansion and Retrenchment." In Carl le Grand and Toshiko Tsukaguchi-le Grand, eds., *Women in Japan and Sweden: Work and Family in Two Welfare Regimes*, 17–44. Stockholm: Almqvist and Wiksell International.

———, ed. (2002). *Making Men into Fathers.* Cambridge: Cambridge University Press.

Hobson, Barbara, and Marika Lindholm (1997). "Collective Identities, Women's Power Resources and the Making of Welfare States." *Theory and Society* 26: 475–508.

Hochschild, Arlie (1997). *The Time Bind: When Work Becomes Home and Home Becomes Work*. New York: Metropolitan/Holt.

Hoekman, Bernard (1996). "Assessing the General Agreement on Trade in Services." In Will Martin and Alan Winters, eds., *The Uruguay Round and the Developing Economies*, 88–124. New York: Cambridge University Press.

Hoffmann, Stanley (1966). "Obstinate or Obsolete? The Fate of the Nation State and the Case of Western Europe." *Daedalus* 95 (Summer): 862–915.

Holloway, Nigel (2001). "The End of Germany AG." *Forbes*, June 11, http://www.forbes.com/global/2001/0611/024.html.

Holt, Richard (1989). *Sport and the British: A Modern History*. Oxford: Clarendon Press.

Holt, Richard, and Tony Mason (2000). *Sport in Britain, 1945–2000*. Oxford: Blackwell.

Hood, Christopher, Oliver James, George Jones, Colin Scott, and Tony Travers (1999). *Regulation Inside Government: Waste-Watchers, Quality Police, and Sleaze-Busters*. Oxford: Oxford University Press.

Höpner, Martin (2003). "European Corporate Governance Reform and the German Party Paradox." Max Planck Institute for the Study of Societies, Discussion Paper 03/4, Cologne, Germany.

Höpner, Martin, and Gregory Jackson (2001). "An Emerging Market for Corporate Control? The Mannesmann Takeover and German Corporate Governance." Max-Planck-Institut für Gesellschaftsforschung, MPIfG Discussion Paper 01/4, Cologne, Germany, September.

Horsman, Mathew, and Andrew Marshall (1994). *After the Nation–State: Citizens, Tribalism, and the New World Disorder*. London: Harper Collins.

Howell, Chris (1992). *Regulating Labor: The State and Industrial Relations Reform in Postwar France*. Princeton, NJ: Princeton University Press.

——— (1998). "Virtual Unionism in France." In Harrick Chapman, Mark Kesselman, and Martin A. Schain, eds., *A Century of Organized Labor in France*, 205–212. New York: St. Martin's Press.

——— (2000). "From New Labour to No Labour? The Industrial Relations Project of the Blair Government in Britain." *New Political Science* 22, no. 2: 201–229.

——— (2005). *Trade Unions and the State: Constructing Industrial Relations Institutions in Britain, 1890–2000*. Princeton, NJ: Princeton University Press.

Huber, Evelyne, and John Stephens (2000). "Partisan Governance, Women's Employment, and the Social Democratic Service State." *American Sociological Review* 65: 323–343.

——— (2001). *Development and Crisis of the Welfare State: Parties and Policies in Global Markets*. Chicago: University of Chicago Press.

Hufbauer, Gary C., and Erika Wada (1997). *Unfinished Business: Telecommunications after the Uruguay Round*. Washington, DC: Institute for International Economics.

Hurwitz, Leon (1987). *The European Community and the Management of International Cooperation*. New York: Greenwood Press.

Hyde, Alan (1993). "Employee Caucus: A Key Institution in the Emerging System of Employment Law." *Chicago-Kent Law Review* 69: 149–193.

IATA (1974). *Agreeing Fares and Rates: A Survey of the Methods and Procedures Used by the Member Airlines of the International Air Transport Association.* 2d ed. Montreal: IATA.

Ikenberry, G. John (2003). "Conclusion: What States Can Do Now." In T. V. Paul, G. John Ikenberry, and John A. Hall, eds., *The Nation–State in Question,* 350–371. Princeton, NJ: Princeton University Press.

ILO (1994). *The Yearbook of Labour Statistics.* Geneva: ILO.

INSEE (2005). "Dépense pour l'emploi." http://www.insee.fr/fr/ffc/chifcle_fiche .asp?ref_id=NATTEF03235&tab_id=68.

International Monetary Fund (1977). *International Financial Statistics Yearbook.* Washington, DC: International Monetary Fund.

Iversen, Torben, Jonas Pontusson, and David Soskice, eds. (2000). *Unions, Employers, and Central Banks.* New York: Cambridge University Press.

Jackson, John H. (1969). *World Trade and the Law of GATT.* Indianapolis, IN: Bobbs-Merill.

——— (1989). *The World Trading System: Law and Policy of International Economic Relations.* Cambridge, MA: MIT Press.

Jacoby, Wade (2005). "Institutional Transfer: Can Semisovereignty Be Transferred? The Political Economy of Eastern Germany." In Simon Green and William E. Paterson, eds., *Governance in Contemporary Germany: The Semisovereign State Revisited,* 21–45. Cambridge: Cambridge University Press.

Japan Times (2002). "Business Leaders Forecast Contraction." February 5.

Jefferys, Steve (2000). "A 'Copernican Revolution' in French Industrial Relations: Are the Times a' Changing?" *British Journal of Industrial Relations* 38, no. 2: 241–260.

Jenkins, Alan (2000). *Employment Relations in France: Evolution and Innovation.* New York: Kluwer Academic/Plenum Publishers.

Jenson, Jane (1986). "Gender and Reproduction: Or, Babies and the State." *Studies in Political Economy* 20: 9–45.

——— (1990). "Representations in Crisis: The Roots of Canada's Permeable Fordism." *Canadian Journal of Political Science* 24, no. 3: 653–683.

——— (1997). "Who Cares? Gender and Welfare Regimes." *Social Politics* 4: 182–187.

Jenson, Jane, and Rianne Mahon (1993). "Representing Solidarity: Class, Gender, and the Crisis of Social-Democratic Sweden." *New Left Review* 201: 76–100.

Jessop, Bob (1991). "Fordism and Post-Fordism: A Critical Reformulation." Lancaster Regionalism Group Working Paper, No. 4, Lancaster, UK, March.

——— (1993). "Towards a Schumpeterian Workfare State? Remarks on Post-Fordist Political Economy." *Studies in Political Economy* 40: 7–39.

——— (1994a). "Post-Fordism and the State." In Ash Amin, ed., *Post-Fordism: A Reader,* 251–279. Oxford: Basil Blackwell.

——— (1994b). "The Transition to Post-Fordism and the Schumpterian Workfare State." In Roger Burrows and Brian Loader, eds., 13–37. *Towards a Post-Fordist Welfare State?* London: Routledge.

Johnson, Chalmers (1982). *MITI and the Japanese Miracle: The Growth of Industrial Policy.* Palo Alto, CA: Stanford University Press.

Johnson, Chalmers, Laura Tyson, and John Zysman, eds. (1989). *Politics and Productivity: The Real Story of How Japan Works.* New York: Ballinger.

Johnson, David, and David Post (1996). "Law and Borders: The Rise of Law in Cyberspace." *Stanford Law Review* 48: 1367–1376.

Johnson, Michael (1998). *European Community Trade Policy and the Article 113 Committee*. London: Royal Institute of International Affairs.

Join-Lambert, Marie-Thérèse, Anne Bolot-Gittler, Christine Daniel, Daniel Lenoir, and Dominique Méda (1997). *Politiques sociales*. Paris: Fondation Nationale des Sciences Politiques.

Jones, Jack (1986). *Union Man: The Autobiography of Jack Jones*. London: Collins.

Jones, S. G. (1988). *Sport, Politics, and the Working Class*. Manchester: Manchester University Press.

Kagan, Robert A. (2001). *Adversarial Legalism: The American Way of Law*. Cambridge, MA: Harvard University Press.

Kahler, Miles, and David Lake (2003). *Governance in a Global Economy*. Princeton, NJ: Princeton University Press.

Kahn, Peggy (1992). "Union Politics and the Restructuring of the British Coal Industry." In Miriam Golden and Jonas Pontusson, eds., *Bargaining for Change: Union Politics in North America and Europe*, 181–212. Ithaca, NY: Cornell University Press.

Kasper, Daniel (1988). *Deregulation and Globalization: Liberalizing International Trade in Air Services*. Cambridge, MA: Ballinger.

Katzenstein, Peter J., ed. (1978). *Between Power and Plenty: Foreign Economic Policies of Advanced Industrial States*. Madison: University of Wisconsin Press.

—— (1984). *Corporatism and Change: Austria, Switzerland, and the Politics of Industry*. Ithaca, NY: Cornell University Press.

—— (1985). *Small States in World Markets*. Ithaca, NY: Cornell University Press.

—— (1987). *Policy and Politics in West Germany: The Growth of a Semisovereign State*. Philadelphia: Temple University Press.

Katznelson, Ira, and Helen Milner, eds. (2002). *Political Science: The State of the Discipline*. New York: W. W. Norton and Co.

Kavanagh, Dennis (1980). "Political Culture in Great Britain: The Decline of the Civic Culture." In Gabriel Almond and Sidney Verba, eds., *The Civic Culture Revisited: An Analytic Study*, 124–176. Boston: Little, Brown and Co.

Kenney, Martin, and David Mayer (2002). "Economic Action Does Not Take Place in a Vacuum: Understanding Cisco's Acquisition and Development Strategy." BRIE Working Paper 148, University of California, Berkeley.

Keohane, Robert O. (1984). *After Hegemony: Cooperation and Discord in the World Political Economy*. Princeton, NJ: Princeton University Press.

Keohane, Robert O., and Helen Milner, eds. (1996). *Internationalization and Domestic Politics*. Cambridge: Cambridge University Press.

Keohane, Robert O., and Joseph S. Nye, Jr. (1977). *Power and Interdependence*. Boston: Little, Brown and Co.

Kindleberger, Charles P. (1971). *American Business Abroad*. New Haven, CT: Yale University Press.

King, Desmond, and Stewart Wood (1999). "The Political Economy of Neoliberalism." In Herbert Kitschelt, Peter Lange, Gary Marks, and John D. Stephens, eds., *Continuity and Change in Contemporary Capitalism*, 371–397. New York: Cambridge University Press.

Kitschelt, Herbert, Peter Lange, Gary Marks, and John D. Stephens, eds. (1999).

Continuity and Change in Contemporary Capitalism. New York: Cambridge University Press.

Knijn, Trudie (1994). "Fish without Bikes: Revision of the Dutch Welfare State and Its Consequences for the (In)dependence of Single Mothers." *Social Politics* 1: 83–105.

——— (1998). "Participation through Care? The Case of the Dutch Housewife." In Jet Bussemaker and Rian Voet, eds., *Gender, Participation and Citizenship in the Netherlands,* 65–78. Brookfield, VT: Ashgate.

Knuth, Matthias (1997). "Active Labor Market Policy and German Unification: The Role of Employment and Training Companies." In Lowell Turner, ed., *Negotiating the New Germany: Can Social Partnership Survive?,* 69–86. Ithaca, NY: Cornell University Press.

Kobrin, Stephen (2001). "Territoriality and the Governance of Cyberspace." *Journal of International Business Studies* 32, no. 4: 687–704.

Koole, Ruud A. (1997). *Politieke Partijen in Nederland: Ontstaan en Ontwikkeling van Partijen en Partijstelsel.* Utrecht, Netherlands: Het Spectrum.

Korpi, Walter (2000). "Faces of Inequality: Gender, Class, and Patterns of Inequalities in Different Types of Welfare States." *Social Politics* 7: 127–191.

Koven, Seth, and Sonya Michel (1993). *Mothers of a New World: Maternalist Politics and the Origins of Welfare States.* New York: Routledge.

Krasner, Stephen D. (1976). "State Power and the Structure of International Trade." *World Politics* 28: 317–347.

——— (1982). "Structural Causes and Regime Consequences: Regimes as Intervening Variables." *International Organization* 36, no. 2: 185–205.

Kume, Ikuo (1998). *Disparaged Success: Labor Politics in Postwar Japan.* Ithaca, NY: Cornell University Press.

Labbé, Dominique, and Maurice Croisat (1992). *La fin des syndicats?* Paris: L'Harmattan.

Ladd-Taylor, Molly (1994). *Mother-Work: Women, Child Welfare, and the State, 1890–1930.* Urbana, IL: University of Illinois Press.

Lake, Marilyn (1992). "Mission Impossible: How Men Gave Birth to the Australian Nation—Nationalism, Gender, and Other Seminal Acts." *Gender and History* 4: 305–322.

Lallement, Michel, and Olivier Mériaux (2003). "Status and Contracts in Industrial Relations: 'La Refondation Sociale,' A New Bottle for Old (French) Wine?" *Industrielle Beziehungen* 10, no. 3: 418–437.

Lange, Peter, and Geoffrey Garrett (1985). "The Politics of Growth: Strategic Interaction and Economic Performance in the Advanced Industrial Democracies." *Journal of Politics* 47: 792–828.

Lash, Scott, and John Urry (1987). *The End of Organized Capitalism.* Oxford: Polity Press.

Laughlin, Richard, and John Broadbent (1997). "Contracts and Competition: A Reflection on the Nature and Effects of Recent Legislation on Modes of Control in Schools." *Cambridge Journal of Economics* 21, no. 2: 277–290.

Lehmbruch, Gerhard, and Philippe C. Schmitter, eds. (1982). *Patterns of Corporatist Policy-Making.* Beverly Hills, CA: Sage.

Leira, Arnlaug (2002). "Updating the 'Gender Contract'? Childcare Reforms in the Nordic Countries in the 1990s." *Nora* 10: 81–89.

Lenoir, Rémi (1990). "Family Policy in France since 1938." In John Ambler, ed., *The French Welfare State: Surviving Social and Ideological Change*, 144–186. New York: NYU Press.

Lessig, Lawrence (1999). *Code and Other Laws of Cyberspace*. New York: Basic Books.

Levy, Brian, and Pablo Spiller, eds. (1996). *Regulations, Institutions, and Commitment: Comparative Studies of Telecommunications*. Cambridge: Cambridge University Press.

Levy, Jonah D. (1999). *Tocqueville's Revenge: State, Society, and Economy in Contemporary France*. Cambridge, MA: Harvard University Press.

―――― (2000). "France: Directing Adjustment?" In Fritz W. Scharpf and Vivien Schmidt, eds., *Welfare and Work in the Open Economy*. Vol. 2, *Diverse Responses to Common Challenges*, 308–350. Oxford: Oxford University Press.

―――― (2005a). "Economic Policy and Policy-Making." In Alistair Cole, Patrick Le Galès, and Jonah D. Levy, eds., *Developments in French Politics 3*, 170–194. Houndmills: Palgrave.

―――― (2005b). "Redeploying the French State: Liberalization and Social Policy in France." In Wolfgang Streeck and Kathleen Thelen, eds., *Beyond Continuity: Institutional Change in Advanced Political Economies*, 103–126. Oxford: Oxford University Press.

Lewis, Jane (1992). "Gender and the Development of Welfare Regimes." *Journal of European Social Policy* 3: 159–173.

―――― (1997a). *Lone Mothers in European Welfare Regimes*. London: Jessica Kingsley.

――――, ed. (1997b). "Gender and Welfare Regimes: Further Thoughts." *Social Politics* 4: 160–177.

Lewis, Jane, and Gertrude Åstrom (1992). "Equality, Difference, and State Welfare: Labor Market and Family Policies in Sweden." *Feminist Studies* 18: 59–86.

Lewis, Peter (1996). "Limiting a Medium without Boundaries: How Do You Let the Good Fish through the Net While Blocking the Bad?" *New York Times*, January 15.

Liebcap, Gary (1989). *Contracting for Property Rights*. New York: Cambridge University Press.

Lieber, Ron (2003). "Banks Now Get Daily Reports on Their Customers." *San Francisco Chronicle*, August 4.

Lindbeck, Assar, and Denis Snower (1988). *The Insider-Outsider Theory of Unemployment*. Cambridge, MA: MIT Press.

Lindblom, Charles (1977). *Politics and Markets: The World's Economic Systems*. New York: Basic Books.

Locke, Richard, Thomas Kochan, and Michael Piore (1995). *Employment Relations in a Changing World Economy*. Cambridge, MA: MIT Press.

Loriaux, Michael (1991). *France after Hegemony: International Change and Financial Reform*. Ithaca, NY: Cornell University Press.

Loth, Wilfred, William Wallace, and Wolfgang Wessels, eds. (1998). *Walter Hallstein: The Forgotten European?* London: Macmillan.

Lowenfeld, Andreas F., ed. (1981). *Aviation Law: Cases and Materials*. New York: Mathew Bender.

MacLean, Nancy (1999). "The Hidden History of Affirmative Action: Working Women's Struggles in the 1970s and the Gender of Class." *Feminist Studies* 25: 43–78.

Maillebiau, Eric, and Mark Hansen (1995). "Demand and Consumer Welfare Impacts of International Airline Liberalization." *Journal of Transport Economics and Policy* 29, no. 2: 115–136.

Majone, Giandomenico (1994). "The Rise of the Regulatory State in Europe." *West European Politics* 17, no. 3: 77–101.

—— (1996). *Regulating Europe.* London: Routledge.

—— (1997). "From the Positive to the Regulatory State: Causes and Consequences of Changes in the Mode of Governance." *Journal of Public Policy* 4: 139–167.

Mann, Michael (1986). "The Autonomous Power of the State: Its Origins, Mechanisms, and Results." In John A. Hall, ed., *States in History*, 109–136. London: Basil Blackwell.

Manow, Philip (1997). "Social Insurance and the German Political Economy." Max-Planck-Institut für Gesellschaftsforschung Discussion Paper 97/2, Cologne, Germany. November.

Manow, Philip, and Eric Seils (2000). "Adjusting Badly: The German Welfare State, Structural Change, and the Open Economy." In Fritz W. Scharpf and Vivien Schmidt, eds., *Welfare and Work in the Open Economy.* Vol. 2, *Diverse Responses to Common Challenges*, 264–307. Oxford: Oxford University Press.

Mares, Isabela (2003). *The Politics of Social Risk: Business and Welfare State Development.* Cambridge: Cambridge University Press.

Marquand, David (1988). *The Unprincipled Society: New Demands and Old Politics.* London: Jonathan Cape.

Marsden, Christopher (2000). *Regulating the Global Information Society.* New York: Routledge.

Marsh, John S., and Pamela J. Swanney (1983). "The Common Agricultural Policy." In Juliet Lodge, ed. *Institutions and Policies of the European Community*, 54–76. New York: Saint Martin's Press.

Marshall, T. H. (1963). "Citizenship and Social Class." In *Class, Citizenship, and Social Development: Essays by T. H. Marshall*, 67–127. London: Heinemann.

Martin, Cathie Jo (2000). *Stuck in Neutral: Business and the Politics of Human Investment Policy.* Princeton, NJ: Princeton University Press.

Marx, Karl (1999). *Capital.* Oxford: Oxford University Press.

Maswood, Javed (2002). *Japan in Crisis.* New York: Palgrave Macmillan.

Mathews, Jessica T. (1997). "Power Shift." *Foreign Affairs* 76, no. 1: 50–66.

Maul, Silja, and Athanasios Kouloridas (2004). "The Takeover Bids Directive." *German Law Journal* 5, no. 4: 355–366.

McCall, Leslie (2001). *Complex Inequalities: Gender, Class, and Race in the New Economy.* New York: Routledge.

McGuire, Steven (1997). *Airbus Industrie.* New York: St. Martin's Press.

Mériaux, Olivier (2000). "Éléments d'un régime post-fordiste de la négociation collective en France." *Relations Industrielles/Industrial Relations* 55, no. 4: 606–638.

Meyer, Bruce D., and Dan T. Rosenbaum (1998). "Welfare, the Earned Income Tax Credit, and the Employment of Single Mothers." Joint Center for Poverty Research Working Paper, No. 2, Northwestern University (Evanston, IL) and University of Chicago (Chicago, IL), May. http://www.jcpr.org/labormothers.html.

Meyer, John W., John Boli, George M. Thomas, and Francisco O. Ramirez (1997). "World Society and the Nation–State." *American Journal of Sociology* 103, no. 1: 144–181.

Michel, Sonya (1999). *Children's Interests/Mothers' Rights: The Shaping of America's Child Care Policy.* New Haven, CT: Yale University Press.

Middlemas, Keith (1995). *Orchestrating Europe: The Informal Politics of European Union, 1973–95.* London: Fontana.

Millward, Neil, Alex Bryson, and John Forth (2000). *All Change at Work? British Employment Relations 1980–1998, as Portrayed by the Workplace Industrial Relations Survey Series.* New York: Routledge.

Millward, Neil, and Mark Stevens (1986). *British Workplace Industrial Relations, 1980–1984: The DE/ESRC/PSI/ACAS Surveys.* Aldershot, UK: Gower.

Milward, Alan (1992). *The European Rescue of the Nation–State.* Berkeley: University of California Press.

Ministry of Employment, Labor, and Social Cohesion (2003). "La Négociation Collective en 2003." http://www.travail.gouv.fr/publications/publications_f .html.

Ministry of Finance (2001). *Projet de loi de finances pour 2002.* Paris: Ministry of the Economy, Finance, and Industry.

Mink, Gwendolyn (1998). *Welfare's End.* Ithaca, NY: Cornell University Press.

Miura, Mari (2002a). "From Welfare through Work to Lean Work: The Politics of Labor Market Reform in Japan." Ph.D. diss., Department of Political Science, University of California, Berkeley.

——— (2002b). "Playing without a Net: Employment Maintenance Policy and the Underdevelopment of the Social Safety Net." Annual Meeting of the American Political Science Association, Boston, MA, August 29–September 1, 2002.

Moran, Michael (1991). *The Politics of the Financial Services Revolution: The USA, UK, and Japan.* New York: St. Martin's Press.

——— (2003). *The British Regulatory State: High Modernism and Hyper-Innovation.* Oxford: Oxford University Press.

Moravcsik, Andrew (1997). "Taking Preferences Seriously: A Liberal Theory of International Politics." *International Organization* 51, no. 4: 513–553.

——— (1998). *The Choice for Europe: Social Purpose and State Power from Messina to Maastricht.* Ithaca, NY: Cornell University Press.

Mosley, Layna (2003). *Global Capital and National Governments.* Cambridge: Cambridge University Press.

Mulgan, Aurelia (2002). *Japan's Failed Revolution: Koizumi and the Politics of Economic Reform.* Canberra: Asia Pacific Press.

Muller-Jentsch, Walther (1995). "Germany: From Collective Voice to Co-Management." In Joel Rogers and Wolfgang Streeck, eds., *Works Councils: Consultation, Representation, and Cooperation in Industrial Relations,* 53–78. Chicago: University of Chicago Press.

Murphy, Anna (2000). "In the Maelstrom of Change: The Article 113 Committee in the Governance of External Economic Policy." In Thomas Christiansen and Emil Kirchner, eds., *Committee Governance in the European Union*, 98–114. New York: St. Martin's Press.

Myles, John, and Paul Pierson (2001). "The Comparative Political Economy of Pension Reform." In Paul Pierson, ed., *The New Politics of the Welfare State*, 305–333. Oxford: Oxford University Press.

National Life Finance Corporation (2003). *Annual Report*. Tokyo, Japan.

National Statistics (2004). "Low Income: Fewer Children in Poverty in Recent Years." October 8. http://www.statistics.gov.uk/cci/nugget_print.asp?ID=333.

Nelson, Barbara (1990). "The Origins of the Two-Channel Welfare State: Workmen's Compensation and Mothers' Aid." In Linda Gordon, ed., *Women, the State, and Welfare*, 123–151. Madison: University of Wisconsin Press.

Nelson, Robert, and William P. Bridges (1999). *Legalizing Gender Inequality: Courts, Markets, and Unequal Pay for Women in America*. New York: Cambridge University Press.

Newman, Abraham (2003). "When Opportunity Knocks: Economic Liberalization and Stealth Welfare in the United States." *Journal of Social Policy* 32: 179–197.

——— (2005). "Creating Privacy: The International Politics of Personal Information." Ph.D. diss., Department of Political Science, University of California, Berkeley.

Newman, Abraham, and David Bach (2004). "Self-Regulatory Trajectories in the Shadow of Public Power: Resolving Digital Dilemmas in Europe and the United States." *Governance* 17, no. 3: 387–413.

New York Times (1998a). "Airlines Coddle High Fliers at Expense of the Coach Class." April 1.

——— (1998b). "US and France Reach Air Accord." April 9.

——— (2003). "Two US Agencies Investigate JetBlue over Privacy Issues." September 23.

Nihon Keizai Shimbun (2003). "Takenaka: Tough on Major Banks, Lenient toward Small." October 1.

Nimmer, David (2000). "A Riff on Fair Use in the Digital Millennium Copyright Act." *University of Pennsylvania Law Review* 148: 673–742.

Noam, Eli M. (2001). *Interconnecting the Network of Networks*. Cambridge, MA: MIT Press.

Noble, Charles (1997). *Welfare as We Knew It: A Political History of the American Welfare State*. New York: Oxford University Press.

North, Douglass, and Barry Weingast (1989). "Constitutions and Commitment: The Evolution of Institutions Governing Public Choice in Seventeenth-Century England." *Journal of Economic History* 49: 803–832.

Nugent, Neil (2001). *The European Commission*. New York: Palgrave.

Nyberg, Anita (2000). "From Foster Mothers to Child Care Centers: A History of Working Mothers and Child Care in Sweden." *Feminist Economics* 6: 5–20.

Oatley, Thomas, and Robert Nabors (1998). "Market Failure, Wealth Transfers, and the Basel Accord." *International Organization* 52: 35–54.

O'Brien, Richard (1992). *Global Financial Integration: The End of Geography*. London: Pinter.

O'Connor, Julia S., Ann Shola Orloff, and Sheila Shaver (1999). *States, Markets,*

Families: Gender, Liberalism, and Social Policy in Australia, Canada, Great Britain, and the United States. Cambridge: Cambridge University Press.

OECD (1999a). *Employment Outlook.* Paris: OECD.

——— (1999b). *OECD Economic Surveys, 1998–1999: Germany.* Paris: OECD.

——— (2000a). *OECD Economic Surveys 2000: Netherlands.* Paris: OECD.

——— (2000b). *OECD Health Data.* Paris: OECD.

——— (2001a). *OECD Economic Surveys 2000–2001: Germany.* Paris: OECD.

——— (2001b). *Employment Outlook.* Paris: OECD.

——— (2004a). *Economic Outlook No. 75: Annual and Quarterly Data.* Paris: OECD.

——— (2004b). *Social Expenditure Database.* Paris: OECD.

——— (2005). *Employment Outlook.* Paris: OECD.

Ohmae, Kenichi (1991). *The Borderless World: Power and Strategy in the Interlinked Economy.* New York: Harper and Row.

——— (1995). *The End of the Nation State: The Rise of Regional Economies.* New York: Simon and Schuster.

Olson, Mancur (1982). *The Rise and Decline of Nations: Economic Growth, Stagflation, and Social Rigidities.* New Haven, CT: Yale University Press.

Orloff, Ann Shola (1991). "Gender in Early US Social Policy." *Journal of Policy History* 3: 249–281.

——— (1993a). "Gender and the Social Rights of Citizenship: The Comparative Analysis of Gender Relations and Welfare States." *American Sociological Review* 58: 303–328.

——— (1993b). *The Politics of Pensions: A Comparative Analysis of Britain, Canada, and the United States, 1880–1940.* Madison: University of Wisconsin Press.

——— (1999). "Motherhood, Work, and Welfare: Gender Ideologies and State Social Provision in Australia, Britain, Canada, and the United States." In George Steinmetz, ed., *State/Culture*, 291–320. Ithaca, NY: Cornell University Press.

——— (2001). "Ending the Entitlements of Poor Single Mothers: Changing Social Policies, Women's Employment, and Caregiving in the Contemporary United States." In Nancy Hirschmann and Ulrike Liebert, eds., *Women and Welfare: Theory and Practice in the United States and Europe*, 133–159. New Brunswick, NJ: Rutgers University Press.

——— (2003). "Markets Not States? The Weakness of State Social Provision for Breadwinning Men in the US." In Lynne Haney and Lisa Pollard, eds., *Families of a New World*, 217–245. New York: Routledge.

Ornston, Darius, and Olli Rehn (2006). "An Old Consensus in the 'New' Economy? Institutional Adaptation, Technological Innovation, and Economic Restructuring in Finland." In John Zysman and Abraham Newman, eds., *How Revolutionary Was the Digital Revolution? National Responses, Market Transitions, and Global Technology.* Palo Alto, CA: Stanford University Press.

Osborne, David, and Ted Gaebler (1992). *Reinventing Government: How the Entrepreneurial Spirit Is Transforming the Public Sector.* Reading, MA: Addison Wesley.

Osborne and Clarke Law Firm (2002). "New German Securities Acquisition and Takeover Act Enacted." January. http://www.osborneclarke.com/publica tions/text/germansecurities.htm.

Ostry, Sylvia (2004). "The World Trading System: In the Fog of Uncertainty." Speech delivered at Lehigh University, April.

O'Sullivan, Mary (2000). *Contests for Corporate Control: Corporate Governance and Economic Performance in the United States and Germany.* Oxford: Oxford University Press.

Oum, T. H., W. G. Waters, and J. S. Yong (1992). "Concepts of Price Elasticities of Transport Demand and Recent Empirical Estimates: An Interpretative Survey." *Journal of Transport Economics and Policy* 26: 139–154.

Padioleau, Jean (1981). *Quand la France s'enferre: La politique sidérurgique de la France depuis 1945.* Paris: PUF.

Parkinson, John E. (1993). *Corporate Power and Responsibility: Issues in the Theory of Company Law.* Oxford: Clarendon Press.

Paul, T. V., G. John Ikenberry, and John A. Hall, eds. (2003). *The Nation–State in Question.* Princeton, NJ: Princeton University Press.

Pedersen, Susan (1993). *Family, Dependence, and the Origins of the Welfare State: Britain and France, 1914–1945.* New York: Cambridge University Press.

——— (2004). *Eleanor Rathbone and the Politics of Conscience.* New Haven, CT: Yale University Press.

Pedler, Robin (2002). "Chiquita Declares War and Wins: Bananas-Transatlantic Trade Dispute." In Robin Pedler, ed., *European Union Lobbying,* 201–228. New York: Palgrave.

Peltzman, Samuel (1976). "Towards a More General Theory of Regulation." *Journal of Law and Economics* 19: 211–240.

Pempel, T. J., ed. (1990). *Uncommon Democracies: The One-Party Dominant Regimes.* Ithaca, NY: Cornell University Press.

Pempel, T. J., and Keiichi Tsunekawa (1979). "Corporatism without Labor? The Japanese Anomaly." In Philippe Schmitter and Gerhard Lehmbruch, eds., *Trends toward Corporatist Intermediation,* 231–270. Beverly Hills, CA: Sage.

People Jobs Opportunity (1992). London: HMSO.

Peterson, Jonathan (2004). "SEC Split on Aiding Investor Challenges." *Los Angeles Times,* March 8.

Petrazinni, Ben (1996). *Global Telecom Talks: A Trillion Dollar Deal.* Washington, DC: Institute of International Economics.

Pierson, Paul (1994). *Dismantling the Welfare State? Reagan, Thatcher, and the Politics of Retrenchment.* Cambridge: Cambridge University Press.

——— (2000). "Increasing Returns, Path Dependence, and the Study of Politics." *American Political Science Review* 94, no. 2: 251–268.

——— (2001). "Coping with Permanent Austerity: Welfare State Restructuring in Affluent Democracies." In Paul Pierson, ed., *The New Politics of the Welfare State,* 410–456. New York: Oxford University Press.

Piore, Michael J., and Charles F. Sabel (1984). *The Second Industrial Divide: Possibilities for Prosperity.* New York: Basic Books.

Platenga, Janette (1998). "Double Lives: Labour Market Participation, Citizenship and Gender." In Jet Bussemaker and Rian Voet, eds., *Gender, Participation and Citizenship in the Netherlands,* 51–64. Aldershot, England: Ashgate.

——— (2002). "Combining Work and Care in the Polder Model: An Assessment of the Dutch Part-time Strategy." *Critical Social Policy* 22: 53–71.

Poggi, Gianfranco (1990). *The State: Its Development, Nature and Prospects.* Palo Alto, CA: Stanford University Press.

Polanyi, Karl (1944). *The Great Transformation: The Political and Economic Origins of Our Time.* Boston: Beacon Press.

Pollitt, Christopher, Jeremy Lonsdale, and Xavier Girre (1999). *Performance or Compliance? Performance Audit and Public Management in Five Countries.* Oxford: Oxford University Press.

Porter, Theodore M. (1995). *Trust in Numbers: The Pursuit of Objectivity in Science and Public Life.* Princeton, NJ: Princeton University Press.

Power, Michael (1997). *The Audit Society: Rituals of Verification.* Oxford: Oxford University Press.

Preston, Ron (2004). "Software Patents Abused." *Network Computing*, May 13. http://www.networkcomputing.com.

Prigge, Stefan (1998). "A Survey of German Corporate Governance." In Klaus J. Hopt, Hideki Kanda, Mark J. Roe, Eddy Wymeersch, and Stefan Prigge, eds., *Comparative Corporate Governance: The State of the Art and Current Research*, 943–988. Oxford: Oxford University Press.

Pring, Richard (2001). "Managing the Professions: The Case of Teachers." *Political Quarterly* 72, no. 3: 278–290.

Purcell, John (1993). "The End of Institutional Industrial Relations." *Political Quarterly* 64, no. 1: 6–23.

Quadagno, Jill (1990). "Race, Class, and Gender in the US Welfare State: Nixon's Failed Family Assistance Plan." *American Sociological Review* 55: 11–28.

Ramesh, M. (2003). "Globalisation and Social Security Expansion in East Asia." In Linda Weiss, ed., *States in the Global Economy: Bringing Democratic Institutions Back In*, 83–98. Cambridge: Cambridge University Press.

Ray, Jean-Emmanuel (2004). "Les curieux accords dits 'majoritaires' de la loi du 4 mai 2004." *Droit Social* 6 (June): 590–600.

Regan, Priscilla (1995). *Legislating Privacy.* Raleigh: University of North Carolina Press.

Reich, Robert (1999). "Clinton's Leap in the Dark." *Times Literary Supplement*, no. 4999 (January 22): 3–4.

Reid, Margaret (1988). *All Change in the City: The Revolution in Britain's Financial Sector.* Basingstoke: Macmillan.

Reskin, Barbara, and Irene Padavic (1994). *Women and Men at Work.* Thousand Oaks, CA: Pine Forge Press.

Reynaud, Jean-Daniel, Sami Dossa, Josette Dossa, and Pierre Maclouf (1971). "Les évènements de mai et juin 1968 et le système français de relations professionnelles." *Sociologie du Travail*, no. 1 (January–March): 73–97.

Rhodes, Martin (2000). "Restructuring the British Welfare State." In Fritz W. Scharpf and Vivien Schmidt, eds., *Welfare and Work in the Open Economy.* Vol. 2, *Diverse Responses to Common Challenges*, 19–68. Oxford: Oxford University Press.

—— (2001a). "Globalization, Welfare States, and Employment: Is There a European 'Third Way'?" In Nancy Bermeo, ed., *Unemployment in the New Europe*, 87–118. Cambridge: Cambridge University Press.

—— (2001b). "Political Institutions and Welfare State Restructuring: The Impact of Institutions on Social Policy Change in Developed Democracies." In Paul Pierson, ed., *The New Politics of the Welfare State*, 165–194. Oxford: Oxford University Press.

Rhodes, R. A. W. (1997). *Understanding Governance: Policy Networks, Governance, Reflexivity and Accountability*. Buckingham: Open University Press.

Richards, John (1999). "Toward a Positive Theory of International Institutions: Regulating Postwar International Aviation Markets." *International Organization* 53: 1–37.

Richardson, Jeremy (1994). "Doing Less by Doing More: British Government, 1979–1993." *West European Politics* 17, no. 3: 178–197.

Richardson, Tim (2002). "South Korea Broadband in League of Its Own." *Register*, October 14. http://www.theregister.co.uk.

Rissel, Dirk (2002). "Overview of the New German Takeover Law." *Eurojuris Law Journal*, March. http://www.eurojurislawjournal.net/RA/Rissel/Overview-of-the-new-German-Takeover-Law.html.

Rivas, Jose (1999). *The EU Merger Regulation and the Anatomy of the Merger Task Force*. Boston: Kluwer Law International.

Rodrik, Dani (1997). *Has Globalization Gone Too Far?* Washington, DC: Institute for International Economics.

——— (1998). "Why Do Open Economies Have Larger Governments?" *Journal of Political Economy* 106 (October): 997–1032.

Roe, Mark J. (1991). "A Political Theory of American Corporate Finance." *Columbia Law Review* 91: 10–67.

——— (1993a). "Some Differences in Corporate Structure in Germany, Japan, and the United States." *Yale Law Journal* 102: 1927–2003.

——— (1993b). "Takeover Politics." In Margaret Blair, ed., *The Deal Decade: What Takeovers Mean for Corporate Governance*, 321–353. Washington, DC: Brookings Institution.

——— (1994). *Strong Managers, Weak Owners: The Political Roots of American Corporate Finance*. Princeton, NJ: Princeton University Press.

——— (1998). "Codetermination and German Securities Markets." In Klaus J. Hopt, Hideki Kanda, Mark J. Roe, Eddy Wymeersch, and Stefan Prigge, eds., *Comparative Corporate Governance: The State of the Art and Current Research*, 361–372. Oxford: Oxford University Press.

——— (2003). *Political Determinants of Corporate Governance: Political Context, Corporate Impact*. Oxford: Oxford University Press.

Rosenau, James, and J. P. Singh (2002). *Information Technologies and Global Politics*. Albany: State University of New York Press.

Rothstein, Bo (1998). *Just Institutions Matter: The Moral and Political Logic of the Universal Welfare State*. Cambridge: Cambridge University Press.

Rouvinen, Petri, Pekka Yla-Anttila, Ari Hyytinen, and Laura Paija (2006). "Finland's Emergence as a Global Information Technology Player: Lessons from the Finnish Wireless Cluster." In John Zysman and Abraham Newman, eds., *How Revolutionary Was the Digital Revolution? National Responses, Market Transitions, and Global Technology*. Palo Alto, CA: Stanford University Press.

Royal Commission on Trade Unions and Employers' Associations (1968). *Report*. London: HMSO.

Ruggie, John G. (1983). "International Regimes, Transactions, and Change: Embedded Liberalism in the Postwar Economic Order." In Stephen D. Krasner, ed., *International Regimes*, 195–232. Ithaca, NY: Cornell University Press.

Ruggie, Mary (1984). *The State and Working Women.* Princeton, NJ: Princeton University Press.

———— (1988). "Gender, Work, and Social Progress: Some Consequences of Interest Aggregation in Sweden." In Jane Jenson, Elisabeth Hagen, and Ceallaigh Ready, eds., *Feminization of the Labour Force*, 172–188. New York: Oxford University Press.

Saguy, Abigail (2003). *What Is Sexual Harassment? From Capitol Hill to the Sorbonne.* Berkeley: University of California Press.

Samuels, Richard (1987). *The Business of the Japanese State: Energy Markets in Comparative Perspective.* Ithaca, NY: Cornell University Press.

———— (2003). "Leadership and Political Change in Japan: The Case of the Second *Rincho.*" *Journal of Japanese Studies* 29, no. 1: 1–31.

Samuelson, Pamela (1999). "Intellectual Property and the Digital Economy: Why the Anti-circumvention Regulations Need to be Revisited." *Berkeley Technology Law Journal* 14: 1–49.

Sandholtz, Wayne, and Alex Stone-Sweet (1998). "European Integration and Supranational Governance." *Journal of European Public Policy* 4, no. 3: 297–317.

Saraceno, Chiara (1994). "The Ambivalent Familism of the Italian Welfare State." *Social Politics* 1: 60–82.

Saville, John (1986). "An Open Conspiracy: Conservative Politics and the Miners' Strike, 1984–85." In Ralph Miliband, John Saville, Marcel Liebman, and Leo Panitch, eds., *Socialist Register, 1985/86*, 295–329. London: Merlin Press.

Scharpf, Fritz W. (1984). "Economic and Institutional Constraints of Full-Employment Strategies: Sweden, Austria, and West Germany, 1973–1982." In John H. Goldthorpe, ed., *Order and Conflict in Contemporary Capitalism*, 257–290. Oxford: Clarendon Press.

———— (1985). "Die Politikverflechtungs-Falle: Europäische Integration und Deutscher Föderalismus im Vergleich." *Politische Vierteljahresschrift* 26, no. 4: 323–356.

———— (1991). *Crisis and Choice in European Social Democracy.* Ithaca, NY: Cornell University Press.

———— (1997). *Games Real Actors Play.* Boulder, CO: Westview Press.

Scharpf, Fritz W., and Vivien Schmidt (2000a). "Introduction." In Fritz W. Scharpf and Vivien Schmidt, eds., *Welfare and Work in the Open Economy.* Vol. 2, *Diverse Responses to Common Challenges*, 1–20. Oxford: Oxford University Press.

———— (2000b). "Statistical Appendix." In Fritz W. Scharpf and Vivien Schmidt, eds., *Welfare and Work in the Open Economy.* Vol. 1, *From Vulnerability to Competitiveness*, 337–372. Oxford: Oxford University Press.

————, eds. (2000c). *Welfare and Work in the Open Economy.* Vol. 1, *From Vulnerability to Competitiveness.* Oxford: Oxford University Press.

Schmid, Gunther (1996). "The Dutch Employment Miracle? A Comparison of Employment Systems in the Netherlands and Germany." Discussion Paper FS 96–206, Wissenschaftszentrum Berlin für Sozialforschung.

Schmidt, Vivien (1996). *From State to Market? The Transformation of French Business and Government.* Cambridge: Cambridge University Press.

Schmitter, Philippe C. (1977). "Modes of Interest Intermediation and Models of Societal Change in Western Europe." *Comparative Political Studies* 10 (April): 7–38.

—— (1979). "Still the Century of Corporatism?" In Philippe Schmitter and Gerhard Lehmbruch, eds., *Trends towards Corporatist Intermediation*, 7–52. Beverly Hills, CA: Sage.

Schneider, Ben Ross, and Bianca Heredia, eds. (2003). *Reinventing Leviathan: The Politics of Administrative Reform in Developing Countries.* Miami, FL: North-South Center Press.

Schor, Juliet (1992). *The Overworked American: The Unexpected Decline of Leisure.* New York: Basic Books.

Schultz, Vicky (2000). "Life's Work." *Columbia Law Review* 100, no. 7: 1881–1964.

Schumpeter, Joseph (1950). *Capitalism, Socialism, and Democracy.* 3d ed. New York: Harper and Row.

Schwartz, Andrew (2006). *The Politics of Greed: Privatization, Neo-Liberalism, and Plutocratic Capitalism in Central and Eastern Europe.* Lanham, MD: Rowman and Littlefield.

Schwartz, Herman (2000). "Internationalization and Two Liberal Welfare States: Australia and New Zealand." In Fritz W. Scharpf and Vivien Schmidt, eds., *Welfare and Work in the Open Economy.* Vol. 2, *Diverse Responses to Common Challenges,* 69–130. Oxford: Oxford University Press.

Scott, James (1998). *Seeing Like a State: How Certain Schemes to Improve the Human Condition Have Failed.* New Haven, CT: Yale University Press.

Securities and Exchange Commission (2003). *Proposed Rule: Security Holder Director Nominations,* 17 CFR PARTS 240, 249 and 274, Release nos. 34–48626; IC-26206; File No. S7–19–03, RIN 3235-AI93 (October 14, 2003; modified October 17, 2003). http://www.sec.gov/rules/proposed/34–48626.htm.

Shaffer, Gregory C. (2003). *Defending Interests: Public-Private Partnerships in WTO Litigation.* Washington, DC: Brookings Institution Press.

Shameen, Assif (2004). "Korea's Broadband Revolution." *Chief Executive,* April. http:www.chiefexecutive.net.

Shannon, Claude Elmwood (1993). "A Mathematical Theory of Communication." In NJA. Sloane and Aaron D. Wyner, eds., *Claude Elmwood Shannon: Collected Papers,* 5–83. New York: IEEE Press.

Shapiro, Carl, and Hal R. Varian (1999). *Information Rules: A Strategic Guide to the Network Economy.* Boston: Harvard Business School Press.

Shaw, Eric (1994). *The Labour Party since 1979: Crisis and Transformation.* New York: Routledge.

Sherman, Laura (1998). "Wildly Enthusiastic about the First Multilateral Agreement on Trade in Telecommunications Services." *Federal Communications Law Journal* 51, no. 1: 61–110.

Shonfield, Andrew (1965). *Modern Capitalism: The Changing Balance of Public and Private Power.* Oxford: Oxford University Press.

Siim, Birte (1994). "Engendering Democracy: Social Citizenship and Political Participation for Women in Scandinavia." *Social Politics* 1: 286–305.

Skocpol, Theda (1979). *States and Social Revolutions: A Comparative Analysis of France, Russia, and China.* Cambridge: Cambridge University Press.

—— (1992). *Protecting Soldiers and Mothers: Political Origins of Social Policy in the United States.* Cambridge, MA: Harvard University Press.

————— (1995). *Social Policy in the United States.* Princeton, NJ: Princeton University Press.

————— (2000). *The Missing Middle: Working Families and the Future of American Social Policy.* New York: W. W. Norton.

Slomp, Hans (2002). "The Netherlands in the 1990s: Toward 'Flexible Corporatism' in the Polder Model." In Stefan Berger and Hugh Compton, eds., *Policy Concertation and Social Partnership in Western Europe: Lessons for the Twenty-first Century,* 235–247. New York: Berghan.

Sochor, Eugene (1991). *The Politics of International Aviation.* Iowa City: University of Iowa Press.

Social Trends (2004). *34: 2004 Edition.* http://www.statistics.gov.uk/downloads/theme_social/Social_Trends34/Social_Trends34.pdf.

Souriac, Marie-Armelle (2004). "L'articulation des niveaux de négociation." *Droit Social* 6 (June): 579–589.

Spar, Debora (1999). "Lost in (Cyber)space: The Private Rules of Online Commerce." In A. Claire Cutler, Virginia Haufler, and Tony Porter, eds., *Private Authority and International Affairs,* 31–51. Albany: State University of New York Press.

SPD und Bündnis 90/Die Grünen Bundestagsfraktionen (2000). "Entwurf eines Gesetzes zur Reform der gesetzlichen Rentenversicherung und zur Förderung eines kapitalgedeckten Altersvorsorgevermögens." Berlin, November 14.

————— (2001). "Zur Reform der Arbeitsförderung: Eckpunkte der Fraktionen SPD und Bündnis 90/Die Grünen vom 3. Juli 2001 für ein Job-Aktivieren, Qualifizieren, Trainieren, Investieren, Vermitteln-Gesetz." Berlin, July.

Sport England (2002). "Sport England's Aims." http://www.sportengland.org.

Statistics Bureau (1998, 2003). *Employment Status Basic Survey.* Ministry of Public Management, Home Affairs, Posts, and Telecommunications. http://www.stat.go.jp/data/shugyou/index.htm.

Steinberg, Richard H. (1998). "Institutional Implications of WTO Accession for China." IGCC Policy Paper no. 41, Institute on Global Conflict and Cooperation, La Jolla, CA.

————— (2002). "In the Shadow of Law or Power? Consensus-Based Bargaining and Outcomes at the GATT/WTO." *International Organization* 56, no. 2: 339–374.

————— (2004). "Judicial Law-Making at the WTO: Discursive, Constitutional, and Political Constraints." *American Journal of International Law* 98, no. 2: 247–275.

————— (forthcoming 2007). *The Formation, Transformation, and Deformation of Trading States.*

Steinberg, Richard H., and Timothy E. Josling (2003). "When the Peace Ends: The Vulnerability of EC and US Agricultural Subsidies to WTO Legal Challenge." *Journal of International Economic Law* 6, no. 2: 369–417.

Steinmo, Sven (2003). "Bucking the Trend? Social Democracy in a Global Economy: The Swedish Case Up Close." *New Political Economy* 8, no. 1: 31–48.

Steinmo, Sven, and Duane Swank (2002). "The New Political Economy of Taxation in the Advanced Capitalist Democracies." *American Journal of Political Science* 46, no. 3: 642–655.

Steinmo, Sven, Kathleen Thelen, and Frank Longstreth, eds. (1992). *Structuring Politics: Historical Institutionalism in Comparative Analysis*. New York: Cambridge University Press.

Stephens, John (1996). "The Scandinavian Welfare States: Achievements, Crises, and Prospects." In Gøsta Esping-Andersen, ed., *Welfare States in Transition: National Adaptations in Global Economies*, 32–65. London: Sage.

Stern, Robert (2001). *Services in the World Economy*. Ann Arbor: University of Michigan Press.

Stevens, Beth (1988). "Blurring the Boundaries: How the Federal Government Has Influenced Welfare Benefits in the Private Sector." In Margaret Weir, Ann Orloff, and Theda Skocpol, eds., *The Politics of Social Policy in the United States*, 123–148. Princeton. NJ: Princeton University Press.

Strange, Susan (1995). "The Defective State." *Daedalus* 124, no. 2: 55–74.

———— (2000). *The Retreat of the State: The Diffusion of Power in the World Economy*. Cambridge: Cambridge University Press.

Streeck, Wolfgang (n.d.). "High Equality, Low Activity: The Contribution of the Social Welfare System to the Stability of the German Collective Bargaining Regime." Unpublished manuscript, Cologne, Germany.

———— (1984a). "Co-determination: The Fourth Decade." In Bernhard Wilpert and Arndt Sorge, eds., *International Perspectives on Organizational Democracy. Vol. 2*. Chichester, NY: Wiley.

———— (1984b). "Neo-Corporatist Industrial Relations and the Economic Crisis in West Germany." In John H. Goldthorpe, ed., *Order and Conflict in Contemporary Capitalism*, 291–314. Oxford: Clarendon Press.

———— (1995). *Works Councils: Consultation, Representation, and Cooperation in Industrial Relations*. Chicago: University of Chicago Press.

———— (2003). "From State Weakness as Strength to State Weakness as Weakness: Welfare Corporatism and the Private Use of the Public Interest." MPIfG Working Paper 03/2, Max Planck Institute for the Study of Societies, March.

Streeck, Wolfgang, and Philippe C. Schmitter, eds. (1985). *Private Interest Government: Beyond Market and State*. Beverly Hills, CA: Sage.

Streeck, Wolfgang, and Kathleen Thelen, eds. (2005). *Beyond Continuity: Institutional Change in Advanced Political Economies*. Oxford: Oxford University Press.

Strelow, Markus, and Jan Wildberger (2002). "The New German Takeover Act—A New Opportunity for Private Equity?" *Thompson Venture Economics*, April 29. http//www.ventureeconomics.com/buy/protected/ZZZ4HGCLBZC.html.

Summers, Clyde W. (1993). "Employee Voice and Employer Choice: A Structured Exception to Section 8(A)(2), in Symposium on the Legal Future of Employee Representation." *Chicago-Kent College of Law* 69: 129–148.

Supiot, Alain (2001). *Beyond Employment*. New York: Oxford University Press.

Swenson, Peter (1991). "Bringing Capital Back In, or Social Democracy Reconsidered: Employer Power, Cross-Class Alliances, and Centralization of Industrial Relations in Denmark and Sweden." *World Politics* 43, no. 4: 513–544.

———— (1997). "Arranged Alliance: Business Interests in the New Deal." *Politics and Society* 25, no. 1: 66–116.

———— (2002). *Capitalists against Markets: The Making of Labor Markets and Welfare States in the United States and Sweden*. Oxford: Oxford University Press.

SZW. *Sociale Nota.* Various years. The Hague, Netherlands: SDU.

Tallon, Peter (1978). "European Air Transport in a Holding Pattern." *Interavia* 34, no. 11: 1030–1032.

Terry, Michael (1983). "Shop Steward Development and Managerial Strategies." In George Sayers Bain, ed., *Industrial Relations in Britain*, 67–91. Oxford: Basic Blackwell.

Tharakan, P. K. M., and J. Waelbroeck (1994). "Determinants of the Anti-Dumping and Countervailing Duty Decisions of the European Communities." In Mathias Dewatripont and Victor Ginsburgh, eds., *European Economic Integration: A Challenge in a Changing World*, 181–199. New York: North-Holland.

Thelen, Kathleen (1991). *Union of Parts: Labor Politics in Postwar Germany.* Ithaca, NY: Cornell University Press.

——— (1999). "Why German Employers Cannot Bring Themselves to Dismantle the German Model." In Torben Iversen, Jonas Pontusson, and David Soskice, eds., *Unions, Employers, and Central Banks*, 138–169. New York: Cambridge University Press.

——— (2001). "Varieties of Labor Politics in the Developed Democracies." In Peter A. Hall and David Soskice, eds., *Varieties of Capitalism: The Institutional Foundations of Comparative Advantage*, 71–103. Oxford: Oxford University Press.

Tilly, Charles (1975). *The Formation of National States in Western Europe.* Princeton, NJ: Princeton University Press.

Tirole, Jean, and Jean-Jacques Laffont (1993). *A Theory of Incentives in Procurement and Regulation.* Cambridge, MA: MIT Press.

Titmuss, Richard (1987). "Welfare State and Welfare Society." In Brian Abel-Smith and Kay Titmuss, eds., *The Philosophy of Welfare: Selected Writings of Richard Titmuss*, 141–156. London: Allen and Unwin.

Tonnelson, Alan (2000). *The Race to the Bottom.* Boulder, CO: Westview Press.

Trampusch, Christine (2002). "Die Bundesanstalt für Arbeit und das Zusammenwirken zwischen Staat und Verbänden in der Arbeitsmarktpolitik von 1952 bis 2001." Working Paper 02/5, Max-Planck-Institut für Gesellschaftsforschung, May.

Tribe, Laurence H. (1996). "Taking Texts and Structure Seriously: Reflections on Free-Form Method in Constitutional Interpretation." *Harvard Law Review* 108: 1221–1303.

Trumbull, Gunnar (2002). "Policy Activism in a Globalized Economy: France's 35-Hour Work Week." *French Politics, Culture, and Society* 20, no. 3: 1–21.

Tsebelis, George, and Xenophon Yataganas (2002). "Veto Players and Decision-making in the EU after Nice." *Journal of Common Market Studies* 40: 283–307.

Turner, Lowell (1991). *Democracy at Work: Changing World Markets and the Future of Labor Unions.* Ithaca, NY: Cornell University Press.

Tyson, Laura D'Andrea (1992). *Who's Bashing Whom? Trade Conflict in High-Technology Industries.* Washington, DC: Institute for International Economics.

Tyson, Laura D'Andrea, and John Zysman (1989). "Development Strategy and Production Innovation in Japan." In Chalmers Johnson, Laura D'Andrea Tyson, and John Zysman, eds., *Politics and Productivity: The Real Story of How Japan Works*, 59–140. Cambridge, MA: Ballinger.

UK Sport (2002). *Sport in the UK—History of UK Sport.* http://www.uksport.gov
.uk.

Undy, Roger, Patricia Fosh, Huw Morris, Paul Smith, and Roderick Martin
(1996). *Managing the Unions: The Impact of Legislation on Trade Union Behaviour.* Oxford: Clarendon Press.

US Bureau of Labor Statistics (2005). *Employment Characteristics of Families in
2004.* Washington, DC: United States Department of Labor. Accessed March
13, 2006, at: http://www.bls.gov/news.release/pdf/famee.pdf

Vagts, Detlev F. (1966). "Reforming the 'Modern' Corporation: Perspectives from
the German." *Harvard Law Review* 80 (1966): 23–59.

Vail, Mark I. (2003a). "The Delicate Politics of Negotiated Political Change: The
State and Social Partners in Contemporary French Social-Protection Reform." Paper presented at the annual meeting of Southwest Political Science
Association, San Antonio, TX, April 16–19.

——— (2003b). "Rethinking Corporatism and Consensus: The Dilemmas of
German Social-Protection Reform." *West European Politics* 26, no. 3: 41–66.

——— (2005). "Beyond the Frozen Welfare State: Recasting Welfare Capitalism
in Contemporary France and Germany." Ph.D. diss., Department of Political
Science, University of California, Berkeley.

van der Veen, Romke, and Willem Trommel (1999). "Managed Liberalization of
the Dutch Welfare State." *Governance* 12, no. 3: 289–310.

van Kersbergen, Kees (1995). *Social Capitalism: A Study of Christian Democracy and
the Welfare State.* London: Routledge.

van Rijckeghem, Willy (1982). "Benelux." In Andrea Boltho ed., *The European
Economy: Growth and Crisis,* 581–609. Oxford: Oxford University Press.

van Toren, Jan Peter (1996). *Achter Gesloten Deuren? CAO-overleg in de Jaren Negentig.* Amsterdam: Welboom.

Vernon, Raymond (1971). *Sovereignty at Bay.* New York: Basic Books.

Viner, Jacob (1950). *The Customs Union Issue.* New York: Carnegie Endowment
for International Peace.

Visser, Jelle (1999). "The First Part-time Economy in the World: Does It Work?"
AIAS-CESAR Research Paper, Amsterdam.

Visser, Jelle, and Anton C. Hemerijck (1997). *"A Dutch Miracle": Job Growth,
Welfare Reform and Corporatism in the Netherlands.* Amsterdam: Amsterdam
University Press.

Vitols, Sigurt (1995). "Corporate Governance versus Economic Governance:
Banks and Industrial Restructuring in the US and Germany." Discussion
Paper FS I 95–310, Wissenschaftszentrum Berlin fur Sozialforschung, Berlin,
November.

———. (2001). "Varieties of Corporate Governance." In Peter A. Hall and David
Soskice, eds., *Varieties of Capitalism: The Institutional Foundations of Comparative Advantage,* 337–360. Oxford: Oxford University Press.

Vogel, David (1986). *National Styles of Regulation: Environmental Policy in Great
Britain and the United States.* Ithaca, NY: Cornell University Press.

——— (1995). *Trading Up: Consumer and Environmental Regulation in a Global
Economy.* Cambridge, MA: Harvard University Press.

——— (1996). "Why Businessmen Distrust Their State: The Political Consciousness of American Corporate Executives." In *Kindred Strangers: The Uneasy*

Relationship between Politics and Business in America, 29–72. Princeton, NJ: Princeton University Press.

Vogel, Ezra (1979). *Japan as Number One: Lessons for America*. Cambridge, MA: Harvard University Press.

Vogel, Steven (1996). *Freer Markets, More Rules: Regulatory Reform in Advanced Industrial Countries*. Ithaca, NY: Cornell University Press.

——— (1999). "When Interests Are Not Preferences: The Cautionary Tale of Japanese Consumers." *Comparative Politics* 31, no. 2: 187–207.

——— (2005). "Routine Adjustment and Bounded Innovation: The Changing Political Economy of Japan." In Wolfgang Streeck and Kathleen Thelen, eds., *Beyond Continuity: Institutional Change in Advanced Political Economies*, 145–168. Oxford: Oxford University Press.

——— (2006). *Japan Remodeled: How Government and Industry Are Reforming Japanese Capitalism*. Ithaca, NY: Cornell University Press.

Waltz, Kenneth (1970). "The Myth of Interdependence." In Charles Kindleberger, ed., *The International Corporation*, 205–223. Cambridge, MA: MIT Press.

——— (1979). *Theory of International Politics*. Menlo Park, CA: Addison-Wesley.

Weaver, Kent (2000). *Ending Welfare as We Know It*. Washington, DC: Brookings, Institution Press.

Weber, Steven (2001). "Introduction." In Steven Weber, ed., *Globalization and the European Political Economy*, 1–28. New York: Columbia University Press.

———. (2004). *The Success of Open Source*. Boston: Harvard University Press.

Weiner, Norbert (1954). *The Human Use of Human Beings: Cybernetics and Society*. Boston: Da Capo Press.

———. (1965). *Cybernetics: Or Control and Communication in the Animal and the Machine*. Cambridge, MA: MIT Press.

Weir, Margaret (1992). *The Politics of Jobs*. Princeton, NJ: Princeton University Press.

———, ed. (1998). *The Social Divide: Political Parties and the Future of Activist Government*. Washington, DC: Brookings, Institution Press.

Weir, Margaret, Ann Shola Orloff, and Theda Skocpol, eds. (1988). *The Politics of Social Policy in the United States*. Princeton, NJ: Princeton University Press.

Weiss, Linda (2003a). "Guiding Globalisation in East Asia: New Roles for Old Developmental States." In Linda Weiss, ed., *States in the Global Economy: Bringing Democratic Institutions Back In*, 243–270. Cambridge: Cambridge University Press.

——— (2003b). "Is the State Being 'Transformed' by Globalisation?" In Linda Weiss, ed., *States in the Global Economy: Bringing Democratic Institutions Back In*, 293–317. Cambridge: Cambridge University Press.

———, ed. (2003c). *States in the Global Economy: Bringing Democratic Institutions Back In*. Cambridge: Cambridge University Press.

Wetenschappelijke Raad voor het Regeringsbeleid (1990). *Een Werkend Perspectief. Arbeidsparticipatie in de Jaren '90*. Reports to the Government 38. The Hague: SDU.

Weyland, Kurt, ed. (2004). *Learning from Foreign Models in Latin American Policy Reform*. Baltimore, MD: Johns Hopkins University Press.

White House (1997). *Framework for Global Electronic Commerce*. Washington DC: White House Position Paper. 1 July.

Whitehouse, Gillian (1992). "Legislation and Labour Market Gender Inequality: An Analysis of OECD Countries." *Work, Employment and Society* 6: 65–80.

Wiedemann, Herbert (1980). "Codetermination by Workers in German Enterprises." *American Journal of Comparative Law* 28: 79–92.

Wilcox, Brian, and John Gray (1996). *Inspecting Schools: Holding Schools to Account and Helping Schools to Improve*. Buckingham, UK: Open University Press.

Wilcox, Clair (1972). *A Charter for World Trade*. New York: Arno Press.

Wilks, Stephen (1999). *In the Public Interest: Competition Policy and the Monopolies and Mergers Commission*. Manchester: Manchester University Press.

Williams, Linda Faye (1998). "Race and the Politics of Social Politics." In Margaret Weir, ed., *The Social Divide: Political Parties and the Future of Activist Government*, 417–463. Washington, DC: Brookings Institution Press.

Williamson, Hugh (2001). "Germany Acts to Limit Hostile Takeovers." *Financial Times*, July 11. http://www.ft.com.

Williamson, Oliver E. (1996). *Mechanisms of Governance*. Oxford: Oxford University Press.

Windmuller, John P. (1969). *Labor Relations in the Netherlands*. Ithaca, NY: Cornell University Press.

Wolff, Alan William, and Thomas R. Howell (1999). "Trust-Busting in Asia: Trade Policy at the Newest Frontier." In Richard H. Steinberg, ed., *Partners or Competitors? The Prospects for US-European Cooperation on Asian Trade*, 105–136. Boulder, CO: Rowman and Littlefield.

Woo-Cumings, Meredith, ed. (1999). *The Developmental State*. Ithaca, NY: Cornell University Press.

Wood, Robert W. (2001). "Germans in the News Again." *M&A Tax Report* 10, no. 2: 8.

Wood, Stewart (2001). "Business, Government, and Patterns of Labor Market Policy in Britain and the Federal Republic of Germany." In Peter Hall and David Soskice, eds., *Varieties of Capitalism*, 247–274. Oxford: Oxford University Press.

World Bank (1972). *World Development Indicators*. Washington, DC: World Bank.

——— (1997). *World Development Report: The State in a Changing World*. New York: Oxford University Press.

——— (2001). *World Development Indicators*. Washington, DC: World Bank.

Wright, Erik, Janeen Baxter, and Gunn Elisabeth Birkeland (1995). "The Gender Gap in Workplace Authority." *American Sociological Review* 60: 407–435.

Young, Alisdair R., and Helen Wallace (2000). *Regulatory Politics in the Enlarging European Union: Weighing Civic and Producer Interests*. Manchester: Manchester University Press.

Young, Michael (1991). "Structural Adjustment of Mature Industries in Japan: Legal Institutions, Industry Associations, and Bargaining." In Stephen Wilks and Maurice Wright, eds., *The Promotion and Regulation of Industry in Japan*, 135–166. London: Macmillan.

Zacher, Mark, with Brent Sutton (1996). *Governing Global Networks: International Regimes for Transportation and Communications*. Cambridge: Cambridge University Press.

Zehetmeier-Mueller, Ruth, and Richard Ufland (2002). "A New Era for Public Takeover Transactions in Germany Has Begun." *Legal Week Global,* April 17– May 14. http://www.legalweek.net/ViewItem.asp?id=8571&Keyword=take over.

Ziegler, J. Nicholas (1997). *Governing Ideas: Strategies for Innovation in France and Germany.* Ithaca, NY: Cornell University Press.

——— (2000). "Corporate Governance and the Politics of Property Rights in Germany." *Politics and Society* 28, no. 2: 195–221.

Zippel, Kathrin S. (2006). *The Politics of Sexual Harassment: A Comparative study of the United States, the European Union, and Germany.* New York: Cambridge University Press.

Zumbansen, Peer (2002). "The Privatization of Corporate Law? Corporate Governance Codes and Commercial Self-Regulation." *Juridikum* 3: 32–40.

Zysman, John (1977). *Political Strategies for Industrial Order: State, Market, and Industry in France.* Berkeley: University of California Press.

——— (1983). *Governments, Markets, and Growth: Financial Systems and the Politics of Industrial Change.* Ithaca, NY: Cornell University Press.

——— (2006). "Creating Value in a Digital Era: Exploring the Experimental Economy." In John Zysman and Abraham Newman, eds., *How Revolutionary Was the Digital Revolution? National Responses, Market Transitions, and Global Technology.* Palo Alto, CA: Stanford University Press.

Zysman, John, and Abraham Newman, eds. (2006). *How Revolutionary Was the Digital Revolution? National Responses, Market Transitions, and Global Technology.* Palo Alto, CA: Stanford University Press.

Contributors

JOHN W. CIOFFI is Assistant Professor of Political Science at the University of California, Riverside. He is completing a book entitled *Public Law and Private Power: The Comparative Political Economy of Corporate Governance Reform in the Age of Finance Capitalism.*

PETER COWHEY is Professor of Political Science and Dean of the Graduate School of International Relations and Pacific Studies at the University of California, San Diego. His books include *Policy in Japan and the United States, Managing the World Economy: The Consequences of Corporate Alliances,* and *When Countries Talk: International Trade in Telecommunications Services.*

ANTON C. HEMERIJCK is Director of the Netherlands Council for Government Policy (WRR) and Senior Lecturer in the Department of Public Administration, Leiden University. He has published widely on issues of comparative social and economic policy, including *A Dutch Miracle* and *Why We Need a New Welfare State.*

CHRIS HOWELL is Professor of Politics at Oberlin College. He is the author of *Trade Unions and the State: The Construction of British Industrial Relations Institutions* and *Regulating Labor: The State and Industrial Relations Reform in Postwar France.*

JONAH D. LEVY is Associate Professor of Political Science at the University of California, Berkeley. He has published *Tocqueville's Revenge: State, Society, and Economy in Contemporary France* and *Developments in French Politics 3.*

MARI MIURA is Associate Professor of Political Science at the Faculty of Law, Sophia University, Tokyo, Japan. She has authored *The Lost Decade and Beyond: Japanese Politics in the 1990s*.

MICHAEL MORAN is WJM Mackenzie Professor of Government at the University of Manchester, UK. He has written a number of books on comparative regulation and government-business relations, including *The British Regulatory State: High Modernism and Hyper-Innovation* and *Governing the Health Care State*.

ABRAHAM NEWMAN is Assistant Professor of International Relations at the Edmund Walsh School of Foreign Service at Georgetown University. He is the co-editor (with John Zysman) of *How Revolutionary Was the Digital Revolution? National Responses, Market Transitions, and Global Technology* and is completing a book on the international politics of data privacy.

ANN SHOLA ORLOFF is Professor of Sociology, Gender Studies, and Political Science at Northwestern University. She has published widely on sociology and gender, including *Remaking Modernity*, *States, Markets, Families*, and *The Politics of Social Policy in the United States*.

GENE PARK is a doctoral candidate in political science at the University of California, Berkeley. Park is currently a visiting scholar at the Japanese Ministry of Finance, where he is researching Japan's Fiscal Investment Loan Program.

JOHN RICHARDS is Director of Marketing for Collaboration at Microsoft. Richards has published extensively on the regulation and economics of services industries (telecommunications, computing, and aviation), including articles in *International Organization*, *Japanese Journal of Economics*, and multiple edited volumes.

RICHARD H. STEINBERG is Professor of Law at the University of California, Los Angeles, and Senior Scholar in the Division of International, Comparative, and Area Studies at Stanford University. His most recent books are *The Evolution of the Trade Regime: Economics, Law, and the Politics of GATT/WTO* and *The Greening of Trade Law: International Trade Organizations and Environmental Issues*.

MARK I. VAIL is Assistant Professor of Political Science at Tulane University. Vail is completing a book entitled *Beyond the Frozen Welfare State: Recasting Welfare Capitalism in Contemporary France and Germany*.

JOHN ZYSMAN is Professor of Political Science at the University of California and Co-Director of the Berkeley Roundtable on International Economy (BRIE). Zysman's books include *How Revolutionary Was the Digital Revolution? National Responses, Market Transitions, and Global Technology*, co-edited with Abraham Newman, *The Highest Stakes: The Economic Foundations of the Next Security System*, and *Governments, Markets, and Growth: Finance and the Politics of Industrial Change*.

Index